ANTONIONI

ANTONIONI *Centenary Essays*

Edited by Laura Rascaroli and John David Rhodes

A BFI book published by Palgrave Macmillan

First published in 2011 by
PALGRAVE MACMILLAN

on behalf of the

BRITISH FILM INSTITUTE
21 Stephen Street, London W1T 1LN
www.bfi.org.uk

There's more to discover about film and television through the BFI.
Our world-renowned archive, cinemas, festivals, films, publications and learning resources are
here to inspire you.

Palgrave Macmillan in the UK is an imprint of Macmillan Publishers Limited, registered in
England, company number 785998, of Houndmills, Basingstoke, Hampshire RG21 6XS.
Palgrave Macmillan in the US is a division of St Martin's Press LLC, 175 Fifth Avenue, New
York, NY 10010. Palgrave Macmillan is the global academic imprint of the above companies and
has companies and representatives throughout the world. Palgrave® and Macmillan® are
registered trademarks in the United States, the United Kingdom, Europe and other countries.

Cover design: couch
Cover image: *Il deserto rosso* (Michelangelo Antonioni, 1964), Film Duemila/Francoriz
Text design: couch
Set by Cambrian Typesetters, Camberley, Surrey
Printed in China

This book is printed on paper suitable for recycling and made from fully managed and sustained
forest sources. Logging, pulping and manufacturing processes are expected to conform to the
environmental regulations of the country of origin.

British Library Cataloguing-in-Publication Data
A catalogue record for this book is available from the British Library
A catalog record for this book is available from the Library of Congress
10 9 8 7 6 5 4 3 2 1
20 19 18 17 16 15 14 13 12 11

ISBN 978–1–84457–384–4 (pb)
ISBN 978–1–84457–385–1 (hb)

Contents

Acknowledgments

For assistance with translations, we would like to thank Chiara Alfano. We thank the School of English, University of Sussex, for research support. We also thank Rebecca Barden and Sophia Contento at BFI Publishing for their enthusiastic support of this project.

This book should have included an essay by the late Peter Brunette (1944–2010). We wish here to remember Peter's enormous contribution to Antonioni scholarship, to the study of Italian cinema and to film studies. We dedicate this book to his memory.

Notes on Contributors

JACOPO BENCI is a visual artist who lives and works in Rome. His work encompasses photography, video and film and installation; it has been shown in galleries, museums, festivals in Italy and around the world. His most recent solo exhibitions are 'A Possible Itinerary 1981–2011' (MLAC, 'Sapienza' University of Rome, 2011) and 'Sentieri invisibili' (Hybrida Contemporanea, Rome, 2010). He has published on Italian film-making in the edited collections *Cinematic Rome* (2008) and *Rome: Continuing Encounters Between Past and Present* (2011), and in the journal *Filmwaves* (2007). Since 1998 Benci has been the Assistant Director for Fine Arts at the British School at Rome where he has coordinated over forty exhibitions of resident artists and architects. In 2006 he curated the exhibition 'Responding to Rome: British Artists in Rome 1995–2005' at the Estorick Collection in London.

FRANCESCO CASETTI is Professor in the Humanities Program and the Film Program at Yale University. He has previously taught at Università di Genova, Università di Trieste and the Catholic University of Milan and he has been Visiting Professor at the University Paris III, at the University of Iowa and the University of California, Berkeley. He is the co-founder of the Permanent Seminar on the History of Film Theory, an international network of scholars. His research is on film theory, film and modernity, and post-cinema. Major publications include: *Inside the Gaze: The Fiction Film and its Spectator* (1998), *Theories of Cinema: 1945–1995* (1999) and *Eye of the Century: Film, Experience, and Modernity* (2008). Together with Roger Odin, he co-edited the 1990 special issue of *Communications* (no. 51) entitled 'Télévisions/Mutations'.

ALEXANDER GARCÍA DÜTTMANN is Professor of Philosophy and Visual Culture at Goldsmiths College, London, and Visiting Professor in the Department of Photography at the Royal College of Arts. He is the author of numerous books, including *Visconti: Insights into Flesh and Blood* (2008), *Philosophy of Exaggeration* (2007), *Between Cultures: Tension in the Struggle for Recognition*

(2000) and *At Odds with Aids* (1997). His most recent book is *Participation: Consciousness of Semblance* (2011).

DAVID FORGACS is Guido and Mariuccia Zerilli-Marimò Professor of Contemporary Italian Studies at New York University. He is the author of *Rome Open City* (2000) and *Mass Culture and Italian Society: From Fascism to the Cold War* (with Stephen Gundle, 2007) and the editor of numerous volumes including *The Antonio Gramsci Reader* (2000) and *Robert Rossellini: Magician of the Real* (with Sarah Lutton and Geoffrey Nowell-Smith, 2000).

ROSALIND GALT is Senior Lecturer in Film Studies at the University of Sussex. She is the author of *The New European Cinema: Redrawing the Map* (2006) and *Pretty: Film and the Decorative Image* (2011), as well as co-editor with Karl Schoonover of *Global Art Cinema: New Theories and Histories* (2010). Her research focuses on issues of geopolitics, aesthetics and sexuality in modern cinema, and has appeared in journals such as *Screen, Discourse, Cinema Journal* and *Camera Obscura*. Her recent publications include articles on the 1960s Catalan avant-garde, cinematic masochism and the question of Europe in the films of Michael Haneke.

ROBERT S. C. GORDON is Reader in Modern Italian Culture at Cambridge University. He has published widely on twentieth-century Italian literature, cinema and cultural history. He is the author or editor of several books on the work of Primo Levi, including *Primo Levi's Ordinary Virtues* (2001). His study of cultural responses to the Holocaust in Italy will appear in 2012. His work on cinema includes the books *Pasolini: Forms of Subjectivity* (1996) and *Bicycle Thieves* (2008), DVD and Blu-ray audio commentaries on Pasolini's *Teorema* (2007) and *Bicycle Thieves* (2011), and articles and essays on Holocaust cinema, early film and literature, 'Hollywood on the Tiber' and censorship.

MATILDE NARDELLI is currently a British Academy Postdoctoral Fellow at University College London and is working on a book on cinema in the gallery since the 1960s. She wrote her PhD thesis on Antonioni and experimental film-making and is interested in the dialogue between 'commercial' and 'experimental' cinema, and between cinema, art and other media. Recent and forthcoming publications include articles on Antonioni (in *The Soundtrack* and *Object*), cinema's obsolescence in contemporary art (in *The Journal of Visual Culture*) and the photobook as a kind of cinema (in *Framing Film*).

KAREN PINKUS is Professor of Italian and Comparative Literature at Cornell University, where she is also a minor field member in Studio Art. She has written

x

widely in the areas of Italian culture, literary and visual theory. Her most recent books are *The Montesi Scandal: The Death of Wilma Montesi and the Birth of the Paparazzi in Fellini's Rome* (2003) and *Alchemical Mercury: A Theory of Ambivalence* (2009). Her current research is centred on the potential role of the humanities in confronting climate change.

LEONARDO QUARESIMA is Professor of Film History and Director of Cinema Studies at the University of Udine, Italy. He has published widely on Weimar cinema (Riefenstahl, Ruttmann, Balázs), on silent cinema, on genre and on style. He is the editor of *The Tenth Muse: Cinema and Other Arts* (2001) and of the new edition of Siegfried Kracauer's classic *From Caligari to Hitler: A Psychological History of the German Film* (2004). He is on the editorial boards of *CINEMA & Cie* and *Bianco e Nero* and has been visiting professor at the universities of Paris III, Bremen and Salzburg.

LAURA RASCAROLI is Senior Lecturer in Film Studies at University College Cork, Ireland. Her work has appeared in journals such as *Screen, Framework, Film Criticism, Italian Studies, Studies in French Cinema* and *New Cinemas*. She has authored three monographs with Ewa Mazierska: *From Moscow to Madrid: European Cities, Postmodern Cinema* (2003), *The Cinema of Nanni Moretti: Dreams and Diaries* (2004) and *Crossing New Europe: Postmodern Travel and the European Road Movie* (2006), and has co-edited with Patrick O'Donovan *The Cause of Cosmopolitanism: Dispositions, Models, Transformations* (2011). Her monograph on essayistic non-fiction, *The Personal Camera: Subjective Cinema and the Essay Film*, was published in 2009.

ANGELO RESTIVO is the author of *The Cinema of Economic Miracles: Visuality and Modernization in the Italian Art Film* (2002) and, more recently, the essay 'From Index to Figure in the European Art Film: The Case of *The Conformist*', which appeared in *Global Art Cinema: New Theories and Histories* (edited by Rosalind Galt and Karl Schoonover, 2010). His current book project explores the relationship between cinematic form and processes of (post)modernisation. He is Associate Professor of Film Studies at Georgia State University and directs the doctoral programme in Moving Image Studies.

JOHN DAVID RHODES is Senior Lecturer in Literature and Visual Culture in the School of English at the University of Sussex. He is the author of *Stupendous, Miserable City: Pasolini's Rome* (2007) and *Meshes of the Afternoon* (2011), and the co-editor of *Taking Place: Location and the Moving Image* (with Elena Gorfinkel, 2011) and *On Michael Haneke* (with Brian Price, 2010). His essays have appeared in *Film History, Framework, Log* and *Modernism/Modernity*. He is a founding co-editor of the journal *World Picture* (www.worldpicturejournal.com).

KARL SCHOONOVER is an assistant professor of film studies at Michigan State University. He is the author of the forthcoming book *Brutal Vision: The Neorealist Body in Postwar Italian Cinema* (2011) which rethinks canonical conceptions of neo-realism's humanism, exposing how these films use spectacular views of injury, torture and martyrdom to place the filmgoer at the centre of a postwar geopolitics of international aid. In addition to his work on Italian cinema, he has written essays on classical film theory, the history of photography and slow cinema. He is also the co-editor with Rosalind Galt of *Global Art Cinema: New Theories and Histories* (2010).

MICHAEL LOREN SIEGEL completed his PhD in the Department of Modern Culture and Media at Brown University. His dissertation examined the films of Dario Argento in relation to transformations in Roman urbanity in the years following the economic miracle. He has published and presented on Argento and the Rome of neo-realism. He is currently visiting faculty in Modern Culture and Media at Brown and Screen Studies at Clark University.

Laura Rascaroli and John David Rhodes

INTERSTITIAL, PRETENTIOUS, ALIENATED, DEAD: Antonioni at 100

At a moment at which we might yearn for the death of the conversation about the 'death of cinema', about the medium's replacement by any number of audiovisual technologies, platforms and regimes, we feel that there might be something productively untimely in turning our attention to Antonioni. (Timely for us, the present moment marks the hundredth anniversary of his birth.) His films were, we might say – the best of them anyway – unfashionably fashionable. Unlike the raw and nervous edges of the new wave cinemas that dominated the period in which he graduated into artistic maturity, Antonioni's films were highly polished, sculpted, expertly joined together – but nonetheless shocking, jarring and 'difficult'. They were – like fashion – entirely of their moment, drenched in contemporaneity, documents of a time and place, and of a way of being. But by saying this we also mean to suggest that – like fashion – they risked their own obsolescence. By taking this risk in the most radical terms, they became timeless. That is to say, they did not become eternally relevant: rather, they became stubborn monuments of aesthetic will, documents of a hardheaded – even embarrassing – insistence on posing the largest, most universal questions (who are we? where are we? why are we?) in the concrete materials of an artistic medium and in the language and materiality of the historical moment of their making.

Approaching the figure and work of Michelangelo Antonioni a century after his birth, one is confronted with a number of persistent critical tropes about his oeuvre, with a substantial, if in great part dated, body of critical work and, perhaps, also with the sense that all has already been said and written on the director of the malady of feelings, of filmic slowness and *temps mort*, of the crisis of the postwar bourgeoisie, of epistemological uncertainties, of modernist difficulty and even boredom, of aestheticism and the hypertrophy of style, of narrative opacity. And yet, Antonioni today powerfully escapes the reach of old categorisations that have attempted to congeal his figure once and for all into an inert monument of modern cinema. His continued influence on world film-makers and the new pressing questions that his films raise today for contemporary audiences call for a renewed critical effort.

1

This volume of new essays takes on the task in the knowledge of the need and importance of approaching Antonioni's work with the eyes of a new century, from the vantage point of new methodological approaches, and with the sense that his position in the history of modern cinema is not fixed once and forever, but is mutating and still uncharted in its extraordinary richness and propulsive, experimental innovativeness. At each viewing, Antonioni's films renew the sense of a profound enigma, which the critical paradigms listed above attempt unsuccessfully to demystify and crystallise in established and definitive 'explanations' and categories.

Such an enigma, coupled with the impression of a commanding significance and import, was also experienced by Antonioni's early audiences, and is epitomised by spectatorial and critical reactions to the groundbreaking *L'avventura* (1960) – the film that single-handedly propelled Antonioni into the gotha of the 'difficult modernists' and that seemed instantly to win him an enduring place in the history of the cinema, while also attracting derision and gaining him many detractors. *L'avventura* was a defining moment in the history of film, as it became immediately evident; but the problem of capturing and, precisely, defining the essence of such uniqueness and importance is at the core of the question of the history of scholarly efforts on Antonioni's cinema.

In order to investigate this question, one could turn to the open letter that was addressed to Antonioni with the aim of communicating to the director its authors' own understanding of the features of his unique achievements. The letter is evidence of a tear opened by *L'avventura* at its first appearance, of the rupture and interruption that the film inflicted on its unsuspecting cosmopolitan audience, of a crisis in the language of criticism.

Let us begin by recalling the famous episode of the first screening of *L'avventura* at the 13th Cannes Film Festival. Michelangelo Antonioni and Monica Vitti, director and protagonist of the film, emerged from the projection in tears, devastated by the audience's scathing reaction, but awoke the following morning to find, hanging from a wall in the hall of their hotel, a typewritten letter of support signed by a long list of directors, technicians, actors and critics (among many others, Roberto Rossellini, Georges Sadoul, Janine Bazin, Anatole Dauman, André S. Labarthe and Alain Cuny). The short letter read:

> Conscious of the exceptional importance of Michelangelo Antonioni's film, *L'avventura*, and appalled by the demonstrations of hostility it has aroused, the undersigned professionals and critics wish to express all their admiration to the author of this film.[1]

This brief letter suggests that the significance of *L'avventura* was immediately detected and acknowledged by the people who were in the know; in other words, by those who made films and wrote about them. The professionals of the cinema found the reaction of the rest of the audience revolting, so much so that they were compelled to dissociate themselves publicly from it and express their admiration for the director through a signed letter of testimony.

Antonioni's ideal spectator of the 1960s, the one he had fully addressed for the first time only with *L'avventura*, was certainly not the acritical consumer who is often associated with mainstream cinema; but, as it became apparent, neither was she the keen patron of Cannes – a festival which, while traditionally sensitive to both the glamorous and the commercial sides of the cinema, had also always prized quality and indeed overindulged the auteurs (symptomatically, Fellini's *La dolce vita* won the Palme d'or in 1960, followed by Buñuel's *Viridiana* the year after). If Cannes' habitués booed it, *L'avventura*, in 1960, must have truly looked like an alien object. What is striking in this letter, which according to accepted historiography precipitated the decision to arrange a second screening and, subsequently, of awarding to Antonioni the Prix du Jury (shared with *Kagi* by Kon Ichikawa), is that the film is not compared to other films that were shown at the same festival, nor is it described as beautiful, powerful, moving or aesthetically striking, but purely and epigrammatically as a work of 'exceptional importance', and, therefore, as a unique, incomparable and arresting work, a watershed, after which – one is tempted to extrapolate from the short testimonial – the cinema will never be the

3

same. The reasons, however, are not explained; arguably, because it was impossible – the film defied definition. All the emphasis in the letter is, tellingly, on *L'avventura*'s exceptionality and uniqueness, thus on the experience of seeing it for the first time without firm points of reference. It is a film that produces a void, hollows out the space around it, demands new forms of language with which to address it.

That experience cannot, of course, be fully repeated; *L'avventura*, after rapidly entering all critics' 'top tens' of best films of the decade (and beyond), has been seen, written about and anatomised countless times, and has been referenced and alluded to directly and indirectly by generations of film-makers. The committed young cinephile/critic/film professional of today, in many ways the heir to Antonioni's ideal spectator of the early 1960s, will be able to rely on a complex network of meanings and expectations when encountering the film for the first time. The sensation of the lack of artistic references and of the cultural void that made of *L'avventura* an alien object in 1960 has been tempered by decades of film-making, as well as of scholarship and criticism on the film and on Antonioni's oeuvre. Yet, arguably, some of the same effect of striking alienness continues to be part of each viewing of *L'avventura*.

In what follows we address some thinking to Antonioni's work under the terms by which it has been both abused and praised, terms that have served to name and categorise his work. We turn (and return) to these so as to orientate readers to some of the major conceptual tendencies in Antonioni's reception, but we do so in a spirit of dialectical engagement in order to understand what truth content might still be found lurking in these terms.

Interstitial

While the early connoisseurs did not even attempt in their letter to articulate *L'avventura*'s 'exceptional importance', another open letter addressed to the director by an intellectual twenty years and eight films later tried by contrast to deal directly with this issue. Roland Barthes wrote his famed encomium 'Cher Antonioni ...' in 1980 to mark a prize presented to the director by the City of Bologna. The letter, first published posthumously in *Cahiers du cinéma* in the same year, is a reflection on the role of the artist. Barthes borrows what he sees as some of the features of Antonioni's work to define the three virtues that, in his mind, define the artist: vigilance, wisdom and fragility. Antonioni, then, becomes the ideal artist for Barthes, whose tribute is simultaneously a succinct appraisal of the director's entire oeuvre.

Barthes's text is at times rather dense and allusive; this is perhaps unsurprising, given the difficulty of the task at hand. And the word 'difficulty', indeed, surfaces already in the second paragraph, with specific reference to the Modern's difficulty

4

at following the mutations of history.[2] The argument is that Antonioni is a true Modern because of his treatment of thirty years of history; Barthes uses one term in particular to characterise such a treatment: 'subtlety'. Antonioni's subtlety has to do with openness ('your art consists in leaving the road to meaning open'),[3] ambiguity and instability of meaning. Barthes works here with concepts that have been regularly associated with Antonioni's cinema, such as epistemological doubt, the vertigo of the uncertainty of subjectivity, the intensity and persistence of a gaze that insists on looking at things that the artist was not asked to look at, and for longer than seemed necessary. Antonioni is thus said to epitomise the artist who challenges conventional ways of seeing and disturbs the safety of established modes of perception.

While these concepts are not new, and indeed form the better part of much of the existing scholarship on Antonioni's oeuvre, something exciting animates Barthes's letter; this something lies in the point at which Barthes tries to capture the essence of Antonioni's 'exceptional importance', to use the Cannes letter's expression. Barthes declares he will not discuss the 'how' (the scenes, the shots, the montage, whose analysis he leaves to the true film experts), but does engage with the effects of Antonioni's subtle openness, which, he proposes, produces a 'vacillation', a 'vibration' of the represented object. The object – and, one could argue, the film itself – vibrates. Barthes compares this vibration to the work of painters such as Matisse or Braque, who observe the object until the idea itself of the object disappears; or, even better, to Oriental art, which captures the object 'in that rare moment in which the whole of its identity falls brusquely into a new space – that of the Interstice'.[4] While Barthes is here talking of Antonioni's entire oeuvre, he also indicates the film which gives a 'stupefying demonstration' of the Interstice: *L'avventura*, needless to say.

It is the alienness of the interstitial space created by *L'avventura* in 1960 that made its bodies, landscapes, objects – indeed, the screen itself – vibrate. The film's vibration, in other words, is that of an art object that is in the plenitude of its identity, and yet that also falls into a void, because of an obstinate, subtle, open gaze that is directed to the world. And it is these same qualities of obstinacy, subtlety and openness that continue to vibrate at each viewing of Antonioni's films, and that today take on a novel relevance at the turn of a new century.

Pretentious

Manny Farber, in his famous essay 'White Elephant Art vs Termite Art', takes Antonioni up as a major example of the pejorative category (that of the 'white elephant'). 'Termite' art 'feels its way through walls of particularisation, with no sign that the artist has any object in mind other than eating away the immediate boundaries of his art, and turning these boundaries into conditions of the next achievement'.[5]

European art cinema, however, fares badly in this polarised discursive context; it is too indebted, in Farber's terms, to the tradition of the 'densely overwrought European masterpiece'.[6] Most of Farber's examples of the 'termite' tendency are collected from Hollywood genre film-making. His emphasis on the 'ornery', 'go-for-broke' ethos from which 'termite' art will issue leads him even – albeit it with some ambivalence – to include in his canon 'the TV debating of William Buckley'.[7] Obnoxious neo-conservatism thus wins entry into Farber's reverse-snobbish demotic-elite; European 'artiness', however, bars one access to this boys' club.

Farber claims that 'the common quality or defect' of 'white elephant' art (his favourite examples are Antonioni, François Truffaut and Tony Richardson) is 'fear, a fear of the potential life, rudeness, and outrageousness of a film'.[8] Thus, Antonioni sins against his medium by approaching it like painting: 'Antonioni gets his odd, clarity-is-all effects from his taste for chic mannerist art that results in a screen that is glassy, has a side-sliding motion, the feeling of people plastered against stripes or divided by verticals and horizontals.'[9] When, at the beginning of *La notte* (1961), Antonioni pictures the nymphomaniac's encounter with Giovanni, he has her, in Farber's terms, 'backed against a large horizontal stripe of a white wall'. The result: 'a pretentiously handsome image that compromises the harrowing effect of the scene'.[10]

It is worth returning to this jaundiced take on Antonioni's work not only because Farber's terms of abuse have remained consistent in negative appraisals of the director's oeuvre, but also because they permit us to see something that is true about this work. Farber is right: Antonioni does approach cinema like a painter, which is to say that, despite the stylishness of the surfaces of his images, his cinema is impure – it is derived from a variety of artistic and cultural sources and intervenes not only in the history of cinema, but in the history of aesthetic modernism. Farber is right: Antonioni's cinema takes itself too seriously, and the problem of its doing so extends from its desire to want to be something other than cinema – not more than cinema, just not cinema on its own or *purely* on its own terms.

Of course, the title of one of Antonioni's most famous essays would seem to undercut this assertion: 'Making a Film is My Way of Life'.[11] We might assume that the title implies that cinema – the specific medium of film – becomes the true, unique path to the real, the authentic. And yet what does Antonioni actually intend by this title? He says: 'Making a film … is living … While I am shooting a film, my personal life is not interrupted; in fact, it is intensified.'[12] Film and life name permeable boundaries, modes of being. Thus, if painterliness – by which we might mean a keen interest in the visual and spatial relations among bodies, objects, surfaces and monuments – is something that preoccupied the living Antonioni, then it will be no surprise that it preoccupies his cinema. His cinema – despite the frequent severity of his forms, a severity that would seem to limit what can be on-screen, in the frame – declares its openness to the world and the world's influence; in making

this declaration it runs the risk of being, at times, rather uncinematic – too fascinated by other forms, and of using cinema less as a specific medium (with its 'own'
laws) and more as a way of bringing various media into contact with one another.
Cinema, like life, is radically impure: this is what Antonioni means. For Farber, this
is pomposity, 'wet towels of artiness and significance'.[13] We prefer to see this,
instead, as a serious form of humility: of taking the film's relation to the world seriously. Such seriousness will mean that the film that results will exhibit – even the-
atricalise, perhaps – its madness, its obvious investment in the aesthetic, in the
other arts, and in film's relation to them. We don't intend to suggest that there are
not moments in some Antonioni films (or indeed, entire films in his oeuvre) when
we wince with the recognition that his self-consciousness has missed its target. But
such are the wagers of an intentional comportment towards art-making. Why is seriousness sometimes so embarrassing? Because it so obviously risks exposure, failure,
bathos? If so, then seriousness – pretentiousness, even – may actually be the mode
in which we (like Antonioni) run the greatest risk of encountering our humble position vis-à-vis the world's complex immensity.

Alienated

Along with ennui, uncertainty, solitude, separation, emptiness, misapprehension,
malady, crisis (but – also – painful slowness, tediousness, boredom), alienation is
one of the most frequently encountered terms (and tropes) in critical writings on
Antonioni. Notoriously, Andrew Sarris coined a neologism that neatly (and somewhat dismissively inasmuch as it is suggestive almost of a trade name or a brand)
captures and synthesises all these semantic and discursive fields: Antoniennui.[14]

Critical explorations of alienation in Antonioni have broadly followed two
routes: one sociological, which readily associates his plots, settings and characters
with a historically specific postwar bourgeois existential crisis; and the other modernist, which sees alienation as one of the prime thematic preoccupations of an
entire cultural and artistic epoch. The two areas, of course, conflate and overlap.
When attempting to capture the essence of Western European modernist cinema,
John Orr points to its bourgeois class formation and interests, factors which are
deemed to be responsible for the sense of frailty and anxiety of its images – 'For the
central problem of the post-war bourgeoisie lies in its profound crisis of values.' Of
course, it is at this point that Orr gestures precisely towards Antonioni.[15]

Without proposing to reject historicist and sociological approaches, or to deny
Antonioni's belonging to a specific transnational cultural and artistic milieu, which
indeed he both profoundly shaped and represented in an exemplary fashion, one
does experience an urge to move beyond this established critical framework and
think about Antoniennui as something highly distinctive and yet difficult to locate

and demarcate; and also to go beyond the mere naming of the set of filmic techniques and procedures that the critical literature tends to see as directly responsible for the production of 'alienation' (a camera that shuns emotional proximity, a decentred human figure, gazes directed off-screen, rarefaction of dialogue, narrative ellipses, long sequence shots and slow camera movements).

Alienation in Antonioni has to do both with the subject and with aesthetics. On the one hand, the on-screen subject appears to experience a displacement, a separation from herself and the world, an awkwardness of being, a tangible discomfort in the face of the raw presence of space and the palpable flow of time; on the other hand, we witness equally the emergence of an aesthetic of anxiety somewhere, ineffably, amid the rigorous formalism of the frame, the pictorial flatness of the surface, the sophisticated texture of the image, the orchestrated disposition of bodies and objects, the deliberate vectors of gazes and movements. Antonioni's aesthetics are at once arresting and perturbing; the characters' anxiety, expressed through the tension of bodies and gazes, reflects a broader disquiet that resides in unfathomable ways in the categories of form, of the distribution of objects and of the grain of both sounds and images.

Sigmund Freud's essay of 1919 on the uncanny is an attempt to conceptualise an aesthetic of anxiety, one which has to do precisely with the subject and with the art form.[16] Far from wanting to psychoanalyse Antonioni and his characters, there may be something to be gained by briefly recalling that Freud's description of the *unheimlich* as that which is strangely familiar may resonate with Antonioni's aesthetics. Yet, rather than focusing on Antonioni's frequent use of the double (a figure that Freud discusses in his essay as a typical occurrence of the uncanny in art), one could productively turn to the evocative passage in which Freud recalls walking, on a hot summer afternoon, through the deserted streets of a provincial Italian town which was unfamiliar to him, and finding himself unable, in spite of repeated detours, to avoid returning to a particular street. Freud reads his own uncanny feelings triggered by this experience in light of the compulsion to repeat. But what is most interesting here is undoubtedly the sense of a human habitat from which he wishes to separate himself, but which defies all his efforts to do so, as well as his awareness that his presence was beginning to be noted – that he felt uneasy about becoming the object of insistent gazes.

Over and over again, Antonioni's characters, not unlike Freud, find themselves in spaces that similarly elicit uncanny feelings. They walk through deserted streets in the morning light, accompanied by the distinct sound of their steps on the tarmac; stand in the abstract darkness of the night next to tall, rattling flagpoles; uneasily survey a storm approaching on the horizon; look from a balcony at surrounding anonymous buildings, and wince when they notice a man at an open window; happen to walk in the middle of a frightening, violent fight in the suburban periphery; stand awkwardly in a square, objectified by searching sexualised gazes; are compelled to run away after hearing a scream coming from a boat hidden in the fog. In all of these and in countless other examples, these characters harbour the violent desire to separate themselves from the environment that contains them and in which (by which?) they feel scrutinised. It is their embodied presence that turns urban and natural habitats into uncanny and mysterious compositions of buildings, objects and bodies; and it is the obstinate, subtle, open gaze directed at them that makes them vibrate and fall – as Barthes put it in his letter to Antonioni – into the space of an interstice.

In the affective sphere produced by the unfamiliar familiar, what is not at home for Freud is – of course – the human ego, which is thus alienated from itself, from its own embodied experience. Antoniennui may well be the alienation of the subject from itself; but it is also and decidedly the distinctive way in which this alienation is cinematically generated by forms distributed in spaces, by relationships between images and sounds, by directions of gazes and trajectories of bodies, by the rhythm of presences and voids, and by the obstinate look of the camera – all of which combine to materialise a true aesthetics of anxiety, one which reveals to us the foreignness of our home (and our foreignness to our world).

Dead

Another term that is frequently invoked in Antonioni's cinema is *le temps mort*: dead time.[17] Antonioni's films are 'full' of empty moments, directionless passages in which the seconds and minutes crawl by. The term, borrowed from the French, abuts on another borrowed from the history of painting: *la nature morte*, or 'still life', in English. These terms – *le temps mort* and still life – point to an important nexus of concerns in Antonioni's work.

If we take the French term literally, then it might be said to name something about narrative temporality, or an attitude towards narrative in Antonioni's cinema. Antonioni's cinema is one in which, very often, too little, or nothing at all seems to be happening. Places are shown before and after human actors arrive at and depart from them. The camera may seem to absorb itself in the pictorial interest of an object, building, or place, irrespective of what is meant to be happening near, in, or at it. Or else we follow a character who seems to be 'killing time', just existing, fiddling with the edges of things. The most famous sequence in which all of these tendencies come together might be the opening of *L'eclisse* (1962) in which the film establishes its own autonomous interest in certain complexities of the visual and material array of Riccardo's house. There are times when the camera and the character seem to be absorbed in looking at the same object, although we never learn what the character thinks about what she is looking at. And then there is the wonderful moment – one that detractors of Antonioni's cinema might find too obvious – when Vittoria idly plays with an empty picture frame on Riccardo's desk, inserting one object (an ashtray) and then another (a small abstract sculpture) into the empty frame, trying out the possibilities of framing.

If too little is happening in such a passage of *temps mort*, then *temps mort* names a problem of narrative economy. *Temps vivant*[18] would be time animated by human eventfulness – or at the very least by the character's telling us what she feels while she goes on doing nothing, killing time. In these dead moments 'nothing happens'. Time passes, but only passes, which is what makes it dead. The sheer passage of time in the film seems to mark or materialise time as time, time as the index of our common finitude, our fealty *to* time as we move, minute by minute towards non-existence.

However, as all of the foregoing examples, but in particular, Vittoria's pointless rearrangement of objects in an empty frame – itself obviously an analogy of Antonioni's own labour – suggest *temps mort* is not just a matter of narrative economy but of pictorial economy, as well, like *la nature morte*, the still life. This genre of painting (in many historical periods the lowliest, the least prized in the history of the arts, at least up until modernism) names the way in which representation meets its own specular allegory. Pictorial representation, broadly speaking, seeks to still, to abstract, to cut from the flow of time some small piece of the real and to deliver it out of time, and over to human consciousness, which might just have overlooked it. In the still life, painting chooses to focus its attention on things (not on the actions of humans appropriate to history painting) – and on things, moreover, that have been abstracted from human presence which may be felt to linger behind in the image in some purely indexical way (a half-drunk glass of wine, a half-eaten joint of meat, used, soiled cutlery). These things are either inorganic, or doomed to become thus – to be consumed and excreted, or else to rot, decay, become mere matter, formless, dead. The dead things arranged for our consumption – for our visual pleasure (which is itself predicated on or against death) – reflect on and embody the deadness of representation itself, the abstraction involved in any act of picturing. The term 'still life' touches on the oxymoronic heart of visual representation, which, in Jean-Luc Nancy's terms, *can only be* representation in its attempt both to touch and to withdraw from the world.[19] In theatricalising – in a moving image (one that too-notoriously consists of so many countless still lives, so many still frames per second) – the condition of the still life as Antonioni does at the beginning of *L'eclisse*, his cinema asks us that we consider the cinema as itself something dead – not dead in the sense of having 'outlived' its usefulness or currency as a medium, but dead in that it participates in the inorganic nature of the aesthetic itself.

What claims do the dead make on us? In moral or historical terms, the dead – who in truth demand nothing – mutely ask to be reckoned with, or at least remembered. But we can easily ignore them; most often we do. Their demands, in fact, exert appallingly little claim on our attention. Antonioni's still lives and dead times, however, *do* make demands on us. When his cinema asks us to look for longer than might otherwise have been comfortable at this or that object, we feel that we are being asked to work, to participate in, to share in the dead life of the film. Such a sharing of labour is what is being talked about when his films are described as 'demanding'.[20] They would not demand so much of us were they not already dead, did they not already insist on their deathliness as one of their major preoccupations. We do not mean, in any strict sense, that it is only the 'difficult' modernist text – with its durations, dilations and disjunctions – that can bring the spectator back to life, as Brechtian film theory might teach us. And yet, we do not disavow that these films may promise exactly such revivification: surely the hisses at Cannes are the rumours of indignant human life – an indignation, however, that addresses itself to a surface that cannot hear or respond to its complaints. Antonioni's dead times and still lives run the risk of boring us – boring us by making us feel like we are doing too much work, work that might be better done by his films telling us what to think or believe, what to grant importance to, what to ignore or let go. The sophisticated spectator who does not experience – or who disavows – boredom in Antonioni's dead cinema misses something important. The tedious work we feel like we are doing – a kind of muted, sedate busyness in front of the screen – *is* frustrating, for the cosmopolite cinephile who is willing to be challenged, as well as for the 'average' viewer who expects to be entertained. Here is a sensitive critic, Norman N. Holland, writing on Antonioni's mature work of the early 1960s at close historical range: 'When I first saw *L'avventura*, the film bored, annoyed, frustrated, and infuriated me. Inspired by the critics, I tried again. The second time, knowing nothing was going to happen, I made what turns out to be the necessary gesture of surrender to Antonioni: waiting without hope or expectation. Then I loved the film.'[21] Holland's account gives us the busyness required by the film, but a busyness that must turn into its opposite – a kind of death, or in Holland's terms a 'surrender' – in order for pleasure, insight, knowledge – that is to say, a living engagement with the film and its world, and the film as a part of our world – to be achieved. Adam Phillips has said that the value of frustration is that it 'contains the possibility of discovering a new want'.[22] Antonioni's dead time aporetically summons a lively participation whose obverse is a kind of deathly stillness, that produces – in another turn, or following an interval – a means towards a lively re-cathexis of the world, its objects, persons and things – those still living and those already dead.

The lessons of Antonioni's intersitiality, pretentiousness, alienation and deathliness are felt in many of those forms of cinema and audiovisual representation that today feel most alive. We think especially of contemporary East Asian cinema, the work of auteurs like Apitchatpong Weeresethakul, Jia Zhangke, Tsai Ming-liang and many others.[23] The 'slow' cinema of these and other directors clearly owes a

11

debt to Antonioni's formal vocabulary, and what is certainly compelling about these artists is that they draw on Antonioni's work as a reservoir of formal technique. But much more powerfully they appeal to it also as a means of recording, reckoning with and intervening in East Asian economies, revealing them to be over-determined and dizzying modernisations, with their own concomitant hypertrophy of cities and radical urbanisation of the countryside. After all, the contexts of Antonioni's own stylistic development were comparable – namely the rapid changes in Italian life in the postwar period. His patient and often obtuse way of looking not only searched for the odd juxtapositions of Italy's uneven development, it also sought to dilate time, to introduce a kind of languor into a historical context that had sold its soul to speed. In adopting and adapting Antonioni's strategies, contemporary East Asian directors are not merely declaring a cinephiliac love of European art cinema; rather, they are inserting their films into the social materiality of the political and economic history that links 1950s Italy to twenty-first-century China. What we witness, uncannily, is the recurrence of an insistent, enigmatic, unpredictable gaze.

*   *   *

Because Antonioni's cinema is, in our view, so richly and complexly imbricated in history, in a thinking of history, and in thinking, it is all the more urgent to revise commonly held perceptions that his work is frozen in time, apolitically stylised and stylish to the point of insipidity. Like the contemporary directors who make so much of his example in so many unexpected ways, we believe that Antonioni's work is still capable of teaching us, precisely, unpredictable lessons, of teaching us how to look again – not only at the films themselves, but at the world, its places and peoples.

The first section of the volume, 'Modernities', identifies a set of ways in which Antonioni's films may be said to illuminate specific areas of their precise historical moments, while simultaneously being profoundly shaped by its material embodiments and discursive expressions. By turning their gaze with keen attention to the relationship of his work inside distinct social, ideological and artistic contexts, the four chapters in this section bring to light instances of Antonioni's profound engagement with the contingent nature of historical processes. Read together, they present us with the image of an artist deeply embedded in his own time, and yet endowed with a powerful capacity for synthesis that produces essential and commanding visions of our shared modernities.

Starting from a careful examination of previously undetected sources, Jacopo Benci traces the reasons for the path that, in the early 1940s, brought Antonioni from his native Ferrara to Rome, thus illuminating a period of the director's biography that has hitherto remained rather nebulous. The connections and relationships unearthed by Benci resonate in compelling ways with the outcomes of Antonioni's artistic and intellectual development; against a biographical backdrop, Benci turns his attention to the embeddedness of Antonioni's developing cinematic practice in two decades of social, economic and architectural life in Rome. While clarifying the ways in which Rome shaped Antonioni's early career, Benci also identifies the contours of a (cinematic) city that is specifically his. It is precisely by challenging the critical trope of Antonioni's formalism as timeless abstraction that Laura Rascaroli's chapter tackles the historical resonances of the inorganic in his cinema. The essay identifies a progression in the attention devoted by Antonioni to the object in his work of the 1960s, and comes to focus on *Blow-Up*'s (1966) complex imbrication with precise transnational artistic discourses of the decade. Formalism is elucidated as a framing that is not abstracted from the world, but that in fact produces a range of aesthetic, critical and ideological discourses which speak to and of the world's presentness; Antonioni's understanding of the modern condition is thus understood as developing within a specific set of current artistic and sociological preoccupations.

Angelo Restivo takes issue in his chapter with the overriding reception of *Zabriskie Point* (1970) as the disappointing and preposterous product of the director's utter misunderstanding of the US circa 1970 (and as a failure of all the tenets of art cinema); the chapter compellingly argues that – far from being unrealistic, clichéd and simplistic, as it was then characterised by its critics – the film reveals today an extraordinary appreciation of the social and ideological tensions and contradictions of its present time and society. While somewhat dated even in its day, *Zabriskie Point* has now come to express in powerful ways the revolutionary potential that Benjamin recognised in the outmoded. Through a broad engagement with the figures of the detective and the reporter in narrative cinema, especially that of Hollywood, Robert S. C. Gordon uncovers the popular tropes mobilised by *The Passenger* (1975) both in character construction and narrative development, and points to a field of transgeneric meanings and archetypes which destabilises, but also paradoxically reinforces, the 'art-house' reading of this film. *The Passenger* thus comes to be situated in a dialogical relationship with popular culture, while Antonioni's play with cross-generic hybridisations and deconstructions is shown to resonate with the specific development of New Hollywood modernism.

Aesthetic concerns are central to the understanding of an author whose work has profoundly challenged and changed the limits of cinema as a popular art and medium, and continues to be a focus for connections and echoes within multiple artistic fields today. The chapters collected in the second section, 'Aesthetics', engage with the category of art in ways that highlight the configurations of Antonioni's specific working practices, and simultaneously make claims as to how his films may be said to shape, challenge and refigure our understanding of the principles of art and beauty.

Turning to Antonioni's early documentaries, Leonardo Quaresima argues against their status as 'minor works' and also their assignment to the sphere of neo-realist humanism, showing through meticulous investigation how their iconographical

13

sources and their visual emphases reveal a tendency to abstraction that tempers their ostensibly realist aesthetics and that produces effects of destabilisation and uncertainty. Thus reconsidered and refigured, Antonioni's early non-fictions point to the future stylistic developments of his artistic maturity, but are also fully restored to their aesthetic autonomy. In Rosalind Galt's contribution, the picturesque is characterised according to its double value as representational strategy and as mode of experience; redeemed from the traditional accusations of aesthetic inferiority and political backwardness, it reveals its centrality in historical debates on class, landscape and social change. By articulating the visible and the invisible in the image, and by capturing instances of personal and social anxiety, the picturesque in *L'avventura* brings to the fore states of class tension and fears of revolution, and catalyses key discourses on the transformation of space in capitalist development. Contending with the concept of participation in art as it impinges on questions of aesthetic seriousness, Alexander García Düttmann interrogates the manner in which spectatorial participation occurs in between immediacy and mediation. While Antonioni's *Il provino* (1965) never allows the spectator to forget the constructedness of its subject matter – a screen test in a film studio – it also elicits unmediated participation as an abstract remainder of melodrama. In its rendering of the quasi-simultaneity of participation and observation, the film thus demonstrates Antonioni's acute sense of the possibility and the impossibility of art. Writing against the grain of the established critical understanding of Antonioni's attitude towards actors, and arguing for his deep interest in developing the expressiveness of their bodies, voices and faces, David Forgacs reconstructs the specificity of Antonioni's directorial practice both from interviews and through textual exegesis. The focus on Antonioni's use of actors reveals new depths to his developing aesthetic approach, which also finds an echo in his uninterrupted interest in the foregrounding of both acting and performance.

The book's third section, 'Medium Specifics', brings a powerfully revisionist urge to bear on the encounter with Antonioni. These three essays ask us to reconsider Antonioni's relation to the media in which he worked. Whereas it is all too seductive to think of Antonioni as devotee of 'the cinematic', in fact, as these essays reveal, his work is impure. His films play with and bear the traces of the conditions of a historical reality which proves to be multi-mediatic. Matilde Nardelli calls into question the typical critical tendency to view *Blow-Up* as little more than a treatise on the vagaries of photographic indexicality and instead asks us to consider the film's insistence on photography's reproducible 'plurality'. In doing so, Nardelli transforms our understanding of this film. By grounding its discourse on photography in sharply defined historical and art historical contexts, Nardelli reminds us that one of *Blow-Up*'s major lessons is that photographs never exist singly, but plurally, and, therefore, in a condition of unruly difference, not in the supposed veracity of the singular. Francesco Casetti's essay on Antonioni's experiment in video and colour, *Il mistero di Oberwald* (1980), made for Italian television, asks us to restore what has often been considered as nothing more than an idiosyncrasy back to the heart of Antonioni's canon. This film's strange itinerary through electronic and analogue modes of registration, storage and exhibition illustrates an anti-systemacity that was always at the heart of Antonioni's production. Moreover, in Casetti's provocative reading, *Il mistero di Oberwald* illustrates and anticipates cinema's contemporary susceptibility to what he calls 'relocation': its tendency to migrate across platforms, exhibition sites and aesthetic categories. Michael Loren Siegel compels us to look again at one of Antonioni's least-loved films, *Identifiazione di una donna* (1982). Whereas most critics have been somewhat embarrassed by this film's failure to meet the standards of Antonioni's earlier work, Siegel forces us to encounter the film in its historical context, one characterised by what he calls 'the image and media saturation' of Italian culture in the early 1980s. Contrary to critics who have tried to recuperate *Identificazione* aesthetically, Siegel argues for the historical necessity of recognising and embracing (at least critically) the film's vulgarity. For what it puts on display is just how the deregulation of Italian television made itself felt in the texture of everyday life.

The book's final section is titled 'Ecologies', and the essays gathered here all prompt a consideration of how Antonioni's cinema continues to matter in our contemporary era of looming and already present environmental disaster, of accelerated – and frequently interrupted – economic development. Karl Schoonover examines how Antonioni's interest in the visual poetics of waste summons a critique of Italian neo-realism's rhetoric of (but impatience with) contingency. According to Schoonover, Antonioni's films are willing to waste time and to traffic with waste in order to question a modern and modernist interest in productivity and the production of value. Karen Pinkus invites us to acknowledge Antonioni as the 'poet laureate of climate change'. Pinkus's argument is that Antonioni's work forces us to question many of the bromides and comfortable truisms of climate change discourse, in particular our belief that 'the natural' and 'the human' constitute separate or separable categories. In a fascinating reading of *Il deserto rosso* (1964) as proleptically attuned to the problem of climate change, Pinkus argues that Antonioni's blurring of the boundaries between the natural and the technological obliges us to return to a more radically human perspective on our place in the world. Last, John David Rhodes traces how Antonioni's style develops inside and in relation to a landscape of intensive postwar development in the Italy of the 'economic miracle'. Antonioni was consistently interested in the potential of urban and industrial development to offer rich materials for the purposes of stylistic visual abstraction. Style becomes, for Antonioni, not merely a by-product of development, but a means of critically apprehending its mediation of near and far, a way of understanding film's place and intervention in the abusive landscapes of late capitalism.

15

These essays do not seek, by any means, to exhaust Antonioni's work nor to offer a summation of its enduring influence. We have not tried to curate this collection so as to treat his oeuvre with any claim to systematicity, or with any overarching narrative framework in mind. We have sought to illustrate the vividness of a certain centenary look motivated by a fascination with Michelangelo Antonioni and with conditions of how, in a cultural moment different from his, we encounter him today. The uses to which Antonioni has been and continues to be put are a cultural fact. But, of course, what we unfailingly find in his work is a signature resistance. Antonioni is indissociable from the scholarship which has marked the reception of his oeuvre, and the essays collected here testify to his continuing influence on each of us as we view his films. But what we seek to identify here also are the conditions of a fragile and contingent new beginning. These essays, then, represent a point of departure for new adventures in understanding his work and its place in world culture.

Antonioni's world remains ours. Night is forever falling at the intersection where Vittoria and Piero fail to meet at the end of *L'eclisse*. The yellow fumes are still being exhaled from the factory we see at the end of *Il deserto rosso*. Antonioni's cinema is concerned with the world. Our concern with his cinema will embody, at best, a passionate concern for the world that this cinema has made us see, so beautifully and so strangely.

Notes

1. Transcribed from the documentary by Gianfranco Migozzi, *Michelangelo Antonioni. Storia di un autore* (*Antonioni: Documents and Testimonials*, 1966), trans. LR and JDR.

2. Roland Barthes, 'Cher Antonioni …', *Cahiers du cinéma* no. 311 (May 1980), pp. 9–11; reprinted in English translation in Geoffrey Nowell-Smith (ed.), *L'avventura* (London: BFI, 1997), pp. 209–13 (p. 209).

3. Barthes, 'Cher Antonioni', p. 210.

4. Ibid., p. 211.

5. Manny Farber, *Negative Space: Manny Farber on the Movies* (New York: Praeger, 1971), pp. 135–6.

6. Farber, *Negative Space*, p. 134.

7. Ibid., pp. 136–7.

8. Ibid., p. 142.

9. Ibid.

10. Ibid., p. 143.

11. Michelangelo Antonioni, 'Making a Film is My Way of Life', in Antonioni, *The Architecture of Vision: Writings and Interviews on Cinema*, ed. Giorgio Tinazzi and

Carlo Di Carlo, trans. Marga Cottino-Jones (New York: Marsilio, 1996), pp. 14–17. The essay was originally published in Italian as 'Fare un film è per me vivere', in *Cinema nuovo* no. 138 (March–April 1959).

12. Antonioni, 'Making a Film is My Way of Life', p. 15.

13. Farber, *Negative Space*, p. 143.

14. In 'No Antoniennui', a review originally published in *The Village Voice* on 29 December 1966; reprinted in Roy Huss (ed.), *Focus on Blow-Up* (Englewood Cliffs, NJ: Prentice-Hall, 1971), pp. 31–5.

15. John Orr, *Cinema and Modernity* (Cambridge: Polity Press, 1993), p. 7.

16. Sigmund Freud, 'The Uncanny', in *The Standard Edition of the Complete Psychological Works of Sigmund Freud*, vol. XVII: *An Infantile Neurosis and Other Works*, ed. and trans. James Strachey (London: Hogarth, 1917–19), pp. 217–56.

17. Seymour Chatman titles a section of one his chapters on the 'great tetralogy' (*L'avventura, La notte, L'eclisse* and *Il deserto rosso*) 'The New Montage and *Temps Mort*', *Antonioni, or the Surface of the World* (Berkeley and Los Angeles: University of California Press, 1985), pp. 125–31.

18. We realise that one misses the definite article in this case, whereas its lack has been naturalised in the English appropriation of *temps mort*.

19. 'The distinction of the distinct is therefore its separation: its tension is that of a setting apart and keeping separate which at the same time is a crossing of this separation.' Jean-Luc Nancy, 'The Image – the Distinct', in *The Ground of the Image*, trans. Jeff Fort (New York: Fordham University Press, 2005), pp. 1–14 (p. 3).

20. Karl Schoonover has brilliantly linked art-cinema performance and spectatorship to questions of labour (that of the film actor *and* the film spectator). Cf. 'Wastrels of Time: Slow Cinema and Its Laboring Subjects', paper delivered at 2011 Society for Cinema and Media Studies Conference, New Orleans, Louisiana.

21. Norman N. Holland, 'Not Having Antonioni', *The Hudson Review* vol. 16 no. 1 (Spring 1963), pp. 94–5.

22. Adam Phillips, 'The Value of Frustration: An Interview with Adam Phillips', with Jane Elliott and John David Rhodes, *World Picture* no. 3 (Summer 2009), <http://worldpicturejournal.com/WP_3/Phillips.html>

23. For a discussion of the mobilisation of Antonioni in the Taiwanese new wave, and especially in Edward Yang and Tsai Ming-liang, see Angelo Restivo, *The Cinema of Economic Miracles: Visuality and Modernization in the Italian Art Film* (Durham, NC: Duke University Press, 2002), pp. 159–64.

Modernities

Jacopo Benci

IDENTIFICATION OF A CITY:
Antonioni and Rome, 1940–62[1]

A Possible Biography

> Leave me alone, let me spend my life drop by drop, in this silence that is really my style
> … So if silence is my religion, let me be this way. And do not talk about me.
> Michelangelo Antonioni[2]

In the preface to his recent case study on *L'avventura* (1960), Federico Vitella pointed out the partial unreliability of published biographical information on Antonioni, 'often undermined by a deliberate sidetracking put in place by the director himself, reluctant to spread "sensitive" information about his creative process'.[3] The title of Renzo Renzi's 1992 book, *Antonioni, una biografia impossibile* (*Antonioni, An Impossible Biography*), referred to Antonioni's reticence in providing details about his life. In her discussion of Antonioni's 1955 film *Le amiche*, Anna Maria Torriglia stressed the relevance of a past never fully disclosed or explained yet continuing to haunt the present. For Antonioni,

> the present is just an enigma that can be solved only by exploring the past. It is not
> possible to know or make sense of an action in the present if we do not understand what
> lies behind it and do not launch ourselves into an inquiry – a true 'journey' – into the
> past.[4]

The aim of this essay is twofold: first, to trace the personal and intellectual journey that brought Antonioni from his native Ferrara to Rome in 1940; second, to examine how, over the following decades, he formed the image of Rome to be found in his films from *N.U.* (1948) onwards.

The study of a wide range of sources, including some previously overlooked ones, affords a more thorough picture of the intellectual milieu within which Antonioni built his visual and cultural framework, as well as a better understanding of the motivations informing the choice of locations for his films.

Ferrara, 1912–39

Michelangelo Antonioni was born in Ferrara on 29 September 1912, the second son of 'self-taught middle-class' parents.[5] His father was a staunch fascist; yet, Antonioni said in 1967, 'at the time of the March on Rome, as he did not want to participate, he was seized and beaten savagely'.[6] The teenage Michelangelo attended *ginnasio*, preparatory school for classical studies, but completed his secondary studies at a technical institute.[7] As an *avanguardista*, he adhered 'in a sentimental and confused way' – he recollected in 1978 – to fascism and its rituals; 'some of their acts reminded me of *Bandiere all'Altare della Patria* by Balla, as some of their rallies reminded me of Boccioni's *Retata*. But later, I had such a reaction to that ideology that everything was wiped out.'[8]

Antonioni enrolled at the Faculty of Economics and Commerce of the University of Bologna, where he graduated on 12 July 1938.[9] In interviews, he talked about the lack of cultural stimuli in Ferrara in the 1930s, and claimed he owed his literary education to his friends Lanfranco Caretti, later a renowned philologist, and the writer Giorgio Bassani, both of whom studied literature in Bologna[10] and distinguished themselves in the Littoriali della Cultura e dell'Arte, yearly cultural contests among students of Italian universities, held between 1935 and 1940 under the aegis and control of the Fascist Party.[11] In 1985 Antonioni said,

> [Ferrara] is a city with an important artistic tradition. In the twentieth century painters such as De Pisis, De Chirico (a good part of his metaphysical painting was created in Ferrara), futurists such as Funi and Depero lived for some time in Ferrara. Strangely, this historical and cultural ferment disappeared during Fascism, and there was almost nothing left of it. There were only three or four of us – Giorgio Bassani, Lanfranco Caretti and I – to form a sort of literary coterie.[12]

Such claims may be read to downplay the influence on the young Antonioni of the cultural ambience of Ferrara and its determining political and social factors.

By 28 March 1935 he had begun writing for the Ferrara newspaper, *Corriere Padano*, to which he regularly contributed film reviews, articles and stories for over five years.[13] The paper's founder, the fascist leader Italo Balbo – one of the four main planners of the March on Rome with which Mussolini came to power – was its chief editor for a brief period in 1925, after which he entrusted it to his close collaborator and friend, the journalist Nello Quilici.[14] Balbo, Quilici and the Jewish lawyer Renzo Ravenna, the city's *podestà* (mayor) from 1926 to 1938, set the political and cultural climate of Ferrara during Antonioni's formative years.

As chief editor of *Corriere Padano*, as well as writer, cultural organiser and patron of the arts, Nello Quilici had links with intellectuals such as Papini, Soffici, Pirandello, Casella, artists like Achille Funi, the futurist 'aeropittore' Tato, De Pisis,

Campigli, Martini and prominent fascist personalities such as Dino Grandi and Giuseppe Bottai.[15] In the mid-1930s the cultural page of *Corriere Padano* allowed – as Lanfranco Caretti remarked – 'for an unusual freedom, at least in the literary field, and made it possible for us to discuss the writers whom we deemed significant', such as Eliot, Joyce, Kafka, Mann, Proust, Valéry.[16] In 1941, Antonioni would write about Quilici with admiration and fondness:

> One did not understand how a man could read so much, yet on whatever publication – political, historical, economic, artistic, literary – one questioned him, he was aware, he knew it, he criticized it … [T]he sympathy he extended to me, was a source of pride for me.[17]

Antonioni's favourite writers in the 1930s included Conrad, Gide, the Russians ('there was always a Russian novel on my desk'), Kafka, Montale and Svevo, though he 'felt closer to Penna and Campana and Pavese'. He also 'read film books like crazy, Canudo to Spottishwoode [sic], Chiarini and Arnheim to Barbaro, Balázs to Vertov'.[18]

During his university years, Antonioni developed an interest in theatre, taking part in student companies as an actor, playwright, art director; for a time, he directed the theatre company of the GUF (Fascist University Group) in Ferrara.[19] He obtained a distinction in film criticism and scriptwriting at the 1936 Littoriali in Venice, and participated in the 1937 Littoriali in Naples. In 1938 he was a fiduciary of the Ferrara CineGUF.[20] Besides his intellectual exploits, he was a regular at Ferrara's Tennis Club Marfisa, and his excellence as a tennis player helped him to improve his social status: 'I was surrounded by the Ferrara aristocracy and by its rich bourgeoisie that came from an aristocratic rural background.'[21]

After graduation, while continuing to direct the GUF theatre, Antonioni took up a job at the Ferrara Chamber of Commerce,[22] but was eager to break out of the boundaries of a provincial city like Ferrara. In the spring of 1939 he started contributing to the Rome-based fortnightly journal *Cinema*, founded in 1936 and directed from October 1938 to July 1943 by Benito Mussolini's son, Vittorio. The editorial board of *Cinema* included Rudolf Arnheim (who left Italy in 1939 because of the racial laws), Francesco Pasinetti, Gianni Puccini and, later, Giuseppe De Santis, Mario Alicata, Pietro Ingrao, Carlo Lizzani. Though directed by Vittorio Mussolini, *Cinema* – as Vito Zagarrio has pointed out – 'ended up putting together an anti-fascist editorial staff, and fostering, indeed, through the instrument of culture, a progressive political stance'.[23]

Antonioni's first piece for *Cinema* was a four-page illustrated article, entitled 'Per un film sul fiume Po' ('For a Film on the River Po') and published in the 25 April 1939 issue. The director and film historian Carlo Lizzani, who was a contributor to *Cinema* from 1942 onwards, has provided a possible explanation of why the editors of *Cinema* published such a long article by a young and hardly known journalist from a northern provincial town:

The most important factor we shared then was the idea to get out of the film studios, and discover Italy in its various aspects, from north to south, which we did not know at all. In fact, we Romans looked with curiosity to those who (like Antonioni) came from the north. I remember that at that time we liked those images, those photographs of the Po that he brought to *Cinema*, they impressed us and gave us the idea that he was bringing a contribution to the knowledge of an Italy that was not known, just as we did not know Ciociaria, or Piedmont.[24]

Over three years before shooting his first cinematic work, *Gente del Po* (*People of the Po*, 1942–47), Antonioni sets out the reasons for choosing the river as a subject, and raises questions about the form (documentary or fiction) and approach this film should take. The relationship between the landscape and its inhabitants is defined in the article in terms of *Stimmung* or atmosphere: 'People of the Po *feel* the river. We do not know in what way this *feeling* is made concrete, but we know that it is widespread in the air and that it is experienced as a subtle charm.'[25]

Ferrara to Rome, 1939–40

Determined to move to Rome, Antonioni turned to Nello Quilici for advice and help.[26] In the summer of 1939, in Venice, Quilici introduced and recommended Antonioni to Vittorio Cini.[27] One of Italy's most prominent entrepreneurs, a friend and fellow citizen of Italo Balbo's, Cini was the High Commissioner of the Universal Exposition of Rome, E42 (also known as EUR, Esposizione Universale di Roma), set to celebrate the twentieth anniversary of fascism. Cini determined the future of EUR by advising Mussolini that the exposition be located in the Tre Fontane area and that it should become a permanent district, a 'new town', a 'metropolis provided with the most modern facilities, seamlessly linked to the historical centre'.[28]

Quilici also secured Antonioni a job as contributor to *Volandum*, the bi-monthly magazine of Italy's flag carrier, Ala Littoria, edited by Quilici's sister Mariula. Antonioni went to Rome from time to time for this job.[29] His first article for *Volandum*, an illustrated feature on the contribution of aviation to world cinema, appeared in the September–October 1939 issue.[30]

Vittorio Cini offered Antonioni a job as one of his personal assistants at E42, yet Antonioni's permanent move to Rome probably did not take place until the summer of 1940. On 15 April 1940 he was in Ferrara, where he had his last meeting with Quilici. He was in Ferrara again on 29 June, when the news came of the deaths of Balbo and Quilici at Tobruk on the previous day.[31] At the beginning of June, a few days before Italy entered the war, Antonioni flew to Libya to write a two-part feature for *Volandum*, which was published in the May–June and September–October 1940 issues of the magazine.[32] The articles are enjoyable, if light, collections of

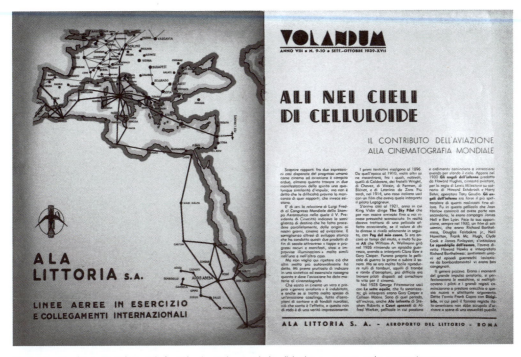

The front page of Antonioni's first article for *Volandum*, 'Ali nei cieli di celluloide', on aviation in the cinema (courtesy Folco Quilici, Rome)

25

impressions and anecdotes on Libya and its climate, the similarity between daily life in the colonies and in the Italian provinces, the difference between Tripoli and Benghazi, excursions by car. Italo Balbo – founder and owner of the *Corriere Padano*, Minister of the Air Force, renowned aviator – was governor of Libya from 1934 until his death on 28 June 1940; Antonioni's visit to Tripoli and Benghazi for the *Volandum* reportages should be seen as part of Balbo's plan to popularise his activities as governor.[33] In regards to Antonioni's receipt of fascist patronage, this was not unusual for young intellectuals at the time (though it did not prevent them from gravitating towards anti-fascism); however, these connections and relationships have been rarely if at all examined by critics, and his collaboration with *Volandum* has so far gone entirely undetected and unexplored.[34] Given the frequent emphasis on air travel across Antonioni's oeuvre (for example, in *L'eclisse* [1962] and *Zabriskie Point* [1970]), as well as the attention that scholars such as Noa Steimatsky have paid to the 'aerial' as the key to understanding Antonioni's impulse towards abstraction, the *Volandum* articles should inform and enrich the genealogy of these concerns.[35]

In Rome, Antonioni took up his job at the E42 headquarters, Palazzo degli Uffici.[36] He later recalled that the job was very well paid, but Cini was rarely seen at the office; Antonioni resigned after a few months, because 'I could not bear to lose time in unnecessary work, which absorbed me without giving me anything.'[37]

In alto: Villaggio Luigi di Savoia — In basso: Via di Bengasi

Taccuino Volante

INTRODUZIONE ALLA LIBIA

Dopo tre ore circa di Mediterraneo — un Mediterraneo macchiato dall'ombra delle nuvole come da inchiostro, — l'orizzonte si definì. Fu dapprima una macchia incerta, d'un colore violaceo sbiadito, poi la macchia ripulì i suoi contorni, s'allungò per un buon tratto di mare, prese un color seppia chiaro e l'Africa si rivelò ai nostri occhi. Devo dire subito che per essere la prima volta che la vedevo l'Africa mi parve, dall'alto, una terra estremamente retorica. Rossa, come infocata, consolata da rade macchie verdastre, dall'apparenza arida e afosa; e poi le case bianche, tutte bianche di Bengasi. Era un tornare indietro con gli anni, ai tempi dei nostri primi fervori giovanili per questa terra, questo caldo, questa sabbia.

Ed ecco che scendendo tutto invece mutò. E tanto mutò che la seconda — per così dire — impressione fu esattamente l'opposto della prima. Dov'era il solleone che dissecca la terra e pesa sui cervelli? Dov'erano i cinquanta all'ombra che infiacchiscono gli uomini? Passi per il ghibli, che non è cosa di tutti i giorni, ma quella placida brezza che veniva dal nord a temperare il meriggio, a dargli sapor di mare, di spiaggia adriatica, mi deluse veramente. Come essere a Rimini.

È chiaro che ambedue le impressioni dovevano risultare sbagliate. Un paese non si dà al primo sguardo, per quanto sottile la sensibilità di chi vi capita. Ma sul momento nel ritrovarmi attorno quell'aria casalinga ci rimasi male. E

solo una più ampia e attenta visita potè riscattare codesta impressione.

Così il metter piede per la prima volta in terra africana non mi procurò, come avevo pensato, alcuna emozione. Certo recarsi in Libia oggi è appena uscir dalla porta di casa. Fui colazione a Roma e pranzi a Tripoli o a Bengasi. Hai ancora nelle orecchie il brusio della fontana dell'Esedra, non c'è il distacco, il senso della lontananza. Ma forse, come già m'avvenne di constatare ad altri viaggi, la questione è più generale. Ed è in noi, nel nostro essere all'altezza dei tempi. Indubbiamente vivamo tempi scettici. Non si crede più a niente, si è corrotti da una vita irta d'esperienze, si prova ritegno ad abbandonarsi. E capita così che luoghi lungamente accarezzati con la fantasia non eccitino più il nostro stupore. Si finisce per non credere nemmeno alle lontananze. S'arriva nei passi carichi di diffidenza, l'animo vigile, disposto ad accettar ogni sorpresa col beneficio d'inventario, l'occhio preparato a ogni bellezza la più estranea: si guarda e si ha vergogna della meraviglia. In noi uomini moderni, scanzonati la meraviglia è una debolezza. Sarà forse necessaria l'inimmaginabile novità d'un arrivo a New York, che attragga e atterrisca insieme, per giustificare il nostro sbalordimento.

Ma dopo alcuni giorni di permanenza in Libia, via via che scoprivo o credevo di scoprire qualche cosa, nasceva l'interesse, nasceva l'amore e quindi l'entusiasmo. Quando partii, i nomi dei luoghi che non avevo veduti, Gadames, Cufra, Derna, ecc., mi mulinavano nel cervello come le mete più belle che spirito turistico possa desiderare. Di quelli che

The frontispiece of the first part of Antonioni's reportage from Libya in *Volandum*, 'Taccuino Volante. Introduzione alla Libia' (June 1940), with an aerial photograph of one of the settlers' villages (courtesy Folco Quilici, Rome)

He found employment as editorial secretary of *Cinema* thanks to Gino Visentini, a collaborator of the renowned writer-publisher Leo Longanesi.[38] Antonioni's stint as editorial secretary of *Cinema* was brief. He recalled, 'Gino Visentini left, and for a time afterwards, I was left alone to edit the magazine. Then I had some disagreements with Vittorio Mussolini's secretary, Rosario Leone.'[39] He was eventually

26

sacked without any severance pay; Pasinetti and then Puccini and De Santis took over the magazine.[40] The following period was not easy for Antonioni:

> I lived in poverty in Rome. I was hungry. I hated Rome, because it was a world too different from mine. I felt corruption getting into my nose, my ears, my eyes. I knew it ended up involving everyone. None of those I considered my friends gave me a hand. I spent a few months really alone. … Rome is a difficult, hostile city. My father had money – he was then a small industrialist – and wanted me back in Ferrara. But I refused and lived by selling tennis trophies; I had boxes full of them that I'd won in tournaments during college days. I pawned and sold them all.[41]

Antonioni's professional links with Ferrara were cut off with the deaths of Balbo and Quilici. Quilici's sister Mariula, however, continued to employ and support him, and he contributed film and book reviews, articles, reportages and short stories to *Volandum* until July 1943.[42] Nello Quilici's son Folco has recalled:

> My aunt told me, 'Antonioni came into my office every other day, as he put together the magazine'. His contribution to *Volandum* didn't just entail the articles that he wrote; he oversaw the whole magazine, because my aunt was busy with her work as head of the press office of Ala Littoria. His involvement in *Volandum* was much more substantial than it appeared, and I understand that it was essentially what allowed him to keep himself in Rome. Also, my aunt recommended him highly to the chief editor of the newspaper *Il Messaggero*, who was a close friend of hers and my father's. So my aunt made sure that Antonioni contributed articles to the newspaper, which probably came out unsigned.[43]

Antonioni stayed in Rome in order to pursue the path of film-making. At that delicate moment of transition, through the *Cinema* group Antonioni found new contacts, opportunities, intellectual and artistic stimuli.

Encounters and Experiences in Rome, 1940–47

In late 1940, alongside De Santis and Massimo Mida (Gianni Puccini's brother), Antonioni enrolled in the film direction course at Centro Sperimentale di Cinematografia at the invitation of its director Luigi Chiarini and of Umberto Barbaro, critic and professor at the Centro.[44] Massimo Mida recalled,

> The year we spent at the Centro was important for us, not only for the value of teachers, but also because we were able to rely on theoretical activity such as that of the journal *Bianco e Nero*, and the translations, made by Chiarini and Barbaro, of books by

Pudovkin, Béla Balázs, and Arnheim who had published a kind of summary of his famous book *Film as Art* in one of the first issues of *Bianco e Nero*. Of course, one must add to all this the meetings that took place in salons-laboratories such as those of Arnheim, Alicata, Luchino Visconti, that slowly clarified what was to be our commitment both as intellectuals and as anti-fascists.[45]

Among Antonioni's teachers at the Centro Sperimentale was the critic, historian, theorist, screenwriter and director Francesco Pasinetti. Born in Venice in 1911, the first student in Italy to graduate with a thesis on the cinema from the University of Padua in 1933, he wrote for newspapers and magazines (including *Cinema*, *Bianco e Nero* and *Primato*) and published five books on cinema.[46] Pasinetti moved to Rome in the mid-1930s and took an apartment at Viale di Villa Massimo 24.[47] From 1936 he taught screenwriting at the Centro Sperimentale, and acted as director of the school from 1948 until his untimely death in 1949.

Antonioni had already met Pasinetti and his brother, the writer Pier Maria (P. M.) Pasinetti, since both contributed to *Cinema*.[48] As Antonioni recalled in 1980, 'Francesco Pasinetti was for us – I mean not only the students of the Centro, but all those who worked in the cinema at that time – a kind of symbol, somehow we identified him with the cinema.'[49] The two young men became close friends, and Pasinetti even invited Antonioni to lodge at his home.[50] The acquaintance with the Pasinetti brothers, who belonged in a family of bourgeois intellectuals and artists and were widely read and travelled, certainly helped Antonioni broaden his cultural horizons.

At the Centro Sperimentale, Antonioni met Letizia Balboni, a film-making student and occasional contributor to *Cinema*. They married on 21 November 1942 and took lodging with Francesco Pasinetti. When in 1945 Pasinetti married Letizia's sister Loredana, the two couples shared the same apartment. One of five daughters of a Venetian antiques dealer, Letizia was, according to Francesco Maselli (who was Pasinetti's student at the Centro Sperimentale in 1947 and Antonioni's assistant director and co-scriptwriter in 1948–53), 'an intelligent, open-minded, courageous, and very intellectual woman; she was widely read and had a sort of rational supremacy on Michelangelo'.[51] In the late 1940s, both Francesco Maselli and Loredana Balboni would witness how Letizia pointed Michelangelo's attention towards authors such as F. Scott Fitzgerald, and how she suggested that a film should 'tell one story in order to actually narrating another one'.[52]

In the summer of 1941 Antonioni was drafted in the army; he served for a year and a half without leaving Rome.[53] He worked with Massimo Mida and Rosario Leone on the screenplay of *Un pilota ritorna* (*A Pilot Returns*, 1942) written by Vittorio Mussolini and directed by Roberto Rossellini. The protagonist was played by Massimo Girotti, later to star in *Ossessione* (1943), *Caccia tragica* (*Tragic Pursuit*,

1947) and *Cronaca di un amore* (1950).[54] In late 1941, Antonioni contributed an article to the monographic issue 'Stile italiano nel cinema' ('Italian Style in the Cinema') of the quarterly *Aria d'Italia*, a luxury magazine published in Milan by Daria Guarnati, a wealthy art collector and a friend of the architect Gio Ponti.[55] Among the contributors to the cinema issue of *Aria d'Italia* were Pasinetti, Puccini, De Santis, Visconti, Augusto Genina, Enrico Fulchignoni and Gio Ponti. In his article 'Architettura "nel" cinema – Idee' ('Architecture "in the" Cinema – Ideas'), Ponti called for a cinema in which architecture would be an active element of the film rather than background:

> Imagine a film that starts with an 'empty scene' dominated by the architecture ... and where the architecture sings like a musical prelude before the action starts; imagine, after the story has ended, again an 'empty stage', where the architecture alone still lives, deserted now by the actors, as in a metaphysical finale ... Architecture, like music, not only echoes and mirrors the mood of the character, not only it is his landscape, but it is in itself a character, which intervenes with its independent powers.[56]

Ponti's call for an active role of architecture in cinema, and his suggestion that the action is bracketed by shots of empty architectural spaces, foreshadows the later works of Antonioni, especially – and uncannily – the ending of *L'eclisse*.

At the beginning of 1942, Antonioni was introduced to Luchino Visconti by Puccini and De Santis; he recalled in 1978, 'I began to hang around with his group more and more frequently until both of us went to the Po, Luchino to shoot *Ossessione*, and I to shoot *Gente del Po*.'[57] He then worked as co-scriptwriter and assistant director for the Scalera Film production of *I due Foscari* (*The Two Foscaris*, 1942) directed by Enrico Fulchignoni. Fulchignoni's cinematographer, Ubaldo Arata, came to appreciate Antonioni's thinking on cinema and recommended him to the producer Michele Scalera.[58] In the summer of 1942, Antonioni obtained a leave to go to France as assistant to Marcel Carné in *Les visiteurs du soir*, a Scalera co-production.[59] Later in the same year, thanks to the support of Minoccheri, director of the documentary department of Istituto Luce (the state-controlled newsreels and documentary production centre), Antonioni took a film crew to the Po valley to shoot *Gente del Po*, the documentary he had envisaged in 1939.[60]

After the armistice of 8 September 1943 and the subsequent German occupation of Rome Antonioni – who had secretly joined the liberal-socialist Partito d'Azione[61] – was in serious danger, having refused to join the Fascist Republican army. He took refuge for a few months in the Abruzzo, in the house of Antonio Pietrangeli, one of the editors of *Cinema*. Later he returned to the capital, and hid with Giorgio Bassani in Pasinetti's apartment. On the eve of the liberation of Rome, Antonioni earned some money translating from the French Paul Morand's *Monsieur Zéro*.[62] After the liberation, from 22 June 1944 to 12 April 1945, Antonioni was the film critic for the Rome edition of the Partito d'Azione newspaper, *L'Italia Libera*. In November 1944 he co-founded, with Visconti, De Santis, Zavattini, De Sica and Camerini, the Associazione Culturale Cinematografica Italiana (ACCI, Italian Cultural Cinema Association). Among its activities, the ACCI organised screenings of films that had been banned under fascism, introduced by writers, artists and film-makers such as Moravia, De Chirico, Guttuso, Lattuada, Soldati and Pietrangeli.[63]

On 20 January 1945 Visconti's production of Cocteau's *Les parents terribles*, the first work he directed for the theatre, premiered at Teatro Eliseo in Rome. Its huge success established Visconti's reputation as a master *metteur en scène*.[64] Antonioni later stressed the importance Visconti's theatrical work had for him:

> I followed the readings of the texts, the rehearsals, all the performances. I was learning.
> ... Watching him work was wonderful, I spent my evenings in that way. Through him I
> mastered the space where the actor is brought to play, and then projected it in reality in
> my own way.[65]

In the spring 1945, Antonioni worked with Pietrangeli and De Santis on a film script for Visconti provisionally titled *Furore*; a story about four prostitutes on the Anzio war front. After the project folded, Antonioni became a contributor to the journal *Film d'Oggi*, alongside Pietrangeli, De Santis, Puccini, Mida and Lizzani.[66] Between 1945 and 1947 he would write for several other magazines, such as *Film Rivista*, *Risorgimento* and *La Fiera letteraria*.[67]

From August 1945 to September 1946, Antonioni worked with Pietrangeli and Guido Piovene on the script of another Visconti film project, *Il processo di Maria Tarnowska*, the story of a murderous love intrigue among Russian aristocrats in Venice. An article in the magazine *Film Rivista* of 15 April 1946 described Visconti and his collaborators at work in a room at the San Giorgio Hotel in Rome: on the walls, photographs of Venice locations chosen by Visconti, historic images of the defendants, their friends and relatives, of crowds, diplomats, journalists, photographs of plays staged by Visconti and the actors who played them, and 'some beautiful Vespignani drawings of ruins of bombings and trains'.[68] Antonioni was to be Visconti's assistant director for *Tarnowska*. After the project was abandoned, he co-scripted – with De Santis, Zavattini, Umberto Barbaro and Lizzani – *Caccia tragica*, the first film directed by Giuseppe De Santis, starring Massimo Girotti and Andrea Checchi.

In April 1947 the ACCI became the Circolo Romano del Cinema (Rome Film Club); Antonioni was among its founders, and Cesare Zavattini was its president.[69] The Circolo organised a memorable premiere of *Ladri di biciclette* (*Bicycle Thieves*) on 21 November 1948 at the Cinema Barberini, with director, writers and actors in attendance.[70] As director Francesco Rosi recalled,

The Circolo matinees at Cinema Barberini were packed right from 10 AM. Visconti went to see the films of Rossellini, who in turn went to see those of De Sica … You could find Antonioni, De Santis, Amidei, Zavattini, Suso Cecchi D'Amico, Fellini, assistants, scriptwriters … It produced an extraordinary movement of ideas, a unique cultural climate.[71]

The variety of Antonioni's activities during this period reveals that not only was he deeply embedded in the historical experience out of which cinematic neo-realism emerged (and to which it responded), but he was also actively involved in the cinematic culture of neo-realist film-making itself, as well as in the critical apparatuses that mediated its theorisation and reception.

Documentaries, 1947–49

In 1947 Antonioni retrieved and edited what was left of the footage for *Gente del Po*, which had been taken to Venice after the armistice and partly ruined. The documentary was screened on 2 September at the Venice Film Festival. His second documentary *N.U.*, shot between 1947 and 1948, was shown at the 1948 Venice Film Festival, where it won a Nastro d'Argento, the prize for best documentary of the National Union of Cinema Journalists. Between 1949 and 1950 Antonioni shot five more documentaries, *L'amorosa menzogna* (which won another Nastro d'Argento), *Superstizione*, *Sette canne, un vestito*, *La villa dei mostri* and *Vertigine*. He planned several others, while trying to find financial backing for his first full-length feature.[72]

In the late 1940s Antonioni taught for a short period at the Centro Sperimentale. He was one of the examiners for admission at the directors' course of the Centro, and in this role, at the end of 1947, he met the young aspiring film-maker Francesco Maselli.[73] Despite their difference in age (Maselli was still a teenager, being born in December 1930), for the next six years their friendship was to be professionally and culturally influential for Antonioni.

Maselli was born in Rome into a family of bourgeois intellectuals.[74] Luigi Pirandello, a family friend, was his godfather; through his parents and his older sister Titina, a painter, Maselli was personally acquainted with cultural personalities such as Bontempelli, Savinio, Casella and Ungaretti, and had a wide knowledge of the arts. He took part in the Rome Resistance in 1943–44 and became a member of the Communist Party in 1945. From 1949 to 1953 Maselli was Antonioni's assistant director and co-scriptwriter; they chose together many locations for *L'amorosa menzogna*, and in 1952 Antonioni entrusted to Maselli the task of location scouting for *La signora senza camelie*.

N.U. and *L'amorosa menzogna* – Antonioni's two most important documentaries of the late 1940s alongside *Gente del Po* – portray humble, poor people. In

31

several of Antonioni's later films the main characters belong to the middle class, yet there are clues pointing to their lower-class origins (Guido and Paola in *Cronaca di un amore*, Clara in *La signora senza camelie*, Clelia in *Le amiche*, Claudia in *L'avventura*, Vittoria in *L'eclisse*). This interest in humble class origins resonates with literary prototypes such as Jay Gatsby[75] but also, if not with Antonioni's own background, certainly with that of his parents. Talking about *Cronaca di un amore* in 1980, Antonioni said to Seymour Chatman: 'You remember the movie is about money? And what I remember about myself is that I didn't have any money at that time. And that's very important, because I looked at that story from a certain angle.'[76]

Such a statement should be contextualised in the social and economic situation of the immediate postwar period. Between 1939 and 1945 the cost of living had increased by twenty-three times; living conditions in Rome were extremely difficult.[77] Francesco Maselli recalled, 'we were all extremely poor. Michelangelo was really poor, he had only one pair of trousers. Every night he carefully put them under the mattress, to keep them neatly pressed. It was a sorry thing.'[78] Recalling his visits to Rome at the end of the 1940s, the Bolognese film critic Renzo Renzi wrote,

> we met at Otello alla Concordia on Via della Croce, ... where I remember being at the table with young filmmakers, journalists, singers; filmmakers who were all still assistant directors, Rosi, Bolognini, Ferreri, Maselli ... Like many members of that group, Antonioni, accompanied by his wife Letizia Balboni, was sometimes in poor economic conditions, which I think brought him to skip a few meals. But his determination to stay in Rome to make films ... was as strong as steel.[79]

After the death of Quilici in 1940, another sudden loss struck Antonioni when Francesco Pasinetti, his brother-in-law, friend, colleague and former teacher, died of an aneurism on 2 April 1949. Loredana returned to Venice, while Letizia and Michelangelo rented a flat near the Vatican in the Via della Conciliazione.[80] Soon afterwards, when Antonioni finally found financial backing for his first feature, *Cronaca di un amore*, the couple moved to a top-floor apartment at Via Archimede 44 in the affluent Parioli, a district favoured by film-makers at that time.[81] Letizia's relationship with Michelangelo, however, had become strained and she abandoned him in 1954; their marriage was eventually annulled.

But Antonioni's links with the Pasinettis and the Balbonis were not severed. P. M. Pasinetti, who had taken up a professorship in Italian and comparative literature at UCLA in 1949, co-scripted *La signora senza camelie* and played a brief cameo role in the film as a diplomat. In late 1953 Loredana Balboni married the Venetian industrialist and film producer Antonio Pellizzari.[82] She moved back to Rome in 1958, and her Piazza di Spagna apartment became a literary salon where artists, writers and film-makers met regularly.[83] There she introduced Antonioni to American photographer and journalist Milton Gendel, the Rome correspondant of

Art News, and a regular in the salons of the Roman bourgeoisie where writers and artists met. In 1959 Gendel, as partner (and later husband) of British aristocrat Lady Judy Montagu, and advisor of painter Frances McCann, director of the Rome–New York Art Foundation, would give Antonioni access to the Tiber Island locations for Sandro's apartment (the Gendels' apartment) and the art gallery (the Rome–New York Art Foundation) for the Rome prologue of *L'avventura*.[84]

Francesco Maselli witnessed how Antonioni, during the long years when his economic position was precarious and his success was still uncertain, devoted himself tirelessly to weaving a network of relationships with film producers and other potential backers, and forging links with wealthy and influential people who could help him to make films that seemed to have little commercial potential, and with like-minded intellectuals who would advocate what he intended to do, which did not always have the understanding and support of the critics.[85]

Identification of a City

Most people are blind in their own country; they can't see at all. What does a Roman know of Rome? Only his own itinerary.
Michelangelo Antonioni[86]

Antonioni's April 1941 review of the film *Tosca* (begun by Jean Renoir and Visconti, and taken up by Renoir's collaborator Carl Koch when Italy entered the war) gave him the opportunity to describe the Rome cityscape as a cinematic subject:

Wandering the streets of Rome means to see an unexpected perspective opening before one's eyes at every turn; long straight streets lead to scenery of extraordinary architectural harmony; statues and fountains lurking behind corners, rise before you as you turn: blissful patterns of ancient cities! And of Rome in particular. Precisely because of this feature, she seems very suited for cinema. In fact, let us think of camera movements. What better, more truthful, yet more fantastic means of expression to give the eye a sense of this sudden opening up of perspectives, of cityscapes, and so forth? … [I]nventive wit and architectural harmony are so ubiquitous even in the most hidden and unexpected corners of Rome, that the camera, because of its mobility, is the most suited instrument for capturing those qualities.[87]

This article, which was written, we should remember, less than a year after Antonioni's move from Ferrara, makes no mention of what lay beyond Rome's historical centre. The city's landscape is one of 'perspectives' and 'scenery', statues and fountains, architectural harmony. After the war, however, in his documentaries and films of 1948–53, his attention would shift to the industrial Rome of factories,

33

refineries, brick furnaces, workshops, and the trajectories of people belonging in the entire spectrum of society: beggars, street sweepers, workers living in shanties and council housing, middle-class people in the old centre and in new residential quarters. What were the causes of this shift?

The change in Antonioni's perspective must be understood in the context of the dramatic changes that Rome and Italy underwent between 1943 and 1948. According to urban historian Italo Insolera, a new Rome was coming into being:

> During the war and black market years, the Romans were forced to discover their own
> city. ... The well-off people went to look for eggs and chicory in the 'borgate', and the
> inhabitants of the 'borgate' had become accustomed to go into Rome every day, to trade
> on the black market or drive the jeeps [used for public transport]. Internally displaced
> persons lived in schools, and slums were to be found not only in the distant countryside,
> but at Campo Parioli or Campo Artiglio, in residential areas or white-collar
> neighbourhoods. ... The social system of the city had been turned upside down, and
> poverty had brought everyone close together. Rome in 1945 was a different entity than in
> 1940, and above all it was known in a different way by its inhabitants.[88]

Antonioni's way of dealing with Rome is consistent with the neo-realist approach to location shooting; we are shown that the city's poor are not confined to the peripheral *borgate*, but can be found near the upper-class district of Parioli as well as in the *rioni* in the city's heart.

Francesco Rosi, who was assistant director in *I vinti* four years after working with Visconti on *La terra trema* (1948), understood Antonioni's approach to location in the context of the neo-realist tradition:

> Cinema then insisted on the environment [*ambiente*, also meaning 'setting', 'location',
> 'surroundings'], as much as the choice of performers. In Antonioni, the choice of an
> environment was crucial also for the description of a character. The environment in a film
> is closely related to the presence of certain actors, it is essential to justify certain decisions.
> Antonioni was trying to give a very precise image of the social dimension. In this, he was a
> child of neorealism; his interest in the social element to pull out of a film came from that.[89]

In several interviews and statements, Antonioni emphasised the importance of location in his way of constructing films, and its precedence over characters and their stories. The following quotations epitomise the centrality of the real location to Antonioni's aesthetic:

> Some filmmakers want to tell a story and choose 'a posteriori' the decor that suits them
> best. For me, the process is reversed. The subject of my films is always born of a
> landscape, a place, a location where I want to shoot.[90]

In general, I decide upon the outdoor locations before writing the shooting script. ... I need to have the surroundings of the film clearly in mind. There are times too when an idea for a film comes to me from a particular place.

I have to see the location while I am writing, not after. I cannot describe a landscape without knowing it. ... [I]f I'm making something in the street, I have to know which street I am talking about. I want to see first, then I place the characters. Actually, the streets give me the idea for the scene.[91]

Antonioni's emphasis here should be linked to the positions taken in the early 1940s by several contributors of *Cinema*. Giuseppe De Santis wrote in April 1941,

The importance of a 'landscape', and the choice of it as a fundamental element within which the characters should live, almost bringing on them the signs of its impact ... are aspects of a problem almost always resolved in the cinema of other countries, never in our cinema.[92]

Antonioni's approach broadened and developed such positions. One of his distinctive contributions to the understanding of the city through cinema was his topographical accuracy (revealed by comparing his films with the location incongruities of the films of De Sica and Rossellini), which would grow increasingly consistent from *N.U.* to *L'eclisse*.

35

N.U. (1948)

Antonioni's second documentary *N.U.* was shot a few months before De Sica's *Bicycle Thieves*. The two works share several locations and the portrayal of hardship in the aftermath of the war.[93] *Bicycle Thieves* showed the unemployed Antonio Ricci and his family living in the council housing estate of Val Melaina in the far northern outskirts of Rome; *N.U.* showed men sleeping in a florists' stall in Piazza di Spagna, or on a street in Trastevere, and living in poor housing at Monte del Gallo with the dome of St Peter's in sight. According to Steven Jacobs,

Antonioni borrows from neorealism the meticulous selection of locations and great care for settings, but the urban landscape no longer functions as an illustration of the social context of the characters ... Antonioni retains from the documentary genre and the aesthetics of neorealism an interest in the environment, but leaves out any didactic intention.[94]

The visual language of *Gente del Po* related essentially to cinematic sources, such as Jean Vigo, Carné and Dreyer.[95] Antonioni's postwar works such as *N.U.* and *L'amorosa menzogna* reveal a growing architectural and pictorial awareness, which would become a distinctive and significant feature of his language. Antonioni's way of observing and framing urban landscape was informed by the works of Mario Sironi and Lorenzo Vespignani. As Francesco Maselli recalled,

> we were very strongly infatuated with the painter 'par excellence' of urban sites, Sironi. Sironi was an artist who greatly influenced and affected the imagination and soul of many of us. He was like a model – even with all the ambiguity of his fascism – charged with an extraordinary synthesis, an extraordinary expression of the urban landscape. Antonioni's love for Vespignani was equally strong. ... I want to stress the fact that, although nothing was further removed from Antonioni than a direct figurative influence, in the metropolitan atmosphere of *N.U.* and *L'amorosa menzogna* there was certainly a dramatic charge that somehow reflects the figurative climate of that period.[96]

In *N.U.*, the dispossessed – the dustmen, the poor, the needy, the disabled – are associated with blues and jazz music, in a manner that is suggestive of and consistent with the role that American literature, cinema, photography and music played for anti-fascist and proto-neo-realist Italian culture in the late 1930s and 40s.[97]

Among the Italian forerunners of *N.U.* are Francesco Di Cocco's documentary *Il ventre della città* (*The Belly of the City*, 1932),[98] which illustrates how edible supplies are produced and distributed to the city of Rome, and *Nulla si distrugge* (*Nothing is Destroyed*), an INCOM documentary screened at the 1940 Venice Film Festival and described by Antonioni as 'an excellent short film that documents the use of waste in the city of Milan. You would never imagine what can be derived from garbage – textiles, grease, tin, paper, steel, fertilizers and more.'[99]

N.U., however, distances itself from the celebratory tone of the city symphony-type films; the voice-over commentary points to a different set of concerns, to a different face of the city:

> Who are the street cleaners and how do they live, these humble and silent workers whom no one looks at and talks to? This does not seem to concern us. The street cleaners are part of the city as something inanimate. Yet no one takes part in the life of the city more than they. How do they see it?[100]

The dustmen are involved not in *flânerie* but in tough, humble work, which begins at dawn in a poor suburb by a railway, and continues unnoticed among a wide range of locations, ancient and modern, 'high' and 'low', in the historic city and the suburbs.[101] The Rome revealed by the incessant wandering of the dustmen includes historic landmarks such as the Pincio, Piazza del Popolo, the Quirinal, St Peter's, the

N.U. (1948): the last shot, reminiscent of Lorenzo Vespignani's drawings and etchings of postwar Rome: a street cleaner walking towards Piano di Pietra Papa, in the south-west periphery

Spanish Steps, Tiber Island, the Baths of Caracalla, the Forum, the Gianicolo, but also the working-class districts of Trastevere, the Ghetto, Piazza Vittorio, San Lorenzo and middle-class neighbourhoods and monuments built under fascism, Viale Eritrea, Ponte Duca d'Aosta and Viale Mazzini. Antonioni's camera proceeds further to show the viewer a semi-rural dimension existing alongside the colossal buildings of Mussolini's Rome: the suburban Valle dei Casali, where Armando Brasini's 1930s neo-baroque Buon Pastore convent looms over the horizon, or the area below the Monte Mario hill, in which, near the large apartment buildings of the Viale Mazzini one can see pigsties where pigs eat garbage collected by the dust-men. At the end of his workday, a dustman returns to his hovel at Monte del Gallo, from which we can see the dome of St Peter's. Another dustman – like a silhouette in a Vespignani drawing – walks away, over the train tracks, towards the then-unbuilt open space of Piano di Pietra Papa.

In his preface to *Il primo Antonioni* (1973), Carlo Di Carlo pointed out the influence on Antonioni of John Grierson's seminal text *First Principles of Documentary* (1932–34).[102] Antonioni's *N.U.* seems to respond to Grierson's contention that:

> realist documentary, with its streets and cities and slums and markets and exchanges and factories, has given itself the job of making poetry where no poet has gone before it, and where no ends, sufficient for the purpose of art, are easily observed.[103]

In his lengthy article 'Marcel Carné, parigino' ('Marcel Carné, Parisian'), published in *Bianco e Nero* in 1948 (but largely written in 1942–43 and published in part in *Primato* in May 1943), Antonioni quoted from a 1933 article by Carné, 'Quand le cinéma descendra-t-il dans la rue?' ('When will the Cinema Go Down into the Street?'), in which the French director urged film-makers 'to describe the simple life of humble people, to depict the atmosphere of hard-working humanity which is

37

theirs'.[104] A similar point was made in an article by Mario Alicata and Giuseppe De Santis on the significance of Giovanni Verga for the renewal of Italian cinema, published in *Cinema* in late 1941. Alicata and De Santis wrote, 'We want to bring our camera to the fields, ports, factories of our country: we are convinced that one day we will create our best movie following the slow, tired pace of the worker who returns to his home.'[105]

The final shot of *N.U.* puts into images what Alicata and De Santis had envisaged. Carlo Lizzani has remarked on this film:

> For us, that continued to be one of the righteous ways to look at Rome, that is, not the picture postcard way: 'I'll show you precisely the Rome of the river, the living city'. We were pleased when we saw a dirty corner, and I, as a Roman, liked the Rome of *N.U.* It was also a Rome that was against the respectability of the landscape.[106]

L'amorosa menzogna (1949)

Shot in the early months of 1949, *L'amorosa menzogna* is a short film – part documentary, part fiction – about the stars of the hugely popular photographic comic books known as *fotoromanzi* ('photo-novels'). The subject interested Antonioni so much that he developed it into a script, *Caro Ivan* (*Dear Ivan*), which he sold to producer Carlo Ponti (Ponti entrusted it to Federico Fellini, who made it into his first masterpiece, *Lo sceicco bianco* [*The White Sheik*, 1952]).[107]

The *fotoromanzi* were aimed at working-class audiences. Antonioni's camera, turning its back to the historic centre, follows *fotoromanzi* actors and their fans (working girls, delivery boys, soldiers on leave, housemaids, mechanics) around a city of workshops, warehouses, peripheral thoroughfares, tram stops, council housing estates, wine shops, hairdressers, dairies and newsagents. *L'amorosa menzogna* takes

L'amorosa menzogna (1949): working-class Rome. The inner courtyard of a 'casa di ringhiera' at Via degli Equi 26, San Lorenzo

38

the spectator from Via Tuscolana to Via dei Lucani in the working-class district of San Lorenzo; from the merry-go-rounds at Piazzale Clodio, to a chromium-plating work-shop in the inner courtyard of a 'casa di ringhiera' at Via degli Equi 26, San Lorenzo, where the *fotoromanzi* star Sergio Raimondi is greeted by female fans and a little girl dancer.[108] The film eventually takes the viewer to a tavern in Primavalle (the camera lingers on a street corner long enough for us to read the name on the plaque, Via Lorenzo Litta), and ends with the mildly ironic everyday vignette of the *fotoromanzi* star Anna Vita missing the no. 19 tram at Piazza Zama.[109] This is a remarkable top-ographical and sociological variety in a film that is just over ten minutes in length.

Antonioni's keen observation of working-class people and suburban Rome was not purely documentary, but was also informed by an intense awareness of aesthetic values. Francesco Maselli, who went with Antonioni in search of locations for *L'amorosa menzogna*, recalled,

> he warned us … that in a strongly characterized metropolitan environment, it was necessary to get rid of any presence of greenery – a cypress tree, a bush – because greenery spoils, softens everything; even when shooting in black and white, it creates a splash of colour. … I once found a really striking image that had a wonderful aura, but Michelangelo said 'No' and I asked, 'Why not?' He replied, 'Can't you see there is a post that gets in the shot from the right? Don't you realize that it spoils everything?' I was stunned, then I realized this was an extraordinary lesson because that bit of post indeed ruined the emotional purity and the figurative power of that image.[110]

39

The notions of 'emotional purity' and 'figurative power' of images should be seen in the context of Italian art movements of the first half of the twentieth century, such as metaphysical painting, Valori Plastici and magic realism. Antonioni's vision was shaped by his appreciation of the works of Sironi, De Chirico and Morandi.[111] Indeed, the shot where a delivery van stops at a newsstand, with a slender smokestack

L'amorosa menzogna (1949): a Sironiesque cityscape

towering in the background, is strongly reminiscent of Mario Sironi's *Urban Landscapes* of the early 1920s.

The Rome Episode of *I vinti* (1952–53)

Antonioni's second feature *I vinti* (*The Vanquished*, 1952–53), funded by the Catholic production company Film Costellazione, dealt with the discomfort of post-war youth, which manifested itself through crime. The film consists of three episodes, set in Paris, London and Rome; today the English episode is unanimously considered the best of the three, and a forerunner of Antonioni's mature style. The French and especially the Italian episodes, however, suffered heavy censorship.

Stefania Parigi has traced the history of the Rome episode. Antonioni wrote the screenplay with Giorgio Bassani and Suso Cecchi D'Amico in 1951, based on the story of a young neo-fascist, Achille Billi, whose body had been found in a boat near Ponte Risorgimento in April 1949, and whose death was attributed to suicide or the struggle between moderate and radical factions of neo-fascism. In the first draft of the screenplay, a young man named Arturo Bolla is a member of a radical group that pushes the neo-fascist party, Movimento Sociale Italiano (MSI), to undertake violent actions. In a later draft, the young man (named Arturo Botta), along with other neo-fascists, carries out a bomb attack on the Ministry of Interior. The attack fails, and the MSI (which secretly incites but officially condemns the conspiracy) expels Arturo, who commits suicide.[112] The introduction of the bomb attack was probably suggested by events that just preceded the production of the screenplay: on 13 March 1951, the Legione Nera (Black Legion) claimed two terrorist attacks against the Ministry of Foreign Affairs and the US Embassy in Rome. On 3 June, the police arrested twenty-one people for attempted reconstitution of the outlawed Fascist Party, and as responsible for terrorist attacks in Rome during the previous two years. In the city council elections of 25 May 1952, the MSI obtained 15.6 per cent of the votes, not only in middle-class districts but also in working-class neighbourhoods and *borgate*. According to a confidential police report to the Ministry of the Interior, the MSI 'intended to penetrate all layers of society, particularly blue-collar workers and students'.[113]

Shooting for the Rome episode began on 7 July 1952. Five days before, the Film Production Division of the Presidency of the Council of Ministers' General Directorate of Entertainment issued a 'Precautionary review – Memorandum' regarding the submission of the script for *I vinti*. The memorandum stated,

> the subject [of the movie] is thorny and insidious in view of the final revision, given the apparent morbidity that is present in these juvenile crimes, more or less inspired by real events. ... Also, it implies a hard and heavy condemnation of modern bourgeois society,

40

which is made entirely responsible for the crimes recounted. ... [T]here is a danger that this critique will bring benefit to enemy propaganda rather than the corrective function of contemporary morality that the filmmakers intended by embarking on a film of this genre. ... The film, as it is conceived ... far from suggesting explicit remedies and forthcoming solutions, ends up being an indictment aimed at society at large, and an apocalyptic warning cry. ... The choice of Antonioni as director of this film exacerbates the above concerns.[114]

The memorandum also specified for the Rome episode – crucially, as we will see – 'we recommend changing the view of Campo Parioli on page 170 of the script'.[115]

The Christian Democrat producers at Film Costellazione, Turi Vasile and Diego Fabbri, intervened heavily in the screenplay, making the political position of the protagonist, rechristened Claudio Valmauro, contradictory and unclear. When I vinti was premiered at the Venice Film Festival, on 8 September 1953, the critics' reactions to the Italian episode were so negative that the producers asked for Antonioni to re-edit it, removing some shots, adding others, changing the sequence of events and, above all, turning the protagonist into a wealthy young man who smuggles cigarettes for rather unclear reasons. In 1978, Antonioni recalled with some bitterness:

[N]eo-fascism was a topic that interested me. I had found a story that I liked – the story of a young man who commits suicide so that it appears that he has been killed by his political enemies. This story excited me very much. But censorship prevented me from shooting the film, and so I had to settle for another guy who smuggled cigarettes.[116]

41

The first version of the Rome episode was eventually retrieved in 2004, allowing for a comparison with the remake. Besides the changes introduced in the plot and the motivations of the protagonist, there are important differences in terms of locations and their significance. In both versions, the episode opens at night at Claudio's parents' home at Via Brenta 10, in one of the luxury apartment buildings of Quartiere Coppedè (c. 1919–26). This choice of location seems hardly accidental, given the quarter's strong association with late decadent taste of the poet, writer, aviator and proto-fascist political agitator Gabriele D'Annunzio. As historian Richard Bosworth noted, in the Coppedè

the ambiguities of the regime in its early days, still coloured by a Liberal and D'Annunzian inheritance, are vividly displayed ... Here, apartment blocks are ornamented with mosaics of scenes from Dante and look for all the world like the Victoriana of Dante Gabriel Rossetti and Edward Burne-Jones transposed south.[117]

In the original version, we first glimpse Claudio getting off the no. 135 bus at Largo Forano on the corner of Viale Somalia, one of the areas of intensive apartment buildings for the middle class, begun under fascism and completed during the Christian Democrats' hegemony from the late 1940s onwards. Claudio wanders through the buildings under construction, eventually reaching a slum, where he visits his accomplice Spartaco, a factory worker. Antonioni's camera shows the outside of the shanties, the dirt streets and then takes the spectator inside the shack where Spartaco lives with his wife. The slum, which seems to be on the edge of town, was actually not far from Via Flaminia and the Porta del Popolo. It was known as the Campo Parioli, and the Parioli hills with their luxury apartment buildings can be glimpsed in the background. As Francesco Rosi recalls:

> The choice of Campo Parioli in *I vinti* is characteristic of a cinema that is strongly affected by the neorealist revolution. All directors who were interested in portraying Italy chose topics that could serve as a guide to the representation of the contrast between the bourgeoisie and the poor classes. The people who lived in Campo Parioli had no means, they were refugees who had no choice. Therefore an environment like Campo Parioli was suited to be used as a place of belonging for the character of Spartaco [Gastone Renzelli], and to be put in contrast with the life of a bourgeois like Claudio [Franco Interlenghi], who lives in the Quartiere Coppedè. Indeed Renzelli, who had worked in Visconti's *Bellissima*, was an 'ossarolo', he worked at the slaughterhouse collecting bones.[118]

For a keen spectator in 1953, the reason for a factory worker like Spartaco to be living in a slum rather than in council housing would have been clear. The bombings of 1943–44, and the flight of the population of Lazio and Abruzzo from the war front, brought into Rome masses of refugees and internally displaced persons. During the 1950s, 12,066 families, totalling 48,336 people, lived in precarious and illegal housing (shanties, ruins, caves) in the city and its suburbs. Most of the adult male inhabitants were industrial workers, only a small part of them unemployed. Almost all of the dwellings had no drinking water supply and over 60 per cent had no latrines.

42

I vinti, Italian episode, original version (1952–53): the middle-class youth Claudio visits the blue-collar worker Spartaco at the latter's shanty at Campo Parioli, with the affluent Parioli district in the background

I vinti, Italian episode, remake (1952–53): the view from Marina's penthouse on the Parioli hill, with the fascist-era sports complex, and the shanties of Campo Parioli in the background

Later on, Claudio goes to the luxurious penthouse apartment of his girlfriend Marina. From the windows of Marina's house on the top of the Parioli hills, we get the reverse view; below the affluent Parioli neighbourhood lie the 1930s sports complex used for 'Campi Dux' and fascist youth organisations' rallies and, in the background, a settlement of shanties that in 1957 was still inhabited by 1,484 people.[119]

In the first version of the episode, Marina then drives Claudio to the factory where he carried out a bomb attack. In the remake, the car ride no longer has a clear destination; but in both versions, the wide avenue on which they travel is easily identifiable as Via Cristoforo Colombo, formerly called Via Imperiale and conceived by the planners of the E42 as 'the axis of the future urban development ... a true backbone of the new commercial and residential Rome, between Piazza Venezia, "brain and heart of the Urbs", and the E42; ... overambitious premise for a new master plan of the imperial Rome'.[120] For the Holy Year of 1950, the Christian Democrat mayor Rebecchini resumed construction of the road, which had ground to a halt in 1943, and built the monumental 'suburban hotels' on which Antonioni's camera lingers.[121]

For the remake, Antonioni shot a new night-time sequence, with Claudio's meeting with cigarette smugglers who arrive with a motorboat from the mouth of the river. The location was the area he had previously used for *N.U.*, with the Purfina refinery, the Marconi Bridge under construction and the adjacent Lungotevere San Paolo and Pietra Papa. This south-western stretch of land along the Tiber, developed since the late nineteenth century as Rome's industrial and services area (with the city's slaughterhouse, gasworks, market halls, a power station, refineries, warehouses and freight yards), was repeatedly used by directors such as De Sica (*Sciuscià* [1946] and *Bicycle Thieves*) and Rossellini (*Europa '51* [1952]), and later by Pasolini in *Accattone* (1961) and Bertolucci in *La commare secca* (1962).

Antonioni's choice of this area, filmed late at night, casts it as a wilderness, a still uninhabited area, a permeable edge of the city where cigarette smugglers weave an unlikely relationship with a wealthy young idler from Quartiere Coppedè.

43

La signora senza camelie (1953)

The troubled production of *La signora senza camelie* overlapped with the making of *I vinti*. Compared to the films that preceded and followed it, the film is much more plot- and character-driven, and indoor and dialogue scenes predominate. Yet, a comparison of the screenplay published in 1973 by Carlo Di Carlo in *Il primo Antonioni* (transcribed from the film and reviewed by Antonioni) and a 1953 type-script screenplay held in the Biblioteca Chiarini of the Centro Sperimentale di Cinematografia shows that the locations for the film were chosen with painstaking accuracy in relation to the characters and their social position.

Most consistent with the significance of place in Antonioni's previous and subsequent work was the scene in which the diplomat Nardo and the actress Clara drive in his car to a deserted wasteland where they can talk safe from prying eyes.[122] In the distance, silent witnesses to their meeting, we see the distinctive silhouettes of the Palazzo degli Uffici, Palazzo della Civiltà Italiana and Santi Pietro e Paolo, landmarks of the first phase of construction of EUR.

While Antonioni and Maselli were preparing and shooting *La signora senza camelie*, the destiny of the EUR site was being debated at local and national government levels. On 19 April 1952, in the Borromini Hall of the Oratorio dei Filippini – where in 1928 he had first proposed the expansion of Rome towards the sea – Virgilio Testa (commissioner for E42 of the fascist Governorate of Rome, and commissioner for EUR from 1951 to 1973) presented his plan for salvaging the complex, which would become 'A modern district in a modern Rome'. The elegant public burst into a long applause when Testa announced that the technical superintendent of EUR would be Marcello Piacentini, who during the fascist period had been 'official architect to the government, Secretary of the Royal Academy, President of the National Committee on City Planning, director of the magazine *Architettura*, official organ of the Fascist Syndicate of Architects'.[123]

44

La signora senza camelie (1953): the diplomat Nardo and the failed actress Clara, with the Palazzo degli Uffici, Palazzo della Civiltà and Sts Peter and Paul in the background

In almost unbroken continuity of men, offices and locations between fascism and the Christian Democrat era, Virgilio Testa's plan was aimed at demonstrating that the original purpose of E42 – its function as exhibition complex – was still viable. The existing roads and buildings were restored; the Via Cristoforo Colombo was completed and bus lines connected the new district to the city centre; the Rome trade fair was moved from Piazzale Clodio to EUR. Finally, between June and October 1953, the Agricultural Exposition, EA53, took place.[124]

The fatuous and selfish Nardo is described in the script of *La signora senza camelie* as 'a tall man of about thirty-six, elegant and slightly snobbish, just about enough for an old-fashioned career diplomat'.[125] His age, which sets his birth date around 1917, implies that his career began under fascism and continued under the Christian Democrats – as was the case for E42/EUR; and as it would be implied for Anna's father, a retired diplomat, in *L'avventura*. These details, along with the film's subtle, but extremely precise use of locations, suggest Antonioni's awareness (and implied critique) of the continuity between prewar and postwar governments.

Tentato suicidio (1953)

The script of Antonioni's segment for the omnibus film *L'amore in città* (*Love in the City*, 1953) was published in 1973 by Carlo Di Carlo, alongside an earlier and longer version of the script, with topographical indications and brief contextualisations for the stories of attempted suicides that the film narrates. In the revisions of the initial script – which were certainly undertaken to avoid the censorship that had hit *I vinti* – Antonioni reduced some contextual details and eliminated some stories, in particular that of a housemaid who lived – again – at Campo Parioli, in 'a sordid hovel, with a makeshift bed and a handful of other rickety furniture'.[126]

Antonioni filmed extensively in suburban Rome, in the *borgate* on the edge of an empty countryside. In doing so, his point of reference – rather than Rossellini and De Sica – was Visconti. The extraordinary eight-minute documentary *Appunti su un fatto di cronaca*, filmed by Visconti in the Primavalle *borgata* in 1951, condensed in a small number of powerful shots the story of Annarella Bracci, a twelve-year-old girl who was raped, killed and thrown into a well. Reminiscent of Visconti's shots of Primavalle is the panoramic shot of Quarticciolo in *Tentato suicidio*'s story of Rosanna Carta, which takes us from a row of tenements to a ditch (which would later become a large avenue, Viale Palmiro Togliatti) to another row of tenements and eventually to the shanties where Rosanna lives.[127]

Although many of the protagonists of *Tentato suicidio* live in poor peripheral areas (e.g., Rosanna Carta at Quarticciolo, Maria Mobili at Val Melaina), misery and despair also exist in the historic centre of Rome, as shown in the story of Lena

45

Tentato suicidio
(1953): Rosanna
Carta's haunts at the
Quarticciolo
neighbourhood. The
ditch dividing the two
rows of tenements will
be later filled in to
become the Viale
Palmiro Togliatti

Rossi, whom we see coming out of a tenement on the Lungotevere Testaccio; she walks along the east bank of the Tiber from Ponte Palatino, with the Tiber Island in the background, to Ponte Mazzini, looking for a place to drown herself. It is a tragic walk that Antonioni filmed on a clear sunny day that gave the monuments and the river itself the benign aura of the picture-postcard film.

Antonioni approaches the story of middle-class teenager Donatella Marrosu, an aspiring actress, with a marked degree of irony and ambivalence. Unlike the other women, she has enough money to live in 'a small guest house in the so-called "existentialist" district of Rome' (as the voice-over says), Pensione Forte of Via Margutta. She hangs out at the trendy Baretto of Via del Babuino and owns a Vespa, which we see when she visits a petrol station in Piazza di Spagna. She is the only one willing to show – literally – the scar of her suicide attempt; and the only one who is asked if her attitude is a pose.

The last episode, the story of the unhappy love triangle of Maria Mobili, her lover Giacomo and his wife Marcella, was excised from the film in 1953, and only

Tentato suicidio
(1953): Maria Mobili's
lover Giacomo near
the Val Melaina council
estate

recently restored. Despite the distancing implicit in the voice-over introduction of the episode ('This is a factory worker, who through error and misfortune experienced a sad love story'), the subject was unacceptable to the censors.[128] Maria Mobili worked at Lanificio Luciani, a large wool factory in the north-eastern suburban Via di Pietralata, and lived in the council housing estate of Val Melaina – the home of fictional character Antonio Ricci in *Bicycle Thieves*. In 1953, though no longer as isolated from the city as was the case in 1948, Val Melaina still appeared as it did five years earlier. In Robert Gordon's words, this neighbourhood is 'clearly beyond the urbs, with open land between there and the start of the built environment'.[129] Another *Bicycle Thieves*-related location of Maria's story is Corso Sempione, near Piazza Sempione. After the theft of his bicycle, Antonio Ricci picks up his son Bruno almost exactly where Maria sees Giacomo and Marcella at the no. 137 bus stop and decides to commit suicide.[130]

The use of *Bicycle Thieves*-related locations in *Tentato suicidio* implicitly comments on and criticises De Sica's film which, despite its having cast non-actors for its main roles, disregarded precisely Zavattini's appeal to getting rid of scripts to make films with real stories of real people. (One should not forget that Zavattini, who had scripted *Bicycle Thieves*, was the force behind *L'amore in città*.) *Tentato suicidio* largely refrains from the pathos and overt exposure of social injustice that characterised *Bicycle Thieves* and focuses on what would be called Antonioni's 'neorealismo interiore' ('inner neo-realism').[131] In 1958, Antonioni impugned *Bicycle Thieves* in relation to the development of his own concerns:

> Today … what's important is to see what's inside the man whose bicycle was stolen, what his thoughts and feelings are, how much is left inside of him of his past experiences, of the war, of the postwar period, of everything that happened to our country.[132]

Clearly Antonioni's minutely careful – often mutely, unemphatically specific – use of Roman locations in his films of the 1950s offers us a key for understanding his critical approach to the contradictions of life in postwar Italy, but also to the shortcomings and blind spots of the neo-realist film-making that had initiated the project of looking at Rome (and all of Italy) with new eyes.

Continuities and Reappearances

Antonioni's reticence as an explicit commentator on politics is belied by his use of locations which becomes in his work a kind of coded political discourse. His films express an intense awareness of the legacies of fascist urban politics as well as the gross distortions of Rome's accelerated urban development during the years of economic growth in the 1950s and early 60s. Antonioni's films of that period, indeed, feature the recurring presence of building sites: they range from large-scale apartment blocks in *I vinti*, to low-income houses at Via Monte Bianco in the Montesacro district in *Tentato suicidio*, from upper-middle-class 'palazzine' at Via Piccolomini off the Via Aurelia Antica in *L'avventura*, to the building site at EUR's Viale del Ciclismo in *L'eclisse*.

The careful use of these locations suggests that he was well aware of one of the most striking aspects of the distorted modernisation of Rome, the 'speculazione edilizia' – a politically driven real-estate speculation.[133] In this, he unobtrusively sided with the campaigns conducted since the mid-1950s by leftwing politicians and intellectuals such as Aldo Natoli and Antonio Cederna, as well as the weekly magazine *L'Espresso*, denouncing the responsibilities of Società Generale Immobiliare (General Real Estate Company, usually known simply as *the* Immobiliare) and other developers, whose interests were supported and represented by the Christian Democrats. The Immobiliare, one of the leading Italian construction companies and the biggest in Rome, was the protagonist of the urban transformation of the capital between the 1950s and early 60s. As noted by historian Vittorio Vidotto,

> Vatican capital ... made Immobiliare one of the mainstays of the economic initiatives of the Holy See. ... In the political polemics of those years, Immobiliare was singled out as the very symbol of speculation. ... There was no doubt that Immobiliare was a powerful party, and the Christian Democrat administration was not willing to curb its initiatives.[134]

Federico Vitella has pointed out that four of the male characters in *L'avventura* – including the protagonist Sandro, an architect – work directly or indirectly in the construction industry, a hardly coincidental detail at the time of the late 1950s building boom and its social and political implications.[135]

The issue of the new 'city that rises' is addressed in the Roman prologue of *L'avventura*, in the anti-rhetorical and ironic manner typical of Antonioni. Yet the brief conversation between the builder and Anna's father, and the contrast between Anna and her father, visually matched by the contrast between the 'palazzine' under construction and the dome of St Peter's, hint at Antonioni's awareness of the issues raised with the 'Corrupt capital, infected nation' campaign launched by *L'Espresso* in December 1955 against real-estate speculators and their Christian Democrat supporters in the city government.[136] Is it merely coincidental that in the final sequence of *L'eclisse*, Antonioni's camera ostentatiously follows a man who reads *L'Espresso*?

In the short story 'La rovina dell'umanità', Alberto Moravia described the appearance of the south-west outskirts of Rome in the immediate postwar years:

> beyond the Tiber I saw the abandoned building sites of E42, the palace with all the arches that looks like a dovecote, the church with the dome, and the columns that do not

support anything and resemble the wooden columns of a construction game for children. Behind me was the industrial area of Rome: the blast furnaces with long plumes of black smoke, the warehouses of the factories, full of windows; the low and wide cylinders of two or three gasometers, the tall and narrow cylinders of the silos.[137]

The 'palace that looks like a dovecote' had been a familiar image for Antonioni since his move to Rome in 1940, when he worked at E42's Palazzo degli Uffici. On 25 April 1940, a colour photograph of Palazzo della Civiltà Italiana with a wooden actual-size mock-up of one of the monumental sculptures (a half-futurist, half-metaphysical mannequin) featured on the front cover of issue 92 of *Cinema*, which contained two articles by Antonioni.[138]

As we have seen, EUR appeared in *La signora senza camelie* in 1953. In the same year, after ten years of abandonment and decay, the exposition complex was the site of the Rome Trade Fair and the Agriculture Exposition of Rome, whose acronym EA53 echoed the fateful E42. Within a decade, EUR had been 'transformed from a stretch of uncompleted and abandoned buildings in the most modern and organized neighbourhood in Rome'.[139] For *L'eclisse*, begun exactly a year after the 1960 Olympics, Antonioni cast EUR as one of the film's leading characters. Several of the district's landmarks feature in the outdoor shots.

Some hark back to the quarter's fascist origins, such as the Palazzo della Civiltà Italiana, the dome of Saints Peter and Paul, and the foundations of Giovanni Michelucci's unfinished open-air amphitheatre by the artificial lake. Some – the 'mushroom' water tower, the Velodrome, the ENI steel and glass tower – refer to the rebranding of EUR, begun in 1952 and completed in 1960 with the Olympics, as Rome's exemplary 'modern district', its residential garden city, rechristened 'quartiere Europa'.

Yet others hint at continuity between past and present. The Palazzo dello Sport, built for the 1960 Olympics, performed the very same task (and in the very same location) as the unrealised giant metallic arch Adalberto Libera had conceived for E42: that of perspective backdrop for the Via Imperiale at the south end of the exposition complex.[140] The architect who co-designed the Palazzo dello Sport was none other but Marcello Piacentini, who in 1938 had drawn the final plan for E42.[141] As architectural historian Tullia Iori noted, 'Piacentini plays a key role … in the general layout of the [Palazzo dello Sport] project, in 1954, when he recovers the ideas developed before the war for a circular Altar of Peace, converted now into a sports facility.'[142]

What are we to make of this collection of landmarks and their relationship with the past? When Vittoria and Piero, at her mother's apartment, look at a photograph of her parents in front of a shack, or one of her father in uniform, she fails to give any historical reference, and speaks only of 'poverty' and 'war'. They do not discuss politics, do not comment on places and buildings they happen to pass by and through; yet Antonioni's camera lingers long on those same places and buildings, even on a manhole cover bearing the acronym 'EUR'.

49

The past in Antonioni's films is not – or is only marginally – the *distant* past of which Italy is so rich, be it the imperial grandeur of Roman monuments, or the splendour of Renaissance palaces. The garbage collectors of *N.U.* eat their lunch near the ruins of the Baths of Caracalla and the Roman Forum, and in *L'eclisse* we see Vittoria and Piero among the mighty pillars of the Stock Exchange and then against the monumental colonnade of the Temple of Hadrian. But in both instances, such landmarks do not appear to be of interest to them. Antonioni's attitude is secular, and as Vittoria is 'not nostalgic for marriage', he does not long for tradition.[143]

But while the distant past may not be of great interest to Antonioni, he certainly has an interest in the *recent* past, and the way in which it looms over the present. This theme recurs in all of Antonioni's films, and at least up to *Il deserto rosso* (1964) it specifically relates to recent Italian history – fascism, African colonies, war, reconstruction – and the ways it has influenced the lives, ways of thinking and material conditions of his characters.[144]

L'eclisse ends a journey that had begun with the arrival of Antonioni in Rome to work as a secretary of Vittorio Cini at E42. Antonioni witnessed the initial phase of that project, and for a short period was directly associated with it. He had come to Rome after five years as a contributor to the newspaper founded by Italo Balbo and directed by Nello Quilici, and after their deaths he would spend another three years working for a magazine directed by Vittorio Mussolini. All this would die – like Giovanna in *Cronaca di un amore* – in 1943, and Antonioni, like many other young intellectuals and artists of his generation, would bring his 'long journey through fascism' to its conclusion by way of a profound critical reassessment of the regime and its material incarnations, the most imposing and enduring of which was architecture.[145]

Yet what seemed defunct at the end of the war took on a new life in the 1950s; at the time of *La signora senza camelie*, EUR would be restored and completed alongside the Via Imperiale/Cristoforo Colombo. Finally, in 1960, the monumental complex designed for what Mussolini called the Olympics of Civilisation[146] would become the site of the Olympic Games, giving EUR a new identity – and completing the task of obscuring and confusing its origin and its meaning.

Is this what Antonioni was addressing? It is maybe no coincidence that after *L'eclisse* Antonioni turned his back on Rome as a setting for his films and, after *Il deserto rosso*, on Italy altogether. Although he would return to Rome for *Identificazione di una donna* (1982), that film is a chronicle of the uncertainties of a director struggling with two differently elusive women and a fictional female character he is unable to pinpoint, rather than an investigation of the history and politics inscribed in a specific urban environment.

At the end of *L'eclisse*, the disappearance of Vittoria and Piero leaves as the sole protagonist the city; but it is a city whose horizon – having given up both its prewar imperial ambitions, and the ideas of renewal and moral cleansing that characterised the postwar period and neo-realism – is the bleak mediocrity of real-estate speculation; a city where any passer-by can resemble another person, and where the 'palazzine', the zebra crossings, the bus terminals are all alike.

Notes

1. I would like to thank Francesco Maselli for generously giving his testimony and a wealth of precise historical details which provided an invaluable contextualisation of Antonioni's work; Paolo Balbo, Loredana Balboni, Milton Gendel, Carlo Lizzani, Folco Quilici, Paolo Ravenna, Francesco Rosi, Gaetano Tumiati, for sharing their knowledge and recollections with me; Carlo Di Carlo, David Forgacs, Laura Rascaroli, John David Rhodes, for their valuable advice; Massimo Sani, Daniele Ravenna, Silvana Tamiozzo Goldmann, Tina Hedwig Kaiser, Michael L. Siegel for their kind help; André Viljoen, David A. Mellor, Pia Gottschaller, Heidi Specker, for giving me opportunities to lecture on various aspects of Antonioni's work. I also thank the staff of the libraries where I carried out research: Biblioteca Luigi Chiarini, Centro Sperimentale di Cinematografia, Rome; Biblioteca Alessandrina, Sapienza University, Rome; Biblioteca dell'Istituto di Teoria dello Stato, Department of Political Science, Sapienza University, Rome; Archivio Storico Iconografico del Socialismo – Fondazione Nevol Querci, Rome; Biblioteca Nazionale Centrale, Rome; Fondo Enzo Siciliano, Casa delle Letterature, Rome; Istituto Gramsci, Rome. Except where otherwise stated, all translations from Italian and French are my own (JB).

2. Michelangelo Antonioni, 'Strada a Ferrara' [1978], in Anna Folli (ed.), *Vent'anni di cultura ferrarese: 1925–1945. Antologia del 'Corriere Padano'*, vol. II (Bologna: Pàtron, 1979), pp. 175–7 (p. 177).

3. Federico Vitella, *Michelangelo Antonioni. L'avventura* (Turin: Lindau, 2010), p. 8.

4. Anna Maria Torriglia, *Broken Time, Fragmented Space: A Cultural Map for Postwar Italy* (Toronto: University of Toronto Press, 2002), p. 143.

5. His parents, Elisabetta Roncagli and Ismaele Antonioni, came from the nearby villages of Bondeno and Pontelagoscuro. Elisabetta was a former factory worker; Ismaele, a railwayman who – according to Antonioni – managed to achieve a good position 'through evening classes and hard work'. Seymour Chatman and Paul Duncan, *Michelangelo Antonioni: The Investigation* (Cologne: Taschen, 2004), p. 184; Tullio Kezich and Alessandra Levantesi (eds), *Cronaca di un amore. Un film di Michelangelo Antonioni* (Turin: Lindau, 2004), pp. 51, 111; Renzo Renzi, *Album Antonioni. Una biografia impossibile* (Rome: Centro Sperimentale di Cinematografia, 1992), p. 183; 'Report about Myself', in Michelangelo Antonioni, *Quel bowling sul Tevere* (Turin: Einaudi, 1995 [1983]), pp. 105–10 (p. 107). Antonioni provided other versions about his father's profession: a 'sales representative', in a 1967 interview with Dacia Maraini in *Vogue Italy*, reprinted in Dacia Maraini, 'Antonioni', *E tu chi eri?* (Milan: Bompiani, 1973), pp. 111–18 (p. 111); and a 'messenger in a factory', in

51

Lietta Tornabuoni, 'Io e il cinema, io e le donne' [interview], *Corriere della Sera*, 12 February 1978, English trans. 'Myself & Cinema – Myself & Women', in Carlo Di Carlo (ed.), *Michelangelo Antonioni* (Rome: Cinecittà Holding, n.d. [2005]), pp. 22–32 (p. 26); Aldo Tassone, *I film di Michelangelo Antonioni. Un poeta della visione* (Rome: Gremese, 2002), p. 6.

6. Maraini, 'Antonioni', p. 118. The same incident occurs to the character of Luisa's father on Antonioni's unrealised script *Le allegre ragazze del '24* (*The Merry Girls of '24*, 1956). See Michelangelo Antonioni, 'Le allegre ragazze del '24', in *I film nel cassetto* (Venice: Marsilio, 1995), pp. 55–62 (pp. 56, 57, 58).

7. Guido Fink, 'Michelangelo Antonioni: A Biographical Sketch', in Seymour Chatman and Guido Fink (eds), *L'avventura* (New Brunswick and London: Rutgers University Press, 1989), pp. 17–28 (p. 18).

8. Anna Folli, 'Michelangelo Antonioni' [interview, 1978], in Folli, V*ent'anni di cultura ferrarese*, vol. II, pp. 333–6 (p. 334).

9. University of Bologna, Historical Archive, online directory, <http://www.archiviostorico. unibo.it/template/listStudenti.asp?IDFolder=143&start=true&LN=IT&nEPP=200& offset=1400&filtro=no> (last accessed 25 August 2010).

10. Tassone, *I film di Michelangelo Antonioni*, p. 10; Fink, 'Michelangelo Antonioni', p. 18.

11. 'Although it may seem paradoxical, the Littoriali della Cultura, organized by the Fascist Party, were vehicles for anti-fascism: it was an internal contradiction of the regime, which, in order to promote youthful energies, ended up – so to speak – nursing vipers in its own bosom.' Paolo Alatri, 'Ricordi e riflessioni sulla mia vita e la mia attività', *Dimensioni e Problemi della Ricerca Storica* vol. 9 no. 1 (1996), pp. 13–46 <http://w3.uniroma1.it/dprs/sites/default/files/214.html> (last accessed 27 August 2010).

12. Aldo Tassone, 'Conversazione' [interview], in Michelangelo Antonioni, *Fare un film è per me vivere. Scritti sul cinema* (Venice: Marsilio, 1994), pp. 204–15 (p. 209); For an English translation, cf. 'Conversation', in Michelangelo Antonioni, *The Architecture of Vision: Writings and Interviews on Cinema*, ed. Carlo Di Carlo and Giorgio Tinazzi, trans. Marga Cottino-Jones (New York: Marsilio, 1996), pp. 230–44. (Elsewhere I have quoted from *The Architecture of Vision* wherever possible; however, the translation of this interview omits some important information.)

13. Anna Folli, 'Introduzione', in Anna Folli (ed.), *Vent'anni di cultura ferrarese: 1925–1945. Antologia del 'Corriere Padano'*, vol. I (Bologna: Pàtron, 1978), pp. xv–xviii (p. xxiv).

14. Ibid.; see also Paul Corner, *Il fascismo a Ferrara 1915–1925* (Rome and Bari: Laterza, 1974), p. 310.

15. See Mimì Quilici Buzzacchi (ed.), *Nello Quilici. L'uomo, il giornalista, lo studioso, il maestro* (Ferrara: Nuovi Problemi, 1941), pp. 47–8, 62, 117, 121; Giordano Bruno Guerri, *Italo Balbo* (Milan: Mondadori, 1998), pp. 183–90.

16. Lanfranco Caretti, in Roberto Cotroneo (ed.), *Giorgio Bassani. Opere* (Milan: Mondadori, 2001), p. lxiv. Nello Quilici's son, Folco, thus recalled that time: 'Antonioni, Bassani, Caretti and other young contributors to the *Corriere Padano* often went to see my father. I do not think he could give them a lot of his time, having to manage the newspaper and write articles, but they spent all afternoon in his studio, three large rooms which doubled as library. My father often went to France, he received foreign magazines, including the *Nouvelle Revue Française*, so maybe they went there to look at these magazines, and when he returned from a trip, maybe they'd ask him about it. In any case, they were always there.' Author's interview with Folco Quilici, 16 February 2011.

17. Michelangelo Antonioni, 'L'ultima lezione', in Quilici Buzzacchi, *Nello Quilici*, pp. 221–6 (pp. 221, 222).

18. Tassone, *I film di Michelangelo Antonioni*, p. 10; Folli, 'Michelangelo Antonioni', in Folli, *Vent'anni di cultural ferrarese*, vol. II, p. 335. The Italian translation of Raymond Spottiswoode's book *A Grammar of the Film* (1935) was published by Edizioni di Bianco e Nero in 1938. Pavese's novel *Paesi tuoi* was published by Einaudi in May 1941; therefore Antonioni's discovery of Pavese should be dated to the summer 1941, when he had already moved to Rome.

19. Author's interview with Paolo Ravenna (son of the *podestà* of Ferrara, Renzo Ravenna), February 2011: 'In the 1930s Antonioni directed *Il Ludovico*, a theatrical satire. Such a spectacle was made possible by the tacit protection provided by Balbo.' See Renzi, *Album Antonioni*, p. 26.

20. Fink, 'Michelangelo Antonioni', p. 18; Tassone, *I film di Michelangelo Antonioni*, p. 8; Michèle Manceaux, '*L'Avventura* sort à Paris' [1960], English trans. in *Sight and Sound*, vol. 30 no. 1 (Winter 1960–61), pp. 5–8, and 'An Interview with Antonioni', in Bert Cardullo (ed.), *Michelangelo Antonioni: Interviews* (Jackson, MS: University Press of Mississippi, 2008), pp. 11–20 (p. 13); Aldo Bernardini, *Michelangelo Antonioni da 'Gente del Po' a 'Blow Up'* (Milan: Edizioni I Sette, 1967), p. 25; Gaetano Tumiati, 'Quando Michelangelo si chiamava Nino', *Ferrara: Voci di una Città* no. 17, December 2002, <http://rivista.fondazionecarife.it/articoli/2002/num.-17/quando-michelangelo-si-chiamava-nino.html> (last accessed 25 August 2010); author's interview with Gaetano Tumiati, 2 March 2011; Gian Piero Brunetta, *Il cinema italiano di regime. Da 'La canzone dell'amore' a 'Ossessione', 1929–1945* (Bari: Laterza, 2009), p. 80; Michelangelo Antonioni, *Sul cinema*, ed. Carlo Di Carlo and Giorgio Tinazzi (Venice: Marsilio, 2004), p. 221.

21. Fink, 'Michelangelo Antonioni', p. 18; Tumiati, 'Quando Michelangelo si chiamava Nino'; Tornabuoni, 'Myself & Cinema – Myself & Women', p. 26.

22. Tumiati, 'Quando Michelangelo si chiamava Nino'. Among the works Antonioni staged in the late 1930s was Pirandello's *O di uno o di nessuno*.

23. Vito Zagarrio, *'Primato'. Arte, cultura, cinema del fascismo attraverso una rivista esemplare* (Rome: Edizioni di Storia e Letteratura, 2007), pp. 199–200. For a contextualisation of *Cinema*, see Orio Caldiron, 'Introduzione', in Orio Caldiron

(ed.), *'Cinema' 1936–1943. Prima del Neorealismo* (Rome: Fondazione Scuola
Nazionale di Cinema, 2002), pp. 9–14.

24. Author's interview with Carlo Lizzani, 15 March 2011.
25. Michelangelo Antonioni, 'Per un film sul fiume Po', in *Cinema* vol. IV no. 68
    (25 April 1939), pp. 254–7, reprinted in Caldiron, *'Cinema' 1936–1943*, pp. 117–20.
    Emphases in the original.
26. Folco Quilici, *Tobruk 1940: Dubbi e verità sulla fine di Italo Balbo* (Milan:
    Mondadori, 2006), p. 126.
27. Vittorio Giacci, 'Biografia', in Vittorio Giacci (ed.), *Michelangelo Antonioni: Lo
    sguardo estatico* (Rome: Fondazione Centro Sperimentale di Cinematografia/BA Film
    Factory, 2008), pp. 139–46 (p. 139).
28. Italo Insolera and Alessandra Maria Sette, *Roma tra le due guerre. Cronache da una
    città che cambia* (Rome: Palombi Editori, 2003), pp. 33, 37; Maurizio Reberschak,
    'Cini, Vittorio', in Alberto M. Ghisalberti (ed.), *Dizionario Biografico degli Italiani*,
    vol. XXV (Rome: Istituto della Enciclopedia Italiana, 1981), pp. 626–34 (pp. 630–1).
29. Folco Quilici, in Giacci, *Michelangelo Antonioni*, pp. 122–3.
30. As early as 1935 Antonioni wrote on unpowered flight for the *Corriere Padano*, cf.
    Folli, 'Introduzione', in Folli, *Vent'anni di cultura ferrarese*, vol. I, p. xxiv. This may
    be the unsigned article, 'Gli agonali di volo senza motore', *Corriere Padano*, 10 April
    1935, p. 4 (author's correspondence with Anna Folli, 2011).
31. Antonioni provided dates and details in his articles 'L'ultima lezione' and 'Ferrara 29
    guigno 1940', in Quilici Buzzacchi, *Nello Quilici*, pp. 221–6 (p. 222) and pp. 3–10 (p. 4).
32. Michelangelo Antonioni, 'Taccuino volante. Introduzione alla Libia', *Volandum*
    vol. IX no. 5–6 (May–June 1940), pp. 55–7; 'Incontri a Bengasi', *Volandum* vol. IX
    no. 9–10 (September–October 1940), pp. 107–11. Antonioni mentioned this first
    journey to Africa only once, in a 1975 interview, without providing any details: 'I was
    [in Africa] as a reporter, to write some features, even when war broke out.' Michele
    Mancini et al., 'Il mondo è fuori della finestra' [interview], in Antonioni, *Fare un film
    è per me vivere*, pp.156–65 (pp. 164–5); English trans. 'The World is Outside the
    Window', in Di Carlo (ed.), *Michelangelo Antonioni* [2005], pp. 48–63 (p. 62).
33. Italo Balbo's son Paolo has recalled, 'My father invited journalists to visit Libya to
    increase public awareness of his plans for improvement, from the archaeological
    excavations to tourism. He believed in the enhancement of the tourist route – Tripoli,
    Sabratha, Leptis, the Gadames Oasis, Sirte and, in Cyrenaica, Benghazi, Derna,
    Cyrene, Apollonia on so forth. The emphasis on travel by car was linked to this
    campaign for the promotion of tourism. It was part of the great expectations about
    how Libya could have become if it were not for the war.' Author's interview with
    Paolo Balbo, 31 March 2011. Paolo Ravenna added, 'Balbo also thought of a great
    documentary on Libya to be commissioned to an important director, and he had his
    eye on Julien Duvivier.' Author's interview with Paolo Ravenna, 17 February 2011.
34. Antonioni's article 'Ferrara 29 guigno 1940' (see note 31, above), which opens the
    June 1941 volume-tribute to Nello Quilici after a preface by Quilici's widow, is a

eulogy for Balbo and his comrades, followed by Giuseppe Bottai's commemoration of Balbo (in alphabetical order; yet a rather striking placement considering that Bottai at the time was Minister of National Education, a member of the Grand Council of Fascism and the force behind *Critica Fascista* and *Primato*). Antonioni's article was previously published with a different title in the Balbo and Quilici commemorative issue of *Volandum*: Michelangelo Antonioni, 'Dietro alla storia', *Volandum* vol. IX no. 7–8 (July–August 1940), pp. 83–6.

35. See Noa Steimatsky, *Italian Locations: Reinhabiting the Past in Postwar Cinema* (Minneapolis: University of Minnesota Press, 2008), pp. 1–39.

36. Palazzo degli Uffici was the first building of the E42 to be completed at the end of 1939.

37. Lietta Tornabuoni, 'Intervista a Michelangelo Antonioni', in Caterina D'Amico de Carvalho (ed.), *Album Visconti* (Milan: Sonzogno, 1978), pp. 6–9 (p. 6).

38. Ibid., p. 6. Leo Longanesi was – among many other things – one of the forerunners of neo-realism, arguing in 1932 and 1933 for an aesthetic that would be 'bare, crude, and very direct'. Ruth Ben-Ghiat, *Fascist Modernities: Italy, 1922–1945* (Berkeley and Los Angeles: University of California Press, 2001), pp. 31, 222, n. 40.

39. Bernardini, *Michelangelo Antonioni da 'Gente del Po' a 'Blow Up'*, p. 26.

40. Ibid.; Tassone, *I film di Michelangelo Antonioni*, p. 12.

41. Maraini, 'Antonioni', p. 118; Pierre Leprohon, *Michelangelo Antonioni* (Paris: Seghers, 1965), p. 13; Pierre Billard, 'Une interview avec Michelangelo Antonioni' [1965], English trans. 'An Interview with Michelangelo Antonioni', in Cardullo, *Michelangelo Antonioni*, pp. 46–69 (pp. 61–2).

42. Antonioni's collaboration to *Volandum* included at least twenty-six articles between 1939 and 1943. Several articles are signed in extenso, others with the initials M. A. Film reviews and articles on cinema – until 1939 almost absent in *Volandum* – are presented as a series of 'Letters to the Editor' signed with the pseudonym Ammonio Sacca (Ammonius Saccas was a philosopher from Alexandria who lived c.175–243 AD and taught Plotinus; Antonioni would use the 'Ammonio' alias again when he wrote the lyrics of *Eclisse Twist* in 1962). Reviews comprise mostly films related with flight, including a three-page feature on cinema and war (vol. X no. 7–8, 1941) and a review of Rossellini's *Un pilota ritorna* (vol. XI no. 3–4, 1942). Starting from the January–February 1940 issue, Antonioni also wrote a column of book reviews, dealing with books about flight, but also books on Italo Balbo (vol. IX no. 11–12, 1940; vol. X no. 1–2, 1941; vol. XII no. 1–2, 1943). Most surprising are the non-cinema-related articles. In the November–December 1939 issue (vol. VIII no. 11–12) there is a three-page article (signed M. A.) on Leonardo da Vinci and flight. For the May–June 1940 issue, besides the first part of his reportage from Libya, he wrote a four-page illustrated feature on the Triennale d'Oltremare fair in Naples. For the March–April 1941 (vol. XI no. 3–4) issue, he contributed a five-page article on 'Fantasy on the Fuselages', discussing images of aircraft 'nose art'. For the May–June

1941 (vol. XI no. 5–6) issue he wrote 'Tobruk, One Year Later', an illustrated five-page article on the ceremonies held in Ferrara for the first anniversary of Balbo's death. There are also two short stories, 'Sowing in Flight' (by Ammonio Sacca, vol. X no. 9–10, 1941) and 'Travel Nostalgia' (by M. Antonioni, vol. XI no. 11–12, 1942). The longest article, published in November–December 1941, based on the true adventure of a Caproni bomber aircraft and its crew, bore a truly Antonionian title, 'L'avventura del Caproni 133. Cronaca di un viaggio miracoloso'.

43. Author's interview with Folco Quilici, 16 February 2011. The chief editor of *Il Messaggero* between December 1932 and July 1941 was Francesco Malgeri.

44. Antonioni attended the Centro for three months only; see Billard, 'An interview with Michelangelo Antonioni', in Cardullo, *Michelangelo Antonioni*, p. 61; Bernardini, *Michelangelo Antonioni da 'Gente del Po' a 'Blow Up'*, p. 27.

45. Massimo Mida, in Vito Zagarrio, *Cinema e fascismo. Film, modelli, immaginari* (Venice: Marsilio, 2004), pp. 249–50.

46. Carlo Montanaro, 'Francesco Pasinetti', in Giovanni Di Stefano and Leopoldo Pietragnoli (eds), *Profili veneziani del Novecento*, vol. 2 (Venice: Supernova Edizioni, 1999), p. 54.

47. Author's interviews with Francesco Maselli, 19 July 2006, and Loredana Balboni, 28 February 2011.

48. Barbara Garbin, 'La "saga" di Pier Maria Pasinetti: itinerario di uno scrittore veneziano e cosmopolita', degree thesis, Faculty of Letters, Ca' Foscari University of Venice, 1999–2000, pp. 5, 7, <http://digilander.libero.it/pmpasinetti/indice_Garbin.htm> (last accessed 30 August 2010). See Antonioni's recollections, 'Note su P. M. Pasinetti', in *Italian Quarterly* vol. 26 no. 102 (Autumn 1985), <http://digilander.libero.it/pmpasinetti/pdf/Antonioni_estratto.pdf> (last accessed 23 August 2010); Manlio Piva, 'P. M. Pasinetti: Alcune immagini di repertorio', in *Studi Novecenteschi* vol. 61 no. 1 (2001) (Pisa-Rome: Fabrizio Serra Editore), pp. 221–41.

49. Michelangelo Antonioni, untitled foreword [1980], in Francesco Pasinetti, *Storia del cinema dalle origini a oggi* (Venice: Marsilio, 1980 [1939]), pp. iii–iv (p. iii).

50. Tassone, *I film di Michelangelo Antonioni*, p. 11; 'Biografia', in Giacci, *Michelangelo Antonioni*, p. 139.

51. Alessandra Levantesi and Francesco Maselli, 'Sui sentieri della memoria', in Kezich and Levantesi, *Cronaca di un amore*, pp. 31–51 (p. 31).

52. Author's interview with Francesco Maselli, 19 July 2006. Loredana Balboni recalled, 'No doubt my sister Letizia had much influence on Antonioni. They were very close. She always collaborated with him, even on the scripts, though uncredited.' Author's interview with Loredana Balboni, 28 February 2011.

53. Fink, 'Michelangelo Antonioni', p. 20. In his 'Cinema e guerra' article in the July–August 1941 issue of *Volandum* (vol. X no. 7–8, p. 72), Antonioni wrote that he was serving in the Army Corps of Engineers, which had a Photography and Cinematography Unit.

54. Antonioni reviewed *Un pilota ritorna* (under the alias Ammonio Sacca) in the March–April 1942 issue of *Volandum* (vol. XI no. 3–4), pp. 32–3.

55. See Silvia Bignami (ed.), *'Aria d'Italia' di Daria Guarnati. L'arte della rivista intorno al 1940* (Milan: Skira, 2008).

56. Gio Ponti, 'Architettura 'nel' cinema – Idee', *Aria d'Italia* vol. 2 no. 7 (Summer 1941), pp. 23–6 (pp. 25, 26).

57. Tornabuoni, 'Intervista a Michelangelo Antonioni', p. 6.

58. Tassone, *I film di Michelangelo Antonioni*, p. 13.

59. *Les visiteurs du soir* was shot in Nice and surroundings between April and September 1942; <http://www.marcel-carne.com/les-films-de-marcel-carne/1942-les-visiteurs-du-soir/fiche-technique-synopsis-revue-de-presse> (last accessed 13 September 2010). During his stay in Nice, Antonioni came across the work of Henri Matisse and read Camus's *The Stranger*. He would write about both after the liberation of Rome, see Antonioni, *Sul cinema*, pp. 209–11, 214–17.

60. Antonioni dated the filming of *Gente del Po* in an interview of 1959: 'While I was filming my first documentary at the end of 1942, Visconti was shooting *Ossessione*.' Anonymous, 'Questions à Antonioni', *Positif* vol. 30 (July 1959), in Carlo Di Carlo and Giorgio Tinazzi (eds), *Michelangelo Antonioni. Entretiens et inédits, 1950–1985* (Rome: Cinecittà International, 1992), p. 33. He would later recall: 'Italian cinema did not portray the poor lower classes in such a harsh way ... At that time, documentaries used to deal with places, works of art ... the valleys of Comacchio carefully cleared of any sign of hardship ... I instead went to the mouth of the Po river, placing at risk Minoccheri, who was my protector within the Istituto Luce and the only one who fought to let me do whatever I wanted.' Aldo Tassone, 'The History of Cinema is made on Film' [interview, 1979], in Antonioni, *The Architecture of Vision*, pp. 193–216 (p. 194).

61. Regarding the political reorientation that took place during the war among the generations that had grown up under the fascist rule, Ruth Ben-Ghiat noted, 'it was the experience of defeat, not the declaration of war, that turned Italians against the regime. ... [S]ome found themselves hoping to lose the war as a way of ensuring the fall of Fascism. Describing this phenomenon in 1944, [Corrado] Alvaro would venture the view that Italians had lived in a state of "moral catastrophe" since the start of the war.' Ruth Ben-Ghiat, 'Liberation: Italian Cinema and the Fascist Past, 1945–50', in Richard J. B. Bosworth and Patrizia Dogliani (eds), *Italian Fascism: History, Memory and Representation* (Basingstoke: Palgrave, 1999), pp. 83–101 (p. 85). The Action Party, founded in 1942 by a group of republican liberal-socialist intellectuals, was 'staunchly anti-fascist but not anti-capitalist, it criticized liberalism without being anti-bourgeois, and proposed a democratic revolution without being doctrinaire; it was therefore well suited to exert a great influence on young people in need of strengthening their reasons for fighting fascism and rebuilding their identity as citizens'. Roberto Chiarini, 'Le origini dell'Italia

57

repubblicana (1943–1948)', in Giovanni Sabbatucci and Vittorio Vidotto (eds), *Storia d'Italia. 4. La Repubblica, 1943–1963* (Rome and Bari: Laterza, 1997), pp. 3–126 (p. 20).

62. Tullio Kezich and Alessandra Levantesi, 'Personaggi e curiosità', in Kezich and Levantesi, *Cronaca di un amore*, pp. 111–23 (p. 111); Tassone, *I film di Michelangelo Antonioni*, p. 15. Antonioni told Tassone he also translated works by Gide and Chateaubriand.

63. Virgilio Tosi, 'L'organizzazione della cultura cinematografica', in Callisto Cosulich (ed.), *Storia del cinema italiano, VII: 1945–1948* (Venice and Rome: Marsilio/Fondazione Scuola Nazionale di Cinematografia, 2003), pp. 497–514 (p. 499); Jean A. Gili, 'C'era una volta la cinefilia', in Gian Piero Brunetta (ed.), *Storia del cinema mondiale. V. Teorie, strumenti, memorie* (Turin: Einaudi, 2001), pp. 397–416 (p. 406). Letizia Balboni was the association's secretary; see Giacomo Gambetti, *Cultura e politica nel cinema di Francesco Maselli* (Florence: Cecchi Gori Editoria Elettronica, 2009), p. 37.

64. D'Amico de Carvalho, *Album Visconti*, p. 115.

65. Tornabuoni, 'Intervista a Michelangelo Antonioni', pp. 8–9.

66. Teresa Antolin, 'La contessa Maria Tarnowska e il conte Luchino Visconti', in Teresa Antolin and Alberto Barbera (eds), *Il processo di Maria Tarnowska. Una sceneggiatura inedita* (Milan and Turin: Il Castoro/Museo Nazionale del Cinema, 2006), pp. 9–31 (p. 22). Antonioni also contributed cover photographs to *Film d'Oggi* (author's interview with Francesco Maselli, 18 January 2011).

67. The literary magazine *La Fiera letteraria*, founded in 1925 and published until 1943, was revived in 1946 by Felice Fulchignoni, brother of Enrico and son-in-law of the architect Marcello Piacentini.

68. Antolin, 'La contessa Maria Tarnowska e il conte Luchino Visconti', p. 22; D'Amico de Carvalho, *Album Visconti*, p. 115; Mario Ferrero, 'Anticipazioni: Maria Tarnowska' [1946], in Antolin and Barbera, *Il processo di Maria Tarnowska*, pp. 423–5 (pp. 424–5).

69. See Robert S. C. Gordon, *Bicycle Thieves* (London: BFI, 2008), p. 8; Renzi, *Album Antonioni*, p. 29; Stephen Gundle, *I comunisti italiani tra Hollywood e Mosca. La sfida della cultura di massa, 1943–1991* (Florence: Giunti, 1995), p. 48; Biblioteca del Cinema 'Umberto Barbaro', <http://www.bibliotecadelcinema.it/bib/bib-chaplin.html> (last accessed 23 August 2010). Again, Letizia Balboni was actively involved in the Circolo activities, see Callisto Cosulich, 'Rifiutato a Venezia, applaudito ovunque', in Kezich and Levantesi, *Cronaca di un amore*, pp. 93–103 (p. 97); Kezich and Levantesi, 'Personaggi e curiosità', p. 112.

70. Antonello Trombadori, 'Zavattini, Picasso e noi nel '49', in *La Repubblica*, 28 October 1989, p. 10, <http://ricerca.repubblica.it/repubblica/archivio/repubblica/1989/10/28/zavattini-picasso-noi-nel-49.html> (last accessed 23 August 2010).

71. Gili, 'C'era una volta la cinefilia', p. 406.

72. The ex-aequo winners of the 1948 Nastro d'Argento were *N.U.* and Francesco Pasinetti's *Piazza San Marco*. Carlo Di Carlo (ed.), *Michelangelo Antonioni* (Rome: Edizioni di Bianco e Nero, 1964), p. 410; Carlo Di Carlo (ed.), *Michelangelo Antonioni 1942–1965* (Rome: Ente Autonomo Gestione Cinema, 1988), pp. 49–50.

73. Levantesi and Maselli, in Kezich and Levantesi, *Cronaca di un amore*, p. 31.

74. The composer Mario Labroca, who wrote the music for Antonioni's *Gente del Po* in 1947, was Maselli's uncle.

75. Besides the direct reference to *Tender Is the Night* in *L'avventura*, Antonioni expressed several times his interest in the works of Fitzgerald, see Antonioni, *The Architecture of Vision*, pp. 89, 165, 233.

76. Seymour Chatman, 'Antonioni in 1980: An Interview' [1977], in Cardullo, *Michelangelo Antonioni*, pp. 155–61 (p. 161).

77. Vittorio Vidotto, *Roma contemporanea* (Rome and Bari: Laterza, 2006), pp. 259–60.

78. Levantesi and Maselli, in Kezich and Levantesi, *Cronaca di un amore*, pp. 31, 51.

79. Renzi, *Album Antonioni*, pp. 39–40.

80. Author's interview with Loredana Balboni, 28 February 2011.

81. Levantesi and Maselli, in Kezich and Levantesi, *Cronaca di un amore*, p. 50.

82. See Giorgio De Vincenti, 'Conversazione sul cinema con Francesco Maselli', in Lino Miccichè (ed.), *'Gli Sbandati' di Francesco Maselli. Un film generazionale* (Turin: Lindau, 1998), pp. 15–41 (p. 27).

83. Author's interview with Loredana Balboni, 28 February 2011.

84. Author's interviews with Milton Gendel, 2006 and 2010. On the Rome locations of *L'avventura*, Jacopo Benci, 'Michelangelo's Rome: Towards an Iconology of *L'Eclisse*', in Richard Wrigley (ed.), *Cinematic Rome* (Leicester: Troubadour, 2008), pp. 63–84 (pp. 64–7); Vitella, *Michelangelo Antonioni*, esp. pp. 19, 110–11, 180–4.

85. Author's interviews with Francesco Maselli, 2006.

86. Antonioni, interviewed by Bert Cardullo, June 1978, in Cardullo, *Michelangelo Antonioni*, pp. 138–9.

87. Michelangelo Antonioni, 'Distrazioni', in *Cinema* vol. 5/1 no. 115 (10 April 1941), p. 240. Actually, *Tosca* shows nothing of what Antonioni writes about, offering just a few vistas of the interior and exterior of Castel Sant'Angelo, the dome of St Peter's in the mist, the Piazza Farnese, some Roman ruins and a few rather nondescript streets.

88. Italo Insolera, *Roma moderna. Un secolo di storia urbanistica* (Turin: Einaudi, 1971), pp. 182–3. See also Mark Shiel, 'Imagined and Built Spaces in the Rome of Neorealism', in Wrigley, *Cinematic Rome*, pp. 27–42 (p. 29). A similar shift in perspective occurred at the same time in the works of Rossellini (compare *Un pilota ritorna* and *Roma città aperta*) and De Sica (compare *I bambini ci guardano* and *Sciuscià*). The term 'borgate' refers both to fascist-era public housing estates that re-housed working-class people who were displaced by the extensive redesign of central Rome under fascism and to various informal shanty towns that grew up around Rome's periphery and that housed recent migrants to the city and those displaced from its centre for any number of reasons.

59

89. Author's interview with Francesco Rosi, 12 February 2011.

90. Michèle Manceaux, 'Ravenne. Dans *Le désert rouge*: Pour la première fois Antonioni parle de son premier film en couleurs' [interview], *L'Express* (16 January 1964), in Di Carlo and Tinazzi, *Michelangelo Antonioni*, pp. 183–6 (p. 183).

91. Billard, 'An Interview with Michelangelo Antonioni', p. 48; Chatman, 'Antonioni in 1980', p. 161.

92. Giuseppe De Santis, 'Per un paesaggio italiano', *Cinema* vol. 5/2 no. 116 (25 April 1941); quoted in Andrea Martini, 'I luoghi dell'intreccio (Antonioni viaggiatore)', in Giorgio Tinazzi (ed.), *Identificazione di un autore. Forma e racconto nel cinema di Antonioni* (Parma: Pratiche Editrice, 1985), pp. 83–90 (p. 88).

93. Filming for *N.U.* (the acronym stands for Nettezza Urbana, municipal cleansing service) took place between 1947 and 1948, while *Bicycle Thieves* was shot between May and October 1948. Tassone, *I film di Michelangelo Antonioni*, p. 58; Gordon, *Bicycle Thieves*, p. 121.

94. Steven Jacobs, 'Between EUR and LA: Townscapes in the Work of Michelangelo Antonioni', in Ghent Urban Studies Team (eds), *The Urban Condition: Space, Community, and Self in the Contemporary Metropolis* (Rotterdam: 010, 1999), pp. 325–42 (p. 329).

95. 'I really loved Vigo's *A propos de Nice*, which I think is a fantastic documentary.' Tassone, 'The History of Cinema is made on Film', p. 211.

96. Francesco Maselli, 'I miei esordi con Michelangelo', in Alberto Achilli et al. (eds), *Le sonorità del visibile. Immagini, suoni e musica nel cinema di Michelangelo Antonioni* (Ravenna: Longo Editore, 1999), pp. 147–52 (p. 147).

97. This is reflected in the precise instructions Antonioni gave for *N.U.* to Giovanni Fusco (who wrote the scores of nearly all of his films until 1964). See Roberto Calabretto, 'Giovanni Fusco: musicista per il cinema di Antonioni', in Achilli et al., *Le sonorità del visibile*, pp. 45–75 (p. 68). Antonioni openly acknowledged the importance of American literature in his formative years: 'My interest in the United States dates from the time when I was at the university. … But my first contacts with America were above all literary, and quite naturally so. I say "naturally", because Pavese's and Vittorini's translations [of American novels] were famous, and there were places in Rome during the war where you could go to find them, despite fascist censorship.' Michelangelo Antonioni, 'A Constant Renewal' [1987], in Michelangelo Antonioni, *The Architecture of Vision*, pp. 319–25 (p. 319).

98. *Il ventre della città* was described by Umberto Barbaro as 'one of the best Italian documentaries, if not the best one' and 'a little gem'. The film's cinematographer was Ubaldo Arata, and its music was written by Mario Labroca (who wrote the score for Antonioni's *Gente del Po* in 1947, see note 74, above). Angela Madesani, *Le icone fluttuanti. Storia del cinema d'artista e della videoarte in Italia* (Milan: Bruno Mondadori, 2002), pp. 48–9.

99. Michelangelo Antonioni, 'La settimana cinematografica a Venezia' (*Corriere Padano*, 5 September 1940), in Folli, *Vent'anni di cultura ferrarese*, vol. II, p. 175.

100. Carlo Di Carlo (ed.), *Il primo Antonioni* (Bologna: Cappelli, 1973), p. 32.

101. On the *flânerie* in Antonioni's later films, see Tina Hedwig Kaiser, *Flaneure im Film: 'La Notte' und 'L'Eclisse' von Michelangelo Antonioni* (Marburg: Tectum Verlag, 2007).

102. Carlo Di Carlo, 'Vedere in modo nuovo', in Di Carlo, *Il primo Antonioni*, pp. 11–19 (p. 14).

103. John Grierson, 'First Principles of Documentary' (1932–34), in Forsyth Hardy (ed.), *Grierson on Documentary* (London: Faber and Faber, 1966), pp. 145–56 (p. 151).

104. Marcel Carné, 'When will the Cinema Go Down into the Street?' ('Quand le cinéma descendra-t-il dans la rue?', *Cinémagazine*, 13 November 1933), in Richard Abel (ed.), *French Film Theory and Criticism 1907–1939: A History/Anthology, Volume II, 1929–1939* (Princeton, NJ: Princeton University Press, 1988), pp. 127–9 (p. 129).

105. Mario Alicata and Giuseppe De Santis, 'Ancora di Verga e del cinema italiano', *Cinema* vol. 6/1 no. 130 (25 November 1941), p. 315; Antonio Pietrangeli, 'Verso un cinema italiano', *Bianco e Nero* vol. 6 no. 18 (25 August 1942), p. 315; quoted in Brunetta, *Il cinema italiano di regime*, p. 210.

106. Author's interview with Carlo Lizzani, 15 March 2011.

107. Tullio Kezich, *Federico. Fellini, la vita e i film* (Milan: Feltrinelli, 2007), pp. 119–20.

108. A 'casa di ringhiera' was a low-income, working-class tenement housing on an interior courtyard, with one long common balcony on each floor. All entrances to the flats were placed on the balcony itself.

109. Several locations of the film – including the tram stop at Piazza Zama – were identified by Francesco Maselli (author's interview, July 2010). Piazza Zama was the end of the no. 19 tram line until 14 April 1949 (see <http://www.tramroma.com/tramroma/rete_urb/tram/storia/cronolog/urbcron_3.htm#8/19>, last accessed 8 August 2010). This detail provides a date *ante quem* for this scene.

110. Maselli, in Achilli et al., *Le sonorità del visibile*, pp. 147–8.

111. See ibid., p. 147; Antonioni, *The Architecture of Vision*, p. 248; Ned Rifkin, *Antonioni's Visual Language* (Ann Arbor: UMI Research Press, 1982), p. 38.

112. Stefania Parigi, 'L'avventura de *I vinti* – L'episodio italiano', in Stefania Parigi (ed.), *I vinti* (Rome: Gianluca & Stefano Curti Editori, 2007), pp. 4–25 (pp. 15–17).

113. Sergio Lambiase and Tano D'Amico (eds), *Storia fotografica di Roma, 1950–62. Dall'Anno Santo alla 'dolce vita'* (Naples: Edizioni Intra Moenia, 2004), pp. 30, 34; Vidotto, *Roma contemporanea*, pp. 272, 433.

114. 'Presidenza del Consiglio dei Ministri, Direzione Generale dello Spettacolo, Divisione Produzione Cinematografica. Revisione cinematografica preventiva – Appunto, 2 luglio 1952', typescript, pp. 5, 7. DVD-ROM contents, in Michelangelo Antonioni, *I vinti*, Minerva Classic DVD (Rome: Gianluca & Stefano Curti Editori, 2007).

115. Ibid. See Parigi, 'L'avventura de *I vinti* – L'episodio italiano', pp. 15–17.

116. Lino Miccichè, 'Antonioni visto da Antonioni' (RAI2 broadcast, Italy, 12 February 1978), in Di Carlo and Tinazzi, *Michelangelo Antonioni*, p. 87.

117. R. J. B. Bosworth, *L'Italia di Mussolini, 1915–1945* (Milan: Mondadori, 2009), p. 443. See Terry Kirk, *The Architecture of Modern Italy, Volume 2: Visions of Utopia, 1900–Present* (New York: Princeton Architectural Press, 2005), p. 34.

118. Author's interview with Francesco Rosi, 12 February 2011.

119. The Campo Parioli was cleared in 1958 when the Comune sold its 22 hectares to INCIS in order to build the Olympic Village. Insolera, *Roma moderna*, pp. 201, 245; Mauro Olivieri, '1925–1981: La città abusiva', in Alberto Clementi and Francesco Perego (eds), *La Metropoli 'spontanea'. Il caso di Roma* (Bari: Edizioni Dedalo, 1983), pp. 290–304 (p. 294); Vidotto, *Roma contemporanea*, p. 280.

120. Giorgio Ciucci, *Gli architetti e il fascismo. Architettura e città 1922–1944* (Turin: Einaudi, 2002), p. 183.

121. Insolera, *Roma moderna*, pp. 241–2.

122. At that time, the still undeveloped area at the intersection of today's Viale Guglielmo Marconi, Via del Mare and Via Cristoforo Colombo was called 'gli sterrati' (the dirt patches); author's interview with Francesco Maselli, July 2010.

123. See Tullia Iori, 'Nervi e le Olimpiadi di Roma 1960', in Tullia Iori and Sergio Poretti (eds), *Pier Luigi Nervi, architettura come sfida. Ingegno e costruzione* (Milan: Electa, 2010), pp. 53–67 (p. 62); George Nelson, 'Marcello Piacentini' (1935), in George Nelson, *Building a New Europe: Portraits of Modern Architects – Essays by George Nelson, 1935–1936* (New Haven, CT: Yale University Press, 2007), pp. 29–37 (p. 30).

124. Luigi Di Majo, Italo Insolera, *L'Eur e Roma dagli anni Trenta al Duemila* (Rome and Bari: Laterza, 1986), pp. 81, 84n16, 89–92.

125. Di Carlo, *Il primo Antonioni*, p. 201.

126. Ibid., p. 264.

127. The script accurately specifies that Rosanna lived between Via Lucera (today Viale Togliatti) and Via delle Palme. Di Carlo, *Il primo Antonioni*, p. 269.

128. The excision was discovered during the restoration of *Tentato suicidio* made by the Cineteca Nazionale in 2001. Cineteca Nazionale (eds), *La memoria del cinema. Restauri, preservazioni e ristampe della Cineteca Nazionale (1998–2001)* (Rome: Fondazione Scuola Nazionale di Cinema, 2001), p. 95.

129. Gordon, *Bicycle Thieves*, p. 65.

130. Di Carlo, *Il primo Antonioni*, p. 272.

131. See Cosulich, 'Rifiutato a Venezia applaudito ovunque', p. 95.

132. Michelangelo Antonioni, 'La mia esperienza' [1958], English trans. 'My Personal Experience', in Di Carlo, *Michelangelo Antonioni* [2005], pp. 10–21 (p. 14).

133. The 'speculazione edilizia' and the issues it entailed were dealt with in various ways in the works of writers and film-makers between the late 1950s and early 60s, from the eponymous short story by Italo Calvino, *La speculazione edilizia* (*A Plunge into Real Estate*, 1957) to Pier Paolo Pasolini's novel *Una vita violenta* (*A Violent Life*, 1959),

to Francesco Rosi's film *Le mani sulla città* (*Hands over the City*, 1963). See Vitella, *Michelangelo Antonioni*, p. 181.

134. Vidotto, *Roma contemporanea*, pp. 283–4.

135. Vitella, *Michelangelo Antonioni*, pp. 180–1. Vitella noted that, before resorting to labels such as 'mystery in reverse' and 'sickness of feelings' in explaining his intentions in making *L'avventura*, Antonioni declared in 1957 that the film's theme was 'the future of the bourgeoisie', and therefore he thought of conveying his project by emphasising its nature of cross-section of class (ibid., pp. 175–6).

136. See Benci, 'Michelangelo's Rome', pp. 64, 79, n. 4.

137. Alberto Moravia, 'La rovina dell'umanità', in *Racconti romani* (1954), quoted in Insolera and Sette, *Roma tra le due guerre*, p. 47.

138. The articles were 'La nuova colonia', an illustrated feature on French actors in Cinecittà, and the interview 'Un tecnico del suono', *Cinema* vol. V/I no. 92 (25 April 1940), pp. 255–7, 287. In October of the same year, an almost identical black-and-white photograph featured on page 7 of the third issue of *Civiltà*, the official magazine of the Universal Exposition of Rome.

139. Vidotto, *Roma contemporanea*, p. 201.

140. Francesco Garofalo and Luca Veresani, 'Symbolic Arch for the E42', in Francesco Garofalo and Luca Veresani (eds), *Adalberto Libera* (New York: Princeton Architectural Press, 2002), pp. 107–9 (p. 107).

141. See Alessandra Muntoni, 'Piano E42, 1937', in Adachiara Zevi (ed.), *Una guida all'architettura moderna dell'EUR* (Rome: Fondazione Bruno Zevi, 2008), pp. 15–16 (p. 16); Alessandra Capanna, 'Palazzo dello Sport 1956–60', in Zevi, *Una guida all'architettura moderna dell'EUR*, p. 34. Piacentini worked on the Palazzo dello Sport with Pier Luigi Nervi.

142. Iori, 'Nervi e le Olimpiadi di Roma 1960', p. 62.

143. In 1960 Michèle Manceaux, interviewing Antonioni on *L'avventura*, defined him 'almost the only Italian director whose work strikes one as entirely secular', and he replied, 'if it is true that I am a secular artist, it is also true that I am part of a secular cultural tradition, both in literature and in the cinema. Svevo, for instance, was a secular writer; so was Pavese. The Italian silent and pre-war cinemas were secular. There has always been this minority in Italy. Even today there are secular cultural groups. So I would say, simply, that if I am a secular artist, I am not some kind of monster.' Manceaux, 'L'Avventura sort à Paris', English trans. (modified), in Cardullo, *Michelangelo Antonioni*, p. 19.

144. See Mark Shiel, *Italian Neorealism: Rebuilding the Cinematic City* (London and New York: Wallflower Press, 2006), p. 103.

145. See Emilio Gentile, *Fascismo di pietra* (Rome and Bari: Laterza, 2007).

146. See Ciucci, *Gli architetti e il fascismo*, p. 180.

63

Laura Rascaroli

MODERNITY, PUT INTO FORM:
Blow-Up, Objectuality, 1960s Antonioni

Annette Messager's concise but eloquent view of the function of the artist resonates compellingly with Antonioni's specific approach to modernity. Writes Messager: 'Mostly, I believe an artist doesn't create something new, but is there to sort through, to show, to point out what already exists, to put it into form and sometimes reformulate it.'[1] Similarly, Antonioni's own strategy vis-à-vis modernity arguably consists in indicating, signalling and displaying the existent or, as we could also say, the present, through an act of framing that produces a multiplicity of aesthetic, critical and ideological discourses. Such a strategy corresponds to a fashioning of the world, a putting of the world into form, which is, simultaneously, a reformulation of the world. The term I here wish to highlight is 'form'; because it is through form especially that Antonioni expresses his vision of modernity. The concept recalls, first of all, that extreme attention to image and style that are so characteristic of his cinema; an attention that many have described as formalism or aestheticism, or as a commitment to 'the surface of the world'. In truth, Antonioni's formalism is a framing of the world that is certainly not an end in itself, as I will endeavour to show.

Antonioni is attentive, as has frequently been remarked, to the condition of modernity intended as an experience of alienation, incommunicability, fracture and absence of meaning; a condition so widespread in the urban West that it almost becomes abstract, and universal. Yet it sometimes tends to be forgotten that Antonioni's modernity is precisely inscribed in strongly historicised bodies, landscapes and objects. His films are full of buildings, artefacts, clothes and accessories that Antonioni chooses not for their stylishness or decorative potential, but on account of their ability to enter into signifying relationships with contemporary extra-textual discourses on art, culture, identity, class, industry, fashion, power, nation. Simultaneously, his objects resist historicisation, not so much because they seem to function symbolically, as has repeatedly been suggested, but because they are irreducible material presences – because they are other-than-subject. These are the two paradoxical poles that define the idea of modernity in Antonioni's cinema: the concreteness of objects and the abstraction of forms, universality and historicity, thingness and no-thingness.

Antonioni's filmic work is widely regarded as very conversant with and even co-identical with the fine arts. His first artistic production was as a painter;[2] frequently in his films there appear 'places which are openly non-narrativized, of a pictorial and visual interest which suddenly takes hold, causes the narrative to err, to wander, momentarily to dissolve'.[3] His manner of framing is noticeably inspired by the observation of the work of painters; Antonioni himself has confirmed his use of modern art as a point of reference and a constant source of inspiration, as he does, for instance, in the following interview:

> I have a great love for painting. For me, it is the one art, along with architecture, that comes immediately after filmmaking. I'm very fond of reading books on art and architecture, of leafing through pages and pages of art volumes, and I like to go to art shows and keep in touch with the latest work being done in art – not just to be *au courant* but because painting is something that moves me passionately. Therefore I believe all these perceptions and this interest have been somewhat assimilated. And, naturally, having followed modern art, my taste and my predilection for a certain style would be reflected in my work.[4]

In the course of the 1960s, Antonioni's cinema directly engaged with the two presiding stylistic sensibilities of the decade: that of modernism and that of pop. The modernist sensibility found incisive expression in the 'tetralogy'. *L'avventura* (1960), *La notte* (1961), *L'eclisse* (1962) and *Il deserto rosso* (1964) focused on precise geographical and cultural aspects of the Italy of the first half of the decade: the Rome and Milan of the construction boom, the old money and the new entrepreneurial bourgeoisie, archaic Southern realities and aggressive Northern industrial development. Italy was here seen through a number of historically defined and representative locations: the timeless and formidable nature of the Aeolian Islands, the untouched, mythical beauties of Sardinia, the baroque architectures of Noto, the hyper-modern development of Rome's EUR, the rich and ostentatious Brianza, the metropolitan centres of culture and business, the industrial Viallassa valley near Ravenna, the Breda factory at Milan's periphery. These places, carefully chosen to express eloquently the features and paradoxes of the incomplete modernisation of the country, were framed in ways that proposed an idea and a vision of the present that was deeply inflected by European modernism and, in particular, as Giorgio De Vincenti has remarked, by the Informal (abstract expressionist) art of the 1950s and 60s.[5] The Pop sensibility, on the other hand, made its appearance in the first film Antonioni shot outside Italy, and in English, *Blow-Up* (1966). *Blow-Up*, like the subsequent *Zabriskie Point* (1970) and *Identificazione di una donna* (1982), presents affinities with Pop Art and other artistic movements which were deeply marked by the return of the object after the abstraction of Informal art.

In truth, objects were already central to Antonioni's cinema prior to *Blow-Up*. Indeed, his interest in objects has often been seen as an important and, indeed, even crucial element of the innovative cinematic language of the tetralogy. For instance, Vittorio Giacci described his camera's avoidance of the human subject and prediction for things as an 'evasive gaze', capable of materialising the consciousness of nothingness.[6] However, this critical approach placed the accent not on the object as such, but on the process of objectification of the human being at work in Antonioni's films of the first half of the 1960s. For instance, in a debate on *L'eclisse* which took place at the University of Milan in 1962, Paolo Gambazzi suggested that de-subjectivation, intended as the reduction of the subject to object, was the central element of this film.[7] This critical approach was inescapably limited, as it failed to give a full account of the uncanny significance of the object in Antonioni's cinema.[8]

Blow-Up represents not only Antonioni's first obvious step in the process of his detachment from modernism and approach to newer artistic forms, which I will here define as proto-postmodern; but also, and in parallel, the film marks the beginning of the evolution of his discourse on objects. In his films of the early 1960s, artefacts were predominantly seen as expression of bourgeois taste and of socio-economic status, as well as symbols of the modernity of the characters and of the times – a modernity which, as already mentioned, was influenced by the Italian modern architectural movement, Razionalismo, by European modernism, the International Style and the forms of Italian design and fashion, and which found a visual correlation in the abstraction of non-figurative Informal art. Consider, for instance, Monica Vitti's and Jeanne Moreau's stylish outfits and accessories in each of the four films: the two lead stars wore clothes characterised by precious fabrics and straight, neat, essential lines that made them look wealthy, fashionable and almost futuristic. Vitti's fashions and haircuts especially stood in contrast with the softer and more markedly feminine, 1950s-looking dresses and hairdos of the other female characters, which remained closer to the high-bourgeois fashions lavishly displayed in *Cronaca di un amore* (1950). Consider also the centrality to the films of the tetralogy of key status-symbol possessions, such as the yacht belonging to Monica Vitti's upper-class friends in *L'avventura*, or Alain Delon's Alfa Romeo in *L'eclisse*. Moreover, in these films recent architectures were framed as eloquent, commanding materialisations of a modern style that was both characteristically international and obviously Italian – as in the iconic example of the futuristic water tower at EUR in *L'eclisse*. Antonioni's framing consistently worked towards a flattened and abstract vision of things and of the world.

In *Il deserto rosso*, the emphasis on material things further intensifies; these are no longer or not exclusively typical status symbols, like cars, yachts, swimming pools, villas, clothes or paintings, but often large and threatening objects that appear

The toy robot in
Il deserto rosso
(1964)

to be endowed with a mysterious, mechanical life. Consider the child's ultramodern toys (especially the tall peripatetic robot, but also the spinning wheel that cannot be tipped over); the factory, which at unexpected times shrieks and exhales steam; the oscillating radio-telescope towers with which the researchers of the University of Bologna listen to the stars; and, finally, the several boats that slide through the fog ominously sounding their horns. All these objects move and make sound in ways that are often experienced by Giuliana (Monica Vitti) as startling and threatening. It is in the meeting with the objects of the world of industry, science and innovation that the disquiet and neurosis of modern living become most evident – even though the relationship of the individual to things is far from being one-dimensional. As Giuliana explains to Corrado (Richard Harris), in fact, she is tied to objects and cannot see herself without them; if she decided to leave forever, she would have to take everything with her.[9]

Antonioni's discourse on objects in the tetralogy, then, is suggestive of the direct association of things with the modern condition, as well as with contemporary bourgeois lifestyles: objects are not only chosen, but also choose individuals and indissolubly tie them to their class and status, and to the requirements of 'modern living'. Thus, they represent people and give them a sense of security, but also immobilise and imprison them. Objects, furthermore, are frequently given emphasis by Antonioni in these films in place of the more customary attention devoted by fiction cinema to the human being; as many critics have remarked, the eye of the camera in the tetralogy ceases to be fully anthropocentric. This move towards the inanimate world is so striking that it appears to endow objects with a mysterious aura, and to make them look like powerful if indeterminate symbols. In *Il deserto rosso* – a work in which the neurosis and alienation already hinted at in the previous three films escalate and become overwhelmingly tangible – the impression of the independent existence of objects increases. Objects, arguably, are here still a function of man, as they emanate from science and technology;

67

however, they also emphasise and compound the dissociation of the human being from his or her environment.

Blow-Up is the film that marks Antonioni's move to filmic forms which can be described as proto-postmodern, and also to a somewhat different type of interest in objects. I here use the term 'proto-postmodern' to describe a phase of Antonioni's cinema, inaugurated by *Blow-Up*, which is marked by a clear detachment from modernism, but which still presents clear traces of ethical discourses that are typical of modernism. This phase is furthermore characterised by the absence of the irony and shallowness that are broadly associated with artistic expressions of postmodernity.[10] Most critics have remarked on the novelty of the film; Seymour Chatman notes, for example, that in *Blow-Up* Antonioni's camera 'turns away from the abstract visual style of the tetralogy and renews its preoccupation with effects of depth'.[11] Furthermore, the editing style and fragmentation of the decoupage conspicuously differ from the long-take approach typical of the previous films. Rather than focusing on editing and camerawork, however, I will concentrate on the key role of framing as a way of putting into form, and on form as a key indicator of specific modernities; and I will focus on the object as the element that catalyses all the discourses that I intend to explore.

A terminological question remains to be mentioned. Thus far, I have used the terms 'thing' and 'object' interchangeably, as synonyms. Although I will continue, to some extent, to use these terms as equivalents, when thinking about *Blow-Up* I mainly refer to objects as being endowed with an aesthetic form and, thus, with a presence that distinguishes them from mere things. This is also why I coin the term 'objectuality' instead of adopting the more ordinary 'thingness'. While the latter is arguably suggestive of the sheer materiality of the inanimate world, the former implies that the things I talk about have an aesthetic as well as commercial or other value, which is attributed to them within a system of cultural, economic and ideological references and thus sets them apart from more generic matter.

Blow-Up: Object Value

> To the modernist, the art object is no longer a mirror of this world or a window into an idealized realm; it is a thing in itself.[12]

It is significant that, at the time of effecting a substantial break with his previous work, Antonioni leaves the country and goes to shoot in the most international of European cities, thus inaugurating a series of films made outside Italy. As he stated in an interview after the release of *Blow-Up*, it would not have been possible to set the story that he had in mind in Rome or in Milan, but only in a city like London.[13] The importance for the film of 1960s London, of its cultural and artistic contexts, cannot be overstated. To begin with, many have recognised in the nameless protagonist, the modish photographer who stumbles upon a suspected murder in a park and becomes obsessed by it, the figure of the best-known photographer of Swinging London, David Bailey, contributor to English *Vogue* since 1960, as well as freelance photographer for the *Sunday Times*, *Elle* and *Glamour*. David Mellor has analysed in detail some of the contemporary avant-garde artistic contexts of this city that influenced the film, from the practice of the photographic representation of contingent bodies, which was 'a critical area of exploration for British artists of this time ... and became a major preoccupation in the era of Pop, with Richard Hamilton as its chief component',[14] to the paintings of the photographer's neighbour, prepared for the film by artist Ian Stephenson.

Other contemporary contexts that need to be taken into account in order to understand their influence on Antonioni's film are the London rock, avant-garde theatre and beat scenes, which at that time were the focus of the experimental cinema of British documentarist Peter Whitehead. While preparing to shoot *Blow-Up*, Antonioni went to Whitehead's Soho flat to see his *Wholly Communion* (1965), a record of the International Poetry Incarnation event with Allen Ginsberg and other poets at the Royal Albert Hall in London on 11 June 1965, and *Charlie is My Darling* (1965), a documentary of the Rolling Stones' first tour of Ireland.[15] According to some critics, Whitehead himself was a model for the figure of the protagonist.[16]

The importance of these cultural encounters was decisive for Antonioni and his historicising approach to London; it was the meeting with Ian Stephenson in March 1966, for example, that persuaded the director to include the figure of the painter in a much more prominent role than the one originally devised in the screenplay. Antonioni made his crew film Stephenson in his studio for two days, dressed his painter-character in the same style, and borrowed from the artist a range of things, including brushes, jars, easels and paintings, to use on the set.[17]

The centrality of objects in *Blow-Up*, and especially those found by the protagonist in the antique shop in Woolwich, has been remarked on more than once. Critics have frequently read them symbolically; for instance, Richard Wendorf believes, rather literally, that the propeller the photographer buys from the antiques shop represents his desire to escape from London, a wish to which he refers once during a conversation with his agent. William Arrowsmith reads these antiques as the representatives of the past, seen in direct contrast with the present, which is in turn symbolised by the city:

> Antiques, and even old junk, are valuable because, in a time of drastic change, they
> represent lost stability, the permanence of the past. They have a potency, cachet,
> talismanic properties, like a piece of petrified wood or a fossil flower or a fish, persisting
> in a world whose momentum of change is so rapid that the object Thomas must have, a
> twenty-year-old World War Two propeller, has become an antique.[18]

If symbolic readings of the antiquarian's objects appear to be authorised by the enigmatic aura that surrounds them, such readings, and especially those that see them as symbols of the past, are ultimately inconclusive and unsatisfactory. The antiques in *Blow-Up*, in fact, are not isolated, but are part of a vast and complex system of things which includes paintings, photographs, cameras, clothes, accessories, artefacts, cars and buildings, all of which could hardly look more current or, indeed, fashionable. As signifiers of earlier historical moments, the objects in the antiques store carry traces of various meanings, some of which are original, some acquired over time. As objects among objects, they are an expression of taste, but also exist in their sheer materiality, which is simultaneously straightforward and opaque, on account of the ways in which Antonioni frames them. This opacity extends to the entire film. *Blow-Up* is a work that transforms the 1960s and its aesthetic into an object and, more precisely, an object of consumption (let us remember that the film was distributed, for the first time in Antonioni's career, by MGM, and that it was to be his biggest box-office success). Indeed, *Blow-Up* itself is an aesthetic object, though in more than one way an ineffable one, as testified to by the rivers of ink that have been spilled by critics in the attempt – constantly frustrated, and at times grotesque in its insistence – to 'explain' the film.

The paradoxical dual value of historicity and opacity, sheer presence and suggestive meaning concerns not only the antiques, but also the modern objects. A telling example is the pair of white Levi's worn by the protagonist, which were one of the most fashionable items of clothing among the London Mods – who, incidentally, adored and copied Italian fashion and design (thus, in this sense, Antonioni's cultural encounter with Swinging London was mediated by the encounter of young Londoners with the image of Italian style and culture). There is, however, in Antonioni much more than a straightforward discourse on style and fashion as a reflection and expression of the present times. One need only think of the protagonist who, precisely like Monica Vitti in *L'eclisse*, wears clothes that literally make him look more modern than the moderns. The photographer's clothes, even if representative of the fashion of the 1960s, cannot be reduced to it; they are, in fact, less dated, more ageless than those worn by many other characters. His blue blazer, sky-blue chequered shirt and white jeans are surely perfect for Swinging London; moreover, they embody the cool mix of casual style and elegance that marks the photographer's look, and signify the place that he feels he occupies in the world; but they are also timeless, perfectly acceptable even today, at the opposite, for instance, of the dresses and hairstyles of some of the girls in the film, but also of many of the men. It is not surprising that the film's costume designer, Jocelyn Rickards, explained in her memoir that 'Antonioni's approach to the design of the film was to look two years into the future of fashion.' Precisely for this reason, she went to Paris to research the fashion houses and the fabric manufacturers, and found inspiration in 'futuristic wonders' such as 'a molten silver tissue

From tramp to modish
photographer:
the protagonist before
and after changing his
clothes in *Blow-Up*
(1966)

that moved like water flowing from a tap, and a matt white jersey that changed colour under different lights'.[19]

In other words, Antonioni certainly paints the portrait of a generation that expresses itself through objects seen as aesthetic choices and as manifestation of a taste which, as Bourdieu reminds us, is first of all an expression of the dispositions of class and of its ideology, and a positioning of the subject in society.[20] Simultaneously, things impose themselves beyond historicising discourses. In this film, indeed, objects display an undeniable opacity, as do entire habitats. Consider again the crucial episode at the antique store. The photographer – who wants to enter the property market at a time of accelerated urban development – intends to buy the entire shop (which is, in this way, itself objectified), but the owner is hostile, and brusquely asks him what he's looking for. 'A landscape', replies the protagonist, apparently offering a random answer to the unfriendly question; the owner replies that he has none. The photographer, then, moves some busts which partly conceal a large Romantic landscape – in other words, a landscape as object.

The landscape painting uncovered by the photographer in the antiques shop in *Blow-Up* (1966)

Landscape has a key importance in *Blow-Up*. The film has often been described as a city film and a portrait of London, and a park features prominently in its story. Several critics have read the park as a site of uncontaminated nature, set in contrast with the artificiality of the city;[21] but the episode of the painted landscape, which immediately precedes the introduction of the park, suggests the opposite: that all landscape can succumb to the condition of being object and that all landscape is, in fact, urban landscape.

It is useful in this sense to recall that the origin of the painted landscape in Western art in the course of the fifteenth century is urban; each landscape presupposes an urban gaze, a gaze from the city.[22] It is the city, initially always present in the painting as architectural element, as window or balustrade, which surrounds, encloses and frames the view. Even when the landscape eventually breaks free of the city, this remains in the composition as a repressed element. It is thus particularly significant that, in the first images in which it appears, the park of *Blow-Up* is framed by architectural elements (two sets of two-storey houses, one on each side of the park's entrance); furthermore, the protagonist enters the park with the intention of photographing it and, thus, of transforming it into a vista, according to that same artificial perspective that is at the base of the pictorial landscape.[23] Finally, when the photographer leaves, the park is for the second time conspicuously framed by an architectural element: the open door of the antiques store, which is itself framed by a bust and some old prints. This last shot constitutes a clear framing of the park in the shape of urban landscape – and also tells us that the photographer, whom we see walking from the park in the background towards the door in the foreground, is contained in that landscape, of which he is but an element.

In this way, and through framing, the park is powerfully connected by Antonioni to the idea of the artificial landscape. In fact, the nature in the park is evidently constructed, manmade and manicured, precisely like the gardens of Rome's EUR in

The photographer framed in the urban landscape

L'eclisse. The landscape is thus itself city, and object; but it is so in ways that are opaque and irreducible – consider how the bucolic idyll that the photographer initially sees soon transforms into something sinister and horrific; and how, in this sequence, it is not the protagonist who sees the park but, conversely, the park that 'sees' the protagonist. I refer to the fact that some time elapses before the photographer finally notices the park, whose presence has already been brought to the spectator's attention by means of the prominence in the soundtrack of the rustle of the leaves in the wind. Through its 'voice', thus, the park appears to call the photographer; and it also seems to 'see' him. In fact, when the protagonist finally turns and looks at it, he is framed from the point of view of the park.

Found Objects: From Pop Art to Proto-postmodern Cinema

In what way can we productively think about this opacity, this irreducibility of the objects in *Blow-Up*? I propose to look at this question within the context of the artistic discourses of the period, especially those linked to Pop, as well as of late modernism and the shift towards a new sensitivity, which Antonioni – attentive spectator of modern art and sensitive interpreter of the present – is ready to recognise, absorb and transform into new cinematic forms.

In this sense, it is first of all necessary to remember that 'the nomination of found objects and prefabricated materials as "ready-made" components of art is the crucial transformative element of early twentieth-century art'.[24] In European and North American art of the 1960s, then, the object acquires absolute importance, and indeed becomes the crossroads of discourses that are fundamental to the passage from modernism to proto-postmodernism. The object, and especially the found object, which, as I will argue, is particularly relevant to *Blow-Up*, has been central

73

to key movements of the 1960s such as Fluxus, Pop Art and Arte Povera.[25] It is also useful to recall how Pop Art has its roots in the Independent Group, founded precisely in London in 1952. In Italy, Pop Art comes into view in 1964, in particular thanks to the Roman Scuola di Piazza del Popolo, represented by artists including Franco Angeli, Giosetta Fioroni, Renato Mambor and Mario Schifano.

Seymour Chatman has noted that, in the trilogy, Antonioni has allowed objects found on the set to influence the narrative of his films; his example is a painting 'found' in the hall of the hotel in Taormina, which appears in *L'avventura*. For Chatman:

> The *objet trouvé* undeniably guarantees the 'thereness' of the real world, not because it is verisimilar but because it really *was* there. ... One consequence of this new kind of realism is that the universe is demonstrated to be basically meaningless. For if this bit of the world is no less and no more worth photographing than any other, questions of moralistic or psychological commentary cannot arise. 'There it is' is all the film is willing to say, 'the neutral surface – make of it what you will'.[26]

The question of the indifference of things is pertinent, but the meaninglessness of the universe is not the only aspect that needs to be highlighted; it is, in fact, opportune to reflect more thoroughly on the complex role played by the found object in the artistic panorama in which Antonioni worked in those years.

74

The wave of renewed interest for Duchamp and his notion of the found object, originally formulated at the beginning of the century, marks the move away from the modernist ideals of abstraction and unrepresentability, and the emergence of the interest in the use and incorporation of things, images and techniques of mass production and popular culture. In the 1960s, Duchamp's works were frequently exhibited, often remade because the originals were lost, as *The Complete Works of Marcel Duchamp*, a catalogue published in 1969, confirms: '1964, Milan: First full-scale replicas issued under the direct supervision of Duchamp on the basis of a blueprint derived from photos of the lost original.'[27] It is easy to note in this passage an almost uncanny resonance with the plot of Antonioni's film, and with the idea of the photograph as replica that replaces and indeed becomes an original that is always already lost. Ideas of replica and questions of reproduction are central to the art of those years, and were suggested precisely by the artists' reflection on everyday objects and on mass production, as well as on photography. Such ideas, in the climate of late modernism, also generated radical reflections on authorship, originality and reproducibility. Consider, for instance, the ample use that was made of photography by Pop artists. As Mellor writes, with special reference to the British artistic environment and the key figure of Richard Hamilton: 'Like Bacon, Hamilton's adaptation of photo-generated imagery was crucial to visual art in London in the mid-sixties, in its collusion with the wider forces of commercial Pop.'[28] Consider furthermore the use of photography made in those same years by a world-famous Pop artist and style icon such as Andy Warhol: 'In the silkscreen paintings that he began to produce in 1962, Warhol pursues inherent multiplicity in the repeated use of screens to produce series of works and in the serial repetition of an image within the space of a single work.'[29] The same Robert Rauschenberg, the precursor of Pop Art who was already famous for his use of everyday objects and materials in his 'Combines' of the 1950s, from 1962 began to incorporate in his art not only found objects but also photographs, thanks to the same silkscreen process used by Warhol. In 1964, year of the sensational arrival of Pop Art at the Biennale di Venezia, Rauschenberg was awarded the prize for best foreign artist, an event that provoked much heated discussion and even controversy, and that certainly Antonioni did not fail to notice.

The interest in objects, incidentally, concerns also literature, and especially the *nouveau roman*; and was discussed in the Italian context by Italo Calvino in his influential essay, 'Il mare dell'oggettività' (known in English as 'The Sea of Objectivity'), originally published in 1960. Writes Calvino:

> It is my impression that we have yet to recognize the turn that has come into effect over the past seven to eight years, in literature, in art, in yet more varied intellectual pursuits, and even in our attitude towards the world. From a culture based on a relationship and contrast between two limits, on the one hand the individual's conscience, will, and judgement, and on the other hand, the objective world, we are now passing into a culture in which the first limit is submerged by the sea of objectivity, by the uninterrupted flux of what exists.[30]

It is thus becoming obvious that *Blow-Up* is in a momentous relationship with a complex constellation of questions that emerge directly from the observation and use of the object in the art of the decade, a use that, since Duchamp, has been marked by an inaccessible opacity, inasmuch as in Duchamp's theory objects are chosen and used as indifferent forms, and as instances of reticent, non-signifying materiality.[31] Simultaneously, they do refer to the historical conditions of reproducibility and multiplicity, which are crucial in negotiating the border between modernism and postmodernism. These objects also pose the key question of what differentiates art from the world of the objects of consumption, fashion, advertising and popular culture, a world that was then in a phase of great expansion. It is not by chance that the protagonist of Antonioni's film is a fashion photographer (and, indeed, a fashionable one) who aspires to be an artist, as is suggested by the book of photographs of London that he is preparing, and by the explicit comparison drawn by the characters between his photographs and the paintings of his neighbour and friend. Similarly, it is not a coincidence that the questions of the mechanical nature and infinite reproducibility of photography are at the core of the film's plot.[32] It is in the 1960s that the debate on the simulacrum, the copy and

75

authenticity develops precisely as part of the reflection on the object. And it is in this context that two further discourses emerge: the debate on the loss of the modernist artist's individuality, uniqueness and subjectivity; and the conversation about the dissolution of the borders that had separated art, style and fashion – a dissolution that *Blow-Up* clearly announces, and that will become progressively accentuated over the following decades.[33]

The importance of the object in *Blow-Up* has arguably been overshadowed in the critical literature by the prevalent epistemological reading of the film as a commentary on the limits of vision and of photography (and thus also of the cinema) and on the unknowability of the real.[34] But Antonioni's discourses on photography as reproduction and on objects as form are not incompatible. The film's things and the protagonist's photographs are placed on the same plane by Antonioni; indeed, they all are found objects.[35] The protagonist is a collector of objects as much as of images. As Megan Williams has noticed, the photographer has in the film the precise function of collecting and discarding objects.[36] To this observation I would add that to him also belong the activities of looking at, touching and surrounding himself with things. Their materiality and form are emphasised by the physicality with which he enters into a relationship with them; he constantly touches them, and not only with his hands; at times, he wraps his body around them.

Such a focus on physicality is not accidental; many of the film's discourses on 'objectuality' – as one might attempt to term the notion of the precise yet enigmatic nature of things as objects – refer in fact to the body. The bodies of the characters themselves are historicised objects; their presentness and modernity are communicated via hairstyles, clothes, accessories, attitudes and gestures that are the expression of precise tastes and tendencies. And it is useful to remember that Antonioni is explicit about the process of objectification that the photographer imposes on his fashion models. Furthermore, the film is opened and closed by two famous sequences dominated by a group of mimes, whose bodies are exalted in their physicality by their performance, make-up and absence of speech. These street artists, who at the start of the film peacefully invade the streets of London in the early morning, and at the end are engaged in a mimed tennis match in the park, have frequently been read as part of the film's discourse on the ambiguity of perception; however, it is useful to remember that in the 'happening', another key artistic phenomenon of the 1960s evoked by the film, each element of the scene – the actor included – becomes an object.

The presence of these mimes further confirms the paradoxical double value of objects in *Blow-Up* – the duality that places them in between thingness and nothingness. The mock tennis match that concludes the film suggests the immateriality and illusion of experience, precisely like the images captured by the protagonist's Nikon, like the corpse that appears and disappears from the park in the space of a few hours, and like the photographer himself, who vanishes from the last frame of

The photographer and his double: touching the corpse in the park

the film. Nevertheless, these objects and these bodies suggest presence as much as they do illusion or intangibility. The photographer throws the imaginary ball back into the tennis court, from which it had escaped, and in so doing he materialises it; and the corpse in the park can not only be seen, but also touched.

The photographer's discovery of the corpse catalyses all the discourses that we have examined so far, and takes them to a new level. Arguably, without this corpse Antonioni's discourse on objects would fail to be as incisive and momentous. The dead body powerfully demonstrates that the duality of objects also makes for their sublimity: the coexistence of being and non-being, of meaning and its absence induces an ineffable and uncanny experience. The corpse, powerful figure of the other-than-subject, is the found object par excellence in the film; and the shots of the protagonist who touches it are undoubtedly the most sublime in a film full of sublime images. By framing together the body of the photographer and his dead alter-ego, his double, Antonioni shows us the object in its value as inhuman copy of the subject, in the encounter with which the subject experiences the fascination of the horror, of the non-human, and runs the risk of dissolution, with all the necessary references to Kristeva.[37] And yet, in a counter-Kristevan reading, it is precisely the encounter with the other-than-oneself that occasions for the photographer his most lucid, if not only, moment of self-awareness in the film. The presence of the corpse implies the absence of the human; by touching it, the protagonist, a man full of certainties on the self, recognises that he is object among the objects, that he is part of the 'sea of objectivity'. The two bodies, dead and alive, are framed together because they are the two faces of the same coin: both are simultaneously subject and object. Both also function in the film as mobiles or movable objects: they are contained in the urban landscape, but they appear and disappear from the frame.

It is precisely this ethical tension – this discourse on the subject, on his being in the world, on his relationship with objects – that indicates the continued belonging

Sublime bodies

of Antonioni's cinema to the sphere of (late) modernism. *Blow-Up*, however, also clearly signals the director's move towards forms and questions that will be typical of postmodern art; as such it is a true *limen* in Antonioni's research on the image, on modernity and on filmic language.

   Blow-Up also opens a dialogue with contemporary art in its recourse to the register of the sublime, which made its return, together with psychedelia, precisely in the period of late modernism. The bodies of *Blow-Up*, because they are so explicitly wrapped in multicoloured garments, exalted by haircuts, make-up and accessories, conveyors of theatrical gestures and attitudes, undoubtedly are sublime objects. And, as objects, they are part of the urban landscape of *Blow-Up*, which contains them all. Commenting on the use of spectacular colours in the urban images of the film, Mellor called attention to the fact that this London, painted in saturated reds and blues, is a truly sublime city: 'This invented, superposed spectacularization of colour within the urban environment suggested an enigma of sight ... Outside of Bill's studio, viewed by Thomas from his car, London was a shifting set of screened and materialized colours – it was Sublime.'[38] Enigmatic and present, tangible yet incommensurable, sublime and pop, the Swinging London of *Blow-Up* is Antonioni's true object, his opaque and beautiful *objet trouvé*, an urban landscape that is distinctively his, and that lies ineffably on the border between modernism and postmodernism.

Notes

1. Annette Messager cited in Stephen Johnstone, 'Introduction: Recent Art and the Everyday', in Stephen Johnstone (ed.), *The Everyday* (London: Whitechapel, 2008), pp. 12–23 (p. 12).

2. Antonioni was a painter at least since the 1970s; some of his work is displayed at the Michelangelo Antonioni Museum in Ferrara.

3. Sam Rohdie, *Antonioni* (London: BFI, 1990), p. 51.

4. Michelangelo Antonioni, 'A Talk with Michelangelo Antonioni on his Work' [1961], in *Michelangelo Antonioni: The Architecture of Vision. Writings and Interviews on the Cinema*, ed. Carlo Di Carlo and Giorgio Tinazzi, trans. Marga Cottino-Jones (New York: Marsilio, 1996), pp. 21–47 (p. 44).

5. See Giorgio De Vincenti, *Il concetto di modernità del cinema* (Parma: Pratiche, 1993), pp. 199–218.

6. Vittorio Giacci, 'Le regard évasif', in Carlo Di Carlo (ed.), *Michelangelo Antonioni, 1942/1965, L'Œuvre de Michelangelo Antonioni*, vol. 1, 2nd edn (Rome: Ente Autonomo di Gestione per il Cinema, 1988), pp. 14–15 (p. 15).

7. Enzo Paci et al., 'Dibattito su *L'eclisse*', in Carlo Di Carlo (ed.), *Michelangelo Antonioni* (Rome: Edizioni di Bianco e Nero, 1964) pp. 87–118 (p. 88).

8. It also ultimately failed to give account of the importance placed by Antonioni on the human figure in relation to objects, spaces and the built environment – a practice on which David Forgacs sheds light in his contribution to this collection.

9. This dualism is also reflected in Antonioni's declarations on his fascination for the aesthetic qualities of the industrial plant, which, however, is both aestheticised and depicted as threatening and poisonous in the film. See Michelangelo Antonioni, 'Red Desert' [1964], in *The Architecture of Vision*, pp. 283–6.

10. Of course, the term 'late modernism' is equally relevant; however, proto-postmodernism is more decidedly suggestive of the novelty that I here wish to emphasise.

11. Seymour Chatman, *Antonioni, or the Surface of the World* (Berkeley and Los Angeles: University of California Press, 1985), p. 153.

12. Arthur Goldwag, *Isms and Ologies: All the Movements, Ideologies and Doctrines That Have Shaped Our World* (London: Quercas, 2007), p. 103.

13. 'È nato a Londra, ma non è un film inglese', *Corriere della Sera*, 12 February 1982; English trans: 'It was born in London, but it is not an English film,' in Antonioni, *The Architecture of Vision*, pp. 89–91.

14. David Alan Mellor, ' "Fragments of an Unknowable Whole": Michelangelo Antonioni's Incorporation of Contemporary Visualities in London, 1966', *Visual Culture in Britain* vol. 8 no. 2 (2007), pp. 45–61 (p. 45).

15. Peter Whitehead, personal communication. At the time, Whitehead was making *Tonite Let's All Make Love in London* (1967), the quintessential Swinging London document, and *Benefit of the Doubt* (1967), a recording of the Royal Shakespeare Company and Peter Brook's anti-Vietnam War show, *US*.

16. Nicole Brenez, 'Peter Whitehead: The Exigency of Joy', *Rouge* no. 10 (2007), trans. Adrian Martin, <http://www.rouge.com.au/10/whitehead.html>

17. Mellor, ' "Fragments of an Unknowable Whole" ', p. 48.

18. William Arrowsmith, *Antonioni: The Poet of Images* (New York: Oxford University Press, 1995), pp. 108–10.

19. Jocelyn Rickards, *The Painted Banquet: My Life and Loves* (London: Weidenfeld & Nicolson), p. 96.

20. Pierre Bourdieu, *La Distinction, critique sociale du jugement* (Paris: Minuit, 1979). At the start of the film, the protagonist is dressed as a tramp, after taking pictures incognito in a shelter for the homeless; when he changes, he literally becomes a modish photographer. In this way, Antonioni underscores the importance of clothes in the definition of a man's social status and persona.

21. The dichotomy nature/culture (and present/past) can be traced, for instance, in the already quoted contribution by William Arrowsmith, and in Andrew Sarris, 'No Antonennui', in Roy Huss (ed.), *Focus on Blow-Up* (Englewood Cliffs, NJ: Prentice-Hall, 1971), pp. 31–5.

22. Françoise Chenet-Faugerat, 'L'invention du paysage urbain', *Romantisme* vol. 24 no. 83 (1994), pp. 27–38 (pp. 28–30).

23. Ibid., p. 30.

24. John Roberts, *The Intangibilities of Form: Skill and Deskilling in Art after the Readymade* (London: Verso, 2007), p. 21.

25. Arte Povera was announced with a manifesto by Celant in 1967, the year after the release of *Blow-Up*.

26. Chatman, *Antonioni or, The Surface of the World*, p. 101.

27. Arturo Schwarz, *The Complete Works of Marcel Duchamp*, quoted in Martha Buskirk, *The Contingent Object of Contemporary Art* (Cambridge, MA: MIT Press, 2005), p. 70.

28. Mellor, ' "Fragments of an Unknowable Whole" ', p. 47.

29. Buskirk, *The Contingent Object of Contemporary Art*, p. 74.

30. Italo Calvino, 'Il mare dell'oggettività', in *Il Menabò di letteratura* no. 2 (1960), reprinted in Italo Calvino, *Saggi 1945–1985*, vol. I, ed. Mario Barenghi (Milan: Mondadori, 1995), pp. 52–60. Trans. LR.

31. On the indifference of found objects see, for instance, Octavio Paz, 'The Ready Made', in Joseph Masheck (ed.), *Marcel Duchamp in Perspective* (Cambridge, MA: Da Capo Press, 2002), pp. 84–9.

32. For a thorough exploration of *Blow-Up*'s discourse on photography see Matilde Nardelli's essay in this collection.

33. 'The notion of the artist as *monteur* in the broad sense is now one of the key moves identifiable with the dissolution of the boundaries between fashion, style and art in our consumerist-led culture.' Roberts, *The Intangibilities of Form*, p. 11.

34. See, for instance, Peter Brunette, *The Films of Michelangelo Antonioni* (Cambridge: Cambridge University Press, 1998), p. 110.

35. Man Ray used to place photographs and found objects side by side in the Surrealist practice, on account of their capacity to manifest the same uncanny configurations of

repressed desires. See Ramona Fotiade, 'From Ready-Made to Moving Image: The Visual Poetics of Surrealist Cinema', in Graeme Harper and Rob Stone (eds), *The Unsilvered Screen: Surrealism on Film* (London: Wallflower Press, 2007), pp. 9–22.

36. In truth, only one is the object that the photographer discards in the film, a piece of the guitar destroyed by Jeff Beck during the concert of the Yardbirds. Megan Williams, 'A Surface of Forgetting: The Object of History in Michelangelo Antonioni's *Blow-Up*', *Quarterly Review of Film & Video* vol. 17 no. 3 (2000), pp. 245–59 (p. 245).

37. Julia Kristeva, *Powers of Horror: An Essay on Abjection*, trans. Leon S. Roudiez (Columbia: Columbia University Press, 1982).

38. Mellor, ' "Fragments of an Unknowable Whole" ', p. 50.

Angelo Restivo

REVISITING *ZABRISKIE POINT*

No discussion of *Zabriskie Point* (1970) – Antonioni's critically maligned film 'about' post-1968 America and its youth culture – can begin without a consideration of its beleaguered production and reception histories. For today, *Zabriskie Point* comes to us as a kind of *film maudit* and, as such, the first questions to ask would be: what stories lie behind it? (Or, if we wanted to add some humour to the proceedings, we could ask the question as Stanley Kauffmann did in his 1970 review of the film – 'How did it happen?'[1] – the kind of question you'd ask if the 'it' were a plane crash or 9/11.) To answer this, we could begin by 'rounding up the usual suspects' – those facile explanations for cinematic disasters which, perhaps correctly, install greed, hubris and megalomania at the heart of the 'will-to-cinema' – if only to get them out of the way quickly, in the case of *Zabriskie Point*. So, for example, we have the brilliant international auteur acclaimed for the work done in his 'native' culture whose attempt to navigate the waters of a foreign culture leads only to shipwreck (positions taken by Vincent Canby and Stanley Kauffmann in their reviews upon the film's initial release[2]). Or: the director whose tight budgets made his works taut and concentrated, finally given the money to do anything he wants, falls prey to a misguided perfectionism (the *Heaven's Gate* [1980] scenario). Or: the director whose reputation as having made visionary films suddenly is charged with (or charges himself with) the mission to make the definitive statement about a culture, an historical epoch, or a collective memory (the *Apocalypse Now* [1979] scenario).[3]

But these specific explanations – which, as I alluded to above, comprise the canon of 'master narratives' of cinematic disaster precisely insofar as they play off of characteristics that might indeed be endemic to the cinema itself, as institution and art form – don't really get us very far with *Zabriskie Point*. In the first place, *Zabriskie Point* was made possible by the fact that Antonioni had already completed *Blow-Up* (1966), a huge commercial success filmed outside his native Italy, a fact which Stanley Kauffmann tries to get around by arguing that 'Britain is still Europe, whatever the British say,' even going so far as to quote Browning in order to ease the continental European's transit across the English Channel.[4] Second, Antonioni never claimed to be making a grand – let alone definitive – statement about America circa 1968; as Antonioni himself explained in 1970, 'a film is not a social analysis, after all. I was just trying to feel something about America, to gain some intuition.'[5] It is doubtless only from the vantage point of recent years that we can understand that *Zabriskie Point* is about, among other things, the moment at which the nation begins to disintegrate as the horizon against which meaning is assigned to words and images; only now that we can understand what Antonioni understood in that 1970 *Times* interview – long before Deleuze's *L'Image-temps*, incidentally – that '[i]t is not a question of reading between the lines, but one of reading between the images'.[6]

In an interview during the shoot with Marsha Kinder – then a fledgling assistant professor at USC – Antonioni wondered why MGM kept asking him about the film's expenses, when many of those expenses Antonioni saw as built into the Hollywood mode of production.[7] Beverly Walker, brought in from the New York Film Festival as a replacement for the two previous public relations people who had fallen by the wayside for one reason or another, noted that union regulations practically doubled the cost of key crew personnel, since all of the Italian crew members Antonioni brought in had to be 'doubled' by a paid American union member.[8] But perhaps what drew the ire of industry people were not those expenses which remained hidden from view – like Michael Cimino's legendary hundreds of takes of an actor twirling a lasso, in *Heaven's Gate* – but rather those that the film not only made fully visible, but indeed revelled in. Especially the film's explosive finale: production designer Dean Tavoularis insisted that miniatures of the Wright-inspired house built into the desert rock near Scottsdale would not be effective, and so a near-full-size replica was built, for the sole purpose of blowing it to smithereens.[9] This was followed up by an orgy of exploding consumer goods, among the airborne debris a loaf of Wonder Bread, which was then a staple of ordinary American households, its television commercials blatantly linking the family to the national future ('Wonder Bread helps build strong bodies twelve ways'), but which must have seemed to the Italians as much a caricature of bread as the suburban housing developments were a caricature of 'community'. Might the industry have thought Antonioni was biting the hand that fed him? It probably didn't help when Antonioni said, in a 1968 *Times* interview, 'But Mao once made an alliance with Chiang Kai-shek, Castro would have taken money from anyone to survive in the mountains, and look at the deals between Ho Chi Minh and the French! ... why can't I work with MGM if it helps me to do what I want to do?'[10]

But the bad blood didn't run only between the studio execs and the 'Italians': the film's American crew members were conservative, disparaging and even went so far as to attempt to sabotage the filming on occasion. Beverly Walker couldn't have put it more bluntly: '[t]heir disapproval and contempt was all-encompassing'.[11] But this was simply mirroring what was happening on a much larger, national scale: the

83

skilled working class felt increasingly threatened by the social movements which *Zabriskie Point* was, at least nominally, sympathetic to. Thus, the post-68 political landscape in the US was quite different from that of Italy (or continental Europe more generally). While in Italy, for example, there were still ties between students/intellectuals and workers – as is attested not only by the history of the PCI but also in, for example, the autonomist movement[12] – in the US in the late 1960s we see the beginnings of a working-class defection from its traditional home in the Democratic Party (in Nixon's so-called 'silent majority', for example), as that party attempted to deal more seriously with issues of decolonisation, race and social justice. In structural terms, signs of crisis were beginning to manifest themselves in the Fordist regime of accumulation, signs which played themselves out – as Kevin Floyd has recently and brilliantly argued – to some measure across the very bodies of the (white) working-class male and its performed masculinity.[13] We will see in due course just how powerfully the Fordist crisis is inscribed in *Zabriskie Point*; for now, suffice to note that it coloured even the production history of the film.

Given the 'bad vibes' that surrounded the film on the production side, it would seem not unreasonable to surmise that these tainted the film's critical reception. But in fact, the reception of the film in the US went way beyond anything a reasonable person might be expected to deduce from the film's chequered production history; indeed, Beverly Walker says that '[n]othing in my short career had prepared me for the merciless critical onslaught against *Zabriskie Point*'.[14] *New York Times* reporter Guy Flatley duly summarised the onslaught, in 1971: the film was 'loathsome and incredibly shoddy', while Antonioni was 'an ignoramus', contemptuous of the US and – in an apparently overheard remark from a critic after a screening – a 'sonofabitch' who 'ought to be shot'.[15] While Vincent Canby and Stanley Kauffmann were more measured in their criticism – Kauffmann painting himself as a champion of Antonioni's pre-*Blow-Up* work – we have already noted how they resorted to the 'explanation' of the artist out of his cultural element. It seems that any and all elements of the film could be singled out by some critic or another for attack: the meeting of students and Black Panthers was unrealistic; the images of LA as pure surface – dazzlingly executed, we should note – relied too heavily on clichéd ideas about the city; the Death Valley 'love-in' seemed arch, or even silly; the image of the police as prosthetic automatons was simplistic (even if we can see in the confrontation footage resonances with the images of the 1968 Democratic Convention police riots in Chicago, which Antonioni saw first-hand as he was tear-gassed along with others in Grant Park); the real-estate development scheme was too caricatured; the climactic explosion sequence was outrageously protracted. But by far the most severe criticism was reserved for the casting of the two leads Mark Frechette and Daria Halprin, and the dialogue the two delivered. Perhaps the one line singled out for most quoting among the critics is the post-coital 'I always knew it would be like this.' But there was plenty of other fodder: the Black Panther who says 'Molotov cocktails is a mixture of kerosene and gasoline; white radicals is a mixture of bull-shit and jive' (which John Burks, writing for *Rolling Stone*, called a 'classic cliché'!);[16] or, 'The people I'm running around with are on a reality trip.' (Interestingly, the *Rolling Stone* piece is littered with the very same argot that it makes fun of: 'Antonioni digs …' [as in 'likes']; 'this cat Taylor's up to no good' ['cat'='man']; 'the balling scene' [i.e., the sex scene]).

But perhaps at this point it would be more productive to settle on two or three issues raised by the critical reception of the film, and scrutinise them more closely as a way to begin to find an alternate route through the film. For example, in the *Rolling Stone* piece, Burks writes the following:

> One extremely curious thing comes during the scene when Daria is doping. They're rapping about something inconsequential, typically, but it's *dubbed*. Their mouths are saying one thing, their voices another. It's rather badly executed. It's as if Antonioni is telling us that it doesn't really matter *what* they're saying. Any rap will do.[17]

It's not likely that Burks knew about the widespread practice of post-dubbing in Italian cinema. And indeed, the mismatching of sound and image is noticeable in the sequence. But what's interesting here is how Burks seems to be stumbling upon something important without really knowing it. It isn't so much what Antonioni is *telling* us that is important here – after all, post-dubbing, as I noted, was quite common in the Italian neo-realist and art-cinema traditions – but what the meeting between that cinematic tradition and the American one actually produces, as a symptom. The mismatch of voice and image is taken to be a sign of 'B-grade' pro-duction values (underground or porn), unacceptable in a product from the A-list studio MGM; but what the dialogue here begins to make us realise is that Hollywood's tradition of 'realism' in dialogue is in fact a highly stylised convention, in which dialogue must always be tied to characterisation and the film's cause-effect chain. Antonioni's dialogue is not designed to function in this way, and the banal-ity of the film's dialogue finds its correlative in *Blow-Up*'s street demonstration scene, where the demonstrators carry placards with 'empty signifiers' ('Stop!'; 'No!'; etc.). This play between abstraction – discourse only signifies within a set symbolic system – and banal realism – that is, that the pop idioms of 1968 actually sounded like that – must have been quite unsettling to audiences of the time, especially given the utopian aspirations that countercultural discourse held then. It must thus have seemed a great rebuke, akin to Kathleen Cleaver's and the Panthers' rebuke to white radicals early in the film, for a foreign director to – consciously or not – have uncov-ered a narcissistic dimension to the discourse of 'the hippies'. A number of extremely interesting conclusions will follow from this (which will be dealt with as we pro-ceed). One: that the framing of the explosions as an eruption of Daria's fantasy into the social field is itself the mark of a radical failure of the symbolic systems of youth

85

culture to 'link' to anything beyond itself (the political failure of 1968). Two: that the issue of 'pleasure' – cinematic and otherwise – is highly overdetermined across the body of the text, with Antonioni's aesthetic of the rarefication of cinematic pleasure being mirrored in the film's subject matter as a real social contradiction, between a 'disciplined' Marxism (exemplified in the film by the Panthers) and 'the politics of experience' (to mobilise a phrase coined by R. D. Laing in this period).

Burks ends his *Rolling Stone* piece with an observation about audience responses to the film after the screenings he attended, and the passage is worth looking at, as it hits on something that still remains a conundrum in any critical approach to *Zabriskie Point*. Burks first describes how the audience members were split between applause and booing, but notes that neither reaction was sustained for very long. He then says, 'It was as if nobody trusted his first reaction. I don't trust *mine*.' Even after a period of forty years, the film has this same power to put spectators in the uncomfortable position of not being able to trust their own first reactions to the film. On more than one occasion, I've brought up the subject of *Zabriskie Point* to some of my more cinephile graduate students. More often than not, their initial reaction is to say, 'What a great film!' But then, almost immediately, they will begin to put conditions and specifications onto their initial enthusiasm, in a way that they would not think to do if the film were, let's say, *L'avventura* (1960). This then suggests that an entire set of interpretive protocols attached to the art film are called into question by *Zabriskie Point*. It becomes clear, for example, that resorting to an unabashed auteurism will not help us through our self-doubting reactions. For if we enumerate all the characteristics of the Antonioni 'signature' that reappear in *Zabriskie Point*, we somewhat forcedly turn the text into a 'good object', by repressing the very obstacles that seem intrinsic to our experience of the film. To be sure, one has to *learn* to see an Antonioni film (here we can recall that *L'avventura* was greeted with boos at its premier at Cannes, for example), and no doubt the film's 1970 reception can be largely explained by the fact that a good percentage of the film's audience was 'untutored' in Antonioni's style. But, in a work like *L'avventura*, the spectatorial process of learning to see is integrally bound up in the formal systems of the film – the immersion in cinematic duration, the relentless expectation of 'the event', the bodies' relations to space – so that understanding (or appreciating) the film completely coincides with the experience of viewing it, and one hardly needs to impose a predetermined interpretive grid over the film in order to 'get' it. This is why one does not 'mistrust' one's reactions to *L'avventura*. And to the extent that one feels the need to impose such an interpretive grid over *Zabriskie Point*, then to that extent the film remains a 'failure', by all the aesthetic criteria of the art film. What I wish to propose, then, is that it is the film's confrontation between Antonioni's formal system and the American landscape that makes it such a strange and beautiful film. This meeting is very much embedded in history: but what the film produces is the *unreadable historical sign*, and it is this that gets attached to

various scraps of 'bad' dialogue or acting, or other signs of excess, and which produces a kind of spectatorial mistrust, even among viewers today.

In what was clearly meant to be a criticism of the film, Burks remarked –
remember, this is at the moment of the film's release – that '*Zabriskie Point* seems
almost a period piece.' Looking at the film decades later, more than one critic[18] has
proclaimed the film as decades ahead of its time. Perhaps the biggest paradox of
Zabriskie Point is that these two things go together: that the film is 'always already'
both outmoded and anticipatory. These two words bring us quite naturally to
Walter Benjamin: to his notion, from the surrealism essay, of the revolutionary
potential that lies hidden in the outmoded; as well as to his notion that the catastrophe of history lies less in extraordinary events than in the continual repetition
of the everyday.[19] The outmoded is a charged fragment that stands outside the
repetitive cycles of capitalist production; as such, it has the potential to arrest
the inexorability of 'progress'-as-catastrophe. The short-circuiting of temporality
in *Zabriskie Point* performs, I would argue, a similar kind of operation: provided,
of course, that we see all those signs of *Zabriskie Point*'s 'failure' rather as
charged fragments, lying in wait, signifiers in a historical moment in which it was
impossible for them to cohere.[20]

The Screen: Abstract Expressionism Meets Pop

The opening (credit) sequence of *Zabriskie Point* – the Black Panthers speaking
before a group of white students – is in some ways a reprise of the opening sequence
of *Il deserto rosso* (1964): the camera is initially out of focus, turning the visual field
into a kind of abstract colour field until, slowly, figures begin to emerge from the
ground. But *Zabriskie Point* takes the technique one step further, by repeating the
same strategy with the auditory field. Initially, what the characters are speaking is
barely audible against the 'background' of a low, percussive beat which seems to
envelope or interiorise the scene. Thus, from the very first moments of the film, a
play between interiority and exteriority is set up which will carry through the film
in various formal ways; however, what we initially can take from this strategy is that
Antonioni is announcing a kind of limit to 'documentary' filming, insofar as the link
between word and act is fundamentally unclear, haunted by an insistent, if formless,
interiority. Ultimately, it will be useful to characterise this problematic as one of
affect; now, however, suffice to say that this validates our earlier observation about
the 'problem of dialogue' in the film as being less about the authenticity of the
speech and more about the violation of the (Hollywood) expectation that speech
and action connect seamlessly.

Throughout the 1960s, as Antonioni pushes his exploration of cinematic indexicality to its limits, the figure–ground relationship comes to interest him intensely.

As Rosalind Krauss has so brilliantly shown, while one current within modernism – let's call it modernism's 'triumphalist' mode – was heavily invested in a rationalist abstraction of vision as such, another current, which Krauss connects to 'the optical unconscious' and to artists like Marcel Duchamp and Max Ernst, continued to produce work which showed the limits to this triumphalist project.[21] Lacan was perhaps the one who most thoroughly theorised the obstacles to any rationalisation of visuality, in his seminar sessions on 'The Gaze as Object-a',[22] though to be sure he drew upon what amounted to an extended examination of the problem by contemporaries such as Sartre, Merleau-Ponty and Caillois. In sum, the argument was this: we have, on the 'rational' side, the eye which gathers in the light so as to bring a world into focus (and in alignment with geometral perspective); on the other side, we have the embodied subject, surrounded by a light which is a generalised luminence, who in essence is 'captured' by the enveloping light. Here, where the subject is taken into the picture – says Sartre – is where the subject 'haemorrhages' into her surroundings. As figure dissolves into ground, the subject, in Roger Caillois's words, 'feels himself becoming space'.[23]

In the mid-1960s, Antonioni's exploration of figure–ground relations is most easily seen in the final shot of *Blow-Up*, when the photographer is absorbed into the grassy background. (This shot can be seen as the logical culmination of other bodies-becoming-space: for example, the patriarchal corpse which disappears from the film; or, indeed, the more generalised 'becoming-ground' which occurs to the photographic figures as they are blown up.) In *L'eclisse* (1962), we see a similar kind of play with figure and ground, when Vittoria (Monica Vitti) steps into a photograph of the Kenyan savannah, or in her walk under the canopy of trees as she 'disappears' from the film. I have argued elsewhere that this destabilisation of figure–ground relations in Antonioni is the direct result of the meeting between a cinematic legacy of neo-realism and the profound spatial transformations that occurred as Italy experienced the economic miracle. In other words, the unreadability of the historical event, the event which is visible only second-hand through its effects, is what underwrites Antonioni's systematic exposure of the structure of the gaze within the photographic image. Perhaps the most sublime examples of this procedure are in *Il deserto rosso*: here, the brilliant eruptions of primary colours are distributed eccentrically throughout the film, as if to express Giuliana's dissolution, her absorption by space. The colours only 'come together' in the recounted fantasy of the girl on the deserted island, where in the end the 'non-organic life' of the rock formations takes on the quality of flesh.[24]

In *Zabriskie Point*, of course, the desert is real. It is certainly to Antonioni's credit that he understood the profound relationship between the city of Los Angeles and the desert, and, further, between those and something fundamental in the American imaginary. Such a vision can be traced backward at least as far as Nathaniel West, and forward to Robert Towne's script to Polanski's *Chinatown*

(1974). And indeed, even among the film's severest critics one can find some of them appreciative of the film's bravura presentation of Los Angeles, with its awesome horizontality replicating itself to the horizon line. (Baudrillard has noted how the European exurb, however connected to the American idea, does not really replicate its effect: La Defense, for example, is surrounded by a ring road which bounds and constricts it, whereas in the US the idea is that the 'monstrous' development can replicate itself to infinity. In *Zabriskie Point*, this finds expression in the Sunny Dunes real-estate scheme.)[25] One of the film's earliest views of LA is illustrative of what happens when Antonioni's investment in figure–ground relations meets the Pop Art of the LA cityscape. The image seems to be that of a giant, corrugated billboard picturing a cow, and advertising beef; but the image begins moving to the left, as we realise that we are looking at the side of a truck, while what is gradually unveiled as the truck moves away is yet another flat picture plane depicting a cattle ranch, which turns out to be the façade of the trucking company. Here, it isn't just that Antonioni is playing with the clichéd depthlessness of Los Angeles, but rather that the proliferation of images within the built space presents us with a problem of vanishing points. In a very real sense, then, Antonioni's play with figure and ground reaches a kind of limit point in Los Angeles, for Antonioni's earlier procedure of allowing the gaze to erupt in the visual field depended upon a reliability of the vanishing points. If we return briefly to the theory of the gaze, we can say that what Antonioni was doing in his previous five films was throwing outward, into the visual field, the screen that arises when the subject (or object) is enveloped by light. If the screening operation is a kind of defence mechanism which preserves our proprietary 'interest' in the integrity of the perspectival field, then its eruption into the visual field is a mark of our 'haemorrhaging' into the picture itself.

But as the built environment is given over more and more to the image, the function of the screen begins to take on new valences. Jean Baudrillard has described this process as a 'refraction', and it is worth quoting at length his description of the Roxy in LA (in the mid-1980s):

> Today, no staging of bodies, no performance can be without its control screen. This is not there to see or reflect those taking part, with the distance and magic of the mirror. No, it is there as an instantaneous, depthless refraction. Video, everywhere, serves only this end: it is a screen of ecstatic refraction. As such, it has nothing of the traditional image or scene … its goal is *to be hooked up to itself*. Without this circular hook-up, without this brief, instantaneous network that a brain, an object, an event, or a discourse create by being hooked up to themselves, without this perpetual video, nothing has any meaning today. The mirror phase has given way to the video phase.[26]

This might be thought of, in Deleuzian terms, as a kind of post-Fordist assemblage between image, body, brain and object. To illustrate the effect of this refractive or

Blow-Up (1966)

scattering assemblage on Antonioni's construction of the visual field, we might turn to a striking shot that occurs in *Blow-Up*, as the photographer is doing a photo shoot in his studio. In this shot – a kind of 'send-up' of perspectivism – a series of screens are placed before the models, who are arranged on a 'false' perspectivial line. Here, geometral perspective – so essential to Antonioni's earlier explorations of figure and ground – is supplanted by a distribution of screens, through which are refracted a phantasmagoria of commodities, or bodies as pure image. In *Zabriskie Point*, this principle of screening becomes a central formal device for the presentation of Los Angeles, and especially of the Los Angeles spaces where capital is most concentrated. Thus, for example, our first view of the urban environment comes when Daria is returning to the office building of Rod Taylor's real-estate firm, where she does temp work and has returned to retrieve the book she left on the roof of the building. The lobby of the building is presented as a series of refractive planes – note in the background the way the wall of the elevator bank is distortedly reflecting both the two security men inside the lobby and also the trees and automobiles on the other side of the glass entrance. We can say that the architecture here aspires to a kind of total, 'ecstatic' visibility, reinforced by the video surveillance monitors which are tucked away under the circular reception counter. If Antonioni's Italian films depended so heavily on a point of occlusion in the visual field, the hint of an 'outside' that might forestall the absorption of the body by space, in America we arrive at a kind of self-containment in the image, a circular hook-up which admits of no outside.

This should lead us to better understand the function of the desert in the film. Death Valley must be seen as a strict correlative to the refractive architecture of LA, with the 'synthesis' of the two being the desert house which is exploded at the film's end. For the desert – as a Deleuzian 'smooth space' – presents us with the same problems of vanishing points, perspective and figure–ground relations as do the 'striated',

Zabriskie Point (1970)

or territorialised, spaces of Los Angeles. Once again, Baudrillard's 1986 exploration of America provides us with an entrée towards thinking about this. His opening chapter, 'Vanishing Point', is an examination of the desert as fundamental to under-standing 'America', especially in its postmodern instantiation. The desert calls forth a kind of pure speed, such that the vanishing point becomes the point where *you* vanish: a point of no return. In words that echo the entire previous discussion, Baudrillard writes: 'Movement which moves through space of its own volition changes into an *absorption by space itself* – end of resistance, end of the scene of the journey as such.'[27]

In relation to this claim, one thing we can note is the way in which the journey – America's key figure for the possibility of self-invention – is not simply declared defunct (i.e., concomitant to the closing of the Frontier) but is more interestingly relocated and redefined, as if only now can we see that the movement westward was always less about arriving at a particular place than about throwing oneself towards a point of no return. (Perhaps this is the reason that, in the American imaginary, California is often seen as having moved to 'a higher plane' than the rest of the country; which is why, from the distance of the present, we can see the banalities of the dialogue in *Zabriskie Point* less as a failure of realism than as a sign that the characters have assented to a certain kind of disappearance of the subject.)

The desert, then, is the site of a radical 'becoming-other'. Daria stops at a remote desert outpost to look up a friend who has started there a 'school' for disturbed boys. She stops in a bar/general store where Patti Paige and the 'Tennessee Waltz' play in the background, and the grizzled denizens of the bar stare vacantly into space, as if the optics of the desert had permanently fixed their eyes on some unattainable horizon: it is this same logic of the American desert which von Stroheim had imagined decades earlier, when he set the climax of *Greed* [1924] in Death Valley. What insane idea possessed Daria's friend – whom she never finds, by the way – to relocate a bunch of troubled Los Angeles boys to what is a virtual ghost town? Daria runs into the children – in a scene generally attributed to Sam Shepard and near unanimously reviled by critics – who seem to group and ungroup rhizomatically across and within the ruins of the town, like swarms of flies.

The Deleuzian term for this ongoing process of becoming-other is 'affect'. Thus, the problem that *Zabriskie Point* ultimately brings us to is how affective investments get distributed across a spatial field which, as we've seen, is fundamentally different from that of any of Antonioni's earlier works. This is both the political and the historical dimension of the film, insofar as this spatial system can be seen as an early manifestation of what would only later be called 'post-Fordism'.

Affect and Spectacle

In his Lectures on Spinoza, Deleuze elaborates a careful definition of affect from Spinoza's *Ethics*: affect is the continually modulated power of the body to act, in its continual encounters (or 'mixing,' to use Deleuze's Spinozist term) with other 'bodies'.[28] The bodies one mixes with need not be other humans: one's body can 'mix' with LSD, or a song by the Grateful Dead, or a police officer, or the university or military bureaucracy. Certainly, the 1960s represent a period of greatly heightened affective investments across the social field, and especially, in the US, among young people. And indeed, this period remains, either implicitly or explicitly, a fundamental reference point for contemporary theorists working in the area of affect. The connection is explicit, for example, in someone like Lawrence Grossberg, who in 1992 attempted to understand how the affective investments connected to the rock music formation have become rearticulated into a fundamentally conservative formation which characterises contemporary American political culture.[29]

The question to be posed here is: to what extent do the spatial transformations that have refracted Antonioni's style in all the ways we've seen above work to disarticulate and rearticulate the affective formations that might have produced a revolutionary situation? In *Zabriskie Point*, we can say that there are three key scenes/ situations in which affective intensities move to the foreground: the political action of the students (distributed over several early scenes); the love-in in the desert; and, finally, the explosion of the desert house which stands as a synthesis of the 'networked city' (dominated by the screen) and the desert. The scenes construct a trajectory, from affect, which is fully plugged in to a politicised public sphere, to the complete interiorisation of Daria's fantasy (though I will want to problematise this last point at the end of the essay). This trajectory, then, justifies our initial interpretation of the sound mix of the film's credit sequence, where we suggested that the discourse of the student revolutionaries was haunted by the hum of an insistent, formless interiority.

(It should be noted here that the formal analysis that these scenes will commission here is one that will be done in broad strokes. I must confess that as I began writing this essay, I did not expect the film to present the kinds of derailments of the protocols of textual analysis that it indeed does: how at one moment one finds oneself analysing in intense detail the formal composition of one or two shots, while at another moment one covers a wide swath encompassing five or ten minutes of screen time. But here too there lurks the question of affect: the kinds of affective engagement in spectatorship that earlier works of Antonioni commission are more attenuated in *Zabriskie Point*. But I would attribute this attenuation to the fragmentary qualities that we uncovered at the end of the initial reception study, a fragmentation that comes about from the film's rather unique historical and geopolitical positioning.)

So, what strikes one about Antonioni's presentation of the student occupation of the university is the extent to which the battle seems lost to begin with (which was hardly obvious to radicals in 1969). Again, this is too often (and erroneously, I believe) attributed to Antonioni's presentation of the police as automatons, when it seems more accurate to attribute it to Antonioni's perception of spatial relations in the post-Fordist city. In order to understand this, we might turn to a comparison with Ivan Dixon's great Blaxploitation film released only three years after *Zabriskie Point*, *The Spook Who Sat By the Door* (1973). Dixon's film manages to take the affective intensities produced by the black power movement and allow them to resonate to greater and greater heights, such that it became possible for the film to imagine an armed insurrection come into being out of America's urban slums. But we can argue that its conditions of possibility came from the outmoded, or underdeveloped, urban spaces of the older, Rustbelt cities, spaces which allow something of the social subject to remain hidden from view and so allow for a tactical engagement with the strategies of control; in other words, precisely the kind of space it was the post-Fordist project to demolish, so as to produce heightened visibility in a horizontalised space.[30] And this shift mirrors the shift in Antonioni's aesthetic deployment of the gaze that we have noted earlier in the essay. As we've seen, Antonioni envisioned Los Angeles as a space in which affect was refracted, circulated within a closed feedback loop, and thus failing to connect to an outside.

Given this spatial problematic, the film's affective investments become increasingly 'interiorised', so that by film's end we are left with a pure auto-referentiality of the image itself. But before that, we have the great set piece of the love scene, a scene in which Antonioni seems now to have been attempting to think his way out of the political impasses produced by the very spatial system that so fascinated him. The love scene, that is, attempts to make affective connections transversally, abstractly connecting 'any-bodies-whatever' across the smooth space of the desert. But what remained unclearly thought out in the counterculture was the extent to which this politics of experience could lead to a political engagement with capital itself. Indeed, what was soon to take centre stage in progressive politics in the West was the politics of 'difference' which – valuable though it has been – essentially sidestepped the problem of the construction of the universal which was the utopian idea fuelling Antonioni's vision of the love-in.

Paolo Virno characterises the movements of the 60s and 70s as:

> a defeated revolution – the first revolution aimed not against poverty and backwardness, but specifically against the means of capitalistic production, thus, against wage labor … [T]he social struggles of the 1960s and 1970s expressed non-socialist demands, indeed anti-socialist demands: radical criticism of labor; an accentuated taste for differences, or, if you prefer, a refining of the 'principle of individuation'.[31]

While his central point of reference is the Autonomist movement in Italy – with its strategy of refusal, etc.[32] – one can, without much of a stretch, see, for example, Timothy Leary's call to 'Turn on, tune in, drop out' as expressing a similar refusal of the means of production. Virno's argument – subtle and sophisticated – is that post-Fordism's genius is to install the very strategies of 'communication', 'self-production' and so forth within the production process itself. Another way to put this is to say that the affective investments of the 1960s become rerouted, or rearticulated, into capitalist production.

Thus, perhaps the 'love-in' was also doomed from the start. The idea for this scene was in fact one of the initial and animating ideas of the film, but Antonioni was dissatisfied with the footage almost immediately after he saw the rushes.[33] Why, one wonders. As lyric interludes go – and let's remember, the lyric interlude had become a staple of New Hollywood film-making, with the 'Mrs Robinson' montage from *The Graduate* [1967] being a particularly popular, if unbearably insipid, example of the device – the love-in of *Zabriskie Point* is formally graceful, indeed captivating. Perhaps the answer again lies in an observation made earlier about Antonioni's relationship to cinematic pleasure, to the ways in which that relationship had to shift in

94

Hollywood (especially in a scene which had become a generic convention in the youth film), and most especially, to the ways in which this formally mirrored a real social contradiction within the counterculture. Thus, perhaps the most telling detail in the desert romp is that Daria smokes marijuana, while Mark refuses to.

We are then left with the film's spectacular finale. As we noted earlier, formally the explosion of the house, and then of consumer goods more generally, is book-ended by medium close-ups of Daria such that the images are to be read as her fantasy; and yet, the sequence is of such a protracted length, and of such stunning beauty, that it tends to undo its own articulation as fantasy, and to become something else. So, to begin with, we need to acknowledge – if only to later qualify or reject as overly simple – the idea that the ending suggests that all affective investments have been disconnected from action in the real world and relocated to the interiority of fantasy. While this provides us with a rather neat narrative trajectory, it seems incomplete. For one thing, fantasy is always intimately bound up with affect in ways that might be as likely as not able to fuel social relations and political engagement. To be sure, one does not imagine that Daria is driving off to join a terrorist cell at the end of the film. But then, having been mesmerised by the explosions, one doesn't particularly imagine *anything* about Daria at film's end; she has become irrelevant.

Instead, the film asks us to invest in the image per se. The irony here is that as the object world is systematically destroyed, the image becomes more and more beautiful, more and more 'for-itself'. On one level, of course, this continues the allegory of *Blow-Up*: the centre of energy of late capitalism shifts from the production of objects to the production of images. Finally, then, what *Zabriskie Point* registers is 'the terrible beauty' of the birth of the postmodern simulacrum, the representation which functions not so much in its relationship to 'truth' as in the very blankness of its meaning. The turmoil of the film is that of the sign positing itself as its own point of referentiality, unanchored from the framing discourses which would have guaranteed both its meaning and its truth. It is precisely this that throws all the signifiers of everyday life up for grabs in the film, and it is precisely this that was unreadable in 1970.

95

Notes

I originally began thinking about *Zabriskie Point* as a collaborative project with Richard C. Cante. Indeed, we co-wrote and presented at a conference a paper entitled 'Revisiting *Zabriskie Point*'. When I was invited to write for this collection, Richard graciously consented for me to write a single-authored piece on the film. Obviously, this essay is indebted to work that was done collaboratively with Richard and, while there are arguments here that evolved as I was working on this essay, many of the key ideas running through it were developed in collaboration with Richard.

1. Stanley Kauffmann, '*Zabriskie Point*' [review], *The New Republic*, 14 March 1970, p. 29.

2. Kauffmann, '*Zabriskie Point*', p. 29. Vincent Canby, 'Screen: Antonioni's *Zabriskie Point*' [review], *New York Times*, 10 February 1970, p. 47.

3. To be sure, *Apocalypse Now* was not the kind of critical or commercial failure that *Heaven's Gate* and *Zabriskie Point* were. But all of the disasters and craziness associated with its production – including Coppola's 'pick ending A or ending B' stunt at Cannes – led many to believe it was heading in that direction.

4. Kauffmann, '*Zabriskie Point*', p. 29.

5. Guy Flatley, '"I Love This Country." Antonioni Defends *Zabriskie Point*', *New York Times*, 22 February 1970, D15.

6. Ibid.

7. Marsha Kinder, '*Zabriskie Point*' [interview], *Sight & Sound* vol. 38 no. 1 (Winter 1968/69), pp. 26–30 (p. 30).

8. Beverly Walker, 'Michelangelo and the Leviathan: The Making of *Zabriskie Point*', *Film Comment* vol. 28 no. 5 (September 1992), pp. 36–49 (p. 45).

9. Ibid., p. 46. The replica was constructed within eyeshot of the actual house, near Scottsdale, Arizona.

10. Lawrence M. Bensky, 'Antonioni Comes to the Point', *New York Times*, 15 December 1968, D23.

11. Walker, 'Michelangelo and the Leviathan', p. 40.

12. In the decades following World War II, the Italian Communist Party (PCI) was the second largest political party in Italy. Though it was consistently locked out of all national ruling coalitions by a system of shuffling political alliances dubbed the 'penta-partito', it nevertheless successfully governed at the local level (most notably, in the Comune di Bologna). This differed dramatically from the US postwar experience, where any vestiges of Popular Front thinking were systematically attacked so as to produce 'the Cold War consensus'. Since these attacks very often were played out through a fantasmatic construction of the homosexual as medicalised pervert (e.g., in the Army–McCarthy hearings), it is not difficult to see how working-class American males might distance themselves from any lingering Depression-era progressivism. See Robert Corber, *In the Name of National Security* (Durham, NC: Duke University Press, 1993); and also Kevin Floyd, *The Reification of Desire: Toward a Queer Marxism* (Minneapolis: University of Minnesota Press, 2009).

13. Floyd, *The Reification of Desire*, chaps 1–2.

14. Walker, 'Michelangelo and the Leviathan', p. 49.

15. Flatley, '"I Love this Country"'.

16. John Burks, 'Fourteen Points to *Zabriskie Point*', *Rolling Stone* vol. 53 no. 7 (March 1970), n. p.

17. Ibid.

18. Most of my knowledge of this comes from personal conversations with film scholars and critics, who think very highly of the film. But Beverly Walker wrote in 1992, 'To view the film today is both to marvel at its prescience and to experience a bygone era.' Walker, 'Michelangelo and the Leviathan', p. 49.

19. Walter Benjamin, 'Surrealism: Last Snapshot of the European Intelligentsia', in Peter Demetz (ed.), *Reflections* (New York: Schocken, 1978), pp. 177–92; Walter Benjamin, 'Theses on the Philosophy of History', in Hannah Arendt (ed.), *Illuminations* (New York: Schocken, 1968), pp. 253–67.

20. Giuseppe Mazzotta has done an elegant reading of *Zabriskie Point* from the point of view of the play of image and sign, though moving in a quite different direction than I do here. See Giuseppe Mazzotta, 'The Language of Movies and Antonioni's Double Vision', *Diacritics* vol. 15 no. 2 (Summer 1985), pp. 2–10.

21. Rosalind Krauss, *The Optical Unconscious* (Cambridge: MIT Press, 1993), pp. 13–27.

22. Jacques Lacan, *Seminar XI: The Four Fundamental Concepts of Psychoanalysis*, trans. Alan Sheridan (London: Hogarth, 1977), pp. 67–121.

23. See Krauss, *The Optical Unconscious*, pp 68–88, 111–13.

24. Angelo Restivo, *The Cinema of Economic Miracles: Visuality and Modernization in the Italian Art Film* (Durham, NC: Duke University Press, 2002), chaps 6–7.

25. Jean Baudrillard, *America*, trans. Chris Turner (New York: Verso, 1988), pp. 16–17.

26. Ibid., pp. 36–7.

27. Ibid., p. 10.

28. Gilles Deleuze, *Lectures on Spinoza*, <http://deleuzelectures.blogspot.com/2007/02/on-spinoza.html>

29. Lawrence Grossberg, *We Gotta Get Out of This Place: Popular Conservatism and Postmodern Culture* (London: Routledge, 1992), *passim*.

30. The relationship between the political power of the multitude and the structures of urban space can be traced at least as far back as Baron Haussman's 'urban renewal' of Paris, such that the grands boulevards provided an interruption to the tactical (and revolutionary) appropriation of urban space. During the 1960s, the Situationist International was engaged in developing a politics of space. Also central is Michel de Certeau, *The Practice of Everyday Life*, trans. Steven Rendell (Berkeley: University of California Press, 1984).

31. Paolo Virno, *A Grammar of the Multitude*, trans. I. Bertoletti et al. (New York: Semiotext[e], 2004), p. 111.

32. Strategies of absenteeism, refusal to pay for public transit or utilities, squatting and so on, which became central in the workers' movements in Europe after 1968.

33. According to Beverly Walker, Antonioni said to Marsha Kinder during the Death Valley shoot, 'I know immediately when something is wrong.' Walker, 'Michelangelo and the Leviathan', p. 44.

Robert S. C. Gordon

REPORTER, SOLDIER, DETECTIVE, SPY:
Watching *The Passenger*

As Virginia Woolf might have said, 'On or around March 1960 the nature of film changed.' At a distance of around half a century from the explosive emergence of the category of modern art cinema – that cinema of the European auteur along with its cult-like, mostly young, highly educated and intellectual audiences, ready to be baffled by new cinemas, and with the money and leisure time to indulge such a strange shared passion – some of its peculiarities, and its historical specificities and continuities, now come into clearer focus than was possible at the time. In particular, the game of difference that it played in relation to its competition and principal objects of contempt (and none-too-oblique fascination) – whether that was the *cinéma de papa* in France, the classical Hollywood narrative and its studio production machine, or the churned-out *filoni* of pepla and soft porn in Italy – looks all but up. Art-house auteurs, using the same technological apparatus, the same structures of production (if in their often eccentric and improvised European guises), and often enough the same actors or stars, as their more commercial, studio-bound, '*metteur en scène*' colleagues, were simply occupying a niche, often a loss-leading niche with bags of cultural prestige attached, within an overarching transnational production system. The art film followed patterns of regulation, reiteration and exhaustion as recognisable under the label of genre as they are as fragments of philosophical reflection on celluloid, or something similar. The art film needs and deserves to be watched again by way of that relation with genre.

It is in this spirit that the films of perhaps the most intellectually, visually and narratively demanding (for which read pleasurably boring) of the Italian auteurs, Antonioni, deserve acknowledgment as acutely aware of the workings of genre, of the recurrent topoi of global, Hollywood-led film and, indeed, of popular narrative genres in general, even as his films recalibrated them in subtle and sophisticated ways. Antonioni is nothing if not the high modernist and visual formalist of European cinema and, just as earlier formalist narratologists cut their teeth on the popular genre of the folktale, using its structures of simplicity as a means to map recurrent, complex patterns of narrativity in general, of *sujet* and *fabula*, so we might suggest that Antonioni's work is more attuned to the two-dimensional arche-types and binary patterns of popular and genre storytelling than his more blinding visual and formal geometries might indicate. In his early career, after all, Antonioni forged his style not only on exquisitely observed documentaries of the Po valley, but also on what we might call, in the context of the 1950s, a 'woman's film' like *Le amiche* (1955) and a melodrama like *Cronaca di un amore* (1950). And as more than one critic has pointed out, even his breakthrough into fully fledged auteurist bafflement of his audiences *L'avventura* (1960) – famously booed at its first outing at Cannes, as all 'great' new artists must be at one time or another – shared its bold-est plot move, although none of its tone or narrative pitch, with its near-contempo-rary *Psycho* (1960): in both films a strong and attractive female protagonist is simply cut out of the picture, killed off, after the first reel. The game and the enigma really are the same.

Above all those that followed *L'avventura*, one film suggests itself as an ideal case study for teasing out this other Antonioni, a film made memorable – a little less boring, certainly, and perhaps a little less overwhelmingly auteuriste also[1] – by a series of strong presences from other worlds: the New Hollywood charisma and raw star presence of Jack Nicholson; the erotic enigma of Maria Schneider, globally notorious as the art-house/soft-porn lover of Marlon Brando in Bertolucci's *Last Tango in Paris* (1972); and by the young screenwriter Mark Peploe, whose script was put together in collaboration with a key voice in the structuralist moment in film theory, Peter Wollen.[2] Nicholson's breakthrough in *Easy Rider* had come in 1969, the same year as Wollen's book *Signs and Meaning in the Cinema* had argued from a high structuralist-formalist position that 'auteurs' were more textual effects than all-seeing artists carving out crystalline masterpieces in celluloid.[3] The film thrown up by Peploe–Wollen–Antonioni–Nicholson–Schneider (etc.) was *The Passenger/Professione: Reporter* (1975): and, alongside its many auteurist tics and effects, it does indeed contains a panoply of tropes and archetypes from auteur-decentring threads of film history, film production and film narrative, starting with the apparently bland non-Italian term in its Italian title.

David Locke, the film's protagonist played by Nicholson, is – as the Italian title points out in its ID-card formula – a reporter.[4] In the enigmatically drawn-out first sequences of the film, Locke is holed up in a North African desert town (filmed around Fort Polignanc, Algeria), trying to make contact with rebel groups engaged in a postcolonial, anti-government struggle. (They are later identified as the 'United Liberation Front', and although the country is never named, the situation seems based on Peploe's personal connections with Chad, as he explains in his commen-tary.[5]) When Locke finds on his return that his recently made hotel acquaintance, Robertson, has suddenly died, he takes the fateful decision – at this point, quite mys-terious and unmotivated (except by the fierce expressions of frustration and detach-ment we have seen in Nicholson in the desert, and by a recalled or recorded snippet

99

of conversation between him and Robertson) – to swap places with the dead man. He carefully and quietly switches hotel rooms, passport photos and clothes with Robertson: the work (the sweat and care) of changing identity is followed with meticulous attention. Locke will spend the rest of the film wandering around Europe trying to become Robertson, to discover who he was, to decipher and meet his commitments and appointments (Robertson's notebook-diary is a talisman here, with its code of girls' names), to take on his cause (which we learn was to supply the rebels with arms: as a mercenary dealer, but also, it is suggested by one of the rebels we meet later on, as a supporter of their struggle).

Meanwhile, the split in Locke/Robertson is neatly paralleled in the splitting of the narrative and audiovisual tracks of the film. Spliced into the primary sequences of Locke's journey, we watch also what we might call the story of his death as an event and the memories of his life that result: his wife's reaction (and her lover's), his work colleagues' tributes, the return of his private belongings and so on. A great deal of the most sophisticated work done by the film – especially in the editing by Antonioni and Franco Arcalli – goes into moments of intercutting, splicing and blurring of these two strands. And we as audience are implicated repeatedly at a third level in this formal game, through the trope of 'watching' of television, of strips and cans of film, of documentary footage, as we too are drawn into the film as mystery or thriller. At several key moments, we cut quite unexpectedly to examples of Locke's previous work as a film-maker-reporter, 'found footage' from his career, fragments of interviews and documentary footage chronicling modern Africa and the violence of decolonisation, only to find in another 'jump' cut as the footage ends, that the 'true' or 'diegetic' audience of this material is Locke's wife and colleague Martin, as they look for material for a film tribute to his career (surrounded in a viewing suite by cans of film reels and strips of film). If Locke is strangely drawn to find out who Robertson was, we – as we watch, and watch others watching – are exploring Locke, trying to work out the mystery of his (futile) escape from himself; and asking what it means to be a reporter by profession.

Locke is, of course, a reporter of a very particular kind, an investigative television journalist, war correspondent and documentarist film-maker, politically committed (although by now, we slowly intuit, rather tired and disillusioned), working in the convulsive and dangerous setting of countries in transition from colonial subjugation to independence, and from there often to dictatorship and civil war. Not without a tinge of satire, the film pointedly pins downs Locke's CV (at least for those of us who can hit a pause button) when he finds himself rooting around his own Notting Hill home like a ghostly thief: looking for money and documents, and finding in passing evidence of his wife's infidelity, he comes across, Mark-Twain-style, a copy of his own *Times* obituary.[6]

The mock-obituary – prepared for by an earlier sequence in a newspaper office, when his file is picked out from thousands of others on dusty archive shelves

Locke's obituary, marked up by his wife, and secretly perused by Locke himself in his Notting Hill home in *The Passenger* (1975)

(memento mori) – hits all the right notes for a contemporary career path of international and investigative journalism, as it was radically redefined and heightened in public profile by the media and global geopolitics of the 1960s and 70s: Columbia University (with its historic Journalism School), Reuters, *The Sunday Times*, *Panorama*, prizes and dangerous locales such as the Congo. Peploe – and it is probably more the screenwriter, who had made documentaries of this kind himself, than the director at the root of these details[7] – is evoking a particular vein of 1960s film journalism, shaped and made possible technically by new lightweight cameras such as the Arriflex 16ST; politically by the protests of the 1960s and the pioneering work of print and television reportage from Vietnam and elsewhere that informed it; theoretically by early 1960s conceptions of 'cinéma vérité' and by early 1970s ideas of the 'New Journalism'; and, in terms of narrative archetype, by a new inflection on an old variation on the figure of the male lead and hero.

There is a rich tradition – both a genealogy and a genre: what we might call a transgeneric archetype – of film-making in Hollywood and beyond centred on the figure of the journalist.[8] Indeed, the journalist, and the fourth estate in general, hold powerful mythical force in American culture and history more generally, as the bystander-chronicler whose telegraph transmissions were present alongside all those Western heroes and pioneers who built the nation, in history and in Hollywood, and who since then have striven to speak truth to and ultimately undo corrupt power, while also all too often tacking close to the seductions of power itself. The great Ur-text for this grandiose role is, of course, *Citizen Kane* (1941). Kane's career as a newspaper man – and indeed the frame story's conceit of a documentary account of his life (not unlike the patchwork film being made for Locke by Martin and others in *The Passenger*) – is central to his charisma, power and ultimate decadence. But the film journalist is a recurrent figure also in comic genres, present, for example, at the heart of the screwball tradition: from Clark Gable caught between the story and the woman in Capra's *It Happened One Night* (1934), to Gregory Peck, and his photographer companion (Eddie Albert), in Wyler's *Roman Holiday* (1953). In comic-book, superhero genres too, the journalist plays a central role: in both Superman and Spiderman stories, both Clark Kent and Peter Parker work for newspapers in their everyday masks, allowing them always to be at the scene of crime and danger, as well as to melt back into their professional roles when needed, perfectly disguised as weak and ineffectual ordinary men. The reporter here is the very essence of the non-heroic, although he somehow also contains the superhero/action hero within. Conversely but similarly, everyday boyishness and the heroic adventurer come together in Tintin, another reporter who is also an ordinary boy, with his dog, getting into all sorts of scrapes. In their weakness, at times even effeminacy or impotence – the glasses say it all – the superhero-journalists point us to a strange gender fluidity in the film reporter role, most richly staged in the three film versions of Ben Hecht's stage comedy *The Front Page* (1931, 1940, 1974). In the first two, and most famously in Howard Hawks' 1940 version with Cary Grant and Rosalind Russell, *His Girl Friday*, brilliant *female* reporter 'Hildy' Johnson is intent on giving up the racket of journalism to get married, but her hard-bitten newspaper editor Walter Burns uses all the tricks in the book to keep her hooked on the story. By 1974, the female 'Hildy' has been turn into a man, played by Jack Lemmon opposite Walter Matthau, in a reprise of the feminised and domesticated nag Felix Ungar, whom he had played, opposite Matthau, in *The Odd Couple* (1968).

If gender roles are fluid and ambivalent at times in this genre, so too are the moral codes of the film journalist. Here, as in several other respects, the journalist and the detective, especially the noir-inflected detective, are close cousins – and this moral dimension is nowhere more evident than in films such as Fellini's *La dolce vita* (1960), among many other things an epigone and remake of *Roman Holiday*, and Alexander McKendrick's *The Sweet Smell of Success* (1957). In both films gossip journalism and the celebrity culture it feeds off are seen at best as morally vapid and at worst pathologically (and sexually) corrupt and corrupting. It is perhaps all the more surprising, then, to find the journalist figure redeemed as a hero in uncovering truth, saving lives and standing up to power in post-Watergate, post-Vietnam America and American film, in a rich new vein, starting in the 1970s, and running from *All the President's Men* (1976) to *The Killing Fields* (1984) to *Good Night and Good Luck* (2005).

How, if at all, does *The Passenger*, and the wandering, destabilised figure of Locke, fit into this complex transgeneric archetype of the reporter in film? The anomalous presence in the previous Hollywood-filled paragraph of the European auteurist icon *La dolce vita* can perhaps offer some indication of the kind of relationship underpinning *The Passenger*'s surprising engagement with popular tropes. *La dolce vita* stands in a sort of viral, parasitic relation to *Roman Holiday*, in this respect: it inhabits the body of the latter but drains it steadily of its vitality. Peck in *Roman Holiday* is initially the cynical hack, immune to love and only interested in the story, in work and money. The pattern of the screwball comedy requires that the cynic be trained into the principles of kindness through circumstance and the heart. The lovers are divided as they should be at the end – they are princess and nobody, after all – but the nobody makes sure he nobly sacrifices his hack story, secretly returning the compromising photos of the princess and so proving his love and becoming the hero instead of the heel. By the time we encounter Mastroianni's Marcello Rubini in *La dolce vita* – he is even called 'agregoripec' at one point – the dynamism of this comic conversion has been drained away: Marcello is marginal to life, indifferent to sex, let alone love, momentarily awakened by the weird phenomenon of the alien blond visitor from Hollywood (Anita Ekberg); but, as the remainder of the film will nihilistically document, he is unable to re-establish any connection with the world around him. He is too emptied out even to appear venal. His role as a journalist pitches him as in some ways a simulacrum of the American journalist-hero, but without even the drive to be a Sidney Falco, let alone a J. J. Hunsecker. He is, of course, also that very European figure of the failed writer, a journalist by accident, disconnected from and disillusioned with himself, with women, his father and the world as a result of his half-acknowledged failure. Marcello is also disconnected from and an embodiment of the Rome he inhabits, a Rome read and lived through the eyes of modern, American celebrity, a Rome raised to the heights of cosmopolitan sophistication and reduced to one dimension by the culture of celebrity.

103

Jack Nicholson's Locke and his half-realised reinvention as Robertson is, similarly, a drained and flattened, decelerated and introverted, and thereby refracted and fragmented reprise of a cluster of tropes and typologies from the tradition of the film journalist. What is enigmatic about the structure of *The Passenger* is that all these lines of resemblance, all of Locke's life and identity as a reporter and so all the residues of a generic motif of the past, precede the film narrative itself, its surface *sujet*: with the exception of the stalled, failed reporterly efforts of the opening few minutes, we never see Locke as a reporter per se and in the present. When Locke becomes Robertson, the film insistently asks – without ever quite answering definitively – does he slough off the skin of the reporter (like Clark Kent taking off those glasses) and begin to make himself (or fail to make himself) anew? Or, more likely, does he never quite escape the patterns and manner of his métier, leaving the rest of the film, in its present tense and its flashbacks as a haunted portrait of the man as a reporter?

In terms of literal resemblance, Locke comes closest in his back-story to that figure of the Western/American journalist confronting the global stage of late-twentieth-century war and genocide: in film history, he is cousin to Sydney Schanberg in *The Killing Fields*, or to the character played by James Woods in Oliver Stone's *Salvador* (1986) or, in a crazed cameo variant, Dennis Hopper in *Apocalypse Now* (1979), a portrait of insanity more skewed but not wholly alien to Locke's state of neutered, meandering emptiness for much of *The Passenger*. In this context, the literal content of the footage from his past is most directly eloquent, in that we see the range of his method and, crucially, his positioning of himself – a point on which much critical energy has been expended – as the passive observer (passenger, not driver).[9] In three sequences of extracts from his previous work, clustered near the centre of the film, we see Locke in professional action, first questioning a shaman, insensitively asking him what is left of his witch-doctor magic, now that he has lived in the West, and struggling to accept the camera being intelligently and disturbingly turned upon him (this kind of journalist is also a kind of ethnologist/anthropologist); then, we see him tamely allowing a dictator to set the tone of his interview questions and answer; and, finally, near the exact centre of the film (at fifty-six minutes), we see the brutal footage of the summary execution of a man (Locke is not present here on film; but we watch his camera watching this horrific event).[10] Much analysis of the film has dwelled on the tension between the bystander asking his unthinking questions or watching passively (the reporter) and the active agent (Robertson the arms dealer, but also the shaman, the dictator, the executed rebel); but even if Locke's doubling were not enough to remind us that this dichotomy already exists within the very dynamic and ethics of the role of the journalist, the genealogy of journalism in film would certainly tell us as much. And these ethics, as *Citizen Kane* chronicled pitilessly, are double-edged: the reporter who takes up arms (Locke who becomes Robertson; Kane/Hearst who starts wars) is in no way making a simple choice between 'being' and 'not being', between surrender and action or resistance.

Both Robertson's arms-dealing and Hearst's war-mongering point to a further cognate role for this war-correspondent figure, that of the soldier. And the soldier is, of course, one of the great narrative – and filmic – archetypes, within the single genre of the war movies but also across any number of others, alongside which and against which the journalist – and Locke in multiple ways, as we will see – defines himself. Aside from the Western journalist-soldier reporting on Third World, post-colonial conflict in the 1970s, several formal, narrative and structural tropes that seem to recur in the film-journalism tradition also turn up, in modified form and function, in *The Passenger*. Several of these tropes are shared by other genres also, since part of the function of genres and their filiations is to process and re-present recurrent patterns and configurations of storytelling and human lives: genres are iterative not only within themselves but also between each other. Take the following examples.

The journalist, with his notebook and newshound mask, is an epistemological animal – searching for knowledge, information and pursuing enquiry.[11] Perhaps closest here to the detective[12] – but also, in different modes, to the photographer, the writer or the artist – the journalist is something of an investigator of the modern world, in search of some kind of truth, engaged in some kind of quest. The endpoint of the search takes the form, classically in the journalist genre, of the 'story', the scoop or headline that clinches success (and typically ends the narrative): in *Roman Holiday*, as we saw, the scoop drives the film's moral dilemma, and only its non-appearance settles and closes the narrative. In *The Passenger*, this pattern of searching and enquiry is powerfully present, but shot through with threads of uncertainty and indeterminacy: there is no story, possibly no rebellion following the failure of Robertson's mission, there is no memorial documentary in the end, and Locke's death has been repeatedly misconstrued and misrecognised right up to the final frames. Locke's first search in the desert, his *vox clamantis*, emblematically ends in failure; his questioning interviews (quest and questioning, of course, share an etymology) turned on their head or rendered useless by his interviewees. But he is not alone. He is also the object of a search: by his wife and friend, who are simultaneously both literally 'making enquiries' about him and his death, and also trawling through his professional film work, exploring and enquiring about his life's work; by the assassins looking for Robertson, who eventually will kill him; and by the camera, the narrative and visual track, and the insistent, exquisite framing of Antonioni's camera, which seeks to set and reset Locke in a certain landscape or visual shape (the famous Barcelona cable-car shot of Locke as 'free' bird; the parable in the Umbraculo). What is more, the film is peppered with emblems of pure chance, enigma and of the emptiness and directionless of pure information, which conspire to deny the value of investigative gathering of data, of quests for truths through riddles and solutions. Robertson's notebook is a central instance of the latter, with its codes, dates and places seemingly mapping out a path for action and for discovery – as well as, of course, being a visual cliché of the journalist's paraphernalia.

Maria Schneider's character seems to behave as a sort of free radical, unnamed, unbound and open to chance, underscored first of all by her entirely enigmatic presence in a shot in London (on a bench outside the modernist icon the Brunswick

Locke peruses
Robertson's notebook
in Munich

Centre as Locke walks by), before she and Locke meet by chance and fall into an absurd, slow journey to nowhere that starts in Barcelona. Of course, the 'story' in the journalistic sense is in the course of becoming, through these dynamics, the 'story' in the narrative sense: and *The Passenger* shows how Antonioni's version of the latter – as ever, meandering, indeterminate, loose in shape and structure – has seeped out of and overtaken a mode born in Locke's identity as a journalist. After his death and after the famous long-take sequence at the end of the film that occludes the murder from our view, several stories and several searches come to an apparently vacuous or random end, not least that of Locke's wife who pointedly 'does not recognise' the dead man.[13]

Another feature that recurs with strange regularity in the genre of journalism movies is a pattern of doubling and tricks of switching, mirroring and makeover that *The Passenger* takes to resonant levels of complexity. From Gregory Peck's Joe Bradley and Eddie Albert's Irving in *Roman Holiday*, to Hunsecker and Falco (*Sweet Smell of Success*), Woodward and Bernstein (*All the President's Men*), Schanberg and Dith Pran (*The Killing Fields*) – and we could add, turning once more to comic-book characters, Tintin and Milou – tales of journalism seem to be frequently enacted by twosomes, often but not always homosocial couples, sometimes played out alongside stories of romantic coupling. In the case of *The Killing Fields*, furthermore, the lead pairing allows the film to stage not gender trouble, but rather the cultural encounter with the 'other' (Dith Pran was, of course, Cambodian; Schanberg, American), another instance of the journalism movie tapping into that ethnographic function of the contemporary journalism that Locke has practised. In reality, these pairings often seem to function and give narrative energy to these films not through a psychology of relationships, but rather through a particular relationship to geographical and filmic space. The journalist pair propel each other, and articulate the journey across, a certain landscape – the city of Rome, the seedier bars around Broadway, secret Washington, genocidal Cambodia – and through a certain quest, and the moral and/or political dilemmas thrown up by these different spaces. The pair's internal dynamic functions as a staging arena for the progress of the quest. In this sense, these couples, or pseudo-couples, are journalistic variants on the buddy-movie couple and, more specifically still, the buddy road movie. Locke and the woman he accidentally falls in with for his final days are just such a couple. Their bond is deliberately opaque, as is their status as distinct subjects in their own right (they are both, in their different ways, empty, nobodies). They do have sex; but they also speak, in stilted and elliptical dialogue, at staged scenes along the way of Locke's flawed and doomed quest for purpose, identity, an ending, a story for himself. And their journey is also carefully staged against the rich, framed landscapes of Barcelona and Almeria, seen through the geometrical eye of Antonioni's camera. Locke's cable-car flight, for example, is echoed by Maria Schneider's moment of windswept 'flight' in which she stands at the back of their convertible car and stretches out towards the receding row of trees along the side of the road.

Of course, Locke and his woman are haunted and framed by the other pseudo-couple of the film, Locke and Robertson. This lookalike pairing, and the process we witness of their exchanging first words, then identities, and then the experience of death with each other, underscores a further dynamic of the journalism genre, which is that of disguise, role-play and makeover. One of several sequences cut from *The Passenger* by its American producers at MGM was a chance encounter in Munich between Locke, as he plays at being Robertson, and a man in a bar who mistakes him for a long-lost friend and plies him with drink and memories. Locke, in his hazy, uncertain state, plays along and drinks and 'remembers', in confused bad faith. As already noted, the reporter-superhero bond is precisely one where disguise seems to fit the anonymous reporter: and in some ways, Locke's transformation into Robertson is a journalist's ploy to get the story through masquerade. Peck in *Roman Holiday* starts out pretending to be a friendly nobody, the ordinary guy who doesn't know who the girl he encounters is, when he happens upon his escaped Princess in Rome. This ploy is mirrored in Wyler's extensive dwelling on the makeover processes that turns the Princess into the ordinary girl for a day (including famously the hacking off of her royal hair to make the character assume Hepburn's star, gamine look), inverting a fairytale topos from Cinderella to 'King for a Day'.

The reporter role, then, in its genre or transgenre function as echoed in Locke's strange destiny, operates at the borders of a number of hyphenated roles – reporter-detective, reporter-solider and, more loosely, reporter-hero. And there is, indeed, one further genre worth mentioning that shadows Locke's story of masquerade and makeover, his play of pretence, multiple passports, disguises and tricks – and indeed of shifting, glamorous locations, pursuit and international danger: that is, the spy movie, and perhaps particularly the James Bond series, begun in 1962 (*Dr. No*) and already nine feature films strong and hugely popular and influential by the year of *The Passenger*'s release in 1975.

The leap from Antonioni to James Bond perhaps goes a little too far (although Bond was also in his way a product of the swinging 60s that produced *Blow-Up* and *Zabriskie Point*; and the Bond films were also led by attractive Anglophone young stars, whose protagonists share *The Passenger*'s clipped, strong and generically English names – David Locke, James Bond. What is made clear in pushing to such a near-absurd juxtaposition is that certain tropes that are deeply embedded in *The Passenger* are shared by a cluster of classic Hollywood genres, their narrative moves and their archetypal male and female leading roles; that Locke's identity as a reporter taps into subtle questions of morality, ideology and subjectivity – as well as the *mise en abyme* dynamics of seeing and viewing – but also into a genealogy of film history that takes in Capra and Hitchcock, as much as Godard or Fassbinder (or rather, one that takes in the genre flirtations of both of these latter). As a final

Locke's wife Rachel
(Jenny Runacre) is
framed by the dingy,
material debris of
Locke's life; strips, cans,
the viewing suite

nod to those other, Hollywood conventions, we can return to a term used more than once above: 'haunting'. *The Passenger* is, after all, also in its own way, a tale of the after-life, a ghost story. As noted, it has been compared in Italy to Pirandello's 'after-life' novel *The Late Mattia Pascal*, whose protagonist Mattia survives at the end of the novel in a sort of phantasmatic half-life, with both his original self and his invented substitute snuffed out. To *The Late Mattia Pascal*, though, we might add another Capra title: *It's a Wonderful Life* (1946).[14] Locke lives a brief limbo in *The Passenger*, between Robertson's death and his own, or Robertson's first and second deaths, or indeed his own first and second deaths. For his wife and colleagues and the world's press, he is already dead, the obituaries written. Our journey with him is a journey from life to an after-life, as well as a sort of reappraisal/judgment on his life. Like James Stewart, although with darker, emptier consequences, by being a ghost and seeing the world without him, Locke crystallises his own failings (as a man, as a reporter) and returns, unlike Stewart, to death at the end. Robertson haunts Locke as a past life for him that never happened; Locke's past haunts his present; and a certain ghostliness, a sign of death, haunts the film as we watch – three corpses prop up the film, at beginning, middle and end – and perhaps, Antonioni would add, because death haunts also those lifeless strips and cans of celluloid hanging in the viewing suite.

*   *   *

Not surprisingly, this is not the first time that *The Passenger* has been read through the filter of genre. In an important contribution, Charles Derry's book *The Suspense Thriller* builds a multifaceted model of the genre named in its title, which Derry sees as derived from and crystallising around the 'shadow' of Alfred Hitchcock.[15] Of the six sub-categories Derry identifies within the 'suspense thriller', the third is what he calls the 'thriller of acquired identity', and it includes, among others, *The Passenger*.[16] The sub-category consists of films in which the protagonist acquires a new identity (or, in a key variant, loses his own identity, through amnesia), and is forced on the run and thereby 'to come to terms with the metaphysical and physical consequences of this identity, and the relationship of this acquisition to a murderous plot'.[17] Derry notes how well *The Passenger* fits the genre template, for all its art-house style: 'despite *The Passenger*'s self-conscious "artiness", the film provides the genre with a relatively accessible work'.[18]

Derry's formulation – the plotline of 'acquired identity', the art-house-genre hybrid, as well as the genealogy of links to Hitchcock – is compatible with the reading offered here. But, in a sense, it is a restricted reading, one intent on collocating the film within a single genre or sub-genre and thereby resolving it taxonomically with a label. Instead, by looking at *The Passenger* through the figure of the journalist-reporter, and through his/her links to an extensive web of transgeneric presences of journalists in film, we have been aiming to destabilise somewhat both simple categories of genre and, similarly, stylistic readings based on the figure of the auteur.

Genre theory has always had a tendency to turn around in circles, never quite settling on what the nature and parameters of its precise object of study should be.[19] Where, for some, genres are useful when they are industry-led labels of studio-bound, serial production practices, for others the patterns of reiteration, expectation and recognition of genre works exist more broadly in form and in spectatorial perception, than in a model of Fordist production. And while certain 'hero' figures inhere to certain classic genres (the detective, the gangster, the dark hero of film noir, the cowboy in the Western), other genres are less determinate, built instead around settings, spaces, moods or plotlines, into which a deliberately variant body of characters are inserted. The figure of the archetypal protagonist who, however, neither historically nor analytically has sustained a specific, single category of genre – such as the reporter in *Professione: Reporter* – seems to sit across this spectrum of approaches, at once complicating and simplifying it. The transgeneric figure suggests that this latter body of characters is itself organisable into a patterned network or system, just as much as the panoply of single genre labels can be conceived also as a 'genre system'.[20] Indeed, we might suggest that one of the driving engines of filmic intertextual reproducibility is the overlaying and intersecting of these parallel systems. An archetype such as the reporter constantly overspills the frame of any single genre, occupying narrative space in a position of agency and subjectivity acted out across genre boundaries, creating transgeneric connections of an often surprising kind.

Theorists of 'genre systems' would certainly recognise in the complexities of the transgeneric motif of the journalist, and *The Passenger*'s acutely self-aware exploration of it, powerful evidence for the plural simultaneity of genre matrices, in this kind of film-making and perhaps in all film-making. There may, however, be a particular historical dimension to this opening up of the system from the single label

109

also: it may be no coincidence that, around the same time as *The Passenger*, New Hollywood – including Nicholson–Polanski's *Chinatown* (1974) – was performing similar hybridisations and dismantlings across a whole range of genres, between Hollywood and art house, producing a string of works that self-consciously used genre mechanisms to question and undermine the very structure of those genres.[21] The figure of the reporter-soldier-detective-spy(-ghost) in *The Passenger* functions as a knowing evocation of its genre backshadows, their multiple transgeneric protagonists and the patterns of representation they bring with them. All these are restaged through Nicholson's emerging, enigmatic trans- and multigeneric New Hollywood persona; through Peploe–Wollen's subjectivity effects in their structuralist mapping of film; and through a questioning and melancholic dismantling of genre and a teasing out of an (Antonioni-esque) enquiry into the very nature of subjecthood, looking at the world and the subject contemplating his own death. We should, in short, be wary of jumping too hastily to the Antonioni part of this long equation, just because of the byline above the title.

Notes

1. It was the first of his mature films not to be scripted by Antonioni himself.
2. Peploe, on his DVD commentary to the film (Sony Pictures, 2006), notes that he and Wollen wrote the treatment of the film during a journey to Spain and North Africa, fitting the narrative to their journey. The two were accompanied by Laura Mulvey, another key figure in the *Screen* moment in film theory: her seminal – and over-cited – essay 'Visual Pleasure and Narrative Cinema' was written in 1973 and published in 1975 (*Screen* vol. 16 no. 3 [Autumn 1975], pp. 6–18): and it would be all too easy, tellingly easy, to map the gender roles laid out in Mulvey's essay to the functions and directions of Nicholson and Schneider in *The Passenger*.
3. Peter Wollen, *Signs and Meaning in the Cinema* (London: Secker and Warburg/BFI, 1969).
4. *The Passenger* was the original intended title of the screenplay and film, but a Polish film with a near identical title existed already (*Passenger*, 1963) and so the current Italian title was substituted for the release in several countries.
5. When in London we see a shot of Robertson's air ticket, with a sequence of destinations that reads as follows: Douala [Cameroon], Fort-Lamy [Chad], Paris, London, Munich. From Munich onwards, as the film goes to some visual and narrative lengths to point out, the journey to Barcelona and around Spain is continued by Avis hire car: modes of transport are key visual markers in this film (jeeps, cars, horse-drawn carriages, cable cars etc.).
6. Italian commentators on the film often compared this aspect of the film to a key work of Italian literary modernism, Luigi Pirandello's 1908 novel, *The Late Mattia Pascal*, in

which the eponymous hero reads on a train returning home from the casinos of Monte Carlo a newspaper report of the discovery of his own mangled body. See, for example, Giovanni Grazzini, 'Antonioni: saper leggere dentro le cose', *Corriere della Sera*, 5 March 1975; Alberto Ongaro, 'Antonioni. Una ricerca nel profondo', *L'Europeo*, 18 December 1975, reprinted as 'An In-Depth Search', in Carlo Di Carlo and Giorgio Tinazzi (eds), *The Architecture of Vision: Writings and Interviews on Cinema* (New York: Marsilio, 1996), pp. 344–51.

7. Antonioni had interests in documentary and reportage himself, of course, but of differing kinds: for example, the photographer of *Blow-Up* is a reporter in his way: and there is a Hitchcock connection here, too, since James Stewart's character in *Rear Window* was a wheelchair-bound photographer who uses his camera to solve a murder, as David Hemmings's character also tries to do. The film project Antonioni abandoned before making *The Passenger*, to have been entitled *Technically Sweet*, set in Brazil and Italy, also had a journalist as a protagonist. And he had just shown his troubled and controversial documentary about China, *Cina Chung Kuo*, in 1972.

8. There is an interesting sub-field of work on journalists in film: see, as a first resource, the 'Image of the Journalist in Popular Culture' project, USC Annenberg, at: <http://ijpc.org/index.html> (accessed 5 August 2010).

9. Nicholson was supposed to be the passenger in the car sequences of the film in Spain with Schneider, to flag up and make sense of the title, but Schneider could not drive and the plan had to be abandoned (Wollen, DVD commentary).

10. Peploe was deeply uncomfortable with the use here of actual footage, filmed in Nigeria, for this sequence, almost falling out with Antonioni over it (DVD commentary). This detail is in itself indicative of the delicate ethics of dealing with 'real' events as filmed for news or documentaries, in reportage or in fiction film narrative, the same issue as is raised more obliquely in the editing of the interview footage with the dictator, followed by 'live' footage from the site of the interview with Locke and his wife.

11. Although tangential, there is an intriguing connection to be drawn here from *The Passenger*'s narrative of enquiry and a model in contemporary Italian intellectual history, linking the film to a vein of 'inchiesta' work in historiography (Carlo Ginzburg's early microhistorical work), narrative and documentary and fiction film (Leonardo Sciascia, Francesco Rosi) of the 1960s and 70s.

12. Between the filming and release of *The Passenger*, Nicholson starred in Roman Polanksi's *Chinatown* (1974), a film drenched in genre, in Hitchcock and in a not dissimilar sophisticated reflection on the hidden indeterminacy and sited, sensory stagings of modern 'quest' stories and their heroes. Of course, it also stands as one of the finest examples of New Hollywood cinema, and thus of a specific form of modernism. Nicholson's roles in *The Passenger*, *Chinatown* and also *The Shining* (1980) all seem to share a kind of hollowing out of genre roles. (I am grateful to this book's editors for this insight.)

111

13. Another misrecognised death that comes to mind is that of Athos Magnani Snr in Bertolucci's *Il conformista* (1970): by the end of the film Athos Jnr, like Locke's wife, has wearily but wisely learned to accept and declare as true the false version of his father's (her husband's) death.

14. And of course, we could and should go back to Hitchcock again: haunting is one of the underpinning motifs of his films, from *Rebecca* (1940) to *Vertigo* (1958).

15. Charles Derry, *The Suspense Thriller: Films in the Shadow of Alfred Hitchcock* (Jefferson: McFarland Press, 1988).

16. Ibid., pp. 175–93 [on *The Passenger*, pp. 184–8]. Other films in the 'acquired identity' sub-group are: *Demoniaque* (1957), *Purple Noon* (1960), *The Third Voice* (1960), *The Running Man* (1963), *Dead Ringer* (1964), *Seconds* (1966) and *Someone Behind the Door* (1971).

17. Ibid., p. 175.

18. Ibid., p. 185.

19. See the useful survey in Pam Cook and Mieke Bernink (eds), *The Cinema Book*, 2nd edn (London: BFI, 1999), pp. 137–231.

20. Ibid., pp. 146–7.

21. Thomas Schatz, *Old Hollywood/New Hollywood: Rituals, Art and Industry* (Ann Arbor: UMI Press, 1983), pp. 27–8. See Cook and Bernink, *The Cinema Book*, p. 144. Schatz points to the genre games played by films such as *Bonnie and Clyde* (1967, gangster movie), *New York, New York* (1977, musical), *The Deer Hunter* (1978, war movie), *Annie Hall* (1977, romantic comedy) and so on.

Aesthetics

Leonardo Quaresima

'MAKING LOVE ON THE SHORES OF THE RIVER PO': Antonioni's Documentaries

In investigations of Antonioni's cinema the references to *Gente del Po* (1947) and the other shorts of the early postwar period seem frequently to be little more than ceremonial gestures, or else professional duties to be paid on account of these films' purely inaugural character; less frequently are these films treated as actual objects of analysis. Essentially, once the tribute has been paid to their place in the author's filmography and to their status as initiators (as in the case of *Gente del Po*) of an entire, decisive season of Italian cinema, the discussion quickly moves to the *major* films and (despite intentions often declared) ends up by relegating the works made before *Cronaca di un amore* (1950) to the role of incunabula, worthy of attention on account of the fact that they display small traces of future developments, but also in full awareness that they exhibit features that separate them from those texts. Something similar happens in regards to Antonioni's essay 'Per un film sul fiume Po' ('For a Film on the River Po'), a point of a consistent – even ritual – reference. My intentions in this essay are twofold. First, I want to demonstrate the foundational centrality of the documentaries made by Antonioni during the 1940s (and of 'Per un film sul fiume Po') to neo-realism. Arguing these films' centrality to neo-realism may involve me in distancing myself from many of the commonplaces of the movement's subsequent self-representation (and historiography). My understanding of neo-realism apprehends it as an aesthetic and communicative project whose humanism is of a piece with its individualistic relativism. This is a neo-realism equally occupied with the 'discovery of Italy' (of its backwardness, of its underdevelopment and of the provinces) and with an attention to its modernisation. Such ambiguities are typical of realism's broad, heterogeneous range of models.

Second, I intend to argue that these shorts (and especially *Gente del Po*, *N.U.* [1948], *L'amorosa menzogna* [1949] and *Sette canne, un vestito* [1949]) should be granted the status of autonomous works, minor only in the sense of their (intrinsic) brevity, but also already mature in their thematic and stylistic preoccupations, and their openness to the most advanced currents (and not only in the cinematic sphere) of European culture in the 1930s.

Let us reread the text first published in *Cinema* in the spring of 1939:

It is not ridiculous to say that the people of the Po Valley are in love with the Po. In fact the river is surrounded by a halo of instinctive attraction, even of love ... The people of the valley 'feel' the Po. How this feeling comes to reification, we do not know. We only know that it is 'in the air' and is felt as a subtle bewitchment ... In other words, a special intimacy, fed by different factors, is established ...

There is another significant point of interest which comes from reflecting particularly on the civilization of the people of the river. A long time ago, the river used to look more serenely romantic ... Neither for men nor for things did the years pass in vain, and for the river too came the time to awaken.

Then it was iron bridges, on which trains clattered along by day and night; it was five-storied buildings spotted with large windows which vomited noise and dust; it was steam boats, factories, smokey chimneys and added channels with concrete piers. In fact, it was a whole modern world, mechanical and industrialized, which had come to upset the old one.

Yet, in the midst of the destruction of their old world, the population had no regrets ... At a certain point, the evolution not only did not disturb them, but in a certain way, pleased them.[1]

We are not struck here so much by the evocation of both old and new: of the anthropological character of the human being, of the eternal repetition of his reasons for existing (and his deepest values), and of the process of modernisation, the transfigurations imposed by the process of industrialisation, which affect individuals over and above its effect on landscapes. These points of reference ground us in the common terms of cultural debate of those years. But the text leans towards the second of the two poles – towards the new: modernisation is seen as a positive process, in correspondence with the people who traverse it. Founding this sympathy for the modern constitutes the text's novelty and its effectiveness, given that this same inclination, this valorisation, is the foundation on which Antonioni's documentaries are built (and this is a foundation more fundamental than what is suggested by superficial accounts of the neo-realist image that have been tenaciously insisted upon by scholars and critics who owe debts to the ideologising conceptions of neo-realism that accompanied the movement's development in the immediate postwar period and in the early 1950s).

Gente del Po begins with images of a modern mill (in the course of its narrative, the film will show us an archaic mill, built on a barge, but it is abandoned, the remnant of a past epoch) and with the traffic of canal boats transporting goods (framed, as we will see below, in such a way as to highlight their belonging to an industrial and not a 'romantic', outdated phase of river transport). *N.U.* opens and closes with the (eccentric, in terms of the thematic development of the film) presence of a train, and while the subsequent sequences appear to revert to an emphasis on under-development (we recall the man who spends the night in an improvised shelter, wrapped in newspapers), the centre of attention turns to an ultramodern truck for the collection of refuse, a machine characterised by lucent and functional metallic shapes, so 'futuristic' in its mechanical and formal conceptions that it produces a true 'attraction effect' on the spectator.

A most futuristic industrial plant is at the centre of *Sette canne, un vestito*. The mechanisation of the collection, of the processes of production – everything refers to technologically advanced modes of production, which were at the vanguard of Italian industry at the dawn of the 1950s. The film's emphasis on modern forms as well as its almost systematically complete exclusion of the artisanal, intensify its thematic orientation. The plant, isolated in the countryside, almost resembles the space station of a science-fiction film. (The voice-over commentary, in an attempt to lessen the spectators' disorientation, makes reference, by contrast, to more familiar models by comparing the factory to a 'mysterious castle'.) The buildings of the factory, framed from below, appear to us like skyscrapers of an American metropolis; the network of the pipes of the chemical plant recalls the configurations (and the imagery) of a new era. Here, as is evident, we are in perfect continuity with the sceneries and modernist-industrial ambivalences of *Il deserto rosso* (1964).[2] The quasi-science-fiction-like imagination[3] manifests itself, accentuated as it is by the protective gear, resembling space helmets, worn by the workers assigned to the picking of the canes. This imagery is balanced out by an iconography typical of an American model of progress, with machines furrowing vast farm lands which recall the iconographic motifs of North American realist paintings (which I will refer to again later).

The rubbish truck in *N.U.*, the industrial structures in *Sette canne, un vestito* and even the cabin of the funicular in *Vertigine* (1950), give life to an original figure, which we could read as an *apparition*: they represent the irruption into the universe of each film of entities imbued with an uncertain and ungraspable meaning; these are like objects from another planet (the science-fiction motif …), presences that surely correspond to a precise function, but one that exceeds the sense of the scene in which they manifest themselves. This situation will acquire a central role in the early feature films and will become one of the distinctive traits of Antonioni's cinema. In *Cronaca di un amore* we think of the shiny surfaces of the cars' hoods that invade the frame in the first encounter between Paola and Guido, or in the scene of the test drive of the Maserati; of the architectures of the artificial lake, the *idroscalo*; of the Milan planetarium; of the gigantic advertising panels in the shape of bottles (where the structure of the tribunes and the patterns in the background of the planetarium seem again to allude to a science-fiction imagination). Or we might think of the spools for cables in the love scene between Aldo and Virginia (the owner of the petrol station) at the periphery of Ravenna in *Il grido* (1957).

117

N.U. (1948); *Sette canne, un vestito* (1949); *Vertigine* (1944)

On a stylistic plane, the early shorts continuously oscillate between a realist aesthetic and another one founded instead on principles of abstraction; the latter term predominates. The situation seems to be both 'surprising' and 'heretical' – compared to the tradition of neo-realism to which the films, with a seminal, even programmatic role, belong, especially in the case of *Gente del Po*. This oscillation marks from the start the whole movement and continues to be felt even in those films that would seem to bear the strongest affinity with the realist impulse. Shortly before Antonioni started the shooting of *Gente del Po*, the photographic book *L'occhio quadrato* by Alberto Lattuada was published by the periodical *Corrente*.[4] This book is usually regarded as one of the manifestos of neo-realist humanism, or at least as paradigmatic manifestation of the balance between the poles of realism and abstraction in the experience of the group of critics (Giansiro Ferrata, Luciano Anceschi) and artists (Raffaele De Grada, Renato Birolli, Ernesto Treccani, and Renato Guttuso as well) who collaborated with *Corrente* between 1938 and 1940.[5] At closer inspection, however, *L'occhio quadrato* actually constitutes one of the most overt denials of this programme and of the idea of a neo-realist humanism. The introductory text actually makes reference to the necessity of founding a new humanism: 'Man awaits to be given back the richness that has been taken from him, the warmth of feelings and relationships, the Christian solidarity.' Its point of origin is the urgency of 'returning to look at men with the *eyes of love*', and when it sets out the relationship between subject and environment it does so on the basis of a close relationship between these two components. Lattuada writes: 'When photographing, I have attempted to always keep alive the relationship of man with things. The presence of man is constant; and even where material objects are represented, the point of view is not that of the pure form of the play of light and shadow, but that of the assiduous memory of our life.'[6]

The photographs, however, contradict this project in the clearest manner. The human life that is shown is one at the margins, both in regards to its social position-ing and its more properly 'narrative' dimension. In many of the shots, the individual is not in the frame: the elements fixed by the photographic camera exclude the human presence as a constitutive – not contingent – off-screen presence. The attention is focused on spaces, architectures, objects and is guided first and foremost by relation-ships between lines, surfaces, volumes. Even when the human figure is part of the pic-ture, the gaze is detached, absent; the subject is only an element among many, but never the centre of orientation or the source of meaning for that which surrounds him.

I do not know if we can be sure that *Corrente* and its milieu impinged definitely on Antonioni's formation, and it is even more difficult to establish whether he was familiar with Lattuada's book.[7] What is certain is that we can trace precise analo-gies and not just generic affinities between the figurative system of Antonioni's shorts and many of the photographs in *L'occhio quadrato*.

Abstraction is thus a constant (and always latent) dimension in Antonioni's post-war documentaries. One of the many projects for short films that he conceived at the end of the 1940s, *Macchine inutili* was to be devoted to the work of Bruno

Alberto Lattuada, *L'occhio quadrato* (1941); *Gente del Po* (1947)

Alberto Lattuada, *L'occhio quadrato* (1941)

Superstizione (1949)

Alberto Lattuada, *L'occhio quadrato* (1941)

N.U. (1948)

Alberto Lattuada, *L'occhio quadrato* (1941)

L'amorosa menzogna (1949)

Alberto Lattuada, *L'occhio quadrato* (1941); *Gente del Po* (1947)

Munari and to be configured as a 'an almost abstract documentary'.[8] Bearing this abandoned project in mind, *Gente del Po* would appear the eloquent and programmatic result of such preoccupations. The opening titles run on a surface characterised by two areas – one bright one dark – and separated by a diagonal line. Some traces present in both zones of the image suggest that this may be a wall (a thin column of bricks on the left-hand side, an opening – possibly a small window? – on the right), but the frame is constructed on the combination of the two surfaces of contrasting luminosity and on the effect of the diagonal line that marks it. Even when the last caption disappears, the lateral panoramic shot that animates the image only slowly inserts itself within a specific context (one of the walls that flanks the opening from where the bags of flour come out). The abstract qualities persist, and the film appears to let go of them only reluctantly. So much has been written on the

Gente del Po (1947)

Sette canne, un vestito (1949)

opening images of, for instance, *La notte* (1961) or *Il deserto rosso*: nobody seems to have noticed that those of *Gente del Po*, a film from the 1940s, put forward a no less radical programme.

An even more pronounced situation manifests itself in *Sette canne, un vestito*. The various stages of the working of the reeds, the treatment of the celluloid after its whitening, its transformation into rigid sheets are the cue to explore compositions of volumes and surfaces, geometries and light effects, the latter making us think of *Lichtrequisit* (1930) by László Moholy-Nagy.

Moreover, the valorisation of the processes and forms of modernisation does not lead exactly in the same direction as that of neo-realist humanism. Even when the narrative focuses on individuals or on a community, with a gesture that intends first and foremost to retrieve them from the shadows in which they were submerged, the gaze moves away from *warmth*, from *participation* (the 'love' evoked by Lattuada). It not only tends to drain away all emotional, pathetic involvement, it even goes so far as to call into question the legitimacy of these very same psychological preoccupations. In *Gente del Po* the family that lives on the barge – the potential collective protagonist of the story and point of focalisation for the exploration of a geographical and human universe – sees its central position progressively eroded by other figures and situations. The presentation of this family unit actually acts to block the currents of the spectator's empathy. The characters are studiously observed from behind as one by one they are 'called' (and not just by the narrating voice-over) as if summoned to a hypothetical stage,[9] a procedure that introduces an artificial, performative model which is clearly distinguished by the 'naturalness' of 'reality'. Only at the presentation of the *putina* (local dialect for little girl) does the spectator have the possibility of a 'frontal' contact with them, of engaging emotionally (through the access to their faces) with this encounter. Up until that moment, all individual, subjective traits are denied to us, as is all access to the characters' most personal emotions.

The more that the human life put on display is marginal, at the limits of civil life, the more the gaze becomes neutral, distant, detached. This attitude is flagrant in *Superstizione* (1949) – a short quasi-ethnographic film about folk beliefs, rituals and cures among Italian peasants – but this is not a limit case dictated by the particularity of the subject. We see it at work in *N.U.* in the long shot of the street sweeper who walks with his girlfriend along the vast, deserted bank of the Roman Lungotevere with the brush still in his hands, and again in *L'amorosa menzogna* in the shot of the two lovers on their bikes against a backdrop of fascist-era working-class, modernist high-rise buildings. Shots and moments like these not only anticipate precisely certain passages in *Cronaca di un amore* (and suggest its sense of the estrangement of characters from their environment, as in the famous sequence of the encounter between Paola and Guido at the *idroscalo*),[10] but also represent two of the 'harshest' manifestations of that modality of vision. In these passages, the film does not appear to leave any hope, any illusion of change, any possibility of human fulfilment, and instead extinguishes these possibilities, in the urban landscape, in the coldest and crudest manner (in a way that is almost cruel).

The 'estrangement' is realised by placing the melodrama of a couple (melodrama constitutes one of the basic points of reference, even in actual generic terms, of

N.U. (1948);
L'amorosa menzogna
(1949); *Cronaca di un*
amore (1950)

Antonioni's cinema) in relation to a 'cold', neutral environment, one inspired by the nature of architectural 'rationalism' of the interwar period. Antonioni's iconography seems to make reference to these things quite clearly.[11]

The gaze may openly take on the models and procedures of the entomologist. In *N.U.* the street sweepers on their lunch break are positioned against a long white wall, at a regular distance from each other, isolated and almost immobile, like insects pinned down in a collector's display box. Some critics have talked of 'statues in a metaphysical painting',[12] or else have evoked, as a point of comparison, John Gay's *Beggar's Opera* (1728). Even bearing these comparisons in mind, however, the position in Antonioni is much harder – and more distancing, insofar as his cinema evokes models of exhibition and of 'spectacle' – not only the exhibiting displays of the curiosities of a Wunderkammer, but also the cinematic screen as itself, an exhibition space, on which the street sweepers are positioned as objects of a spectacle. The solution's effectiveness is such that it recurs in Antonioni's cinema: in his episode *Tentato suicidio* for *L'amore in città* (1953) (a collective film inspired by Zavattini), in which the protagonists of the episode (all of whom have attempted suicide) are summoned together in a vast film studio and positioned against a large white sheet. In its prevention of any possible empathy from the spectator (who might otherwise have been moved by the coincidence between actor and character), this episode inscribes from the start the context of exhibition, of *mise en scène* – particularly in its oscillation between the naturalistic-scientific understanding of this term and the cinematic one. The distancing from *melodrama* – which is nevertheless evoked and posited by the characters and their stories – could not be more decisive; the critique of the neo-realist-humanist model

László Moholy-Nagy, *Stadion in Lyon* (1927); Mario Sironi, *Il molo* (1939)

N.U. (1948); *Tentato suicidio* (1953), episode of *L'amore in città*

promulgated (and re-proposed precisely in this film) by Zavattini could not be more radical and profound.

This approach to the material is rendered even more effective (and more explicit) when the distancing of the subject takes place, as it does in these cases, in the presence of the subject herself. This is the solution that has been much discussed in relation to *Cronaca di un amore*, when, at the end of the encounter of the two protagonists at the *idroscalo* (the appointment that brings the characters together again after many years and that rekindles their love story – thus one of the key moments of the narration of their story), the camera, after accompanying them to their car and following the vehicle while it drives away, moves towards the 'empty' image of the lake.

But critics seem not to have noticed that an even more radical and 'merciless' attitude is already proposed by *Gente del Po*. The sequence I am thinking of is, in my opinion, one of the most beautiful and emotional (not, obviously, in the sense of its producing spectatorial empathy) of Antonioni's entire cinema. It is dusk, the time when 'people are on the river banks'; the voice-over draws our attention to a young man on his bicycle, whom we had already glimpsed in the previous images, while he was crossing the village square. 'Al va a far l'amore in riva al Po' ('He goes to make love on the shores of the River Po'), explains the voice-over (with a sad inflection, it must be admitted), and the images show him immediately after he has reached a young woman who sits with her back to the camera, as he places himself behind her, also with his back to the camera. The depersonalisation of the two lovers (the passion, the intimacy of their love story would have – we might assume – required images of their faces) is accentuated by the visual 'attraction' generated by the man's shirt, dominated, as it is, by the logo of a well-known brand of bicycle written out in elegant art deco typography. It may be that this brand and piece of clothing had for the youth of the 1940s the same function of the T-shirts adorned with logos of the teenagers of today. But certainly, in this particular context, the logo

125

Gente del Po (1947)

– which makes itself conspicuous in the shot of the two characters – has the effect of taking our attention away from the tenderness of 'making love' (which, in the jargon of the 1940s, meant going out with a boy or a girl, dating and not having sex with them) and relocating the entire scene from the point of view of an anomalous and alienating perspective. When the woman turns towards the man, her gaze expresses such resignation, such a lack of prospects that it denies, in the most drastic manner, any connotation of 'happiness', of 'dreams for the future', of hope of change, that could be attributed to the characters or to a situation of this type (a couple at dusk in a moment of intimacy). The woman's gaze is not only disillusioned, hopeless; it is a *desperate* gaze. And her mood is further accentuated by the film's attitude towards this couple: after having submitted to the spectator, for what feels like an uncomfortable period of time, the spectacle of their meeting and her gaze, the film abandons the two characters precisely at the moment at which they appear to ask most forcefully for our solidarity and support. The camera literally abandons them to their destiny as it slowly absents them from the frame by panning right, until it comes to rest on the empty, desolate image of the river: a landscape devoid of vanishing points, devoid of horizon, devoid of any element of dynamism, devoid of any idea of escape and change. As Noa Steimatsky has written in her analysis of this scene, this landscape 'even refuses the consolation of a receding distance'. According to Steimatsky, here 'we witness what is surely the earliest and paradigmatic instance of Antonioni's modernism'.[13]

The relativisation of the human subject's centrality (to the film, its story and its images) is also achieved by questioning the existence of a point of view that could be imputed to such a central position or role. The films adopt other solutions that point to a perceptual estrangement, a disorientation, an unanchoring from an anthropomorphic base of the gaze and of observation. One is reminded of techniques used by the avant-gardes of the 1920s (for instance, of some of the most representative features of László Moholy-Nagy's photographs from this period). We also note the use of figures, spaces and landscapes that impose themselves on the image and on the viewer and that echo metaphysical painting or the cityscapes of Mario Sironi.

Gente del Po (1947); László Moholy-Nagy, No title (1929); *N.U.* (1948); *L'amorosa menzogna* (1949); *Sette canne, un vestito* (1949)

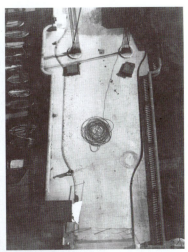

Mario Sironi, *Sintesi di paesaggio urbano,* 1921

Sette canne, un vestito is, without doubt, the film among Antonioni's early documentaries that in the most obvious (and programmatic, because of its having been commissioned by the Italian textile industry) manner accentuates the marginalisation of the individual human subject, and that thus most calls to mind the iconography of Walter Ruttmann's industrial films, in particular, those forms that his *Acciaio* (*Steel*, 1933) directly inserted in the fabric of Italian cinema. But *Sette canne, un vestito*, like the other shorts, realises this objective also through a series of original techniques, principally the emphasis on references that exceed – and indeed, are incongruous with – the proposed context. The estrangement – which here is cultural before being perceptual – is realised via paradigmatic dilations that challenge the linearity and thematic coherence of the narration. This mode of distanciation was explicitly announced in the preparatory text for *Gente del Po*; the river, Antonioni wrote in that article, 'takes on features of African landscape'.[14] In such a strategy – quite apart from their affinities with the avant-gardes of the 1920s, or with metaphysical painting – the documentaries insert themselves into a series of seemingly heterogeneous sources and contexts, all of which nevertheless nourished and influenced the theorisation of neo-realist cinema in the 1940s: Italian

Sette canne, un vestito (1949)

'verismo', as well as French and Russian realist literature; the very different cinematic realisms of Hollywood and Soviet cinema; and French Poetic Realism.[15]

It is thus possible to explain the sudden openness towards North American realist painting (or the cinema of the New Deal) that we see in the image (above) from *Sette canne, un vestito*, in which the harvested rows of cane extend deep into the horizon. Or an openness towards Soviet cinema that we detect in the emphasis on agricultural machinery in another image (above) from the same film. We sense the presence of 'attractions' that are almost 'stolen' from Dada or FEKS (or, once again, from the photograph of Moholy-Nagy – or from Lewis Hine's photos of the construction of the Empire State Building) in images like the one (below) from *N.U.* But it is to the French cinema of the 1930s (the context in which, we should not forget, Antonioni's directorial training took place) that these films most consistently refer (for example, the image from *L'amorosa menzogna* [below]).

Antonioni had been an ill at ease assistant director on the set of Marcel Carné's *Les Visiteurs du soir* (1942). And it is the fairytale, fantastic imagery of

N.U. (1948); *L'amorosa menzogna* (1949)

Gente del Po (1947);
Sette canne, un vestito
(1949); Marcel Carné,
Les Visiteurs du soir
(1942)

that film (but also of all Poetic Realism) that materialises in the image of the white horse we see in *Gente del Po*, an image which is so anomalous in the context of the narrative's severity. (We might also read this as a Zavattinian irruption, perhaps, but this is a context that is, as we have seen, very far from Zavattini). We also see the traces of this imagery in the reference to and image of the 'mysterious castle' of *Sette canne, un vestito*: a gesture that is even more audacious and displacing, especially given the immediate cultural context of modernisation and, formally, given the *Neue Sachlichkeit* contours of Torviscosa plant itself.

Reality in Antonioni's films always tends towards an opaque, suspended, 'intransitive' dimension,[16] one of 'escape' with respect to its functional, 'applied' value. In these landscapes, it is not the enigmatic character of a form, of an object, of a landscape that attracts our attention. The films make use of a montage of primary materials, all of which themselves ought to reside in or refer to precise, stable semantic categories, but the films use these same materials in order to produce effects of destabilisation and uncertainty. These methods are already clearly those that will characterise the so-called 'major' films. I want to insist, however, that these methods ought not to be seen in a genealogical frame of reference. The documentaries of the 1940s are not anticipations – more or less immature – of the subsequent works; they do not find their meaning in the light of what will follow. They are entirely autonomous works, with their own sense of identity. In them we see – already fully formed – methods, aesthetic criteria and stylistic principles that will continue to manifest themselves in the later films – while, of course, continuing to evolve, mutate and be modified, as we would expect. These films possess a complexity and originality that are already fully realised; they should not be understood as mere precursors – or subordinates – to Antonioni's subsequent works.

> It was 1943. Visconti was filming *Ossessione* on the banks of the Po river, and, also on the Po river, a few kilometers away, I was filming my first documentary … As soon as it was possible for me to do so I returned to those places with a camera. This is how *People of the Po Valley* [*Gente del Po*] was born. Everything that I did after that, good or bad as it was, started from there.[17]

This declaration of poetics – inevitably invoked in all of the critical literature on Antonioni – may actually mean much more than has been commonly assumed.

Notes

Translated from the Italian by Laura Racaroli and John David Rhodes.

1. Michelangelo Antonioni, 'Concerning a Film about the River Po', in David Overbey (ed.), *Springtime in Italy: A Reader on Neo-Realism* (London: Talisman, 1978), pp. 79–80. The essay was published originally in Italian as 'Per un film sul fiume Po', *Cinema* vol. IV no. 68 (25 April 1939), pp. 254–7, and republished in Michelangelo Antonioni, *Sul cinema*, ed. Carlo Di Carlo and Giorgio Tinazzi (Venice: Marsilio, 2004), pp. 77–80.
2. I use not unintentionally the term 'continuity': the model I use in the analysis of these films is not the genealogical one (the early documentaries as source of later development), nor the hierarchical one (the early documentaries as a potential that is achieved in later works), but rather a model of autonomy of themes and forms that identifies the working of thematic nuclei and stylistic principles, with their own precise and formed identity, in the different areas represented by the single films (postwar documentaries included), and in which the processes of transformation and evolution, which are certainly present, spring from the relationship with the different contexts (textual and also systemic), but starting from a degree of elaboration, from a 'statute' of the single components that already in the 1940s presents full originality and 'maturity'. For a recent study that takes Antonioni's early documentary work (especially *Gente del Po*) seriously and in relation to some of the terms I employ here, see Noa Steimatsky, *Italian Locations: Reinhabiting the*

Past in Postwar Cinema (Minneapolis: University of Minnesota Press, 2008), pp. 1–39.

3. Plagiarism by prefiguration? The films that spontaneously come to mind are indeed subsequent. Persisting on this line of reasoning, after all, doesn't the same industrial plant in *Il deserto rosso* seem to us to plagiarise by prefiguration the Parisian Centre Pompidou? On the notion of plagiarism by prefiguration see Pierre Bayard, *Le Plagiat par anticipation* (Paris: Minuit, 2009).

4. Alberto Lattuada, *L'occhio quadrato* (Milan: Edizioni di Corrente, 1941). The volume has been republished in 1982 Piero Berengo Gardin (ed.), *Alberto Lattuada fotografo. Dieci anni di Occhio quadrato, 1938/1948* (Florence: Alinari, 1982).

5. See Giuseppe Turroni, *Alberto Lattuada* (Milan: Moizzi, 1977); Antonio Costa (ed.), *Alberto Lattuada: Gli anni di 'Corrente', Cinema & Cinema* no. 56 (September/December 1989).

6. Alberto Lattuada, 'Prefazione a L'occhio quadrato', in *Alberto Lattuada fotografo*, p. 15.

7. Francesco Maselli confirmed it at a conference held in Ravenna on 21–2 May 1999. The oral testimony, however, is not included in the conference proceedings: Alberto Achilli et al. (eds), *Le sonorità del visibile. Immagini, suoni e musica nel cinema di Michelangelo Antonioni* (Ravenna: Longo, 1999). In this volume, Maselli makes instead reference to their common 'infatuation for the painter of the quintessentially urban sites: Sironi' (Francesco Maselli, 'I miei esordi con Michelangelo', in *Le sonorità del visibile*, p. 147).

8. The projects have been transcribed from an Antonioni's notebook in Carlo Di Carlo (ed.), *Il primo Antonioni* (Bologna: Cappelli, 1973), pp. 15–16: '*Macchine inutili*: Painter Munari constructs machines that he calls useless because they serve no purpose. They are not even machines, they are objects of wood, iron, wire combined with a great sense of harmony and irony. When these machines, which must be hanged from the ceiling before a window, move because reached by even the lightest breath of air, they oscillate, creating curious rhythms. An almost abstract documentary.' Munari was an artist and designer who was associated with the Futurists early in his career and was later a founder of the Movimento Arte Concreta (MAC).

9. Seymour Chatman in turn traced in the same film forms of theatrical presentation, starting with the opening titles sequence, put in relation with an 'immediate attention to the existence of the camera' and to 'Antonioni's lifelong attack on cinematic illusion': Seymour Chatman, *Antonioni, or the Surface of the World* (Berkeley and Los Angeles: University of California Press, 1985), p. 8.

10. The circumstance is so flagrant that it did not go unnoticed by Antonioni's scholars. See, for instance, Giorgio Tinazzi, *Michelangelo Antonioni* (Florence: La Nuova Italia, 1974), p. 59.

11. 'Rationalism' (l'architettura razionale) names a movement in Italian architecture associated with the MIAR (Movimento Italiano per l'Architettura Razionale). Giuseppe Terragni, Giovanni Michelucci, Giuseppe Pagano and Piero Bottoni are

among the most famous adherents of Italian rationalism. Their work bears strong (and self-conscious) affinities with the work of International Style modernists, especially those associated with CIAM (International Congress of Modern Architecture). In the beginning of the 1930s rationalism was officially supported by Mussolini's regime.

12. Aldo Tassone, *I film di Michelangelo Antonioni* (Rome: Gremese, 1990), p. 68.

13. Steimatsky, *Italian Locations*, p. 33. Though my analysis is one that I have been developing over many years (and have proposed at several conferences across the 1990s), I only happened to read Steimatsky's work after the completion of the proofs of my essay. I am happily struck by the attention she draws to many of the same elements that I analyse and gratified that she comes to conclusions very similar to my own.

14. Antonioni, 'Per un film sul fiume Po', p. 79. A similar operation of environmental disorientation is all but anomalous in the context of neo-realism. In the epilogue to *Conversazione in Sicilia*, Vittorini writes that 'the Sicily in which [the] story takes place is Sicily only by chance, because I like the sound of the word "Sicily" better than "Persia" or "Venezuela"'. Elio Vittorini, *Conversations in Sicily*, trans. Alane Salierno Mason (New York: New Directions, 2000), p. 2.

15. Elsewhere, I placed the accent on the heterogeneity of references, and above all on the continuity between the theorisation of a new Italian cinema, on the pages of the periodical *Cinema*, in the early 1940s (thus in the context, again, of fascist cinema) and characteristics of neo-realist films (from *Ossessione* to the postwar works); see Leonardo Quaresima, 'Neorealismo senza', in Mariella Furno and Renzo Renzi (eds), *Il neorealismo nel fascismo* (Bologna: Compositori, 1984), pp. 47–73.

16. These are aspects I discuss in 'Da *Cronaca di un amore* a *Amore in città*. Antonioni e il neorealismo', in *Michelangelo Antonioni. Identificazione di un autore*, ed. Comune di Ferrara, Ufficio cinema (Parma: Pratiche, 1983), pp. 39–50.

17. Michelangelo Antonioni, 'Preface to *Six Films*', in *The Architecture of Vision: Writings and Interviews on Cinema*, ed. Carlo Di Carlo and Giorgio Tinazzi, trans. Marga Cottino-Jones (New York: Marsilio, 1996), pp. 57–68 (pp. 65–6).

133

Rosalind Galt

ON *L'AVVENTURA* AND THE PICTURESQUE

Michelangelo Antonioni's 1960 film *L'avventura* re-enacts a history of picturesque-looking relations: a group of young people from the privileged class take a trip into nature for the pleasure of looking at its untamed beauties. They find irregular and rocky islands, a broken-down shepherd's hut and the crumbling remains of former civilisations. These are precisely the themes of the picturesque, a concept that eighteenth-century writers mobilised in an attempt to theorise an aesthetics of landscape both as a representational strategy and a mode of experience. In the work of Sir Uvedale Price, Richard Payne Knight and William Gilpin, the picturesque emerged as a specific aesthetic category, akin to the beautiful and the sublime, but it also described a practice of looking in which members of the landowning class engaged both the created views of their landscaped gardens and the natural scenery of wild tourist destinations such as Sicily. While the picturesque has often been disparaged as either aesthetically tasteless or politically retrograde, it also names an important historical debate on class, landscape and the relationship between visual perspectives and social change. And like the original picturesque, the relationship between observer and landscape in *L'avventura* is underwritten by tensions inherent in economic modernisation, with its concomitant transformations of space and of the human subject, to say nothing of the rapidly changing status of the image in modern forms of representation.

Thus, to pay attention to the picturesque in *L'avventura* is not merely to note a similarity of theme and setting, but to engage material connections between modes of picturing the Italian landscape in the eighteenth century and those in the twentieth. Although associated with British scenes, the picturesque both derives from Italian and became a crucial mode of thinking the Italian landscape. If the wild scenery of Lisca Bianca evokes the gothic landscapes of eighteenth-century picturesque painting, the film's staging of class tensions during the Italian 'economic miracle' equally recalls the fears of revolution that lurked in theories of the picturesque garden written by landowners like Gilpin and Price.[1] *L'avventura* deploys the picturesque to foreground the relationship between the image and modernity, and in particular the transformation of space in capitalist development. Property relations underlie debates over the original picturesque and the descendents of these same tensions over land ownership animate Antonioni's account of Sicily's postwar transformations. Modernity produces equally radical transformations of the image, which the picturesque engages by asking what it is to look 'like an image'. In the eighteenth century, this question opened onto both painting and, with landscaping and architecture, broader questions of aesthetics as experience. In the second half of the twentieth century a similar representational shift underlies the modern revision of the cinematic image, including transformations of sensory experience and subjectivity. By deploying the picturesque, I argue, *L'avventura* brings into startling proximity some of the key discourses on the modern image.

Approaching Lisca Bianca

Almost as well known as *L'avventura*'s anti-mystery plot is the heroic story of its production. Attempting to film on the Aeolian island of Lisca Bianca, in a shoot that was meant to take place in the summer but was delayed until winter by financial problems, the cast and crew encountered an unpredictable and even dangerous environment. Communication with the mainland was difficult, the sea was perilous and, without pay, many of the crew abandoned the project. In a written account of the production, Antonioni says:

135

> Maybe I should say that all this was happening in Panarea, in the Aeolian Islands, and that every morning we went with a boat to shoot on a rock called Lisca Bianca, twenty minutes from Panarea. When the sea was calm we could see puffs of steam come out of the water and dissolve into tiny sulphurous bubbles. But it was never calm. The storm was constant: wind force eight, nine. In that short distance, to get to Lisca Bianca meant literally risking our lives.[2]

This tale of an intrepid crew battling the elements to get the right shots works as a compelling behind-the-scenes story in the genre of classics that almost didn't get made, but it also extends *L'avventura*'s encounter with the picturesque beyond the limits of the text.

Antonioni describes 'a violent storm [that] shakes the sea, the sound of the waves that hit against the breakwater, in the night, are really frightening'.[3] This account is very similar to the role of the rough sea in defining the picturesque, as where Price tells us that 'all water of which the surface is broken, and the motion abrupt and irregular, as universally accords with our ideas of the picturesque; and whenever the word is mentioned, rapid and stony torrents and waterfalls, and waves dashing against rocks, are among the first objects that present themselves to our imagination'.[4] Antonioni thus writes himself into a picturesque scenario, in which not only does the content of the film offer picturesque images but the experience of its production was a picturesque experience. Such an experience is twofold. Its more benign version is the aristocratic walk around the garden – the leisurely pleasure trip that Anna and her friends first envisioned when they left Rome – but its more *adventurous* variant is the expedition to a rugged and possibly dangerous elsewhere. For the eighteenth- and nineteenth-century advocates of the picturesque, such an encounter with the wilderness often meant a trip to Italy and, in particular, to Sicily. When Antonioni suffers rats and cold in Panarea, and approaches Lisca Bianca with 'the only ones ready to follow me whatever the sea', his account of battling the elements and the locals is a modern iteration of a longstanding narrative of picturesque and dangerous Sicily.[5]

In 1777, theorist of the picturesque Richard Payne Knight travelled to Sicily, expanding on his two previous trips to Italy in 1772 and 1773. While the convention of the Grand Tour had made travel to northern Italy common for upper-class British tourists, Sicily was still seen as an adventurous destination. The dangers faced by Knight and his group included plague, bandits, poor transportation and harsh climate – challenges surprisingly similar to those that faced Antonioni. Knight wrote an account of his journey that emphasised both the dangers and the pleasures of the landscape.[6] The group arrived via the Aeolian Islands, and on the approach watercolourist Charles Gore painted the islands from the north. The group was unable to disembark at Stromboli because of a quarantine, but they spent time on both Lipari and Milazzo.[7] Like Antonioni almost two centuries later, Knight produced the Aeolian Islands as a picturesque and dangerous stopping point between mainland Italy and Sicily, to be viewed and represented visually as a mysterious rocky seascape. Once on Sicily proper, Gore and the German painter Jakob Philipp Hackert made a series of watercolours of the island's dangerous views, including what Claudia Stumpf characterises as 'the fascinating and dangerous heights of Mount Etna, news of whose eruptions have alarmed Europe since 1693, or the legendary eddy of Scylla and Charybdis near Messina'.[8] Sicily was at once able to speak of classical civilisation and contemporary European alarm, and this doubleness of past and present, civilisation and modernity, is echoed in Knight's own descriptions. Of Messina – another location for *L'avventura* – Knight says:

> The view is very beautiful and romantic, the Coasts being high and rocky, adorn'd with Towns and Villages … upon approaching nearer this fine Scene looses all its Splendour, and every object assumes an Air of melancholy and dejection … Every thing seems to declare the fatal calamities that have lately overwhelmed this unfortunate City, and reduced it from the highest State of Wealth and felicity to the lowest depth of misery and despair.[9]

Jakob Philipp Hackert, *View of Lipari and Stromboli* (1778): a painting from Richard Payne Knight's expedition to Sicily in 1777; Approaching Lisca Bianca in *L'avventura* (1960)

As in Antonioni's film, that which is beautiful from a distance becomes sad, downtrodden or abandoned when seen in close-up.

We might ask why it matters that the view of a northern Italian director is so similar to the exoticising picturesque imagined by a British tourist two centuries before. The answer is that Knight's memoir is an early iteration of a discourse on the Sicilian picturesque that shapes representation of the islands from 1777 to 1960 and beyond, and which links these particular landscapes to modernity's reshaping of both property and the image. We find from the eighteenth century to the present a series of approaches to Sicily that figure the Aeolian Islands. In 1898, for example, another British writer, William Agnew Paton, published *Picturesque Sicily*, an influential travelogue aimed at the increasing numbers of moneyed north Europeans journeying to the southern parts of Italy. Paton begins with a familiar tale of a dangerous approach to Sicily via the Aeolian Islands:

All night long, from Capri onward, the steamer battled with head-winds and opposing waves, and her unhappy passengers had many reasons to remember that, through the blackness of the starless winter watches, they were passing close to the Aeolian Islands – the ancient home of all the winds. Little control did King Aeolus exert over his subjects that December night. The struggling gales and sounding tempests, escaping from their prison-house, danced aloft in air and hissed along the sea. It was a night of trying experiences and long vigils – the hours lingered remorselessly, the minutes loitered, while darkness brooded over the face of the deep.[10]

Once the morning comes, however, they see the 'Lipari Islands floated athwart the level rays of the rising sun on an ocean of golden light', and the sight of Sicily is presented in explicitly pictorial terms as an 'inspiring picture'. Antonioni approaching Lisca Bianca in a stormy and perilous sea turns out to be a recurrent trope of imagining the Sicilian islands, and one that ends by framing the landscape as a picturesque view for the intrepid outsider.

But if Antonioni engages the northern European discourse on the Italian picturesque, this discourse is simultaneously in conversation with an Italian history that at once invokes and repudiates it. Nineteenth-century Italian culture embraced the idea of picturesque Sicily, developing the idea of the backward yet alluring South as a recurrent theme of post-Risorgimento Italian art and literature. Thus, in Nelson Moe's account, popular magazines like *Illustrazione italiana* disseminated picturesque images of the South among the country's middle and upper classes, and helped create 'the powerful symbolic charge that rural Sicily had for the Italian bourgeoisie' of the period.[11] At the same time, a countercurrent of both scholarship and literary writing began to examine Sicily in a more realist vein. For example, Leopoldo Franchetti's influential *Condizioni politiche e amministrative della Sicilia* (*Political and Administrative Conditions in Sicily*) opened up the sociological study of the Southern Question in what Moe describes, tellingly, as a 'bleak, antipicturesque vision'.[12] More importantly for our purposes, Giovanni Verga's *verismo* in *Vita dei campi* (*Life in the Fields*, 1880) and *I Malavoglia* (*The House by the Medlar Tree*, 1881) articulated the landscape of rural Sicily from a native perspective, responding to the discourse of picturesque Sicily by combining a regionally acute naturalism with social critique. Of course, Verga was a significant influence on neo-realism and, thus, entirely part of Antonioni's cultural imaginary.

Verga's relationship to neo-realism has been widely noted, and has contributed to cinematic representations of the rural south in general, and Sicily in particular, from *La terra trema* (*The Earth Trembles*, Visconti, 1948) to *Stromboli* (Rossellini, 1950). But this cultural terrain explains the frequent criticism of Antonioni as insufficiently political: the extent to which his films reject the representational strategies of neo-realism is precisely the extent to which they hark back to picturesque models of visualising Italy.[13] Angelo Restivo makes this point in different terms, arguing that Antonioni's engagement with form and landscape – for example, 'the ephemeral formal beauties of the River Po' in *Gente del Po* (1947) – makes critics suspicious that he is drifting away from properly leftist realism.[14] And the connection between Verga's reversal of picturesque Sicily discourse and leftist Italian cinema continues into the present day: Nanni Moretti's film *Caro diario* (*Dear Diary*, 1993) features a journey from the Italian mainland to the Aeolian Islands, in close pastiche of those journeys of Knight and Paton in centuries past. Moretti, like Verga, articulates his journey as one of social investigation into Italian identity, but he adds to this history of *verismo* a reflection on the place of these islands in Italian film history. As David Scott Diffrient puts it, 'The tiny island of Panarea, once home to sea gulls and little else, would seem to be a picturesque alternative to Stromboli, were it not for the outdoor cocktail parties, jet-set business dinners, and daily celebrations of bad taste that have replaced Antonioni's pumice caves and white cliffs.'[15] Moretti's contemporary leftist documentary mourns the loss of Antonioni's wild landscape on Panarea and Lisca Bianca, presenting the islands as taken over by a form of tourism even more insidious than Knight's Grand Tour culture. This vision of tacky cocktail parties echoes Italo Calvino's diagnosis of underdevelopment and affluence as the hellish binary of the modern Italian South.[16] For Calvino, of course, *L'avventura* is exactly the film that exposes this structure.

As we approach Lisca Bianca, then, we see that the discourses of Sicily and the picturesque are not randomly aligned in *L'avventura*, but form a tightly woven tapestry of aesthetic and political issues. The two terms – Sicily and the picturesque – juxtapose central issues of Italian identity, visual and literary cultures, and the problem of representation in modernity. And these questions recur: Antonioni himself kept approaching Lisca Bianca in his writings and in film, returning to the trope in a 1983 television segment called *Ritorno a Lisca Bianca*. In this chapter, I will argue that *L'avventura* draws on picturesque Sicily discourse neither as a nostalgic return to an aristocratic visual pleasure nor as an apolitical aestheticising formalism, but rather as a feature of its modern visuality. What it means to look 'like a picture' is an issue riven with the power dynamics of looking at and being in a landscape, underwritten by questions of which Europeans get to look/own and which are framed as exotic displays.

Picturesque Views

In true picturesque spirit, *L'avventura* offers a series of views for the discerning spectator. The opening scenes in Rome prime us for a pictorial mode of looking, with repeated shots containing internal framing devices; thus the view of Anna waiting in the street, framed by the semi-drawn curtains of Sandro's apartment, and the exterior shot of Anna, Claudia and Sandro driving through an ornate arch.

Claudia's scene killing time in the modern art gallery rhymes with the scene later in the film in which she looks out at the landscape, bored by artist Goffredo's paintings of women, but what strikes us as different in the film's images from these avatars of modern art is the emphasis on framing. As Price argues, while the sublime depends on boundlessness, the picturesque is all about framing: 'Infinity is one of the most efficient causes of the sublime; the boundless ocean, for that reason, inspires awful sensations: to give it picturesqueness, you must destroy that cause of its sublimity; for it is on the shape and disposition of its boundaries, that the picturesque must in great measure depend.'[17] These opening scenes place an emphasis on emphatically drawn boundaries, like Sandro's curtains, which produce a self-consciously 'arty' internal frame for a view (of Claudia) that is only visible from one perspective. As with the walk through the picturesque estate, one stops here, and now here, and now there, in order to see the most pleasingly constructed framings.

However, by the time we reach Lisca Bianca, the view is less safely delimited and the boundless ocean requires careful framing to become picturesque rather than sublime. Claudia refuses to swim in the frightening sea, and establishing shots present the spectator with a dramatic rock face and cliffs tumbling into the sea. These views of waves crashing against jagged rocks accord closely with the idea of the picturesque as roughness and irregularity in landscape, which developed from a European adoption of East Asian aesthetics of asymmetry. The idea of *sharawaggi*, or irregularity, was already at play in the designed wildness of 'Capability' Brown's English gardens in the early 1700s, but Knight and Price took Brown's domesticity to task. Knight advocated roughness and variety of terrain in his influential 1793 poem *The Landscape*, and Price (with whom Knight agreed on very little) similarly felt that smoothness was a feature of the beautiful whereas 'the appearance of irregularity', ruggedness and 'sudden variation' were key components of the picturesque.[18] These ideas of irregularity located the picturesque as a framed and delimited variant of potentially sublime landscapes, with framing producing neither the tension of an encounter with the boundless sublime nor the languor of viewing harmonious beauty, but instead a unique spectatorial curiosity about the strikingly composed image.

It is this curiosity that is prompted in the scenes on Lisca Bianca, where Anna and Sandro walk, sit and fight about their relationship while the setting of the rocky island and sky insistently foregrounds their status as figures in a landscape. In one shot, we see Anna from a vantage point higher up on the cliffs, the high angle creating a graphically irregular picturesque composition. Later in the sequence, Claudia stands at the bottom right of the frame while Sandro climbs up to the top left. The characters move around, forming diagonal compositions within the frame, as well as shifting attention uneasily between foreground and background. Our attention contrasts with the apparently uncurious attitude of the groups of tourists, who bicker about their own lives or wander aimlessly around the island. Unlike the expeditions documented by Knight, Paton and even Moretti, these travellers form picturesque compositions for the spectator without being especially engaged in their own sensory experience. It is only when Anna disappears that curiosity is sparked in the characters, and, even then, their interest in her whereabouts is strikingly limited.

For Price, one of the main features of the picturesque is the architectural ruin, and the tumble-down peasant hut is an especially common theme in picturesque art.[19] Italy figures a particularly significant exemplar of this idea in Ruskin's claim that one has to travel to France or Italy to see the true picturesque because the British countryside is in too good condition to create its effects of irregularity and decay.[20] *L'avventura* follows this representational history by introducing a shepherd's hut that Claudia, Corrado and Sandro stay overnight in while looking for the vanished Anna. The cabin is suitably lowly, providing a contrast when Claudia looks out of the window, framed carefully against the sunrise. Outside, Claudia and Sandro are framed again in picturesque fashion, with Stromboli in the background and the horizon very low in the shot. This contrast of decaying architecture with impressively desolate landscapes characterises both the representational history of the picturesque and the visual logic of the film. Once on the mainland of Sicily, for instance, we see long shots of rough and scrubby scenery on the way to Noto, and once in the town the crumbling baroque architecture repeatedly frames pleasurable images of picturesque decay. Moreover, the abandoned village that Claudia and Sandro encounter revisits the architectural ruin in a modern context, offering emptiness and desolation without material degeneration.

Setting and environment have been common themes in Antonioni criticism, although his urban spaces have been more closely studied than his landscapes. Geoffrey Nowell-Smith describes the natural environment in *L'avventura* as 'indifferent, sometimes seen as benign, but more often as hostile', while Seymour Chatman reads it as 'a rich source of textures, lines, and masses'.[21] But Chatman

141

A picturesque view
from Lisca Bianca

ultimately finds the natural landscape less interesting than those of the urban films, suggesting that:

> Precisely because man did not invent it, nature for Antonioni seems not a subject for man's criticism. Whether savage, as the crags of Lisca Bianca, or soft, as the flowery hills of Sicily, its beauty remains mysterious and neutral, untouched by human quandaries, imperturbably itself, filled with details that have no significance for plot yet that are somehow profoundly meaningful in their own way.[22]

This sense of the natural landscape in *L'avventura* as indifferent and mysteriously profound (and therefore essentially ahistorical) touches on both the sublime and the beautiful but precludes what I argue are the socially embedded meanings of the picturesque. Moreover, this evocation of the natural landscape in terms of mysterious beauty limits the ways in which urban space can signify too, forcing it by contrast into figuring a loss of such natural profundity. This binary forms part of the limiting tendency of critics to read Antonioni's form only as evidence of alienated modernity.

As with landscape, themes of modernity and alienation have centred reception of Antonioni's films from the beginning. In 1960, the director himself describes the present as 'a period of extreme instability' and in a typical contemporary review, Tommaso Chiaretti compared him to Camus, attempting to find a new language adequate to the new modern man.[23] Two decades later, Petr Kral described *L'avventura* in terms of 'the omnipresent emptiness' and, more recently, Noa Steimatsky has argued that 'Antonioni's grasp of the landscape as a distanced, alienated terrain recurs as a critical, transformative principle.'[24] Matthew Gandy summarises this literature by pointing out that '[a] range of scholarship has highlighted how the very idea of landscape implies a process of alienation from nature and is an integral element in the development of modern aesthetics'.[25] So far, so familiar. Antonioni is associated with modernity and alienation almost to the point of parody, and at least his urban landscapes have been central to this discourse.[26] But while many scholars have thought about the modernity of Antonioni's settings, their iconophobic insistence that only an austere and sparse visuality can engender a valuable modern aesthetic produces a blindness to Antonioni's deployment of the picturesque.

This is why Peter Brunette refers to Lisca Bianca as 'supremely aesthetic' and finds it curious that 'this emphasis on the "natural" is also consistently accompanied by its *aestheticization*'.[27] Likewise, why so many of the writers who praise Antonioni's modernism simultaneously insist on its visual rigour. Italo Calvino describes *L'avventura* as 'a picture of great, unsparing severity' and describes its style as 'barren, with no ornament or digression'.[28] Chiaretti asks what Antonioni's style is, and answers that his style is 'stylistic "rigor" '.[29] Pascal Bonitzer opens out the debate by seeing 'a search for formal richness' in Antonioni's films from *L'avventura* to *L'eclisse* (1962), but he nonetheless points out that formal richness is always suspect in cinema. Does he find it suspicious himself, or is this suspicion, like *L'avventura*'s modernist ennui, a more general cultural condition? Bonitzer does not clarify, but I think it is the latter. Antonioni elaborates a richness of style that mostly evades the strictures of iconophobic critics, but in valuing his modernity, the critics must perforce limit their palette of aesthetic analysis. Critics seem only able to find value in Antonioni's style insofar as it can be framed in terms of rigour, emptiness and abstraction. Even Steimatsky, whose project revises histories of Italian cinema in important ways, finds locations such as Lisca Bianca and EUR to 'crystallize an "intelligence" of place stripped of "extraneous and decorative elements" as over-coded rhetorical devices that would mediate human presence, and pastness'.[30] For her, ground is crucial *as figure*, reversing and decomposing the traditional hierarchies of visual representation, and yet only in its undecorated stringency can this transformation emerge. The picturesque counters this assumption that decorative style can only ever confound the political, however, offering a way to think of Antonioni's images as at once part of a theoretical history of the image and as embedded within a modern geopolitics.

Property Relations and the Landscape Imaginary

It is apt that Antonioni turned to this aesthetic tradition for a film that explores rural class relations as the picturesque is shot through with geopolitics. The eighteenth-century theorists of the picturesque rarely related their aesthetic projects to their positions on land ownership, but Marxist critics in the twentieth century insisted on the connection. Most significantly, these critiques of the picturesque centred accounts in the power dynamics of spectatorship and spectacle. Raymond Williams argued in *The Country and the City* that the 'very idea of landscape implies separation and observation', and this idea of an aristocratic view on a pleasurably distanced spectacle is echoed by contemporary postcolonial critics such as Fatimah Tobing Rony who sees the 'quaint and the remote' as a central feature of colonial picturesque scenes.[31] Extending the metaphor of distance to one of complete invisibility, John Berger described the picturesque image of the countryside as a 'curtain' behind which the lives of its inhabitants remain hidden.[32] Berger evokes the iconophobic Marxist trope of the image as a veil, hiding the truth of economic relations, but in this case it was often literally true. The picturesque views sketched by Gilpin and others removed people and habitations, or selected landscapes that were uninhabited. At the very least, the advocates of the picturesque landscape, like the colonial wives sketching in India, preferred their spectacular views not to be sullied with unpleasant details like rural poverty.

But the connection between the picturesque image and the material environment from which it is abstracted is often more direct. Several critics of the picturesque have focused on its coincidence with the period of land reform in Britain and Europe, in which enclosure forcibly turned peasants into wage labourers and entire landscapes – along with the rural cultures they supported – were transformed in a violent process of modernisation. At the same moment, the landowning classes feared repercussions from the French Revolution, and many advocated a turn to arms to quell potential peasant uprisings.[33] Thus, Price wrote a pamphlet proposing militias for property owners, and, on a less violent scale, the concept of 'improvement' as a gardening aesthetic often meant wholesale destruction as a striking correlative to the 'improvements' of enclosure. As Horace Walpole put it, in his carefully titled essay *On Modern Gardening*, 'how rich, how gay, how picturesque the face of the country! The demolition of walls laying open each improvement, every journey is made through a succession of pictures.'[34] The modernity that produces a series of views for the aristocratic spectator is enabled by a corresponding series of demolitions, whose effect on the land's inhabitants is not recorded by Walpole. As Macarthur succinctly puts it, 'Those people who were developing an aesthetic appreciation of the landscape of Britain were also in a state of low-level civil war with its inhabitants.'[35]

That Price, Knight and others were closely involved in geopolitical dispute is clear, and it should probably be obvious that those most strongly associated with literally re-forming the countryside for aesthetic purposes would have some connection to those reforming it for economic ends. But, as Macarthur cautions, it is by no means clear that we can simply align picturesque theories with the exploitative land policies of the reactionary aristocracy. While Price espoused a Tory perspective, Knight was a free-thinker who got involved in debates with both Walpole and Price over politics. In response to Knight's rejection of 'Capability' Brown, Walpole said that he 'Jacobinically would level the purity of gardens, would as malignantly as Tom Paine or Priestley guillotine Mr Brown'.[36] The comparisons to Tom Paine and to the Jacobins demonstrate the stakes of landscape aesthetics in this period: Knight was accused of a dangerous radicalism in his attitude to land ownership. In *The Progress of Civil Society* (1796), he wrote specifically on the French revolution, condemning the Terror but also criticising the ancien régime. As Nicholas Penny explains, this was enough to provoke attack from his Tory contemporaries, 'The revolution in France was polarizing society violently and Knight was suspected of being on the wrong side because he was not violently against it.'[37] Moreover, Knight held liberal views on a range of social and cultural issues, supporting divorce and considering that 'Negro people' must have their own canon of beauty different from that of the European.[38] Macarthur concludes that the geopolitics of the picturesque is not so simple, and that its proponents had widely divergent perspectives on modernising land reforms.

I want to deploy this contemporary revisionist approach to the picturesque as a way of rethinking Antonioni's modern reference to the form. Modernist uses of the picturesque in architecture have reimagined the idea of the composed view, but these appropriations have not often reviewed the geopolitics of the form. Thus, Yve-Alain Bois uses the concept to describe both Le Corbusier's constructions of promenade spaces ('a modern picturesque') and Richard Serra's artworks ('a sublime picturesque').[39] Antonioni, of course, is often thought of in terms of architecture, and the series of architectural views that is so crucial to *L'eclisse* might equally form a modern picturesque in Bois's terms. But the focus on landscape in *L'avventura* returns us to the political foundations of the original picturesque. By combining attention to the picturesque as a modern way of constructing space with a reiteration of its historical articulation of struggles over land ownership, I propose that the picturesque re-emerges in Antonioni as a rich signifier of geopolitical disruption.

Following Macarthur's account of the eighteenth-century debate, I argue that we cannot link the modern picturesque directly to a specific political position. Instead, I propose, we can link it to moments of conflict over land ownership. The picturesque emerges precisely as a symptom of tension between the aesthetics of the natural environment and the economics of its exploitation. This is why it is first named in the early modern period and is theorised in detail during an era that encompasses the violent process of enclosure in Britain, the growth of tourism in Italy and European colonial expansion. And this is why it re-emerges in Antonioni's response to the mid-twentieth century 'economic miracle' in Italy. In this historically acute moment of social and physical transformation, a very different enclosure of Rome's grand estates by high-rise suburbs prompts in *L'avventura* another turn to 'picturesque Sicily' as an escape that reflects wilderness back onto that which was vanishing in the urban centres of modernisation. As in the eighteenth-century, the landowning classes in 1950s Italy simultaneously exploited urbanisation by selling their land for property development and bemoaned the loss of green spaces. The tensions that animated the eighteenth-century picturesque – between landowner and peasant, between North and South, and between Europe and its others – are exactly the tensions that structure Antonioni's cinema.

We see these transformations repeatedly coded in *L'avventura*, beginning from the opening sequence in which Anna grumpily listens to her father explain bourgeois etiquette while, around them, Rome's urban expansion encroaches on the family estate. Once in Sicily, the film returns obsessively to images of radical and often violent change of the physical and social landscape, like the shot of a car emerging from a tunnel that foregrounds the graphic cutting of road into mountain. The road offers perhaps too obvious a visual figuration of modernisation, but throughout the narrative Sicily's visible spaces encode transformations of the social order. The police station is a converted villa, and the camera moves away from the characters in order to gaze at the decorative detail of marble and cornicing that is uncharacteristic of

145

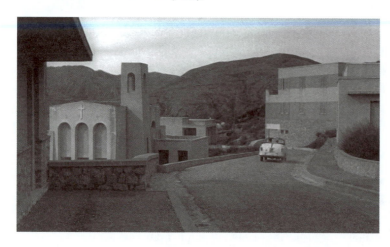

The abandoned
village of Schisina

modern state offices but provides an architectural trace of the building's former aristocratic owners. Where the baroque buildings have not been appropriated for modern use, as in Noto, they are crumbling signifiers of a broader decay in social relations. When the camera focuses on characters, we find a constant investigation of class relations. As Peter Brunette points out, the newspaper report on Anna's disappearance sees her merely as a rich Roman girl (*ricca ragazza romana*), while all of Claudia's social interactions – from her encounter with the petit-bourgeois pharmacist couple to the men who stare at her in Noto – are heavily overlaid with class and gendered tensions.[40]

146

As with the eighteenth-century picturesque, though, the most significant figures of landscape transformation are those that are not visible in the picture. Sicily in the years before *L'avventura*'s production was at the centre of a highly contested land reform programme in Italy's South, designed to modernise agriculture in a way comparable to postwar industrial development. The need for reform was great: land ownership in the South was concentrated in a tiny number of wealthy families, and rural poverty was a pressing problem. Moreover, peasants had been promised large amounts of land in the previous century but never actually given it, and much of this disputed land was left uncultivated by its aristocratic owners. In a situation not dissimilar to that of eighteenth-century England, landlords were anxious about peasant revolt, and in the late 1940s and 50s a series of demonstrations and land occupations brought peasants and landowners into open conflict. This was collective action on a large scale: in 1950, a Sicilian communist leader reported tens of thousands of peasants and landless labourers occupying uncultivated land.[41] The Christian Democrat government eventually passed land reform laws, aiming to expropriate uncultivated land from big estates and allow peasants to buy it, but the laws were weakened by the strong landowning lobby in the party. As Paul Ginsborg points out, only about a quarter of Sicilian peasants got any land at all: landowners sold to their friends rather than have their land taken away, and most of the land acquired by peasants was of very low quality.[42] As a result of this process, land prices trebled in the course of the 1950s and where peasants were given new land, it was often at the price of losing their communities.

We don't see these peasants in *L'avventura*, but, as with the eighteenth-century picturesque, Antonioni's images of landscape contain all the tensions implied by those invisible inhabitants. Think of the scene in the abandoned village: this sequence depicts a transformation that is not explained narratively but articulates a powerful lack of sociality. Where are the people? *L'avventura* makes sure we ask this question as spectators. And in fact, the hauntingly empty village is Schisina, one of a group of hamlets constructed in 1950 to house peasants assigned expropriated land. Separated from their families and communities, their inhabitants quickly abandoned the villages, returning only for the harvest. By 1959, when Antonioni was filming, Schisina was completely uninhabited.[43] Throughout the film, the recent history of peasant activism and incomplete land reform is an unseen presence: the absence of certain people from landscapes does not veil social relations but draws our attention to them. In a film whose narrative centres on a person who disappears from view, that which is not seen must be understood as just as important as what is visible. As with Antonioni's example of the body on the beach in his essay 'The Event and the Image', we cannot have a direct view of this violent shift in property relations, but can only discern it through the lens of its representational traces.[44] Thus, we spend our time in Sicily with a notoriously disengaged group of wealthy people who can't even muster much enthusiasm to search for their vanished friend. As Sandro and Claudia journey from Lisca Bianca to Noto and Messina, Sicily's inhabitants appear mostly as sullen witnesses (the smugglers and shopkeepers) or as hostile observers (the men who mob Gloria Perkins and those who stare at Claudia in Noto). Decadent aristocrat Goffredo prefers to paint women rather than landscapes, and indeed he doesn't even want to look out of the window. It is only Claudia who looks and who sees the political landscape that surrounds her.

In the film's account of an emptied and desolate Sicilian landscape, we have little visual sense of Italy's economic modernisation and, after the opening scenes in Rome, we are faced with a history reflected in the decadent lives of the aristocrats and the crumbling splendour of baroque architecture. Transformation, here, seems limited to the disintegration of the ancien régime. In an obvious way, these images of decay are picturesque in the sense intended by Price when he argued that a Greek temple was beautiful but, in ruin, the same building became picturesque.[45] The broken-down shepherd's hut or the spectacular old buildings in *L'avventura* suggest a similar aesthetic investment in temporal degradation, and if we agree with the commonplace readings of the film as a symbolic account of the Italian bourgeoisie in decline, or of backwardness in the Italian economic miracle, then we must conclude that the picturesque is the form able to stage this political economy. But Price is also the most conservative of the theorists of the picturesque. For him, disintegrating peasant huts were romantically preferable to their owners complaining about their living conditions, and his appreciation of the old fashioned didn't stop him from supporting enclosure. Ruthless modernisation went hand in hand with aesthetic nostalgia. Antonioni's film uses the codes of the picturesque landscape to the exact opposite effect, insisting on a modern aesthetic with which to reveal the social violence of economic modernisation. The unspoken anguish of Claudia in Schisina and the stark compositions which frame her figure in the abandoned village bring together picturesque geopolitics and modernist cinematic style to evoke, rather than veil, social relations. *L'avventura*'s landscapes, pregnant with unseen inhabitants, function as a picturesque in reverse.

Conclusion: Like a Picture

The picturesque is often disparaged in contemporary critical thought for implying an overly pretty composition or a lack of depth and sophistication. Antonioni demonstrates his awareness of this pitfall when Jean-Luc Godard asks him whether he constructs images via abstract forms and details or whether he creates them 'in a pictorial spirit'.[46] It's a loaded question, and Antonioni sidesteps it, clearly realising that while his images might be admirably composed, it would be a mistake to admit that he thinks of them in compositional terms. Godard's suspicion of pictorial spirit is exactly what is at stake in the picturesque: the threat of an image that is like a picture (as if there could be an image that were not like a picture). While, as I have argued elsewhere, a rejection of overly pictorial images suffuses postwar European film culture, the picturesque offers a salutary reminder of the complexities inherent in thinking the modern image.[47] In its original context, the picturesque was not the simple notion of stylistic charm implied by its contemporary detractors but rather produced a transformation of the image as a mode of experiencing the world; what Macarthur tellingly characterises as 'a radical blurring of art and life'.[48] The picturesque asks us what it means to look 'like a picture' and I would suggest that *L'avventura* is particularly interested in investigating that question in a modern cinematic context.

The picturesque is a particular kind of image, and the arguments over its definition inscribe a modern reckoning with the problem of representation. Gilpin defines it in terms of the world viewed, locating as picturesque 'such objects as are proper subjects for painting'.[49] For Price this definition is insufficient because any object that produced a pleasing painting could be picturesque and thus all paintings might be. For him, the picturesque should not simply describe anything pictured, but nor could it come too close to the beautiful by defining only pleasing pictures. Rather, it must refer to a form of picturing that understands itself as such. Knight

shifts the definition definitively to the mode of representation, arguing that the picturesque is only pleasurable for those 'conversant with the art of painting, and sufficiently skilled in it to distinguish, and be really delighted with its real
excellences'.[50] The picturesque is here de-natured and turned into a readable image.
We see traces of this discourse in the common critiques of Antonioni as too
painterly. Film criticism in the wake of neo-realism tended to define the cinematic
in terms of a realist openness and vitalism, and thus to find suspicious any hint of
aesthetic composition, even in the most stylistically overdetermined films. An image
that understands itself as such is, in the context of cinematic realism, a suspicious
image, and one that refers to picturing as a painterly or aesthetic occupation is
doubly so. Thus the attribution of barrenness and rigour to Antonioni is an attempt
to recuperate his formalism as a kind of modernist styleless style.

But this history of the picturesque image does not only turn to Italy for its landscapes; theorists of the picturesque also saw Italy as the origin of the idea. Both Price
and Knight trace the word 'picturesque' to the sixteenth-century Italian *pittoresco*,
and although they have differing explanations of the significance of this national
origin, both accounts are suggestive for reading modern Italian images. For Price,
Italian usage emphasises 'the thing painted' rather than the painted image suggested
in English. Thus, 'The English word naturally draws the reader's mind towards pictures; and from that partial and confined view of the subject, what is in truth only
an illustration of picturesqueness, becomes the foundation of it.'[51] For Price, the
Italian *pittoresco* is to be found in the world itself, before its pictorial representation yet ultimately determined by it. There is a prefiguration of the cinematic profilmic here, whereby real locations form an ontological basis for representational
meaning, but only insofar as they have always already become images. Thus, it matters that *L'avventura* is shot on Lisca Bianca, in Noto and Messina, that it captures
Mount Etna, abandoned villages and postwar public roadbuilding projects before
its lens. But it does not matter in the way of a neo-realist shooting in the present
tense, nor even in the self-reflexive contemplation of the image of *Blow-Up* (1966).
The landscapes of Sicily become legible as aesthetically composed images, always
already entailing a political history of viewing Italy.

Knight's account of the picturesque image supports a materialist poetics: he sees
the Italian *pittoresco* as a historical mode of image-making. He finds it in the development of massing in the paintings of Giorgione and Titian; an innovative technique
that began to depict objects as they are seen by the human eye rather than as they
actually are.[52] The superiority of the picturesque, for him, lies in its production of
a greater realism of vision that, nonetheless, transcends mimesis to create specifically aesthetic effects of light and colour. Again, this definition proleptically figures
the structure of the cinematic image. For Knight, the *pittoresco* signifies 'after the
manner of painters' and this must refer to 'some peculiar mode of representing
[objects] different from simple or common imitation'.[53] After all, if painting simply

149

imitated objects, then 'like a painting' would mean nothing different from 'like life'. To be distinct, the concept 'like a painting' must refer to a mode of visuality, a way of framing and viewing the world that transforms the object through its representational form. Thought of in relation to cinema, the *pittoresco* presents an added turn of the mimetic screw, in which a representation that is not drawn but created out of the material of profilmic reality is nonetheless viewed through the filter of painting. Thus, we see the world, represented with objects of the world, that are themselves observed as if they were painted representations of objects. As with Pier Paolo Pasolini's concept of the cinema of poetry, film's indexicality demands to be read as part of an aesthetics and a politics.[54] If Knight locates the emergence of this visual regime in Italy, I would argue that its modern iteration draws on a comparable cultural history. This is the scandal of Antonioni's style, which pushes beyond neo-realism to create an 'arty' effect, forcing us to view Italian historical realities like a painting, without the straightforwardly cinematic comforts of mimesis.

The modern discourse on the picturesque sought to distinguish good 'painterliness' from bad 'picturesque' images, but *L'avventura* refuses this aesthetic hierarchy and with it a good deal of modernist dogma around the cinematic anti-aesthetic.[55] The final views of the film are unquestionably pleasurable, a series of picturesque compositions that provoke in their sheer aesthetic indulgence. After Sandro's betrayal, Claudia runs outside. We see her from behind, looking out the right side of the frame, her view blocked. Next, we see Sandro's point of view, with Claudia standing in front of a ruined church. As Claudia moves to stand behind Sandro and touches his hair, our view is of both of them, looking out towards the sublime landscape of Mount Etna. The final shot of the film is perfectly symmetrical, yet strikingly uneven. The left side of the screen looks out in depth to Mount Etna while the right is a flat non-view, blocked by a wall. The composition is irregular and dramatically boundaried but it presents a modernist rather than an eighteenth-century picturesque view. Angelo Restivo argues that *L'avventura* represents the last of natural sublime in Antonioni's work, but I find it in some ways the least formless of his films.[56] It is crisply formed, like this final shot so perfectly cut down the middle. Where the sublime calls for a politics beyond representation, the picturesque demands negotiation between image and object. It is inherently concerned with the problem of representation in modernity: what it means to be an image that looks like an image, and how to imagine the relationship between pleasure in the image and the politics of the profilmic world. *L'avventura*'s iteration of the picturesque renews an important debate on the nature of image-making and, moreover, insists on its structuring relationship to modern geopolitics. By travelling to Sicily, the most remote and 'backward' part of Italy, and by forcing this situation of backwardness as his very mode of production, Antonioni reinscribes the geopolitics of the Italian landscape back into the modern history of images.

Notes

1. The 'economic miracle' describes Italy's post-World War II boom, in which rapid social and economic modernisation involved principally large-scale industrialisation and urban development, but also included radical changes to the agricultural economy.

2. Michelangelo Antonioni, 'About Myself and One of My Films', in Seymour Chatman and Guido Fink (eds), *L'avventura* (New Brunswick: Rutgers University Press, 1989), pp. 180–1.

3. Michelangelo Antonioni, 'Je commence à comprendre', *Positif* no. 483 (2001), pp. 47–8. Trans. RG.

4. Sir Uvedale Price, *Essays on the Picturesque as Compared to the Sublime and the Beautiful; and on the Use of Studying Pictures for the Purpose of Studying Real Landscape* (London: Mawman, 1810), p. 57.

5. Antonioni, 'Je commence'.

6. Richard Payne Knight, 'An Expedition into Sicily, 1777', unpublished diary (Weimar, Goethe-Schiller-Archiv MS 25, xliv, 7).

7. Claudia Stumpf, 'The "Expedition into Sicily"', in Michael Clarke and Nicholas Penny (eds), *The Arrogant Connoisseur: Richard Payne Knight 1751–1824* (Manchester: Manchester University Press, 1982), pp. 19–31 (p. 22).

8. Ibid., p. 19.

9. Quoted in ibid., p. 28, original in Knight, 'An Expedition to Sicily', pp. 88–90.

10. William Agnew Paton, *Picturesque Sicily* (New York: Harpers, 1902), pp. 1–2.

11. Nelson Moe, *The View from Vesuvius: Italian Culture and the Southern Question* (Berkeley: University of California Press, 2006), p. 250.

12. Ibid.

13. See, for example, Armando Borrelli, *Neorealismo e marxismo* (Avellino: Edizioni di Cinemasud, 1966), or, for an opposing view, Lino Miccichè, *Il cinema italiano degli anni '60* (Venice: Marsilio, 1975).

14. Angelo Restivo, *The Cinema of Economic Miracles: Visuality and Modernization in the Italian Art Film* (Durham, NC, and London: Duke University Press, 2002), p. 96.

15. David Scott Diffrient, 'Autobiography, Corporeality, Seriality: Nanni Moretti's *Dear Diary* as a Narrative Archipelago', *Journal of Film and Video* vol. 61 no. 4 (2009), pp. 17–30 (p. 22).

16. Italo Calvino, 'Remarks on *L'avventura*', in Chatman and Fink, *L'avventura*, pp. 196–7 (p. 197).

17. Price, *Essays*, p. 84.

18. Richard Payne Knight, *The Landscape: A Didactic Poem* (London: W. Bulmer, 1795), pp. 20–6; Price, *Essays*, pp. 46, 51.

19. Price, *Essays*, p. 51.

20. John Ruskin, quoted in John Macarthur, *The Picturesque: Architecture, Disgust and Other Irregularities* (London: Routledge, 2007), p. 14.

21. Geoffrey Nowell-Smith, *L'avventura* (London: BFI, 1997), p. 36; Seymour Chatman, *Antonioni, or, the Surface of the World* (Berkeley: University of California Press, 1985), p. 112.

22. Chatman, *Antonioni*, p. 112.

23. 'Un entretien avec Antonioni', *Cinéma 60* no. 50 (October 1960), pp. 4–7 (p. 7) (trans. RG); Tommaso Chiaretti, 'Antonioni ou le refus de la banalité', trans. Claire Clouzot, *Cinéma 60* no. 50 (October 1960), pp. 12–21 (p. 12).

24. Petr Kral, 'Traversée du désert: de quelques constantes antonioniennes', *Positif* no. 263, (January 1983), pp. 30–5 (p. 30) (trans. RG); Noa Steimatsky, *Italian Locations: Reinhabiting the Past in Postwar Cinema* (Minneapolis: University of Minnesota Press, 2008), p. 38.

25. Matthew Gandy, 'Landscapes of Deliquescence in Michelangelo Antonioni's *Red Desert*', *Transactions of the Institute of British Geographers* vol. 28 no. 2 (2003), pp. 218–38 (p. 218).

26. John David Rhodes has argued against this critical dogma in 'The Eclipse of Place: Rome's EUR from Rossellini to Antonioni', in John David Rhodes and Elena Gorfinkel (eds), *Taking Place: Location and the Moving Image* (Minneapolis: University of Minnesota Press, 2011), pp. 31–54.

27. Peter Brunette, *The Films of Michelangelo Antonioni* (Cambridge: Cambridge University Press, 1998), pp. 37–9.

28. Calvino, 'Remarks on *L'avventura*', pp. 196–7.

29. Chiaretti, 'Antonioni ou les refus de la banalité', p. 20.

30. Steimatsky, *Italian Locations*, p. 38.

31. Raymond Williams, *The Country and the City* (Frogmore: Paladin, 1975), p. 149. Fatimah Tobing Rony, *The Third Eye: Race, Cinema, and the Ethnographic Spectacle* (Durham, NC: Duke University Press, 1996), p. 84.

32. John Berger, *A Fortunate Man* (London: Penguin, 1967), p. 13

33. See, for example John Barrell, *The Dark Side of the Landscape: Rural Poor in English Painting, 1730–1840* (New York: Cambridge University Press, 1980).

34. Horace Walpole, *On Modern Gardening* (London: Brentham Press, 1975 [1780]), p. 29.

35. Macarthur, *The Picturesque*, p. 8.

36. Horace Walpole, *Correspondence*, vol. XIX (New Haven and London, 1937–74), pp. 338–40.

37. Nicholas Penny, 'Richard Payne Knight: A Brief Life', in Clarke and Penny, *The Arrogant Connoisseur*, pp. 1–18 (p. 10).

38. Macarthur, *The Picturesque*, p. 10.

39. Yve-Alain Bois, 'A Picturesque Stroll Around Clara-Clara', *October* no. 29 (Summer 1984), pp. 33–62 (p. 62).

40. Brunette, *Antonioni*, p. 46.

41. Li Causi quoted in Paul Ginsborg, *A History of Contemporary Italy: Society and Politics, 1943–1988* (London: Palgrave, 2003), p. 128. The original interview is in

Francesco Renda, 'Il movimento contadino in Sicilia', in Pasquale Amato et al. (eds), *Campagne e movimento contadino nel Mezzogiorno d'Italia* (Bari: De Donato, 1979), pp. 557–717 (p. 665, n 10).

42. Ginsborg, *A History of Contemporary Italy*, p. 132.

43. I am very grateful to John David Rhodes and Laura Rascaroli for identifying Schisina.

44. Michelangelo Antonioni, 'The Event and the Image', *Sight & Sound* vol. 33 no. 1 (1963/64): p. 14.

45. Price, *Essays*, p. 51.

46. Jean-Luc Godard, 'Night, Eclipse, Dawn … An Interview with Michelangelo Antonioni', *Cahiers du Cinéma in English* no. 1 (January 1966), pp. 19–29 (p. 28).

47. Rosalind Galt, *Pretty: Film and the Decorative Image* (New York: Columbia University Press, 2011). See especially chapter 5.

48. Macarthur, *The Picturesque*, p. 1.

49. William Gilpin, *Essays on Picturesque Beauty* (London: Blamire, 1792), p. 36.

50. Richard Payne Knight, *An Analytical Inquiry into the Principles of Taste*, 4th edn (London: Luke Hansard and Sons, 1808), p. 146.

51. Price, *Essays*, p. 45.

52. Knight, *An Analytical Inquiry*, pp. 150–1. See also Peter Funnel, 'Visible Appearances', in Clarke and Penny, *The Arrogant Connoisseur*, 82–92 (p. 88).

53. Knight, *An Analytical Inquiry*, p. 148.

54. Pier Paolo Pasolini, 'The "Cinema of Poetry"', in *Heretical Empiricism*, ed. Louise K. Barnett, trans. Ben Lawton and Barnett (Bloomington and Indianapolis: Indiana University Press, 1988), pp. 167–86. See also John David Rhodes's analysis of the essay's politics in Rosalind Galt and Karl Schoonover (eds), *Global Art Cinema: New Theories and Histories* (New York: Oxford University Press, 2010), pp. 142–63.

55. See, for example, Heinrich Wöllflin's account of the *malerisch* (picturesque or painterly) in *Principles of Art History: The Problem of the Development of Style in Later Art* (Mineola, NY: Dover, 1932), pp. 23–7.

56. Restivo, *The Cinema of Economic Miracles*, p. 127.

153

Alexander García Düttmann

QUASI: Antonioni and Participation in Art[1]

Participation in art, if it is to do justice to the demands art makes, seems to be determined by two different aspects. Once they have been told apart, it is difficult to reconcile them. For, on the one hand, participation in art requires immediacy, which lies either in a belief triggered by what is represented in the artwork, by its content, or else in a belief in the artistic representation itself, in the work of art as such. For example, one watches a film and before one is able to really understand it, one feels that there is something there, that there is something significant about this film. Perhaps such a belief, whether it is triggered by the artwork's content or whether it is a belief in the artistic representation itself, cannot be separated from a belief in the body and the world, a belief which, according to Deleuze, may be regained in modern cinema. On the other hand, however, participation in art requires mediation, since a distinction needs to be made between art and non-art, or, to use the terminology of traditional aesthetics, between art and nature. When one participates in a work of art, one must be aware of the fact that it is indeed a work of art, not a product of nature. One has to ask oneself how the artwork was made, why the artist made it the way he made it, how it relates to other, different artworks, what it is that is new about it, how significant it is as an artwork or what it is that constitutes its singular importance. If the two aspects of participation in art are unified in art, and if the demand for immediacy and the demand for mediation stem from the artwork itself, it still remains difficult to reconcile them after they have been told apart because it is not clear how the awareness of the artificiality of a work of art, of its being produced by an artist, can influence the belief in the artwork and in its content. Is there not a point at which this belief calls for a permeability of the boundary that separates art and nature, so that it can be a belief? If I believe that there is something significant about an artwork, if I believe in its content, if, for instance, I feel fear when the artwork represents something terrifying, if this is how I participate in aesthetic seriousness, then I cannot let myself be guided simultaneously by an awareness that it is all just made up and that, not being real, it could also be different. The reality of art is not the reality of nature, and yet they both resemble each

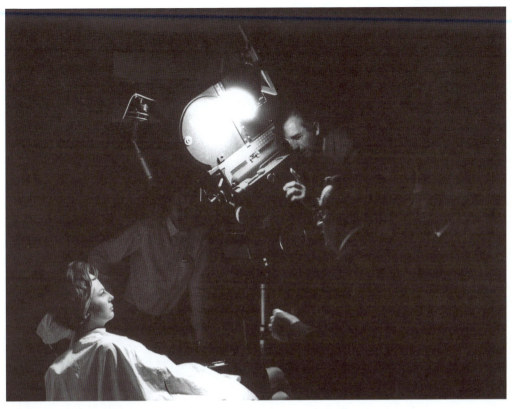

Antonioni films Soraya (*Prefazione: Il Provino*, 1965)

other inasmuch as the immediacy of participation reflects an artistic demand; without it, there would be no aesthetic seriousness and no work of art.

Three anecdotes can serve as an introduction to this text. When I told my friend the art historian Brendan Prendeville that I wanted to write on an almost unknown film by Italian film-maker Michelangelo Antonioni, so as to analyse more closely the unity of, and the relationship between, the two aspects of participation in art, he suddenly remembered a painting by French artist Honoré Daumier, cast largely in browns. It was created around 1860, belongs to the collection of the Neue Pinakothek in Munich, and is sometimes referred to by a double title, *In the Theatre (Melodrama)*, while at other times it is simply called *Drama*. One can see a theatre balcony with a lower-class audience attending a performance. The expression on the faces of the spectators, all painted in profile, is one of intense attentiveness, of shakenness, even of rapture, as if whatever is happening on stage were actually a real occurrence. On stage one recognises three figures frozen in stereotyped, histrionic poses. It is easy for the beholder of the painting to identify them as faceless cardboard figures. There is a woman who turns away in despair; there is a man who lies on the floor and, to all appearances, has been knocked down; and between the two, there is a second man whose forefinger points at the dead or wounded man while he also holds a dagger in his other hand and stretches his arm accusingly towards the woman. Thus the painting doubles the perspective, as if its beholder could see something that the painted audience cannot see, namely the artificiality of the events, the artistic character of a theatre performance *and* the conventional character of what is being represented and of the representation itself. Participation here is not just brought about by an illusion, by an as-if, but reveals itself to be illusionary and unreal. As tempting as it might be, then, to subordinate the perspective of the painted people, who seem captivated by the play and stare at the stage, to the perspective of the beholder, who is aware of the artificiality because of the reflexivity of the painting's artificial character, as tempting as it might be to regard one perspective as the perspective of intelligence and the other one as the perspective of delusion, of a lack of refinement, of stupidity, one must not give in to such a temptation and congratulate oneself. For even the perspective of intelligence must still depend on an as-if, on the representation of the painting; were it not to participate in the representation, in what the painting represents and in the painting as representation, it would immediately collapse into stupidity and prove to be alien to art. It is as if a third gaze were required at this point, a gaze that would observe the beholder's intelligence from behind, as it were, so that its blind spot could become apparent as well, the blind spot caused by an irreducible immediacy. The beholder cannot exempt himself from the audience without turning into a cardboard figure himself. By exempting himself, he falls prey to vanity and shows how much he lacks an understanding of art. He becomes involuntarily entangled in the artificiality of the as-if, in a comedy that exposes him to the people's laughter.

The second anecdote can be found in a text Antonioni published in 1962. The film-maker talks about one of his earliest attempts at making a documentary. Its topic would have been life in a lunatic asylum in northern Italy, and Antonioni would have made it with the aid of the asylum's inmates. Having managed to get permission from the director to embark on such an unusual project, work began. The inmates helped with the preparations for the shoot of the first scene, in which they were to figure themselves. They showed a lot of goodwill and were much more efficient than expected:

> Finally, I gave the order to turn on the lights. I was a bit nervous and anxious. Suddenly, the room was flooded with light, and for an instant the inmates remained absolutely stationary as though they were petrified. I have never seen such expressions of total fear on the faces of any actors. The scene that followed is indescribable. The inmates started screaming, twisting, and rolling themselves on the floor ... In no time at all the room became an inferno. The inmates tried desperately to get away from the light as if they were being attacked by some kind of prehistoric monster. The same faces that had kept madness within human bounds in the preceding calm, were now crumpled and

devastated. And this time we were the ones who stood petrified at the sight ... I have never forgotten that scene. And it was around this scene that we unconsciously started talking about neorealism.[2]

If one wanted to interpret this anecdote, one could say that the madness of the inmates consisted precisely in their lucidity or their good health, in the terror they experienced when confronted with the conditions of art, for these conditions actually amount to a threatening state of emergency. Art as manifestation of a superior power seems to have caused the inmates' regressive behaviour. Did they not show a deeper understanding of art than so-called healthy people who take art for granted, as something that goes almost without saying? From such a perspective, the realism of neo-realism would not be based merely on a behaviour that is different from professional acting and that does not follow the instructions of a film director. Rather, it would be based on the representation of a refusal to participate in art, to partake of its unnatural character or its semblance. The inmates' madness would have resulted from their exaggerated and therefore rigid sense of reality. By not allowing for art at all, this sense would have proven receptive to art's prehistoric heritage, to what is exceptional about it and also repressed when the artwork is split into two different aspects, into the immediacy of participation and the mediating awareness of it. The lunatics obliterated mediation, the awareness of art as art, because they related immediately to the fact of art, and not, as the men and women in Daumier's painting, to what is represented in the artwork. Quite unexpectedly, perhaps, they ended up being faithful to art.

The third anecdote refers to my own distant encounter with Antonioni. I must rely here entirely on my recollection of it. Partially paralysed after a stroke, the moviemaker attended a screening of his film *I vinti* (1953), when an almost complete retrospective of his work took place at the Pacific Film Archive in Berkeley. This was in the early 1990s. After the director of the Film Archive had spoken a few words to welcome her Italian guests, Antonioni simply raised an arm to greet everybody who had come to the screening. The stroke, which had occurred several years before, had left his speech severely impaired. Now the screening was meant to begin. As I watched the film director, I had a feeling that he wished to be present at the screening itself, see his own film one more time, at least in part, while those who accompanied him clearly wanted to leave the cinema. In the row in front of me, two seats had remained empty or had been reserved, for it was on these seats that he and his wife finally sat down. The projection started. Suddenly, distracted by a movement, my gaze wandered from the screen into the dark auditorium. I observed how Antonioni elbowed his wife so as to make her aware of something. Before I knew it, a plane went across the screen, appearing out of nowhere and taking everybody in the cinema by surprise. Antonioni's almost child-like gesture touched me. Had he stayed only for the sake of witnessing the effect of this particular scene on the spectators, or on himself as a spectator? In fact, he left the cinema shortly afterwards, when there was still quite a bit of time left before the film would end. One could interpret his gesture as betraying an awareness of film as something produced intentionally. As he watches his own film repeatedly, the director expects that a scene will work as successfully as it did in the past, and he alerts the other to it, as if he were saying: 'There it is, do you remember? I am sure it will be as good as the first time around!' But perhaps such an interpretation would be too limited. Could one not also maintain that Antonioni's gesture betrayed the impatience of a child who cannot wait for something to happen? The child announces a carefully prepared surprise and yet expects that the announcement will not ruin the surprising effect, that it may even increase it. Hence, the film proves to be alive, each time anew. One does not simply watch it knowingly, unmoved and with a blasé attitude, as if one were watching it after the fact. Perhaps Antonioni's gesture tried to bring together the two aspects of participation and produce the unity of immediacy and mediation that precedes their distinction and separation. The artist sought to mirror himself in the spectator.

Antonioni's concern with the two aspects of participation in art appears in a film he made in 1965 as a kind of preface to *I tre volti* (1965), a portmanteau film consisting of two different episodes. His film is known as *Il provino*, which means 'The Screen Test', and also as *Prefazione*. It circles around a secret screen test that takes place in the middle of the night at the newly built studios of producer Dino De Laurentiis. The screen test is meant to mark the beginning of Princess Soraya's career as a film actress, as if the German-Iranian royalty had been looking for a new role for herself. One of the journalists and photographers who has got wind of the project and has besieged the studio answers the question of why Soraya is trying to become an actress by saying that she is probably tired of playing the role of a princess. The film's first shot shows the letter 'A' formed out of neon tubes; it is the director's initial, of course, but here it also belongs to the name of a newspaper, to a luminous sign attached to the front of a building where the journalists go about their work. Then, later on, there is a further shot which shows four other letters belonging to the same name. In this image, the first letter is separated from the three letters that follow by an empty space. Only when, in yet a different shot, the car of a journalist parks in front of the film studio, will the spectator be able to read the newspaper's full name: *Paese Sera*, a leftwing Roman newspaper founded after World War II at the initiative of the Communist Party. The letters one recognises in the second shot, are 'E', 'S', 'E' and 'R'. Read in sequence, they form 'eser', a word that does not exist but that is reminiscent of the Italian word for being, 'essere'. In *Il provino*, being is, in the first place, the social being of labour performed at a late hour and in an almost empty environment. Such labour is performed by the people working at a newspaper who are putting together the morning edition in their offices and in the printing section, or who stay up all night because they are following up on a developing story or checking on a rumour that could turn into a news item. Such labour is also performed by the people working at the film studio who have arranged for the screen test to take place after hours in order to avoid causing a stir – at this point, most of the employees will have left the building, which contains the actual studio and the producer's offices. When, at the end of Antonioni's film, the men from the newspaper must acknowledge that they have waited in vain, that the princess has left the studio through a back door and has returned to her hotel at the crack of dawn, not giving them a chance to take a snap-shot of her face, the camera moves away to reveal, in a last shot that focuses on the horizon, a motorway and a line of pine trees. The roar of the lorries and delivery vans that now fill the previously empty roads seems to come closer and closer, as if the strangely unreal labour of the people working for the newspaper and in the film studio, who are going home at this hour, has collided with real social labour, with hard work. The irony prompted by this contrast between the serious and the frivo-lous, as it were, also permeates two other scenes in which the men from the news-paper appear. In the first scene, set in the paper's printing section, the journalist is told that there is no space left for a possible, last-minute article on Soraya's acting ambitions: at the moment, an article on the increase of bread prices is in the way. In the second scene, set outside of the film studio, the journalist hears a raven cawing and asks the photographer where the noise is coming from. He is told that the cawing comes from a nearby zoo, created by the producer De Laurentiis specifically for the shoot of *The Bible*, a big spectacular production. Just as Noah sends out a raven that returns to the Ark without having achieved its mission, there is still no land in sight for the newspapermen, for Soraya has not shown her face yet.

However, being in *Il provino* is also the kind of being art produces. It splits into the production of a film, visualised as a creative process that begins with the screen test, and the result of this process, the film which Antonioni has made and which is almost a documentary. The spectator sees how Soraya's face is placed against a dark background; one of its two halves is masked deliberately, so that the other half can be observed more closely. The spectator sees how make-up and lipstick are put on, how mascara is applied to her eyelashes, how a number of wigs, displayed on a shelf and captured in a tracking shot, are ready to be selected, how a studio employee uses an iron to put finishing touches to a red cocktail-dress. While the faces of Soraya and the friend who accompanies her are filmed frontally or in a mirror, so that they look straight into the camera, and while Soraya studies herself in a series of different outfits and on one occasion even throws red fluid at the mirror, as if she were angry, the face of the producer, played by Dino De Laurentiis himself, remains invisible. Either the position of his body is such that it turns away from the camera, or else other bodies come between it and the spectator's field of vision; sometimes the shot allows for the face to appear only in profile, sometimes the producer's head is seen only from behind, thus suggesting that power does not have a face, only a voice that utters decisions, or that faces are expressive and that power must be without expression. When Soraya arrives at the film studio, the neon lights that form a canopy over the driveway have all been switched off. Only the flash of a camera which belongs to the photographer from *Paese Sera* illuminates the scene. Very briefly, the spectator sees a group of people. They hurriedly move from a car to the entrance hall. Later on, the journalist and the photographer will be disappointed, for they will realise that the pictures are worthless. There was no luck during the blind haste; the images don't show the princess's face. As Soraya is getting ready for her screen test in a long and arduous procedure that makes her smoke many cigarettes, her friend reminds her that she has been brought up to hide her feelings and that now she will be asked to exhibit them. It can be gauged from this remark that in the present case the exchange of roles is not simply a transition from one role to another but rather a reversal. Why? Because in the world of the powerful there is not just one form of inexpressiveness; there is the inexpressiveness of power exercised and hence invisible but there is also the inexpressiveness of power represented and hence visible, of power over oneself and over others. For this reason, the split between production and product becomes particularly apparent where it corresponds to the split between expression and inexpressiveness.

Inasmuch as Antonioni's representation of a screen test keeps alerting the spectator to the fact that art is something produced, brought about by an artist, two sequences in his film must be considered that try to elicit an unmediated participation on the spectator's side. On the one hand, Soraya's preparation for her screen test is interrupted by a phone conversation she has with her mother. Speaking in German, she asks her to rush from Munich to Rome on the next available flight, as if she couldn't cope with her life any longer, or as if she no longer wanted to play a role, the role of a princess driven into exile or the role of a budding actress. It seems unlikely that this scene elicits immediate participation. On the other hand, the actual screen test ends with a series of close-ups and long shots that show Soraya wearing an elegant evening gown, a princess who is playing the role of a princess. A spiral staircase has been built on the brightly illuminated set, which resembles a small sunny island in the middle of nowhere. Although there is no upper floor, Soraya comes down this staircase and walks into a large room filled with plants, pieces of furniture, knick-knacks, a chandelier and a Persian rug. Wallpaper with a floral pattern covers the thin wooden walls. The princess exposes herself to an unexpectedly strong draught that penetrates into the room through the open French windows and makes the net curtains inflate. The draught is produced by the large tubes of a wind machine. Romantic piano music is playing but does not succeed in drowning out the noise. Though Antonioni never allows the spectator to forget that this is a screen test in a film studio, and though the artificiality of the situation is underlined by the stark contrast between the false English-style living room and the functional space that surrounds it, it is as if the simulated mood communicated itself to the spectator. This mood is the abstract remainder of melodrama, of an exaggeration of emotions that prompts the two aspects of participation in art to diverge in opposite directions, in the direction of an internal view and in the direction of an external view that cannot be reconciled any more. The mood here signals the beginning and the end of immediate participation.

When turning to the construction of the filmic image, clearly outlined rectangular forms that create a kind of grid correspond to the external view, the view that lets the spectator see the film *as* a film because it is the view of consciousness aware of mediation. These rectangular forms are complemented by the sinuous forms of the curves on the road outside of the studio: they are visible in the dark because neon strip lights have been attached to the railings. Also, Antonioni places an enigmatic structure made out of Perspex in the vicinity of the set built for Soraya's screen test. It is a sort of labyrinth, as if Antonioni had wanted to add a spatial dimension to the sinuous forms of the road curves. A collaborator of the production company gets lost in this labyrinth; at its centre, there is a telephone that he is supposed to reach so that he can call Soraya next door and have a chat with her. The chat, consisting of mildly provocative questions and largely conventional answers, is a pretext to get the screen test going and provide it with some content. Does Antonioni make fun of himself here? His films have been buried under platitudes about alienation in human relationships. To a question she is asked, Soraya replies ironically that everybody is stumbling in the dark, except for a few actors.

What is it, then, that corresponds to the internal view, to the immediacy of participation, in the construction of the filmic image? It is the rambling expansion and proliferation of forms that obscures the clarity of the rectangular and sinuous outlines. There is an early interference which probably remains unnoticed by the spectator. In the studio's entrance hall, which is structured like a grid, the camera moves along a wall adorned with a publicity photo that shows a beautiful woman against a background full of big green leaves. When, towards the end, Soraya is filmed through a screen of plants that populate the set, as if she were trapped in yet another labyrinth, it becomes quite apparent that Antonioni wishes to thwart the strict geometry of forms. For a short while, the storm seems to sweep away the grid. It is under these precarious circumstances that a mood emerges which keeps changing between the genuine and the reified. It is a shabby and mysterious mood.

In Richard Strauss's *Ariadne auf Naxos* (first performed 1912), the listener finds himself ultimately captivated by the *opera seria*, though the fact that it is an exceedingly artificial art form and that it has ceased to be taken seriously is constantly highlighted, so much so that the lament over its loss results in a celebration of its merging with the *opera comica*. In Nabokov's novel *Pale Fire* (1962), which consists of a long commentary on a poem, there is a section depicting an adventurous escape from an imaginary kingdom. At the end of this section, the charlatan who has allegedly written the commentary addresses the reader directly. He believes the reader will have found the narrative amusing. If the reader's amusement were based exclusively on the recognition of literary topoi, it would prove rather artificial. In *Shooting Stars* (1928), Anthony Asquith's first silent movie, one of its protagonists, a character who plays a film actor specialising in the role of a hero, goes to the cinema. He watches himself on the screen, gets all excited and starts applauding when the hero rescues the girl. Later on, he wishes life would be more like cinema.

Two years after *Il provino* was made, Luchino Visconti, with whom Antonioni collaborated in 1946 on the extensive script *Il processo di Maria Tarnowska*, a story told from incompatible perspectives,[3] contributed to the portmanteau film *Le streghe* (1967) with the episode *La strega bruciata viva*. Once again, the producer of the film was Dino De Laurentiis; once again, the film was all about a woman, with Silvana Mangano in different parts; once again, De Laurentiis made arbitrary cuts to the episode without the director's consent; and once again the director repudiated the film's final version. Like Antonioni's portrayal of a princess who does a screen test and is persecuted by the press, Visconti's episode offers both an internal and an external view of the life of a celebrity, each view pointing to one of the two aspects of participation in art. Comparing these films is worth the effort because Visconti does not reduce melodrama to its remainder, to the peculiar emergence of a mood that allows the spectator to participate in the film without mediation. He continues to trust the force of empathy, of identification with a fictional character, in the same manner as Antonioni does when Soraya asks her mother to be by her side. Gloria, a famous actress, faints in a smart Kitzbühl cottage. She has been playing a parlour game and the other guests decide to help her regain consciousness by undressing her, by deconstructing her appearance piece by piece, as it were. First, they remove her startling wig, with all the hair combed up high to form a sort of turban, then they take off her heavy mink eyelashes and the plasters that tighten her skin around her eyes. Before a private assistant restores the actress's image in the morning, the image into which her face has petrified, Visconti shows her in the middle of night, when she is not wearing any make-up. She is speaking on the phone, talking to her husband, an important and influential producer who is overseas. Gloria tells him that she is pregnant, begs him not to force her into having an abortion because of an upcoming film project, and collapses when he refuses to listen to her. 'Underneath the masks that we have been obliged to wear, we, the famous actresses, the witches of the present, are also women of flesh and blood' – this is what the film's trivial message seems to be saying. In a former contribution to a portmanteau film, the episode he made for *Siamo donne* (1953), Visconti had managed to make the same message more appealing by incorporating it into a subtle and profound play of fiction and reality. Here, Gloria's melodramatic scene leaves the spectator indifferent, as if the awareness of the as-if, heightened by the thematisation of artificiality and the lushness of the production, undermined the grounds for immediate participation. The comparison between the two films, between *Il provino* and *La strega bruciata viva*, demonstrates that Antonioni appears to be the director with a more acute sense of the possibility and the impossibility of art, precisely because he does not sacrifice one aspect of participation to the other, and succeeds in transforming immediacy at the very limit of its disappearance, there where a quasi-mood emerges.

Yet isn't participation in art, no matter how immediate, always a feeling, an emotion, an attunement that requires a qualifying adverb, since it can never be real participation, a participation in real life or a participation that partakes of reality? This is exactly the thesis supported by the North American philosopher Kendall L. Walton in his book *Mimesis and Make-Believe*. Walton begins by stressing the double character of participation in art and speaks of a 'dual perspective',[4] distinguishing between participation and observation, which, according to his terminology, does not belong to participation. Thus observation designates the attitude of a spectator who does not simply watch a game but thinks of other possible ways of playing it: 'But imagined participation is not actual participation, and imagined participation, let alone imagining merely that there is a game to participate in, does not constitute involvement in a fictional world. We stand apart from the internal fictional world and observe it through its frame.'[5] Walton explicitly aligns the distinction between the perspective of participation and the perspective of observation with the distinction between an inner and an outer perspective, and emphasises that there is gap which separates both. One cannot participate in a game and observe it at the same time. This is probably why the terminological distinction between participation and observation is important to Walton:

163

> We don't just observe fictional worlds from without. We live in them ... together with
> Anna Karenina and Emma Bovary and Robinson Crusoe and the others, sharing their
> joys and sorrows, rejoicing and commiserating with them, admiring and detesting them.
> True, these worlds are merely fictional, *and we are well aware that they are*. But *from
> inside* they seem actual – what fictionally is the case is, fictionally, *really* the case – and
> our presence in them ... gives us a sense of intimacy with characters and their other
> contents. It is this experience that underlies much of the fascination representations have
> for us and their power over us.[6]

As can be gauged from this quotation, Walton's description of the different perspectives points out their distinctiveness and yet betrays a certain ambiguity. This ambiguity is due to the fact that there is something inherently problematic about participation. It dominates the usage he makes of the adverb 'quasi' when referring to the emotions of the one who participates in art. Precisely because the observer knows that the world of an artwork is fictional, precisely because participation in art is not 'really' or 'actually' the same as participation in the real world, precisely because its immediacy is ultimately determined by a set of special rules, one cannot but ask oneself what it means to 'really' or 'actually' be inside a fictional world, participate in the game of art, follow its rules and have a feeling of proximity and intimacy with fictional characters. Walton realises that the horrified scream of a spectator who watches a horror movie seems 'absurdly out of place' when 'the fictional status of danger is made explicit',[7] but he also realises that participation and observation, or immediate and mediated participation, cannot truly be separated: 'One can hardly do either without doing the other, and nearly simultaneously.'[8] This 'nearly' indicates a simultaneity charged with tension, the simultaneity of a double comportment towards art. Must it then not determine the usage of the qualifying adverb 'quasi' each time that the immediacy of an emotion or a mood caused by the work of art is to be designated?

Walton brings in the hillbilly who does not understand what art is, since he has not learned to apply a decisive criterion of art, namely the interdiction of 'physical interaction' between the real and the fictional world. The hillbilly's naive comportment towards art proves inadequate. Next, the philosopher asks how to understand an emotion of pity or anger provoked by the artwork, an emotion that can be regarded as a 'genuinely emotional experience'[9] but cannot provide a motivation for action; to refer to such a 'physiological-psychological state' he coins the expression 'quasi-emotion'. A 'quasi-emotion' should not be interpreted as being only half an emotion, just as it should not be interpreted as excluding a 'real' emotion, for example 'real fear'.[10] In his book, Walton regularly relies on the difference between the reality of the actual and the reality of the real; yet he does not make this difference explicit, and the way in which he employs the concepts of the actual and the real does not seem to concur with the way in which they are traditionally employed in the history of philosophy. Is he seeking a criterion that will allow him to distinguish a 'quasi-emotion' from a 'real' emotion? That he does not always use 'actual' and 'real' as different concepts and that the conceptual difference itself remains unthematised shows perhaps the difficulty that Walton faces. 'Quasi-fear' is not meant to be a special kind of fear, a 'fictional' fear, for when one relates to a work of art and watches a film, for instance, one can 'actually' experience something that 'fictionally', on the basis of what art or fiction require, is an experience of fear. One does not 'imagine merely *that* one is afraid', rather one 'imagines *being* afraid' and one does so '*from the inside*'; hence the 'remarkably realistic character'[11] of psychological participation. Inasmuch as fiction and reality are not incompatible and something can be true within the context of a work of art, one should never conclude that one does not 'actually' feel fear. However, a fictional truth cannot stand on the same grounds on which a phenomenological description examines an 'actual' feeling. Moods are supposed to be a limit case to the extent that they cannot be located clearly on one side of the divide between 'our actual mental lives'[12] and our 'mental lives' in fictional worlds, at least not with the same accuracy with which thoughts and feelings concerning 'purely fictional objects' can. If, then, a mood can be the remainder of melodrama, as is the case in Antonioni's *Il provino*, this would mean that melodrama would be particularly relevant to an elucidation of the double character of participation in art – but precisely there where it no longer affirms itself as melodrama.

The conceptual vagueness and the tricky malleability of the 'quasi' suggest that, despite all assurances to the contrary, Walton is torn between the immediacy and the mediation of participation in art, or between participation and observation, all the more so as the 'quasi' is designed to render the boundaries more reliable and not to allow for the acknowledgment of a porosity that turns the making of distinctions into a difficult task. This does not entail, of course, that Walton is immune to objections such as the ones Kathleen Stock raises against his 'separatism', or against the manner in which he uses the 'quasi'. If emotions need to be 'quasi-emotions' because the one who participates in a work of art is always aware of the fact that the object or the character to which the emotion refers does not exist in reality, then, Stock claims, it is perfectly possible to recognise that the object or the character in question does not exist in reality, though one does not have to be aware or conscious of this fact; one may well feel an emotion that is not in need of adverbial qualification.[13] The emotion is really a real emotion, as it were, except in the cases when the parentheses placed around consciousness, around the awareness of the non-existence of the fictional object or character, leave a symptomatic mark in the participant's 'mental life'. Yet the argument levelled against Walton, an argument that unhinges his 'separatism', or cancels the separation between reality and fiction that is supposed to be a starting point for participation in art, seems to promote a different kind of 'separatism'. For it amounts to a denial of the quasi-simultaneity of immediacy and mediation to which Walton holds fast so that he can account for participation as participation in *art*, for participation and observation in the domain of fictions.

165

When construing the emotion triggered by a fiction as a 'quasi-emotion', Walton lets himself be guided by the idea of a coherent theory of participation, even though he does not develop the concept sufficiently; at times the 'quasi' seems closer to reality, and at other times it seems closer to fiction, as it were. Conceptually, both tendencies are reflected in the equally problematic quasi-simultaneity of participation and observation, or immediacy and mediation. Stock wishes to renounce the artifice of a 'quasi-emotion' and pays the price of not being able to do justice to art *as* art, to art as something produced intentionally and conventionally by an artist. Thus the hillbilly wins out over Walton after all – and yet he does not. His reaction, for which Stock's counter-argument paves the way, signals that the internal view, the belief in the artist's product, does not simply allow for the external view, the awareness of an artist having produced the work of art. There is a rupture between the two views, as melodrama evidences; viewed from outside, melodrama appears not only as an exaggeration but also as a ridiculous and even vacuous representation. Both in the case of Walton and in the case of Stock the tension between the two aspects of participation, or between participation and observation, is not maintained. Rather, in each case the uncontrollable unity of separation and inseparability is dissolved in favour of separation or inseparability.

It is possible to watch the last scene of Soraya's screen test as if it were nothing but an attempt to denounce semblance, the semblance of art, there where semblance has turned into the kitsch of false romanticism; then one watches it from the external view of an awareness of the as-if, and one almost observes Antonioni as he makes his film. But it is also possible to allow for the mood that emerges in this last scene to have a captivating effect, at least intermittently; then one is likely to watch it from the internal view of immediate participation and to forget for a moment the view from outside, no matter how fragmented the view from inside may be. Independently of how, exactly, one watches the film, one will always have to relate to the other perspective. This is what participation in art means. That such a relation, such comportment towards art, renders conceptual determination somewhat difficult and challenging, can perhaps be taken as a sign of the so-called enigmatic character of art. But it is also the reason for the relevance of participation in art; that is, it testifies to the fact that artworks are never simply a given. One has to measure up to a work of art, participate in it and pass the test, as it were, because the work is merely an audition, the necessary preface to participation.

Notes

1. A German version of this text was published in: *Neue Rundschau*, vol. 4 (Frankfurt am Main: Fischer Verlag, 2009).
2. Michelangelo Antonioni, 'Making a Film is My Way of Life' [1959], in *The Architecture of Vision: Writings and Interviews on Cinema*, ed. Carlo Di Carlo and Giorgio Tinazzi, trans. Marga Cottino-Jones (New York: Marsilio, 1996), pp. 14–17 (p. 14).
3. Michelangelo Antonioni et al., *Il processo di Maria Tarnowska. Una sceneggiatura inedita* (Milan: Il castoro, 2006).
4. Kendall L. Walton, *Mimesis as Make-Believe* (Cambridge, MA, and London: Harvard University Press, 1990), p. 49. Walton defines participation as an achievement of the imagination. We imagine 'from the inside *doing* and *experiencing* things' (p. 212).
5. Ibid., p. 284.
6. Ibid., p. 273. The first emphasis is my own.
7. Ibid., p. 392.
8. Ibid., p. 394.
9. Ibid., p. 197.
10. Ibid., p. 199.
11. Ibid., p. 247.
12. Ibid., p. 252.
13. Kathleen Stock, 'Desires towards Fictional Characters', manuscript 2008, University of Sussex, pp. 3ff.

David Forgacs

FACE, BODY, VOICE, MOVEMENT:
Antonioni and Actors

As a director of actors Antonioni has not had a good press. He himself was partly responsible for this. As early as 1948 he expressed reservations about the methods of directing actors used by Marcel Carné (with whom he had worked as assistant director in 1942 on *Les Visiteurs du soir*) in the following words: 'Carné admires actors, and this is exactly what great directors of actors do not do, Sternberg for example. Indeed Sternberg goes further: he despises them, but in despising them he dominates them.'[1] Later he admitted that on the set of *Cronaca di un amore* (1950) he had slapped the inexperienced Lucia Bosé to undermine her 'natural cheerfulness' and make her cry and had deliberately withheld information from the more experienced Massimo Girotti to keep him in a state of uncertainty and get just the performance he was looking for.[2] He said that Steve Cochran, his male lead on *Il grido* (1957), had shown a lack of intelligence in refusing to do what he asked him, complaining 'I'm not a puppet.' On the same film Betsy Blair, whom by contrast he described as 'a very intelligent actress', gave him 'one of the most terrible and painful' moments of his career when she insisted on going through the script asking him to explain each of her lines.[3] In between *L'avventura* (1960) and *L'eclisse* (1962) his public remarks on the subject of actors included 'an actor does not have to understand', 'the actor is a Trojan horse in the director's citadel' and 'the actor is an element in a particular shot, just as a wall, a tree or a cloud are elements of that shot'.[4]

It is true that some actors who worked with Antonioni defended his unorthodox methods. Monica Vitti was a notable case, though since she was also Antonioni's partner at the time her defence was not seen as impartial. Jack Nicholson also spoke favourably of his experience of working with Antonioni on *The Passenger* (1975) while pointing out that 'to him actors are not the most important thing. They're sort of moving space.'[5] However, other actors were less generous and said they simply found his manner on set frustrating. Jeanne Moreau said of *La notte* (1961): 'Every day I felt morbid, near to suicide. I only knew what was going on from Mastroianni, who was charming, but not from Antonioni.'[6] Carlo Di Carlo has recalled how a

Antonioni filming *La notte* (1961)

furious Richard Harris walked out of *Il deserto rosso* (1964), when it had already overrun its production schedule, after Antonioni had refused to explain why he should move in a particular direction in front of the camera.[7] Mark Frechette stated in a television interview, shortly after the American release of *Zabriskie Point* (1970), in which he had been cast with no previous acting experience: 'I was desperate, working with a guy with his reputation and with what he knows about cinema. I wanted to learn something. But he wasn't teaching. So I got mad.'[8] Christine Boisson, who played Ida in *Identificazione di una donna* (1982), described Antonioni as 'very withdrawn into the depths of himself, particularly when he is working. … You get the impression that he pulls in the people around him and withdraws into a kind of depth, a centre, within himself in order to create his film.'[9]

These statements seem to build up a picture of a director who was aloof and controlling, intolerant of actors who wanted to know too much, even misanthropic. Did he himself not say on one occasion 'I like things very much, perhaps more than people'?[10] It is perhaps understandable not only that little critical attention has been devoted to Antonioni's work with actors but also that critics have sometimes turned away altogether from acting, and from people, in his films and concentrated instead on other aspects, such as their disruptions of conventional narrative structure, their treatment of time or the suggestive properties of architecture, space and inanimate objects. Seymour Chatman excluded actors and acting almost entirely when he defined the central characteristic of Antonioni's post-1960 films as 'narration by a kind of visual minimalism, by an intense concentration on the sheer appearance of things – the surface of the world as he sees it – and a minimisation of explanatory dialogue'.[11]

Yet in reality actors and acting were of considerable interest and importance to Antonioni. His lapidary remarks, such as the one about the actor as Trojan horse in the director's citadel, certainly reflect one aspect of his outlook, but there were many others. It needs to be remembered that some of those remarks were made in discussions with film school students, including students of acting, in other words in particular moments of public self-presentation at a transitional stage of his career, and there was perhaps a dose of curmudgeonliness or of deliberate provocation in them. If one reads the whole of those discussions and interviews one finds other statements that partly conflict with them: 'the director must make the actor understand what he has to do, what he has to represent in the film'; 'acting is one of the means the director can use to express an idea, whether figurative or strictly conceptual'; 'The film actor must work not on the plane of psychology but on that of imagination [*fantasia*]. And imagination switches on by itself, there are no buttons one's fingers can press.'[12]

Antonioni, it must also be remembered, was a director of actors for the screen in a more radical sense than most of his contemporaries. He came to directing from a background in film criticism and close observation of the work of other film directors, as well as in screenwriting, a trajectory similar to that followed later in France by Rivette, Rohmer, Truffaut and Godard, whose early work would be marked, as Antonioni's was, by a profound cinephilia. He did make one excursus into directing for the stage – in 1957, after the release of *Il grido*, when he set up a theatre company in Rome with Monica Vitti and Giancarlo Sbragia – but the experience was short-lived and the following year he started work on *L'avventura* and would never go back to theatre directing.[13] As a film director he treated acting as just one of a number of diverse elements in front of the camera that had to be carefully coordinated with one another. We could contrast this with, for instance, De Sica, who moved into directing from a successful career in film acting and had great empathy with his actors, or Fellini, who started out writing radio sketches and drawing cartoons, or Visconti (with whom Antonioni had worked in 1946 on the screenplay of his unmade film about Maria Tarnowska), who after the war worked both in cinema and theatre and later also in opera. All these directors organised their films around actors and expressive performance in a way that Antonioni would never do. Although a few of his Italian contemporaries, notably Giuseppe De Santis, followed

169

a career path similar to his, and although Rossellini had some affinities with him in deliberately pushing experienced actors into experimental situations (the exemplary case here was with Ingrid Bergman and George Sanders in *Journey to Italy* [1954]), Antonioni was the only one for whom directing films involved such a radical and consistent interrogation of the means of film-making itself.

Film acting can take many forms but it generally operates within a set of technical constraints that distinguish it from theatre acting. First, the actor in front of a camera must move within a limited rectangular frame, formed by the edges of the film, as marked out in the viewfinder or monitor. Within this frame, however, there is much potential for variation. The camera can be set at various angles to the actors and it can move in relation to them; the actor may be positioned at different distances from the lens, from extreme long shot to extreme close-up. The possibility of the close-up means that the face becomes far more important than in theatre acting and so too do little nuances of gesture that would escape a theatre audience seated at a fixed distance from the actors. Second, the script is rarely followed in sequence and the performance is generally broken up, according to the requirements of the production schedule, into scenes or parts of a scene, each of which may involve a separate rehearsal and multiple takes. In between scenes there are changes of camera set-up and sometimes of set, often with long waits for the actor in between. Again, this constraint can become an advantage, allowing small segments of performance to be concentrated on and enhanced through rehearsal. Third, in a film the actor's voice must be recorded through microphones and, if required, mixed alongside music and sound effects. The voice needs to be correctly directed to the microphone, but the lines can be spoken much more softly than on stage, where the voice must be projected into an auditorium. Microphones can capture its slightest nuances, whether it is recorded with direct sound or in post-production over a guide track.

Most directors are perfectly well aware of these aspects of film acting. They are in a sense its basic building blocks. What makes Antonioni's case distinctive is that rather than take them for granted and build up from them, he continued to play around with them, taking them apart and reassembling them in new combinations. It was as if each time an actor stood, moved or made a sound in front of a camera a new and different meaning began to be produced. Take the opening of *L'eclisse*, which he filmed in 1961 when he had already directed seven features. It is far more radical than anything he had done up to that point. It is as if he were reinventing cinema and the actor's function within it. The camera's changing positions and angles start to define the strained relationship between the two characters, played by Monica Vitti and Paco Rabal. The noise of the fan introduces a distinctive soundscape to the scene, as other noises do in later scenes and shots (the ropes smacking the flagpoles, water running out of the pierced rain barrel, the clop clop of the pony trap). It is only after the visual coordinates and sound effects have been set in place

Monica Vitti looks at the EUR water tower in *L'eclisse* (1962)

that the first line of dialogue comes in, over four minutes into the film, and the subsequent lines remain short and spaced wide apart.

In his discussion with film school teachers and students in the year he made *L'eclisse* Antonioni explained that his working method was first to spend half an hour on the empty set or outdoor location to 'feel the environment' and then to call the actors in and start rehearsing the scene.

> It can happen that a particular scene thought out at a desk doesn't work when you drop it into that particular environment and it is necessary to transform it, modify it. A particular line can have a different meaning when spoken against a wall and against the background of a road. Equally, a line spoken by a character in three-quarter view changes value when spoken in full face, just as it can change value if the camera is at a high or low angle. The director (and, I repeat, this is my own way of working) becomes aware of all these things only when he is at the place of work and begins to move characters according to the suggestions that come from being there. For this reason it is extremely rare for me to have shots already fixed in my mind beforehand.[14]

At work here was a principle that comes up repeatedly in Antonioni's statements: it is the director, not the actor, who determines the meaning of the actor's performance in a film. For him the line between director and actor was very clearly drawn and should not be crossed. Steve Cochran had resisted being told what to do because, according to Antonioni, he had pretensions of being a director himself, but that idea was 'simply absurd'. Antonioni described his own position as the opposite of that of Fred Zinnemann, who had said that after he had explained a role to an actor 'the actor must invent everything by himself'. For Antonioni, by contrast, when an actor sought to understand the deep meaning of a scene or a line his spontaneity was compromised and he became 'in a sense the director of himself'.[15] In arguing this, Antonioni was not unique among film-makers. Similar arguments had been put forward by Robert Bresson in favour of using non-actors rather than trained actors. 'When I'm standing in front of an actor', Bresson told students at the Institut des Hautes Études Cinématographiques in 1955, 'the more his power of expression increases, the more mine decreases.' He added 'what matters to me is to express myself, not to let him express himself. For me, the ideal film actor is the person who expresses nothing.'[16] For Antonioni, the actor can speak the lines in a particular way, but only the director can see how their meaning is affected by the position and angle of the camera and by the actor's movements within the set and only the director can hear how the intonation of the actor's voice will mix with the other sounds to be added to the scene and judge if it is right.[17] Here his contrast between Carné and Sternberg is again illuminating. In 'despising' and therefore dominating his actors, Sternberg was able to ensure that there was always a 'perfect fit between the gesture and the psychological moment', whereas in Carné's films the actors 'sometimes exceed the boundaries of their own filmic reality without the director noticing'.[18]

Let us examine briefly these separate elements of the actor's performance – the face, body, voice and movement – in the films of Antonioni's middle period. We can do this by looking at the exemplary case of Monica Vitti. She had had a theatrical training, under Sergio Tofano at the Accademia d'Arte Drammatica in Rome. Antonioni recalled that he first saw her on stage in a Feydeau farce. She then worked for him on the dubbing of *Il grido*. Afterwards they launched, together with Sbragia, the experiment of the joint theatre company. Vitti played Sally Bowles in *I am a Camera*, John Van Druten's stage adaptation of Isherwood's Berlin novels (later readapted as the Broadway musical *Cabaret*) as well as one of two female leads (the other was played by Virna Lisi) in a modern love triangle play, *Scandali segreti*, written by Antonioni with Elio Bartolini.[19] However, it was only when Antonioni cast her in *L'avventura* that he began radically to reshape her acting.

Antonioni described Vitti in 1961 as a 'very modern actress'; 'even in the theatre she never had those attitudes one usually calls "theatrical"'. He remarked that what was really striking about this 'extraordinarily expressive' actress was her 'highly mobile face', which a theatre audience would miss at a distance of 30 metres but which a film could capture.[20] She could stretch her face into comic or grotesque expressions, as she does when she looks in the mirror towards the end of *L'avventura*, or when she grins and dances in blackface in *L'eclisse*. But she could also drain it of expression, give it an existential blankness, as she does when play-ing Giuliana in the opening sequence of *Il deserto rosso* on the wasteheaps. Her face is at once an impenetrable mask, a magnet for spectatorial desire and a channel for empathetic identification.

Vitti is also filmed as a body, often from the back or the side, as repeatedly in *L'avventura*. Whereas an actor in the theatre needs to face or stand at three-quar-ters to the audience, at least when delivering lines, in order for his or her voice to be properly heard, in the cinema this frontality can be completely undone. The micro-phone can be placed in front of the actor when his or her back is turned to the camera, or they can replace their dialogue with a new recording in postproduction. This flexibility of positioning and framing the body in film acting allowed Antonioni to free up the camera to move around Vitti. In that opening sequence of *L'eclisse* she is filmed over the shoulder as she moves objects on the table through an empty frame, then just her legs and feet are filmed under a table, reflected in the shiny floor. The filming of Vitti's body also involved a series of erotic transactions between director and actress, who were in a close relationship during the making of these films. In the three films of 1960–64 in which she plays the female lead, as several critics noted at the time, a back-and-forth slippage occurs between the character in the diegesis and the woman playing that character, between Vitti acting a role and Vitti simply being on screen. She is Claudia, Vittoria, Giuliana but she is also Monica Vitti. This is, perhaps, partly an inevitable effect of the re-use of the same actress in the three films and partly the result of family resemblances between the three characters (consider, for instance, the way each of them pulls back from the first advances of a new lover), but it is not only this. It is also the consequence of the particular way in which Vitti is directed to be on screen, to stand against a par-ticular background, to bring her face in close-up into the frame, to hold up her long thin fingers. Frozen into a series of almost still shots, the beautiful woman momen-tarily leaves the cinematic narrative and re-enters the paratexts of cinema: the fash-ion photograph, the illustrated magazine article about the film star.

Before Vitti was a face or a body in Antonioni's films she was a voice. On *Il grido* she had re-voiced Dorian Gray, the Italian actress who played Virginia. Vitti's distinctive voice, which could be modulated from high and girlish to gravelly to a slightly hoarse laugh, could be heard in its full expressive range when recorded through a studio microphone, more than when she performed on stage. Antonioni then deployed that range in each of the films in which she acted the lead. In *Il deserto rosso*, for instance, when Giuliana tells her son Valerio the story of the girl on the island of pink sand, Vitti's voice is almost hypnotic in its gentleness, whereas when she delivers her monologue to the Turkish sailor at the docks it is nervous and the speech is broken.

In a series of early articles Antonioni had objected to the practice, which had become established in Italy soon after the advent of the talkies, of dubbing all foreign-language films, including films of quality. He noted that this was not done in other countries (in France, for instance, parallel versions were made, dubbed and subtitled) and argued that it was a peculiarly Italian blight. One of its consequences was that the original voice of the actor became separated from his or her face and another voice usurped it. This ran counter to the fact that 'acting – gestures and language – is the result of a single and simultaneous inspiration in the actor'.[21] Matters were made even worse when the Italian dubbing actor sought to emulate or compete with the original actor's vocal performance style. Antonioni, of course, himself used dubbing and dialogue replacement in his films, not only when he cast foreign actors in his Italian films (such as Cochran, Blair, Harris, Moreau, Delon) but also with an Italian actor like Dorian Gray, and from *Blow-Up* onwards he was obliged to produce Italian-dubbed versions of his own English-language films for release in Italy. But, as Carlo Di Carlo noted, he came to take great care over voice dubbing, insisting that the voice, the acoustic properties of the recording space and the nature of the vocal performance be very carefully chosen and controlled.[22]

Finally, the particular ways in which Antonioni directed Vitti's movements are worth noting. In the opening sequence of *L'eclisse*, there is a complex shot which starts with Vitti facing away from the camera, placed just above her head, and looking at Riccardo (Rabal) who stares beyond her into empty space. The camera then dollies very slowly back and to the left as Vitti edges away from Rabal, until she stops at a mark where Rabal is still just in frame, now on the extreme right of the shot. She is facing a mirror in a recess in the room on the extreme left of the shot, and the whole space of the main room now lies exposed between them. Vitti is still looking at Rabal but we now see her reflected in the mirror, so that both actors' faces appear turned towards camera at opposite edges of the frame. Vitti stares at Rabal, then glances very briefly at herself in the mirror, then back at him, then turns on her heels and gasps. As she quickly twists her whole body clockwise, the camera tracks left just a few inches to exclude Rabal and most of the other part of the room from the frame, and we now see only Vitti, and no longer her reflection, which is obscured by her head, nearer to camera and facing us.

One could make various points about this carefully staged take but perhaps the one most relevant to the acting is that it involves a meticulous control of the actors' movements and their relative positions in the frame as well as of their facial expressions. In a sense, any two other actors could have performed this shot, if they had followed the same instructions from the director, except that the director has made these two particular faces, and these two bodies – one motionless, the other nervously in motion – part of the material of the sequence.

Vitti remains a special case, the principal female actor in three of Antonioni's films of 1960–64, and the public face of his cinema in this period. But she was not the only theatrically trained actor whose performance style he made over. Jeanne Moreau, who had started at the Comédie Française before acting in films, and was used to a

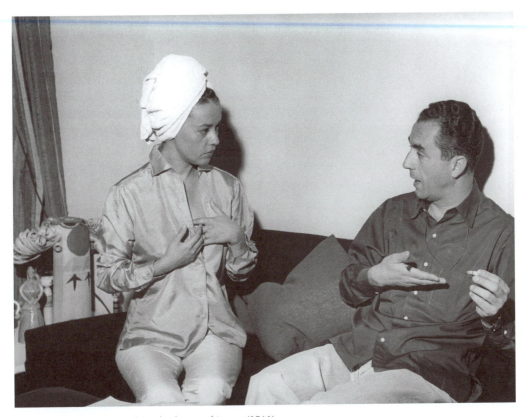

Jeanne Moreau and Antonioni during the shooting of *La notte* (1961)

certain way of preparing a role, complained of being cut adrift by Antonioni's lack of communication on the set of *La notte* and of not being able to identify with her character, Lidia ('I hated acting the wife in that film,' she confided to Penelope Gilliat).[23] Nonetheless, she gives a performance of great range and subtlety. Early in the film, after having visited with Giovanni (Mastroianni) their terminally ill friend Tommaso at the clinic, Lidia/Moreau is filmed from the side crying with her back to the wall. Her chest convulses and she wipes away tears with the back of her hand. At the end she again wipes off a tear, shot this time from a low angle in full-face close-up, after having read to Giovanni his old love letter to her. In her long stroll through Milan her prim walk changes to a flirtatious flounce as she grabs the attention of a man with a sandwich. There is a similar stretching of the actor's range with Lilla Brignone, who plays Vittoria's stock exchange-addicted mother in *L'eclisse*. Her acting background was in Giorgio Strehler's Piccolo Teatro in Milan, then in other companies, and she was renowned for her expressive vocal performances in strong female parts, such as Ibsen's Nora Helmar and Strindberg's Miss Julie. Yet in Antonioni's film the camera concentrates not on her voice, which is kept at a low key, but on her small changes of facial expressions and her slightly matronly walk.

On this stretching of the trained actor the testimony of Vanessa Redgrave, who came from an acting family and had studied in London at the Central School of Speech and Drama, is particularly interesting. She was twenty-eight when she acted in *Blow-Up* and had a famous enough name to be given star billing on some of the posters.

> He was the first director who I'd worked with to whom it was a matter of absolute importance the shape one made as one sat, at what angle one sat, where the chair was, where anything was, and the movement or space between, above, below or transecting, that either a living object – a woman – or an inanimate object made. And as soon as I realized that what was really important to him, and as soon as he realized that I understood what was important to him, and that I wasn't going to get all English and start saying 'Why? 'What? 'If', 'But', we started connecting more precisely because he realized that I wanted to do exactly what he saw could be done, and that no one else could see it but him.[24]

What Redgrave does not mention is that Antonioni actually required quite a wide range of acting skills from her in *Blow-Up*. At one end of the scale was a naturalistic performance of barely controlled desperation in the dialogue in the park scene and again when she comes to the studio to ask for the pictures. In the park she attempts to wrest the camera from the hand of the photographer (like the character played by Redgrave, the one played by David Hemmings is never named in the film, although the screenplay refers to him as 'Thomas') and down on her knees she tugs at the camera strap and tries to bite his hand. He pulls it away and she is then filmed in close-up, panting, nervously moving her hand over her face and adjusting her hair. This was a typically 'expressive' form of acting that her theatre training had helped her produce. At the other end was her willingness to be positioned, as she describes, moved on set by the director, to stand with her weight shifted slightly onto one leg, and also to strip and display her naked back to the camera, in other words to be placed within the photogenic world of modelling and erotic photography that the film here evokes.

This change in her performance style is functional to the story. *Blow-Up* is an interesting film with regard to acting because the relationship between director and actors is ironically doubled in the relationship between the photographer and the people and places he photographs. The photographer stands in as a sort of amoral alter-ego for the film-maker: arrogant, bullying, at once sensually drawn to his female actors and intolerant of their failings. Fashion photography and modelling function here as equivalents for a highly controlled style of film directing. The photographer, like the director, positions his models exactly as he wants them, corrects their errors of performance ('I asked you to smile. What's the matter? Forgotten what a smile is?') and tells them when they may take a break.

Antonioni and David Hemmings on the set of *Blow-Up* (1966)

When the Redgrave character enters the studio she is ostensibly modified by that environment. The photographer makes her stand in front of a roll of coloured paper to try her out ('Not many girls can stand as well as that.' 'Come here. Show me how you sit.') But, having set up this parallel to the world of the film, Antonioni then allows it to break down. The photographer cannot always know or control what his camera records outside the studio. After enlarging the photographs, seeing the pistol in them, going back to the park and finding the corpse, and then returning to the studio to discover that the prints and negatives have been stolen, the photographer is changed. From then to the end of the film David Hemmings acts differently, with fear or bewilderment in his voice and face. Like the Redgrave character in those earlier scenes, the world is no longer in his grasp.

Blow-Up was not the only one of Antonioni's films in which acting and performance were foregrounded and thematised. Immediately before it he had made *Il provino*, the opening episode in the compilation film *I tre volti*, which Dino De Laurentiis produced as a vehicle for Soraya Esfandiary, the ex-wife of the Shah of Iran. Within Antonioni's career this is a perhaps a slight piece of work but it is both intelligent and sensitive in its exploration of performance and the woman's face. During Soraya's screen tests with different wigs and dresses the camera hangs on her face for just a little too long; she becomes distracted and the viewer can begin to scrutinise her. Conversely, in the moments when she is apparently caught off-guard, for instance in the dressing room speaking Farsi to her assistants, she is still being filmed, and the camera follows her, and is therefore still undergoing a screen test.

Three earlier films also centre on performance and the ambiguous line separating it from lived reality: *La signora senza camelie* (1952) and the shorts *L'amorosa menzogna* (1949) and *Tentato suicidio* (1953). The first plays around the slippage between Lucia Bosé and her fictional character, who is, like the 'real' Bosé, an actress of mediocre acting ability, cast for her sultry beauty and her figure, aspiring to play more culturally legitimated roles. The second, at one level a semi-humorous documentary about the world of the photo-romance, depicted as a poor cousin of the cinema, with its melodramatic stories shot in makeshift studios using part-time actors who enjoy minor star status among their working-class female fans, is at another level a representation of an uncanny style of frozen acting, with the performers striking successive poses in front of still cameras so that the resulting photographs can have speech bubbles added and be assembled into a narrative sequence. The third, one of the five short films in the compilation package *L'amore in città* (1953) overseen by Cesare Zavattini and responding to his ideas about a cinema of real life, examines acting more indirectly. Onto a sound stage, in front of a cyclorama, file a number of young men and women who, the voice-over explains, have survived actual suicide attempts and agreed to tell their stories on film. The camera tracks in front of them, picking out their faces as they stare at it or look off-screen. Into this dramatic frame the film inserts the stories of five survivors, all women, who tell and partly re-enact the events leading up to their suicide attempt and in some cases the attempt itself. The voice-over suggests that these real suicide attempts may be viewed as performances, ways in which these women sought to draw attention to themselves. Antonioni said after making it that he thought the women manifested 'an exhibitionist complex' in their willingness to recount and fictionally re-enact their stories to camera. In other words, what one might have assumed to be a private and unrepeatable anguish becomes a repeatable performance. 'They were happy to have tried to take their own lives and to be there talking about it in front of a camera. They were happy to earn some money in such an easy way.'[25]

Let me summarise the main points about Antonioni's work with actors in two general observations. First, although he was highly exacting and demanding as a director, with a clear sense of what he wanted to achieve, he was not, as a certain critical tendency has sometimes portrayed him, and as some of his own remarks might imply, an anti-humanist or abstract film-maker who reduced actors to mere elements in a landscape. There is always a tension in his films between the human presence and the natural or built environment, or between the human figure and an architectural feature or inanimate object. His particular concern was to make his actors work effectively as part of the total *mise en scène*, to light them expressively, to develop the expressiveness of their bodies, voices and faces and their movements within the frame. With these methods of directing he was able to stretch the range of performance of trained actors (most notably Monica Vitti, with whom his directing also involved complex erotic transactions, similar to those of Godard with Anna Karina), and to make others work against the types they had established in their previous films. One notable example of the latter is Alida Valli as Irma in *Il grido*. There are some echoes of her earlier roles, for example as Anna in *The Third Man* (1949), but her performance in *Il grido* is much more radically contained, with hardly any display of outward emotion, except in the scene with her sister where she asks if she is doing the right thing in leaving Aldo. The following scene where, after Aldo has slapped her repeatedly in the street, she ties up her hair and tells him quietly but firmly that it really is now all over, is a masterpiece of this kind of contained acting. The contrast with her performance just three years earlier as the passionate Livia in Visconti's *Senso* (1954) could not be more marked. Yet Antonioni was also skilful in eliciting eloquent performances from untrained actors, such as Carlo Chionetti, who played Giuliana's cold husband Ugo in *Il deserto rosso*, or Mark Frechette and Daria Halprin in *Zabriskie Point*. The scene where Daria hears on the radio the news that Mark has been shot dead on the landing strip is a good example of how Antonioni could direct an untrained actor to stand and breathe expressively. The rest of the emotional charge of that shot is conveyed by the framing – Daria positioned in the left half of the widescreen frame, her back turned to the car – and by the mixing of the dubbed sound.

179

Second, Antonioni not only directed actors, trained or otherwise, throughout his career but his films often foregrounded acting and performance, and indeed in some cases made it a principal focus of attention. Most of his early short documentaries involved performance, not just in the thematic sense I have been describing in *L'amorosa menzogna* and *Tentato suicidio*, but in the more general sense in which much documentary production of that era was scripted and acted, with a careful direction of movement to camera: the family on the barge or the couple on the riverbank in *Gente del Po* (1947), the little comic vignette in *N.U.* (1948) when a man tears up a letter in front of his wife as they cross a bridge and a street cleaner moves in to sweep up the pieces, the staged enactments of magical incantations and prophylactic rituals in *Superstizione* (1949). At a deeper level, the opacity of performance, which leaves uncertain what may lie behind a given action, word or gesture, becomes thematically central to the films of the early 1960s. In *L'avventura* does Sandro (Gabriele Ferzetti) really fall in love with Claudia (Monica Vitti) and she with him? What does she mean in stroking the back of his head in the final scene after he has betrayed her? Conversely, the conscious performance by a character embedded within the diegesis may suggest a desire to escape or the expression of fantasy. One may cite here two other scenes with Monica Vitti: the one already mentioned in *L'eclisse* where, as Vittoria, she enacts in Marta's apartment the colonialist fantasy of going native, and as Giuliana in *Il deserto rosso* simulating sexual arousal after eating the quail's egg. Or one may add further examples of people slipping in and out of performances. One that sustains a whole film is David Locke (Jack Nicholson) assuming, but not assimilating, the identity of the dead Robertson in *The Passenger*.

These two parallel tendencies in Antonioni – the control of an actor's body and voice to obtain desired effects in the edited film, and the making a character's conscious performance part of the film's diegesis, or even (in *The Passenger*) its theme – show just how important and sustained the exploration of acting was in his work as a whole. He was not, to be sure, an 'actor's director', in the sense in which that phrase is commonly understood, but he was an extremely careful and attentive director of actors. This distinction needs to be grasped and its implications fully understood. Antonioni's cinema is non-anthropomorphic, both in the sense that its diegetic world is not made to the measure of human figures and in the sense that its individual shots and framings do not always centre on the human figure and indeed sometimes crop, diminish or exclude it. But this does not mean that it is a cinema in which human beings as such are displaced and superseded by an inanimate world of things, in an anti-humanist or post-humanist sense. Antonioni's films, rather, engage with a tension, a crisis of purposive human action in a world where anomie, coldness or indifference, and the places and rhythms of industrial and postindustrial modernity, can make such action appear difficult, absurd or pointless. This is their repeated central drama, and one finds it again and again, from *Il grido* to *L'eclisse*, from *Il deserto rosso* to *Blow-Up*, from *The Passenger* to *Identificazione di una donna*. Antonioni's analytical approach to film acting – taking it apart into its constituent elements – and his interest in masks and performance are part and parcel of this critical engagement and the repeated restaging of this drama.

Notes

1. 'Marcel Carné, parigino', originally in *Bianco e Nero* no. 9 (1948), pp. 17–47, reproduced in Michelangelo Antonioni, *Sul cinema*, ed. Carlo Di Carlo and Giorgio Tinazzi (Venice: Marsilio, 2004), pp. 111–47 (p. 126). The translations of this and subsequent passages in this chapter are mine – DF. The chapter extends my earlier discussion of Antonioni's work with actors, 'Michelangelo Antonioni', in Paolo Bertetto (ed.), *Action! How Great Filmmakers Direct Actors* (Rome: minimum fax, 2007; also published in Italian), pp. 201–13.

2. 'Cronaca di un amore' (interview with Michele Gandin, *Il Progresso d'Italia*, 14 December 1950), in Michelangelo Antonioni, *Fare un film è per me vivere. Scritti sul cinema*, ed. Carlo Di Carlo and Giorgio Tinazzi (Venice: Marsilio, 1994), pp. 229–32 (p. 230). For English translations of this and all subsequent quotations

from *Fare un film è per me vivere*, see Michelangelo Antonioni, *The Architecture of Vision: Writings and Interviews on Cinema*, ed. Carlo Di Carlo and Giorgio Tinazzi, trans. Marga Cottino-Jones (New York: Marsilio, 1996).

3. 'La mia esperienza' (edited transcript of discussion with students at Centro Sperimentale di Cinematografia, Rome, 31 March 1958), in *Fare un film*, pp. 5–12 (p. 10). Betsy Blair recalled in her memoirs how upset she was when she read these remarks about her reported in *Cahiers du cinéma*; see *The Memory of All That: Love and Politics in New York, Hollywood and Paris* (New York: Knopf, 2003), pp. 275–9. I thank Jacopo Benci for showing me the transcript of his unpublished interview with Blair in 2006 in which she adds further details to this recollection.

4. The statements are, respectively, from 'La malattia dei sentimenti' (transcript of discussion with students and teachers at Centro Sperimentale, 16 March 1961) in *Fare un film*, pp. 20–46 (p. 35); 'Riflessioni sull'attore' (originally in *L'Europa Cinematografica*, July–August 1961) in ibid., pp. 47–9 (p. 47) (he uses the Trojan Horse metaphor also in 'La malattia dei sentimenti', p. 35); 'La malattia dei sentimenti', p. 36.

5. Vitti, interviewed in Gianfranco Mingozzi's documentary *Antonioni: Documents e témoignages* (Italian title: *Michelangelo Antonioni: storia di un autore*) (ONC Canada/IDI Cinematografica Roma, 1966), repeats his words about the actor being only one element of the whole film and needing to play by instinct and not intelligence. She also alludes, without naming names, to 'certain foreign actors' ('qualche attore straniero') who did not understand this and complained that their relations with Antonioni had been difficult. Nicholson's remark is in his commentary on the Sony Pictures DVD of *The Passenger* (2006).

6. Reported in Marianne Gray, *La Moreau: A Biography of Jeanne Moreau* (London: Little, Brown and Co., 1994), p. 54

7. Carlo Di Carlo told me this in an interview in March 2008 when I was researching my audio commentary for *Red Desert* (BFI Video DVD and Blu-ray, 2008; the commentary is also in the Criterion Collection edition, 2010). I am grateful to Carlo Di Carlo also for his replies and suggestions on the present chapter.

8. *The Dick Cavett Show*, ABC, tx 6 April 1970. Frechette and Daria Halprin were guests, along with Rex Reed and Mel Brooks. Reed, who had written a hostile review of *Zabriskie Point*, had just asked Frechette and Halprin what it was like to work with Antonioni after having told them, 'I did an interview with him once in which he said that he despises actors and that he has no use for them at all and actors are like cattle, you walk them through a fence.'

9. Christine Boisson interviewed by Emmanuel Decaux, *Cinématographe* no. 84, special Antonioni issue (December 1982), (pp. 30–3), p. 33.

10. André S. Labarthe, 'Entretien avec Michelangelo Antonioni', *Cahiers du cinéma* vol. 19 no. 112 (1960), pp. 1–14 (p. 8).

11. Seymour Chatman, *Antonioni, or the Surface of the World* (Berkeley and Los Angeles: University of California Press, 1985), p. 2.

12. The statements are respectively from 'La mia esperienza', p. 9; 'Paradossi sugli attori' (originally in *Mondo nuovo*, 27 December 1959) in *Fare un film*, pp. 17–19 (p. 17); 'Riflessioni sull'attore', p. 47.

13. For a well-documented discussion of this theatrical interlude see Federico Vitella, 'Michelangelo Antonioni drammaturgo. *Scandali segreti*', *Bianco e Nero* vol. 70 no. 563 (2009), pp. 79–93.

14. 'La malattia dei sentimenti', p. 29. David Hemmings recalled Antonioni making a similar remark to him during the filming of *Blow-Up* about the way the meaning of an actor's performance changed according to how he positioned the camera. The recollection is in the RAI-BBC documentary *Caro Antonioni*, directed by Gianni Massironi, tx RAI1 1995, and, with the title *Dear Antonioni*, tx BBC2 *Arena*, 18 January 1997.

15. 'La mia esperienza', pp. 10, 9, 10. The remark about the actor who becomes the 'director of himself' is repeated in 'La malattia dei sentimenti', p. 35.

16. ' "Une mise en scène n'est pas un art": Robert Bresson rencontre les étudiants de l'Idhec (décembre 1955)', *Cahiers du cinéma* no. 543 (2000), pp. 4–9 (p. 5).

17. 'La malattia dei sentimenti', p. 36.

18. 'Marcel Carné, parigino', p. 126.

19. Vitella, 'Michelangelo Antonioni drammaturgo'.

20. 'La malattia dei sentimenti', p. 41.

21. 'Vita impossibile del signor Clark Costa' (originally in *Cinema* vol. 105 no. 10 November 1940), in *Sul cinema*, pp. 155–62 (p. 156).

22. See Carlo Di Carlo, 'Nota ai testi sul doppiaggio', in *Sul cinema*, pp. 166–7, and his interview with Flavio De Bernardinis, 'L'invenzione viscerale della modernità', in *Segnocinema* no. 118 (2002), pp. 16–18 (p. 17).

23. The remark is reported in Gray, *La Moreau*, p. 53.

24. The original audio of the interview with Redgrave is in the English edition of Massironi's *Dear Antonioni*.

25. 'Tentato suicidio' (Episodio di *L'amore in città*) (1953)', in *Fare un film*, pp. 69–70. On re-enactment in this film, see the astute discussion by Ivone Margulies, 'Exemplary Bodies: Reenactment in *Love in the City*, *Sons*, and *Close Up*', in Ivone Margulies (ed.), *Rites of Realism: Essays on Corporeal Cinema* (Durham, NC: Duke University Press, 2002), pp. 217–44. See also the interesting recent article by Roberta Piazza, 'Voice-over and Self-narrative in Film: A Multimodal Analysis of Antonioni's *When Love Fails* (*Tentato Suicidio*)', *Language and Literature* vol. 19 no. 2 (2010), pp. 173–95.

Medium Specifics

Matilde Nardelli

BLOW-UP AND THE PLURALITY OF PHOTOGRAPHY

Michelangelo Antonioni's *Blow-Up* (1966) is still probably one of the best-known films 'about' photography, and one in which particular photographs play a prominent narrative and aesthetic part. Not only does photography as an activity permeate the film, but the snapshots of a lovers' tryst that Thomas chances to take in the park constitute a central diegetic and formal motif, on which hang both the murder-mystery plot and the visually arresting sequence in which the photographs are filmed at length by the movie camera as the intrigued photographer enlarges them and scrutinises them in his studio.[1] This complex and conspicuous narrative and aesthetic staging of photography has generated a variety of responses. It has been seen as a philosophical allegory of the nature of reality and our purchase on it; as a more or less conscious exploration of the specific ontology of the photographic image and the structures of seeing and knowing encapsulated within it; as a vicarious meditation on cinema itself – and, often, as all of the above together. In all of these interpretations, photography's status as a reproduction of reality – even, literally, as a take *of* rather than *on* the real – is a crucial focus, however problematic or problematised this status is seen to be in the film. However, as I will argue, *Blow-Up*'s engagement with photography is also inspired by another fundamental sense of both 'reality' and 'reproduction' vis-à-vis the medium. As well as the reality *in* photography, the real captured within the image, the film addresses the reality *of* photography: the material realisation and proliferation of photographs – or, indeed, the 'facts' of photographic production and reproduction which, as we shall see, make photography intrinsically 'plural'. In fact, it could further be said that in fundamental respects *Blow-Up* speaks of the reality of photography in the 1960s – namely, its 'boom' – during which, from magazines and photobooks to family and amateur picture taking, the production and reproduction of photographs multiplied.

Reality Check

While *Blow-Up* is surely familiar to most, it is helpful here to start with a brief recapitulation of its plot, touching in particular on the points important to the discussion to follow. As is well known, the film revolves around Thomas, a successful and somewhat disenchanted fashion photographer in the 'swinging' London of the 1960s, whom Antonioni styled on real-life contemporaries such as David Bailey.[2] As well as doing fashion shoots, Thomas is working on a photobook – a project whose focus on urban degradation and deprivation stands in stark contrast to the glamorous subjects of his other work. It is possibly while out in search of inspiring photo opportunities for this project that he chances upon a couple in a park who attracts his attention, and whose seemingly romantic encounter he captures with a series of furtive, acrobatically taken, snapshots. When the woman notices his presence, her great distress at having been photographed further fuels Thomas's interest in this apparently banal situation. But ignoring her pleas to hand over the roll of film – she will even, somewhat mysteriously, track him down at his studio to try and recover it in exchange for sexual favours – Thomas finally manages to develop the exposures. He then sets out to examine them by printing a selection of enlargements, and enlargements of enlargements, which he arranges as a sequence along the walls of his studio. After further magnification of portions of two of the images, he eventually believes he can discern a gunman and a corpse. The 'objectivity' of this conclusion is not *quite* confirmed in the film, as not only is the final blow-up with the victim's body extremely grainy and almost abstract, but the fact of the murder itself is left unresolved as the story unfolds. When Thomas returns to the spot in the park at night, without his camera, the body seems to be there, yet, when he goes back again in the morning – this time with his camera – there is nothing there (any more). Meanwhile, his studio has been raided and all the negatives and prints taken from it, except for the last, very grainy enlargement. In the final sequence of the film, Thomas sees again a dressed-up group of protesters, the same ones he bumps into at the beginning of the film. They are miming a game of tennis, but when Thomas joins in, and throws back to them the imaginary ball they have lost, the ball can actually be heard bouncing back and forth from one racket to the other. Though unseen and, one would think, imaginary, the ball is in fact, it seems, surprisingly 'real'.

It is easy to see how such a plot encourages speculation on both reality as such and reality *in* photography. And as I have already noted, whether they consider it an existential allegory of the nature of reality and appearance, or a more specific analysis of the ontology of photography and, by extension (in view of their shared material base) of cinema (or, in fact, as is often the case, as a mixture of the above), most scholarly accounts of *Blow-Up* have called upon the notion of photography as a record of the real.[3] For instance, Seymour Chatman has remarked that '[p]hotographs are, of course, by definition visual records of the actual', while the

Russian semiotician Jurij Lotman has suggested not only that '[w]ith respect to reality, photography functions as a reproduction', but that the still photographs specifically function in *Blow-Up* as something 'equivalent to reality itself'.[4] Finally, Amelia Jones, insisting specifically on the 'indexical' and 'analogue' character of photography in its pre-digital life, has recently summarised *Blow-Up* as being 'about chasing down the truth with the photographic apparatus, and within the photographic image'.[5]

However, as the film plot itself almost makes inevitable, most accounts, including the examples above, have also reflected on the ways in which *Blow-Up* complicates or throws into question the reality ostensibly captured by photography. Thus, in the discussion cited above, Chatman argues that the film also shows how photography's 'visual records' are liable to being used 'fictional[ly]'.[6] Crucially, Thomas makes such fictional use not only of his fashion work but also of the very photos within which he wants to discover fact, evidence – for, as others have noted, Thomas's examination of these pictures builds a story out of them. It is as much a construction as a reconstruction of the event, a 'narrativiz[ation]' or 'entexting' which both builds upon, and departs from, their value as records.[7] Lotman has also pointed to the way in which, as well as drawing attention to the 'textuality' of a series of pictures, *Blow-Up* highlights how even a single photograph is always already a text, an interpretation. As the episode in the park is offered twice in the film, first, as shot in colour by the movie camera, and then, through Thomas's black-and-white enlargements, *Blow-Up* allows reflection – or, itself, reflects – on how even an individual photographic image constitutes a take *on* reality rather than simply a take *of* it. For, as Lotman has explained, while we are returned to the park episode by the photographs, that episode, interpreted by Thomas's compositional choices, is also substantially different from the film sequence seen earlier. Lotman highlights in particular its being more in 'close-up' and 'differently arranged', as 'the edges of the photograph have cut off the entire surrounding landscape, focusing only on the two human figures'.[8] If all of this relativises the status of photography as reality by showing it to be a complex representation, a mediation through – at least – eye, camera, film stock and specific format and display of the final image, the film is also seen to challenge this status more radically, by highlighting the medium's inherent opacity and indeterminacy. As critics have often noted, the motif of the progressive enlargements draws attention to how photography may ultimately obscure or even 'lose' the real, rather than help its capture and disclosure. As image yields to grain, the reality *in* photography 'disappear[s] into a general atomic welter',[9] delivering not 'truth' but 'the *diffusion* of truth into surface'[10] – a 'failure' of photography which, in Jones's somewhat schematic reading, is further representative of the 'failure' of a (modernist) model of seeing and knowing the world.[11]

But whether the 'disappearance' or 'diffusion' of the real in the photograph is symbolic of our relation to the world – and even, as Jones suggests, of the point of rupture of a specific epistemic and aesthetic regime – or not, what remains, and is in fact brought into the foreground in this pulverisation, is precisely the material surface of the photograph. Indeed, what, more generally, the concentration on *Blow-Up* as a critique of photography's purchase on the real fails to point out is that what is thrown into relief in this very process is the reality *of* photography itself – or *at least*, and from our historical standpoint, the reality of photography in its pre-digital incarnation. Just as the real in the photographs is problematised and even obscured, the materials and procedures essential to the realisation and experience of photographs (certainly those that were essential to photography before digital-ity) are brought to light. Antonioni himself had in fact underlined this when, com-menting on the short story by Julio Cortázar on which the film is based, he said that he 'was not so much interested in the events as in the technical aspects of photog-raphy. I discarded the plot and wrote a new one in which the equipment itself assumed a different weight and significance.'[12] Perhaps it is even possible to see *Blow-Up* as less preoccupied with photography as the reproduction of reality than with the reality of photography as reproduction *as such*. Or, to put it slightly dif-ferently, *Blow-Up* may be more concerned with the 'how' than with the 'what' of photography, more concerned, that is, with the conditions and processes through which photographs are (or were) generated and circulated than with photographic content and its nature. In fact, as we shall see later, this interest in photography's 'how' may even turn out to be an answer for 'what' photography (still) is.

Production, Reproduction

While photography had undoubtedly been a popular medium more or less from the start, its diffusion had reached new peaks in the years before *Blow-Up*'s release, as developments in camera and printing technologies, coupled with increased affluence, further fostered the taking and consuming of pictures.[13] For a start, cameras were being made at considerably lower costs and in far greater numbers than in previous years as, pioneered by Canon in 1959, their production gradually turned from high-skilled manufacture to line assembly.[14] In the same period, 35mm rollfilm finally overtook plates and film packs as a format of choice in professional photography, particularly as its suppleness and compactness met the practical needs of the bur-geoning field of photojournalism, from reportages from war zones such as Korea and Vietnam to more frivolous features for glossy magazines.[15] An indication of the 'advantages' of this transition can be gained by comparing the photo shoots in *Blow-Up* with the ones represented in a famous Hollywood musical of a few years earlier, *Funny Face* (Stanley Donen, 1957). While Thomas, in Antonioni's film, is all contortions and acrobatics thanks to his compact rollfilm camera, in the earlier film, both photographer and models are rather constrained (and restrained) by the use of

Funny Face
(Stanley Donen,
1957)

Blow-Up (1966)

189

the plate camera.[16] Small-format rollfilm for non-professional use, too, gained in popularity thanks to the development of easy-load, slot-in cartridges, developed for use in simple cameras such as the Kodak Instamatic (launched in 1963) and, over-all, increased automation of camera functions across the spectrum – from automatic exposure in inexpensive family machines to through-the-lens metering in high-quality models – made picture taking a much easier and faster activity. One of the reasons for the immediate popularity of the Nikon F camera – the very camera Thomas sports in *Blow-Up* – when it was launched in the late 1950s was the introduction of an optional film-winding motor drive which enabled the shooting of several pictures per second.

As a whole, these new ranges of equipment contributed to what photographers Martin Parr and Gerry Badger have recently described as 'the great photographic "boom"' of the 1960s.[17] In addition to the flourishing of professional photography, cheaper cameras and increased affluence encouraged the expansion of family and amateur markets: owning more than one camera to take snapshots of everyday life and holidays became common, as did dabbling with more complex equipment as a hobby. In fact, the fields of professional and family or amateur photography might often be connected given that, prior to photographic training's full institutionalisation in art schools and colleges (a process which, indeed, began in the 1960s), many professionals were self-taught. This was largely the case with Don McCullin, the famous British photojournalist – renowned for his hard-hitting coverage of areas of conflicts and deprivation – whom Antonioni commissioned to take the stills for the park sequence, and some of whose photographs also appear in Thomas's photobook project.[18] Furthermore, in a context of radical cultural and aesthetic upheaval, art also became an important locus of photographic production. While the status of photography as art had been debated as early as the medium's invention, it is in this period that photography became a widespread means of artistic production and was itself thoroughly consolidated as art – though, unlike in earlier periods, and not without irony, largely as a tool to mount a *critique* of art and its institutions in the context of emerging movements such as pop, happenings, conceptual and land art.[19]

Meanwhile, technological developments similarly contributed to boost the reproduction of photographs in print media – arguably the mode in which a great, if not the greatest, number of photographs would actually be experienced at the time. Mass-printing methods such as photo-engraving – themselves, literally, a kind of photography before the introduction of digital processes – constitute, as Patrick Maynard acutely argues, a 'most important *re*invention of photography ... without which even "the photograph" today would have a diminished historical significance'.[20] Methods for the reproduction of photographs in ink had been in use since the turn of the century but, as with camera technologies, the introduction of more sophisticated automation in the course of the 1950s and 60s significantly increased the quality, quantity and cost-effectiveness of photographic illustrations in publications. Continual improvements to gravure printing, which saw tests with electronic engraving as early as the late 1940s, facilitated the inclusion of more and more numerous half-tone reproductions in high print-run newspapers and magazines – thus increasing the circulation of photographs in mass-consumption print media while also generating demand for further photographic production.[21] In Italy, the process was so associated with the reproduction and consumption of photographs that *rotocalco* (i.e., rotogravure, as photo-engraving is also called when a rotary press is used) had since the 1930s become the generic name for a cheap, heavily illustrated periodical publication.[22] Yet, in the postwar period, an even more densely illustrated type of *rotocalco* emerged: the photo-novel – or *fotoromanzo* – of weeklies such as *Grand Hotel* and *Bolero Film*.[23] Also popular in France, Spain and Latin America (much less so in the UK and the USA), photo-novels were effectively stories *in photographs*: photographic and romantic versions of the comic-strip cartoon, sequentially arranged and, often, complete with speech bubbles – a phenomenon whose popularity and specific format Antonioni had himself, in fact, explored in the short documentary *L'amorosa menzogna* (*Loving Lie*, 1949) and his script for Federico Fellini's *Lo sceicco bianco* (*The White Sheik*, 1952). Photographic illustrations in books also became more numerous. In addition to the flourishing of heavily illustrated exhibition catalogues, the 1960s saw a boom in the specifically photographic format of the photobook.[24] A growing number of photographers and

Spread from an Italian photo-novel magazine (*Tipo*, March 1953)

191

artists started to see in it a tool suited to their aesthetics, politics and, even, wallets, since technological improvements now made it possible to self-publish illustrated books of sufficient quality at relatively low cost. For some artists, such as the American Ed Ruscha, who is widely acknowledged to have launched the novel format of the artist book with a prolific series of publications including *Twenty Six Gasoline Stations* (1962) and *Some Los Angeles Apartments* (1965) in the course of the 1960s, the photobook was a potentially democratic, multiple and unpretentious object with which to attack prevailing notions of art. For a number of journalists,

Blow-Up (1966)

it constituted a way of articulating their vision more freely or fully than they might otherwise be able to do in the restricted or, even, controlled, context of reportages for the press – an extreme example here being the clandestinely produced exposure of apartheid *House of Bondage* (1967), by the black South African photojournalist Ernest Cole.[25]

The extent to which these developments form a significant context for *Blow-Up* and, in fact, more or less directly inform its thematisation of photography should be obvious enough. Indeed, it is surprising that they are generally ignored in discussions of the film, as they constitute the very premise of its story: Thomas would be simply unimaginable without the innovations in photographic production and reproduced photography which his successful occupation as a fashion photojournalist depends on and, conversely, stimulates. Besides their individual relevance, there is also a more global way in which these developments bear upon *Blow-Up*'s staging of photography. All make visible a single trend: an intensification, and underlining, of what can broadly be described as the plurality of photography. For not only did these developments further seal the experience of photography as an experience routinely 'in the plural' (given that, from the rollfilm to the *fotoromanzo* or the photobook, rarely would one take or encounter a single photograph), but, as we shall see, they also contributed to an awareness of photography's constitutive plurality. And in its foregrounding of the material realisation of photographs, it is this complex sense of photography's plurality that *Blow-Up* cogently reflects – and reflects upon.

192

Types of Plurality

There are two main nuances to what I have suggested we call the plurality of photography, and though they will be discussed at length in what follows, a brief introductory gloss may be helpful here. At a first – literally, 'superficial' – level, photography's plurality is a quantitative and phenomenological matter. In this sense, it describes the sheer numerical proliferation of photographs – their multiplicity and multiplication – and it could thus be characterised as an experiential, or phenomenological, plurality. At a further level, photography's plurality acquires a more qualitative and ontological inflection. In this sense, then, plurality refers to the intrinsic and structural (even if latent or potential) lack of singularity that characterises photography as a technology of reproduction – indeed, as a reproductive process by which, as Maynard argues, even things other than photographs themselves (e.g., text) become reproducible.[26] Both these 'levels' – and their interrelation – are powerfully articulated in *Blow-Up*'s presentation of photography.

Photography is consistently associated with multiplicity – if not, indeed, multiplication – in *Blow-Up*, introduced (towards the beginning of the film itself)

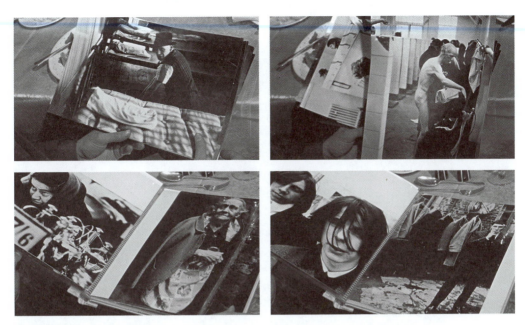

Blow-Up (1966)

precisely through an evocation of numerical abundance, if not excess. Hinted at by the handful of film rolls Thomas hands over to one assistant for development just before the fashion shoot with Verushka, this exuberance is then also more directly suggested by the erotically charged encounter with his model, as the sheer quantity of images being taken is signalled by the increasingly rapid succession of camera clicks. This abundance is further thematised shortly after, as the focus shifts from photographing to actual photographs when Thomas surveys the contact prints from the rolls his assistant has just developed. The characteristic numerousness of these proof images – actual-size positives of negatives, usually in uncut strips of five or six frames, aligned one next to the other on a sheet – is here enhanced by the high number of rolls shot by Thomas, which causes the proofs to extend over several sheets. Their quantity is further emphasised by the movie camera itself, which allows us to identify them as photographic images while leaving their individual contents indistinct by not focusing on them for long or from close enough. When, later in the film, we are shown enlargements of some of these shots, and allowed to see that they are pictures of guests in a dosshouse Thomas plans to include in his photobook, diegesis and aesthetics again put stress on the 'many-ness' of these, and other, photographs. While Thomas mentions to Ron, his agent or co-author, that he will select 'three or four' images from this particular batch, as they flick through the portfolio for the project, framed in close-up by Antonioni's camera, the viewer is made aware of the already large series of pictures that these latter shots will augment. Furthermore, as they converse about what to put at the close

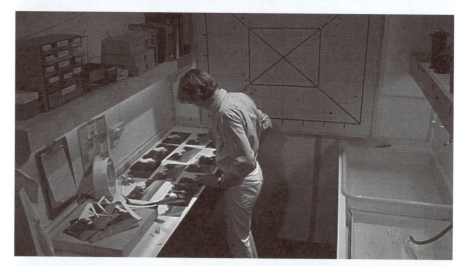

194

of the book, even 'the end' is imagined by Thomas not as one photograph but as a cluster of photographs: the ones of the couple he has just taken in the park (which, having yet to discover anything in them, he describes as 'very peaceful, very still'). Their plurality (in all its complexity) will be visualised subtly and at length in the later, central, scene in which Thomas enlarges and prints a selection of these images and physically groups them as a sequence surrounding him along three sides of his living room.

All of these instances of photographic abundance throughout the film, then, outline what I described above as the experiential plurality of photography: the fact, simply put, that photography is habitually experienced in the plural. Technological and cultural developments have conspired to make photographic production and consumption activities entailing more than one photograph if not, indeed, *many* photographs. In fact, to the extent that the film evokes this experiential plurality of photography, it also in turn makes plurality (vicariously, via cinema) an experience for the viewer who – from the rapid glimpses of the contact sheets to the more ponderous analysis of the park photographs, and from the photo shoot to the dark room – is called upon to engage with a plurality of photographic procedures and images. Precisely because this experiential plurality is shown to start from the very

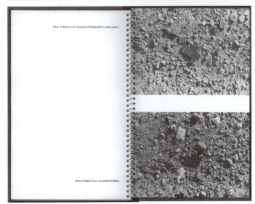

Pages from Ed Ruscha, *Royal Road Test* (1966). © Ed Ruscha. Courtesy Gagosian Gallery

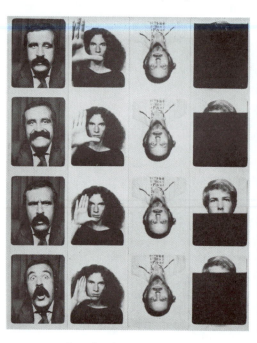

Pages from Franco Vaccari, *Esposizione in tempo reale 4* (1973) (courtesy of the artist)

processes through which photographs are taken and made, a deeper, more fundamental, sense of photography's plurality also emerges.

Blow-Up emphasises, in other words, the plurality constitutive of photography as such. Susan Sontag suggestively summoned a sense of this plurality in the influential essays on photography she wrote in the 1970s.[27] Not unlike the way in which – as I aim to suggest here – *Blow-Up* itself tackles photography, these essays are as much an engagement with the historical reality (the 'boom', as we discussed) of photography from the 1960s onwards, as they are a philosophical contemplation on the medium. In the last of these essays, in which Sontag argues that the sheer quantity of photographic imagery in the Western world is not only a copy *of* the world but, also, a material world in itself, she eventually suggests that even '*one* photograph' – should we chance to come across it – '*implies* that there will be others'.[28] In a nutshell, it is this sense of photography's constitutive plurality that *Blow-Up* itself not only reflects and analyses but also – as we shall see – amplifies and, literally, deepens, articulating it both 'horizontally' and 'vertically'.

But let us unpack Sontag's expression a little. Her characterisation both describes *and* interprets the photograph as a complexly repeatable entity. First, it points to the fact that the photograph – as a class or type of object – is repeatable because it is generated through a series of largely automatic technological procedures. While this is even true of the photograph obtained through early processes such as the daguerreotype, such repeatability is not only greatly facilitated and encouraged but also made more immediately evident, if not 'obvious', by the range and sophistication of automation introduced in the 1960s. In this respect, a photograph *implies* that there will be others because the virtuality of photography is already plural. Even before a picture is actually taken, repeatability and plurality are inscribed in the very conditions of its making, which not only make it possible to generate more than one picture but that – as with rollfilm, for instance – are often *conducive* to the addition of one photograph after another. Second, an individual and specific photograph is repeatable because it is reproducible. In addition to invoking photography's repeatability as an automatised mode of image production (and/or of reproduction of the 'image' in front of the lens), Sontag's 'implies' thus points to the fact that individual photographs are themselves repeatable and, often, actually repeated. For, and largely by applying the same technological processes enabling their production, photographs are reproducible in high numbers by printing copies from the negative (bar exceptions such as daguerreotypes or Polaroids) as well as, as we noted earlier, also often reproduced in even higher quantities in print media.

As photography historians such as David Campany and Blake Stimson have recently argued, these technological attributes of photography have, from very early on, determined its development 'as a medium of multiplicity and accumulation'.[29] This development, moreover, makes 'seriality ... a primary photographic form'.[30] Already introduced at one of photography's famous points of origin, Henry Fox Talbot's presentation of his invention via twenty-four photographs in the publication *The Pencil of Nature* (1844–46), the series went on to become, as László Moholy-Nagy once put it, 'natural' to photography in the course of the twentieth century.[31] From Alfred Stieglitz's almost abstract articulations of clouds (photographic series he called *Equivalents*, c. 1923–31), to 'documentary' projects as varied as those by August Sanders in late-1920s Germany and Walker Evans or Robert Frank in 1930s and 50s America respectively, to the 'fictional' world of the photo-novel, photography largely developed as a medium of series and sequences. If, by the 1960s, seriality and sequentiality had become thoroughly ordinary photographic forms, this was also, to return to this point again, due in great part to their expanding circulation via print media, as the actual multiplication of series themselves across many copies granted them visibility and, with it, 'naturalness' or ordinariness. In slightly different words, this is to say that this 'secondary' mode of photographic reproduction ('secondary', that is, with respect to reproduction from the negative) has often been a 'primary' mode for the diffusion of the photograph – or indeed, precisely, of photographs. The page was certainly conceived as such a primary mode not only in the case of now iconic series such as Walker Evans's *American Photographs* (1938) and Robert Frank's *The Americans* (1958–59), whose original vehicle was the book, but also in the case of the usually more ephemeral and 'consumable' series featured in international or internationally famous magazines such as *Harper's* (a copy of which can be glimpsed in Thomas's studio), *Life* or *Vogue*, whose popularity soared in the 1960s. And, as we have seen, not only is Thomas's activity generally predicated on such serial modes of production and circulation, but, as the film's plot shows, he is specifically engaged in making series for both these kinds of print media – the 'artistic' and 'committed' book as well as the glossy magazine.

Moreover, around the time of *Blow-Up*'s release, the very ordinariness of series and sequences as photographic forms was being aesthetically and conceptually flaunted by work such as Bernd and Hilla Becher's monumental taxonomy of industrial architecture and Ruscha's aforementioned prolific series of photographic books, some of which, such as *Crackers* (1969) and *Royal Road Test* (1967), are mocking elaborations of photo-novels and other forms of photographic narrative (e.g., step-by-step, or 'before' and 'after' demonstrations) common in mass-consumption print-media.[32] For artists such as Ruscha and the Bechers, the photographic series was not only a way of valuing multiplicity over singularity (that is, a means for having the overall effect or meaning of the work reside in a group of pictures rather than in an individual picture, and in reproducible or actually reproduced images rather than in a unique object). It was also a way of engaging formally and theoretically with what was felt to be an open, accretive and expansive medium; a medium, consonant with Sontag's formulation, in which growth and addition are already *implied* in each individual unit.[33] This openness is obvious in the case of the Bechers' extensive, cumulative, inventories. In Ruscha's books, on the other hand, it is, paradoxically, the relative brevity and the random interruption of each photographic series (ending variously at '*twenty-six* gasoline stations', after '*some* Los Angeles apartments' or, even more oddly, after '*various* small fires *and* milk', and '*nine* swimming pools *and* a broken glass') that suggests the potential expansion and inherent openness of the series themselves. The continuation implied by caesura is not unlike the way in which even the last instalment of a serialised photo-novel may exude a certain ongoingness, the promise of continuation – *mutatis mutandis* – in another story.[34]

Through the series and their potential – if not actual – openness, these works manifest what we have been calling photography's constitutive plurality. Indeed, its plurality is articulated, as it were, 'horizontally', by systematically adding one photo next to or after the other in ways which not only suggest the global, cumulative expansion of the medium but that also replicate, or at least evoke, the mechanical repeatability, the unthinking automation, of photography itself. It is this horizontal axis of photography's plurality – the possibility of following one photograph with another, and the technological and cultural incentive to realise that possibility – that is also called upon in *Blow-Up*. In the film, photographs are shown to be taken, made and consumed in – or, even, *as* – series and sequences: accretive, 'open' series and sequences, where one picture leads to and, in fact, almost *produces* another. This is cogently introduced by the rapid camera 'clicks' during the fashion shoot and

198

in the park, suggested by the film's portrayal of Thomas's photobook project (the contact prints, the portfolio he leafs through with Ron) and, finally, most vividly and thoroughly articulated in the sequence dedicated to Thomas's attentive making and studying of his park photographs.

In this central moment in the film, then, not only does Thomas make – that is, develop – the series 'naturally' contained in the roll itself (the series *as* shot) but, out of this, he also makes – that is, generates – a new, further series. The laborious mental and material realisation of this series is dwelled on and explored at length in this remarkable scene. No doubt, we are far from so-called 'real' time: the episode proceeds through temporal ellipses, condensing into minutes a process which, in real life, would have unfolded over a much longer interval. Yet, the film's pace conspicuously slows down, and cinema is as if given over to photography and its stillness as Thomas proceeds to compose this series through a meticulous process of scrutiny, selection and trips to the dark room. The film shows us the series' gradual emergence as a spatial configuration in Thomas's studio, the physical alignment of photographs along the exposed beams and walls, one next to the other. But, through close-ups, zooms and pans on and between the photographs themselves, the movie camera also directs us to – and itself organises – the series' complementarily emerging configuration in time: for Thomas (and, consequently, plot-wise), this serial arrangement in space also has a temporal, and 'narrative', valence – it is a sequence. Not unlike Ruscha's and the Bechers' deadpan series, but with a narrative momentum perhaps closer to the strips of the *fotoromanzo*, Thomas's sequence presents photography's plurality 'horizontally', as a succession of one photograph after the other. In this sense, the scene's photographic display also, self-reflexively, calls upon that 'horizontal' plurality of photographs which *Blow-Up* itself – and cinema more broadly – is at its literal core. If the physical alignment of the photographs in space and the sense of a forward movement in time that Thomas's reconstruction 'applies' to them represent cinema, then it is also true that cinema is, conversely, presented as a particular intensification of the technological and cultural drive to follow a photograph with another: photography's plurality *is* cinema's very structure.

Thomas's construction of his sequence further plays out this drive to make and engage with a series of photographs rather than one photograph.[35] And, again not unlike the photographic series of photo-novels or Ruscha's and the Bechers', Thomas's series, too, signals openness and accretion, *even as* it may seem to reach a certain 'closure'. The very fact that Thomas's series 'ends' twice weakens finality, insinuating a sense that closure may be fundamentally underscored by openness, the possibility of continuation. For, indeed, Thomas first deems his sequence closed, his (re)construction complete, when, having ostensibly detected a gunman in the enlarged detail of one of the photographs, he concludes that he has unwittingly averted a murder, as he excitedly tells Ron on the telephone. But, after an 'interlude' (the famous scene of the sexual frolic with the two aspiring models who turn up at his door to be photographed), Thomas returns to his series and 'opens' it again, adding at least one more picture to it by – as the film now makes a point of showing – rephotographing a detail from a previous enlargement. This second 'end' to his series, a very grainy enlargement (whose resemblance with the semi-abstract paintings by an artist friend of Thomas will later be noted in the film) leads him to think that, rather than having prevented a killing, he has, in fact, witnessed one without quite seeing it – because in this image there seems to be a supine body, half hidden by a bush.

With this addition, the plurality of photography which *Blow-Up* both represents and reflects on becomes apparent under a new light. If Thomas's display – as well as his photographic activity more generally – articulates such plurality by evoking a horizontal vector, a forward movement to the next photograph, then the recursive use of enlargements in his reconstruction also calls into play a vertical vector, a movement *within* individual photographs through which – I believe – the film also proposes a cogent definition of what photography is. For a start, even visually, 'verticality' becomes a marked feature with the introduction of this further enlargement, which Thomas arranges partly 'on top' of the one from which it logically and sequentially derives, and whose logical relation to the previous image is outlined and underlined by the movie camera's descending and ascending panning movement between the two. Quite literally, then, the vertical axis of photography's plurality is configured in superimposition to its horizontal axis. Though enlargements have already featured in Thomas's reconstruction (in fact, all of the prints are, technically, enlargements of the 35mm negatives), this formal language, coupled with the diegetic role of this image, foregrounds the 'blow up' as the conceptual core of the film – for the blow up crucially performs and epitomises photography's plurality.[36] As the image gives way to the grain, the potential seriality of even a single photograph is brought into relief. In its potential to generate further photographs from 'inside' itself, the individual photograph opens onto plurality by implying another which will be after or next to it, but also, logically, *within* it. Although the real captured by the camera may be lost, what is not only maintained but, in fact, quantitatively and qualitatively (or, numerically and intrinsically) pluralised through the process of enlargement, is the photograph itself. Concomitantly, it is precisely the fact of photography *as* a technology – and, indeed, a process – *of* reproduction which is highlighted, and even proposed as a description or definition of what photography is. Besides, this is a reproduction that – surprisingly, if not paradoxically – begets difference. The very process of reproduction by which *another* photograph is produced is also, at the same time, the generation of *an other* photograph, as the same source data (the same negative) engender a different image. Here, phenomenological abundance is underscored, and motored, by ontological plurality; a plurality which, even as the quintessence of a reproductive technology – a technology, therefore, arguably structured through, and for, repetition – contains difference.

*   *   *

As I noted at the start of this essay, discussions of *Blow-Up* and photography have tended to focus on the way in which the film reflects on the medium's ability to capture or represent reality, and largely have overlooked the question of *Blow-Up*'s engagement with the reality of photography – from the many-ness of photographic images to the 'plurality' which is inherent in photographic processes since the medium's inception. Two works, however, a photobook and a film produced a few years after *Blow-Up*, stand out not only as particularly cognate with Antonioni's film but, also, as commentaries on what I believe is *Blow-Up*'s emphasis on photography's plurality and its status as a reproductive process. *Esposizione in tempo reale* (a pun which can translate both as '*Exhibition*' and '*Exposure in Real Time*', 1973), by Italian conceptual artist Franco Vaccari, is a photobook which followed – and completed – Vaccari's contribution to the 1972 Venice Biennale, an installation in which viewers were invited to leave 'a photographic trace of their passage' by making use of the photobooth he had installed in the space of the exhibition. The book, then, collects and reproduces hundreds of the characteristic four-photograph strips viewers took of themselves and, originally, affixed onto the walls of the exhibition. *Blow-Up*'s pursuit of photographic plurality resonates with and is, in fact, amplified by Vaccari's intriguing book, where the reproduction of the automatically (and instantaneously) produced four-unit photo series unfolds – or is complexly 'modulated' – both horizontally, through telescopic arrangements of as many as sixteen strips per page, and vertically, with enlargements of single images from the strips, recurrently blown up to fill the approximately A4-sized page.[37]

A similar dynamic, though pursued by different means, can be detected in *nostalgia* (1971), a film by American photographer and experimental film-maker Hollis Frampton, in which about a dozen of Frampton's own photographs are filmed in close-up as, one after the other, they are burned on a hotplate. Plurality is, again, played out in various ways: not only, on a first level, in the serialised presentation of the photographic prints but also, secondarily, in the voice-over commentary, whose anecdotes about them make each individual photograph ripple with plurality, so to speak (even, indeed, while it is ostensibly being destroyed). The film's commentary produces plurality by linking each individual image to a much larger series (such as a photo shoot) to which it belongs, or by presenting each image as one of many copies from the original negative. And, finally – in what seems a direct, tongue-in-cheek homage to Antonioni's film – *nostalgia* calls upon the blow-up as it closes.[38] Here, the narrator recounts having recently taken what will likely be his last photograph (a last photograph, furthermore, which was the only one he managed to take on the particular occasion). Yet, even this mysterious unique last photograph –

which is rhetorically evoked but not shown in the film – is, in fact, plural, as a strange compulsion to unpack it has meant that, as the voice-over tells us, it has been blown up 'till the grain of the film all but obliterates the features of the image'.

Certainly, these brief accounts do not do justice to either Vaccari's and Frampton's works themselves or the extent of their dialogue with Antonioni's film. However, they hopefully further contextualise *Blow-Up*'s thematisation of photography and, at the same time, point to the particular impact of the film's aesthetic and conceptual engagement with the medium, a meditation on photography that has not only generated a considerable volume of scholarly and artistic responses since the film's release, but whose legacy continues to be strongly felt today. As I hope to have demonstrated, part of the reason for the enduring fascination exercised by the film resides in its complex mixture of, roughly put, 'philosophy' and 'history'. For, in important respects, the film's thematisation of photography can be seen to be informed by, and to give articulation to, the experience of photography's exponential expansion and pluralisation (from faster and easier picture taking, to the 'reproduced' and serial photographs of photobooks and magazines) during the second half of the twentieth century, and particularly the 1960s. It is from an articulation of this experiential plurality of photography that *Blow-Up* also produces a more 'philosophical' reflection on the nature of photography as such. Through its focus on the reality *of* photography (a focus which exceeds the concern with the real *in* the photograph which most scholarly accounts to date attribute to the film), the film proposes that plurality structures not only our experience of photography but also the medium itself. *Blow-Up*, that is, affirms the plurality intrinsic to photography as such – and, indeed, constitutive of it as a technology of reproduction. In fact, *Blow-Up*'s insistence on the figure of the enlargement discloses the 'depth' of such plurality. This pluralisation of photography from 'within' an individual image, through the very processes which should produce a copy, yields difference: reproduction does not suspend or sidestep, but rather generates and sponsors, difference. And perhaps, in so doing, *Blow-Up*'s enquiry into photography's 'how' emphasises 'what' photography is in a way that exceeds the technological specificity of the photochemical era in which the film is itself rooted. Clearly, plurality is still – exponentially – the experiential and constitutive condition of 'photography' (or what still largely goes by this name) in digitality; and even in digitality, where the copy can allegedly be 'perfect', reproduction arguably still realises photography's plurality not only quantitatively but also qualitatively – as difference.

Notes

1. While David Hemmings is never named in the film, the screenplay refers to him as Thomas, and so I will for the sake of simplicity.

2. For a discussion of *Blow-Up*'s relation to the cultural and artistic milieu of 1960s London, see, for example, Peter Lev, '*Blow-Up*, Swinging London, and the Film Generation', *Literature/Film Quarterly* vol. 17 no. 2 (1989), pp. 134–7; and David Alan Mellor, 'Fragments of an Unknowable Whole: Michelangelo Antonioni's Incorporation of Contemporary Visualities in London, 1966', *Visual Culture in Britain* vol. 8 no. 2 (2007), pp. 45–61.

3. For examples of 'existential' readings, see Seymour Chatman, *Antonioni, or The Surface of the World* (Berkeley and Los Angeles: University of California, 1985), esp. pp. 138–52; and David I. Grossvogel, '*Blow-Up*: The Forms of an Aesthetic Itinerary', *Diacritics* vol. 2 no. 3 (Autumn 1972), pp. 49–54. For 'photographic ontology' readings, as well as how this further relates to cinema, see, for example, Amelia Jones, 'Seeing Differently: From Antonioni's *Blow-Up* (1966) to Shezad Dawood's *Make It Big* (2005)', *Journal of Visual Culture* vol. 7 no. 2 (August 2008), pp. 181–203; Jurij Lotman, *Semiotics of Cinema*, trans. Mark E. Suino (Ann Arbor: University of Michigan, 1981 [1973]), pp. 97–105; John Freccero, '*Blow-Up*: From the Word to the Image' [1970], in Roy Huss (ed.), *Focus on Blow-Up* (Englewood Cliffs: Prentice-Hall, 1971), pp. 116–28. The classic discussion on photographic/cinematic ontology is André Bazin's influential essay 'The Ontology of the Photographic Image' [1945], in *What Is Cinema?*, trans. Hugh Gray, vol. 1 (Berkeley: University of California Press, 1967), pp. 1–12.

4. Chatman, *Antonioni*, p. 143; Lotman, *Semiotics of Cinema*, pp. 97–8.

5. Jones, 'Seeing Differently', p. 186.

6. Chatman, *Antonioni*, p. 143.

7. Ibid., p. 149.

8. Lotman, *Semiotics of Cinema*, p. 98. Lotman is here, selectively if not slightly inaccurately, thinking only of some of the enlargements, such as the one in which Vanessa Redgrave's character is seen raising her hand to hide her face and stop Thomas from taking further pictures. However, some of Thomas's photos actually do show quite a lot of the park and, crucially, it is by enlarging the area of the fenced copse to the right of the couple that Thomas believes he can detect a man holding a gun.

9. Chatman, *Antonioni*, p. 152.

10. Jones, 'Seeing Differently', p. 186 (emphasis added).

11. Ibid., p. 187.

12. Quoted in Roy Huss, 'Introduction', in *Focus on Blow-Up*, p. 5 – from foreword to Michelangelo Antonioni, *Blow-Up*, 2nd edn (Turin: Einaudi, 1968), p. 7. Julio Cortázar's short story 'Las babas del diablo' (literally, 'The Devil's Drool', 1963) was translated as 'Blow-Up' when published in English in the collection *End of the Game and Other Stories*, trans. Paul Blackburn (London: Collins and Harvill Press, 1963), pp. 114–31.

13. See for example Mary Warner Marien, *Photography: A Cultural History* (London: Laurence King, 2002); and Colin Ford (ed.), *The Kodak Museum: The Story of*

Popular Photography (London: Century Hutchinson, 1989), esp. David Allison, 'Photography and the Mass Market', pp. 42–59.

14. For this and what follows I have relied on, among others, John Wade, *A Short History of the Camera* (Watford: Fountain Press, 1979) and Brian Coe, 'The Rollfilm Revolution', in Ford, *The Kodak Museum*, pp. 61–89.

15. For a historical overview of photo-reporting see Robert Lebeck and Bodo Von Dewitz (eds), *Kiosk: A History of Photojournalism* (Göttingen: Steidl, 2001).

16. Cf. David Campany, 'From Ecstasy to Agony: The Fashion Shoot in Cinema', *Aperture* no. 190 (Spring 2008), pp. 40–7.

17. Martin Parr and Gerry Badger, *The Photobook: A History*, vol. 2 (London: Phaidon, 2006), p. 6.

18. Don McCullin, *Unreasonable Behaviour: An Autobiography* (London: Jonathan Cape, 1990). For McCullin's contribution to *Blow-Up* see Mellor, 'Fragments of an Unknowable Whole', pp. 49–54.

19. For a general introduction to this, see the '1960–1969' section of Hal Foster et al., *Art Since 1900: Modernism, Antimodernism, Postmodernism* (London: Thames and Hudson, 2004), pp. 434–537. See also: Benjamin H. D. Buchloh, 'Conceptual Art 1962–1969: From the Aesthetic of Administration to the Critique of Institutions', *October* no. 55 (Winter 1990), pp. 105–43.

20. Patrick Maynard, *The Engine of Visualization: Thinking Through Photography* (Ithaca: Cornell University Press, 1997), p. 18.

21. See for example Roy Brewer, *An Approach to Print: A Basic Guide to the Printing Processes* (London: Blandford Press, 1971), esp. pp. 33–4; and Ernest A. D. Hutchings, *A Survey of Printing Processes* (London: Heinemann, 1970).

22. For more on the popular press in Italy, see David Forgacs and Stephen Gundle (eds), *Mass Culture and Italian Society from Fascism to the Cold War* (Bloomington: Indiana University Press, 2007), pp. 35–42 and 95–123.

23. Precursors of the *fotoromazo*, generally text-based summaries of released films with a number of significant illustrations, had been around since the late 1920s. However, it is from the late 1940s that the photo-novel in its photographic comic-strip style emerges and flourishes. See Maria Teresa Anelli et al., *Fotoromanzo: fascino e pregiudizio. Storia, documenti e immagini di un grande fenomeno popolare (1948–1979)* (Milan: Savelli, 1979), and Raffaele De Berti, *Dallo schermo alla carta. Romanzi, fotoromanzi, rotocalchi cinematografici* (Milan: Vita e Pensiero, 2000).

24. An example of this is the catalogue for the 1966 exhibition *The Photographer's Eye*, at the Museum of Modern Art, New York, whose particular layout, in fact, also makes it a photobook in its own right: John Szarkowski, *The Photographer's Eye* (New York: MoMA, 1966).

25. See Parr and Badger, *The Photobook* – see also vol. 1 (2004); Johanna Drucker, *The Century of Artists' Books* (New York: Granary, 2004 [1994]); Anne Thurman-Jaies

and Martin Hellmold (eds), *Art Photographica: Fotografie und Künstlerbücher* (Bremen: Neues Museum Weserburg, 2002).

26. See Maynard, *The Engine of Visualization*, where he suggests that it may be more useful to think of photography *as*, broadly, 'a kind of technology' (p. x) rather than as an activity geared to the making of photographs; for indeed, as he argues, from photogravure to microprocessors, 'there is photography that does not consist in making photographs – at least not as we ordinarily understand those terms' (p. 9).

27. Susan Sontag's essays were collected in her *On Photography* (London: Penguin, 2002 [1977]), though they first appeared, in slightly different versions, in *The New York Review of Books* between 1973 and 1977.

28. Sontag, *On Photography*, p. 166 (emphasis added).

29. David Campany, *Photography and Cinema* (London: Reaktion, 2008), p. 60.

30. Blake Stimson, *The Pivot of the World: Photography and Its Nation* (Cambridge: MIT Press, 2006), p. 30.

31. László Moholy-Nagy, *Vision in Motion* (Chicago: Paul Theobald and Co., 1961 [1947]), p. 208.

32. See Susanne Lange, *Bernd and Hilla Becher: Life and Work*, trans. Jeremy Gaines (Cambridge, MA: MIT Press, 2007); and Richard D. Marshall, *Ed Ruscha* (London: Phaidon, 2003).

33. Cf. Donna De Salvo, *Open Systems: Rethinking Art c. 1970* (London: Tate, 2005).

34. In addition to the aforementioned books, see also Ruscha's *Various Small Fires* (1964) and *Nine Swimming Pools* (1968), whose series indeed take a 'narrative' twist not introduced in the cover title by ending with these unannounced objects (which are, however, mentioned in the title page inside the cover).

35. Cf. Philip Dubois, *L'Acte photographique et autres essais* (Brussels: Labor, 1990 [1983]), p. 154.

36. There is a hint of this, for instance, even in *Funny Face*. At a point, ostensibly through progressive enlargement, two glamorous images of Audrey Hepburn's Jo (one of them an extreme close-up) are derived from a shot in whose composition she was only accidentally framed.

37. For a fuller account see Nicoletta Leonardi (ed.), *Feedback. Scritti su e di Franco Vaccari* (Milan: Postmedia, 2007), pp. 29–31.

38. In fact, Frampton himself once denied that his film made direct reference to *Blow-Up* – though he admitted to having been 'entertained' by it. 'An Evening with Hollis Frampton', 8 March 1973, SR, 70, 22. MoMA Archives, New York, quoted in Rachel Moore, *Hollis Frampton – (nostalgia)* (London: Afterall, 2006), p. 30.

205

Francesco Casetti

TEN FOOTNOTES TO A MYSTERY

'After years of thinking about it, I finally shot a film on video'[1]

In the 1970s and 80s, the state-owned broadcaster, RAI Television, engages in a curious courtship of the cinema.[2] In a first phase, RAI produces a series of quality films that would otherwise have found it very difficult to compete on the market for financial investment. This initiative makes it possible for some directors to make their debut with highly interesting works: in particular, Gianni Amelio with *La fine del gioco* (*The End of the Game*, 1970) and Peter del Monte with *Le parole a venire* (*The Words to Come*, 1970). It is within this same season and in the same spirit that Bernardo Bertolucci's *Strategia del ragno* (*Spider's Stratagem*, 1970) is produced. In a second phase, RAI invites some directors to engage directly with the televisual medium, and to experiment creatively with electronic technology. The occasion also sees the introduction of high-definition video cameras provided by Sony, though these are still analogical and based on televisual technology. It is within this second phase that the production of Michelangelo Antonioni's *Il mistero di Oberwald* (1980) takes place, followed by *Arlecchino* (1983) by Giuliano Montaldo and *Giulia e Giulia* (1987) by Peter del Monte. The initial purpose of this second phase is to obtain a TV product characterised by a visual quality similar to that of film; the standard of high definition is 1,125 lines and, in theory, the definition of this image is close to that of 35mm. Second, these TV products are intended to be exploited in the circuit of film theatres; in particular, *Giulia e Giulia* receives regular theatrical distribution. Third, a political, and undeclared, purpose may also be traced: state television begins to turn into a producer interested in all audiovisual forms, thus leaving behind its simple enjoyment of its sheer monopoly on broadcasting. Another obvious, but even more hidden, aspect of this courtship is the continuation of a form of patronage typical of Italian and European cultures at large: it is right to help artists, especially the young, to help them mature and to affirm their work.

Michelangelo Antonioni shooting *Il misterio di Oberwald* (1980) with a Sony HD camera

'It is the first time that I have taken on a tragic drama, and the impact has been anything but smooth. Let's say that I have done some of my best work to soften the blow'

Il mistero di Oberwald is based on *L'Aigle à deux têtes* (*The Two-Headed Eagle*) by Jean Cocteau, a play in three acts written in 1943 and first performed on 21 December of that same year at the Parisian Théâtre Hébertot, with Edwige Feuillière in the role of the queen and Jean Marais in that of the young anarchist who, wanting to assassinate her, ends up falling in love with her. In 1947 Cocteau had also made a film based on his play, casting the same two main actors, and creating a *mise en scène* that never disguised its theatrical origins. Another example of 'impure cinema', Bazin would have said; but, also, a cinema that still had to be renewed by the linguistic revolution that the *nouvelle vague* was about to introduce.

Antonioni goes back to Cocteau almost with the intention of bracketing the phase of cinema's 'modernisation', which, in the time between the play's first performance and 1980, had been accomplished by the new waves of the 1950s and 60s – and by Antonioni himself. He constructs, in fact, a film in which the staging – the theatrical *mise en scène* – is utterly evident: what we witness is a representation, in every sense of the term. More than the casting of Monica Vitti, the choice of Franco Branciroli, then an emerging actor who was destined for a successful career in the theatre is significant; differently from a Jean-Paul Belmondo, here the young actor is not asked to break established acting conventions, and to conquer a behavioural naturalness, but, on the contrary, to work in an emphatic register, full of pathos.

The result, especially when seeing the film today, is a curious paradox: a work of theatre that aspires to explore the reality of feelings, adapted into a film by a director who had searched for that reality across his entire oeuvre, and that comes to be an extraordinary study of how representation produces effects of falsity.

'Why this choice? It isn't a choice, it's fate. You can also make some irony out of this by saying that the "mystery" is actually in the "why" I made this film'

Antonioni's choice, more than a mystery, seems a confession of the subtle attraction that melodrama exerts on him. It is an attraction that is negated and masked: one by which the adventure in *L'avventura* (1960) never becomes a fully developed love story, but is instead constructed on deviations and abstractions, staked on the randomness of feelings. But it is also an attraction that clearly emerges in the early films, in particular in *Cronaca di un amore* (1950) or in *La signora senza camelie* (1953), in which we are confronted with strong oppositions (between being and appearance), with typical if not archetypal situations (the return of the first fiancée, the *coup de foudre*, the difficulty of explaining oneself), with a search for the sublime (that we see in these films' crucial scenes) and with the prevailing of destiny (it couldn't have happened otherwise …). Yes, Antonioni is a melodramatic director; but he does not want it to be known. Actually, he wants it to be known so little that he becomes, in the eyes of critics and audience alike, the director of incommunicability.

This confession – and this denial – pose a larger interpretative problem. Whom to believe? The author who speaks (and does not say)? The spectator who watches (and often does not see)? Or the work that shows (but through symptoms more than through signs)? *Intentio autoris, intentio lectoris, intentio operis*: never more than in Antonioni's cinema are these in conflict with one another. And never more than in Antonioni's cinema must they be played out in a dialectical manner: the truth consists precisely in their conflict – and in the folds of each. Melodrama of interpretation, indeed.

'I do not want to defend Cocteau – I consider him a talented writer, gifted, yet limited and far removed from modern literary taste. And yet, a certain air of up-to-dateness runs through his play'

What makes a film up to date? In the case of Antonioni, most critics consider him a witness to his time because he represents the crisis of the bourgeoisie, a class incapable of authentic relationships. Undoubtedly, from this point of view Antonioni's films are precious documents even for today's historian. And yet, for *Il mistero di Oberwald* Antonioni devises a different strategy. He says to us, in fact, that he is interested in some of the terms that the film itself puts into play: 'Words like "anarchic", "opposition", "power", "chief of police", "comrade" and "group" belong to our everyday vocabulary.'[3] Thus, the historicity of the film would be linked to its lexicon. These are, of course, words current after the youth revolution of 1968, and that in Italy take on a particular meaning also because the 1970s are the so-called '*anni di piombo*' (the 'years of lead'), marked by the presence of clandestine groups conducting their armed struggle against the state. In 1978 the Red Brigades go as far as kidnapping and assassinating Aldo Moro, the most important politician of the then ruling party, the Christian Democrats. *Il mistero di Oberwald* openly recalls this episode, which was then still very fresh in everyone's memory. But is a lexicon sufficient to recall a historical moment? Are the characters of an anarchist, a queen and a chief of police sufficient to recall a dramatic confrontation between state and anti-state, like the one that bloodied Italy in the 1970s? Perhaps, as well as a lexicon, a syntax would also be required, and thus a narrative fabric capable of bringing to light the social and political intersections that led to the Red Brigades. But Antonioni – to speak in a very synthesising manner – is a director who captures the *air du temps*, but who does not have a sense of history. His historicity is always truncated: he gives us the real that interpellates us, but not the event that transforms us. I believe that this attitude is already present in his essay 'Per un film sul fiume Po' ('For a Film on the River Po'), first published in April 1939 in *Cinema*, and which was followed by the documentary *Gente del Po* in 1943/47. What we find in it is the urge to represent the people and landscapes that characterise that part of Italy in a way that is as alive as possible; but there is also a detachment from what was happening in Italy at that time, including in Po region. By all means, Antonioni captures the real, but he is not interested in the event.

Behind the alternative between the real and the event lies, evidently, a different idea of cinema, which informs film theory from its origins. What matters is not only to decide whether the cinema is a tool that gives us back a reality or that frees our imagination, as in the realism versus anti-realism debate: it is just as important to understand whether the cinema is something that can capture the contingency of the instant or that is, instead, capable of making the fateful moment emerge. Antonioni – and herein lies his modernity – searches for the fateful dimension in the contingent one; in doing so he takes the risk that the fleeting moments might merely become a waiting for the event, or even result in the disappearance of the event altogether. But, indeed, history – with its discontinuities and ruptures – knocks on the door.

'What a sense of lightness I felt in facing those events, so devoid of the complexity of the real, to which we are accustomed!'

Is Antonioni a 'committed' director? I use 'commitment' in the sense that Sartre gives to the term in his essays of the 1940s published in *Temps Modernes*, and that trace the figure of an author who, through his writing – a writing that is, first and foremost, action – intervenes in the present. The time may have come to state that, while Antonioni is not devoted to *irresponsabilité*, nor is he devoted to commitment (I use the two terms that Sartre puts in opposition to one another). As a director, he is interested in the present, but does not feel moved either to intervene in it or to change it. He paints it with the accuracy and ferocity it deserves, but he does not go any farther.

The reason is perhaps found in the second part of his sentence: it is difficult to face the real, because the real is 'complex'. Such complexity is an element of fascination: it is the entanglement of things that attracts us and compels us to narrate them. But the same complexity also restrains us from action: there are no solutions, whether easy or difficult, to the entanglement of things. In other words, the plot must give us the density of a problem; but its conclusions cannot trick us into thinking that there is the possibility of a true intervention. I talk of conclusions because it is precisely the films' endings that give us a sense of the engagement: they not only tell us the direction towards which the story tends, but also the way we would like things to turn out, and thus they function both as omens and as goals.

Antonioni never arrives at these endings. After all, he remains convinced that in life there are only provisional states of equilibrium that have no final solutions. For this reason, *Il mistero di Oberwald* is the least mysterious of his films: at the end we have a real ending, a solution – the exact opposite of what we have, for instance, in the films of the trilogy (*L'avventura*, *L'eclisse* [1962], *La notte* [1961]), whose endings consist of missed appointments, landscapes that empty themselves out and the passage from day to night.

'The electronic system is very stimulating … It is also possible to obtain effects forbidden to normal cinema'

Does something 'specifically cinematic' exist? Does something exist, in other words, that the cinema 'must' do and 'must not' do? The question of the 'specific' is as old as the cinema itself: an American critic, Rollin Summers, writes in 1908:

> Every art has its peculiar advantages and disadvantages growing out of the particular
> medium in which it expresses itself. It is the limitations and advantages of its particular
> means of expression that give rise to its own particular technique. An observation of the

limitations and advantages of motion photography will suggest the particular technical laws of the moving picture play.[4]

Starting from this point, many theorists have worked on what the cinema does best and what is best for it to do. The arrival point is the 'cinematic grammars' of the 1930s, which established what is allowed in the cinema and what is forbidden, precisely in the name of the medium's limits and technical specialities. The most famous is probably Roger Spottiswoode's *A Grammar of the Film: An Analysis of Film Technique*, published in London in 1935, and which had already been translated into Italian by 1938 and published in *Bianco e Nero*, the journal of the Centro Sperimentale di Cinematografia which Antonioni attended in 1942.

From the point of view of the 'filmic grammars', Antonioni is a rather traditional director. We do not find in his work those 'grammatical violations', such as the jump-cut or the sudden shifts in depth of field, which one finds in the cinema from Godard and subsequent film-making. If anything, Antonioni loves 'technical virtuosity' and thus searched for solutions that would push the camera's expressive possibilities. Two famous endings testify to this: that of *Zabriskie Point* (1970), in which the final explosion is recorded in slow motion by fourteen cameras – special cameras that up until that point had only ever been used to make scientific films; and the ending of *The Passenger* (1975), in which the camera, hanging from a crane, moves in a single long take that lasts no less than seven minutes and moves first out of and then re-enters the same room in which David Locke finds his death. But Aldo Tassone recounts that in a short made as a student of the Centro Sperimentale Antonioni already demonstrates his technical prowess, joining with an invisible cut two long sequences, so as to seamlessly transform one character into another.[5]

Classical style and technical virtuosity: is this Antonioni's challenge to what is forbidden in mainstream cinema?

'In short, you realise quickly that it isn't a game, but rather ... a new way of finally using color as a narrative, poetic means'

I confess, openly: for me, one of the mysteries of *Il mistero di Oberwald* is the logic of colour. Thanks to electronics, Antonioni gives to the image diverse and mutable shades of colour: when the Count of Foehn enters, everything turns violet around him; when the sun rises, things take on a whitish reflection; and again, the abundant nature in which the castle is immersed takes on changing hues. As an old semiotician, I tried for a long time to understand whether these chromatic variations constitute a 'colour system' like the one imagined, for instance, by Eisenstein – a system that is not linked to realistic effects, but is dense with symbolism, and which we find experimented with in *Ivan the Terrible* (1944) and explained in essays like 'First

211

Letter About Color' or 'One Path to Color'.[6] Frankly, in spite of much effort, I never managed to identify any 'system'. On the contrary, in fact: it seems to me that Antonioni's activity here is informed by a (healthy) haphazardness and arbitrariness.

Does this mean that Antonioni believes that a text (the film as text) is not undergirded by any structure? Or, even more radically, that a text is a free sequence of images – only bound to the rules of a style? It seems to me that his research on colour in *Il mistero di Oberwald* – so blatantly explicit and so commented upon by critics – masks in reality his profound indifference towards any possible 'system' that acts as a mould, as a scaffold. For Antonioni, a text's architecture does not matter. There are no previous organisations or hierarchies to be obeyed – no order of speech, and even no order of discourse. Antonioni is a true anti-structuralist: for him, a text, even if traversed by constant allusions, is an object characterised by a variable balance and not dominated by any stringent logic.

This is why, rather than continue to research the film's use of colour, I wish to point to another passage of the film, itself linked to electronics, and, I think, rather more decisive: the queen is lying in front of the fireplace, at night, in a moment of calm, wrapped in a blanket; all of a sudden, her body dissolves and only the blanket remains. Power of metamorphosis. Fascination of transmutation not justified by any logic. Antonioni–Méliès: why not?

'Television is in color'

It is exactly across the course of the 1970s that colour television becomes the norm in Europe. Earlier, TV was in black and white. This transformation took place after the one in the cinema: on the big screen colour, which already had been a feature of even early cinema, imposes itself in the 1930s, with Walt Disney's *Silly Symphonies* and Rouben Mamoulian's *Becky Sharp* (1935). Television, instead, turns to colour in 1954 in the US, in 1967 in the UK and in 1975 in Italy. But why does the cinema, at least in the opinion of directors and critics, remain – for so long and ideally – black and white, whereas television immediately becomes colour?

One would have to reconstruct critically the way in which various media progressively conquer a 'reputation' for themselves. The fundamental law is that the introduction of a new medium is required to render the previous medium fully artistic. It is the cinema that makes us think that the theatre has an intrinsic artistic vocation (causing us to forget the countless stage productions that were pure entertainment). Television makes us forget the scant amount of aesthetic consideration that the cinema had hitherto enjoyed. YouTube makes of television a site of formal experimentation. Videogames make comic books look like art books. And so on. A newcomer is needed for a medium to reach the status of city dweller in the aesthetic field. A price, however, is paid – one that I will call a tax on art: in order to acquire an artistic reputation, a medium not only needs a newer competitor on which critics and audiences can concentrate their contempt, but it must also exhibit an element of self-punishment, something that hinders its full potential. Television must adopt filmic formats, as in its prestige dramatic serials. The comic book must remain a book. And the cinema must ideally remain in black and white, like its recognised masterpieces (and maybe even silent, as it was for so long).

In the age of mass media, art is a synonym for permanency, for tradition. A link is needed with a past that may even be invented, mythical. It could be objected that artists nowadays can do whatever they want, outside any canon. This is true; but as Boris Groys has said so well, while artists work to break every possible rule, they continue to dream of something irredeemably old: they think that they will truly be artists only when their work ends up in a museum.[7]

'In no other field do poetry and technology walk hand in hand the way they do in the field of electronics'

The question that always has a bearing on the cinema is its nature as 'mechanical art', as the theorists of the 1920s and 30s used to call it. In the cinema, in fact, technology and art are married like never before and engender, in this way – more than a happy family – a nucleus of potential conflicts.

I do not have the space here to revisit in its entirety the complex relationship between technology and aesthetics in the field of the cinema. I will only make reference to Luigi Pirandello's resolute condemnation (a mechanical reproduction of reality empties itself of its soul, and only gives us back its appearances); to the synthesis prefigured by Jean Epstein (the Bell & Howell is a mechanical brain without human prejudices); and to the new horizon, which is born out of the conjunction of the two terms, theorised by Walter Benjamin (but also, before him, by theorists such as Eugenio Giovannetti in *Il cinema e le arti meccaniche*: the mechanical merged with the human inaugurates an era of artistic democracy).[8] And I also note that neo-realism, so careful to attend to the aesthetic possibilities of photographic reproduction, never addresses itself to any serious reflection on the technical dimension of the cinema: indeed, it places technology in brackets, so much so that the modalities of the recording of the image – and above all of sound – are never truly debated.

The attention paid by Antonioni to technology has its roots both in this contested debate, and in the neo-realist indifference to it. Nevertheless, the encounter with electronics brings him to face a connection that could no longer be ignored. The cinema is a technological art: the adjective demands to be integrated into the noun. What Antonioni certainly does not do is to reverse the order of things in order to conclude that the cinema ought to become an artistic technology, and thus a field in which the accent is placed on the conditions of a making (the technological) rather than on the quality of such making (artistic). In the 1980s this reversal is virtually unthinkable; but, today, it has largely been realised. The cinema has by now abandoned the system of the arts (even if many continue to think in these terms) and has placed itself in an area in which design, informatics services, fashion and tourism dominate. Technical practices, indeed, aimed at creating quality products.[9]

'[T]he magnetic tape is perfectly equipped to take the place of traditional film. In a decade, the game will be over'

The transfer of *Il mistero di Oberwald* onto film stock was, in truth, a disaster: the 16mm did not succeed in rendering – not even minimally – the richness of the work that Antonioni made by electronic means. And the theatrical distribution of the film was practically non-existent. I am not even sure whether the copy I viewed to write these pages derived from the electronic tape or whether it was a transfer from the film stock: a small mystery (another one …) that says much about how the passage from the celluloid strip to the magnetic tape – or to other formats – has not been a simple and linear path.

In any case, it took over ten years for the film and the tape to become interchangeable; actually, they are still not, and probably will never be. In the meantime, the problem has shifted from the support of the image to the environment of the viewing experience. The cinema is still alive, but more and more outside its traditional setting, the cinema theatre. It migrates to domestic home theatres, museums and art galleries, or to means of transport, especially buses and aeroplanes, to the urban screens, but also to computers, tablets, mobile phones. It looks for new territories in which to settle, new spaces to vivify with its images and sounds. If, thus, it still lives, it is not because the film strip has been replaced by tape but, first and foremost, because a gigantic migration has occurred, one which has allowed it radically to colonise spaces that previously were extra-cinematographic or a-cinematographic. This migration of the cinema beyond its traditional borders I have called 'relocation'.[10] This is a trajectory characteristic of other media, like radio and television; it is a trajectory that aims, more than anything, to salvage the permanence of a 'type' of experience that each of these media had delineated; and, finally, it is a trajectory that describes the dynamics of media, and in particular the need for a kind of rootedness and proprietariness that pertains to the experiences that these media have made possible. Better this description of the state of things than concepts, such as that of remediation, which are nevertheless useful.

Why not, then, think of Antonioni's experiment as an episode that finds its place exactly in the archaeology of media relocation?

Notes

Translated from the Italian by Laura Rascaroli and John David Rhodes.

1. The sentences of Antonioni that I have used to title this and each of the following 'footnotes' are all taken from 'Almost a Confession', in *The Architecture of Vision: Writings and Interviews on the Cinema*, ed. Carlo Di Carlo and Giorgio Tinazzzi, trans. Marga Cottino-Jones (New York: Marsilio, 1996), pp. 127–9.

2. On RAI's cinema production, see Alberto Barbera (ed.), *Cavalcarono insieme. 50 anni di cinema e televisione in Italia* (Milan: Electa, 2004); and Vito Zagarrio (ed.), *Cine ma tv. Cinema, televisione, video nel nuovo millennio* (Turin: Lindau, 2004).

3. Antonioni, 'Almost a Confession', p. 128.

4. Rollin Summers, 'The Moving Picture Drama and the Acted Drama: Some Points of Comparison as to Technique', *Moving Picture World* (September 19, 1908), now in Stanley Kauffmann and Bruce Henstell (eds), *American Film Criticism: From the Beginnings to 'Citizen Kane'* (New York: Liveright, 1972), pp. 9–13.

5. Aldo Tassone, *I film di Michelangelo Antonioni. Un poeta della visione* (Rome: Gremese, 2002).

6. Sergei M. Eisenstein, 'First Letter about Color', *Film Reader* no. 2 (1977), pp. 181–4; 'One Path to Color: An Autobiographical Fragment', *Sight & Sound* vol. 30 no. 2 (1961), pp. 84–6.

7. Boris Groys, *Art Power* (Cambridge, MA: MIT Press, 2008).

8. The text by Luigi Pirandello I refer to, originally published in 1915, is *Shoot!: Notebooks of Serafino Gubbio Cinematographer*, trans. Charles Kenneth Scott-Moncrieff (Chicago: Chicago University Press, 2005); the text by Jean Epstein is 'Le Sens I bis', in *Bonjour Cinéma* (Paris: Éditions de la Sirène, 1921), pp. 27–44. For the term 'mechanical art' (which already appears, for instance, in Angiolo Orvieto, 'Spettacoli estivi: il cinematografo', *Corriere della Sera*, Milan, 21 August 1907), see the fundamental contribution by Eugenio Giovannetti, *Il cinema e le arti meccaniche* (Palermo: Sandron, 1930).

9. On the new place of the cinema among the arts of 'making' in the era of the media, and on its decidedly technical dimension, interesting observations may be found in Pietro Montani, *Bioestetica* (Rome: Carocci, 2007).

10. I discussed the concept of relocation in my essays: 'Filmic Experience', *Screen* vol. 50 no. 1 (Spring 2009), pp. 56–66; 'Elsewhere: The Relocation of Art', in Consuelo Ciscar Casabàn and Vincenzo Trione (eds), *Valencia09/Confines* (Valencia: INVAM, 2009), pp. 226–33; and 'Back to the Motherland: The Film Theatre in the Postmedia Age', *Screen* vol. 52 no. 1 (Spring 2011), pp. 1–12. See also Malte Hagener, 'Where Is Cinema (Today)? The Cinema in the Age of Media Immanence', in the monographic issue 'Relocations' of *Cinéma & Cie* no. 11 (Autumn 2008), pp. 15–22. The concept of remediation is put forward by Jay David Bolter and Richard Grusin in their *Remediation: Understanding New Media* (Cambridge, MA: MIT Press, 1999).

Michael Loren Siegel

IDENTIFICATION OF A MEDIUM:
Identificazione di una donna and the Rise of Commercial Television in Italy

Michelangelo Antonioni's *Identificazione di una donna* (*Identification of a Woman*, 1982) closes with a scene of rupture. The final moments consist of a rather campy series of science-fiction-inspired images featuring a tin-foil model of an asteroid-cum-spaceship flying towards abstract colour fields meant to represent outer space and the sun. The scene breaks not only from the film's carefully constructed, 'Antonionian' art-cinema discourse and its contemporary urban diegesis, but it also, in its cheap use of models and postmodernist genre pastiche, seems to betray everything we've come to know about Antonioni as a creator of serious, 'cinematic' images of graceful and resolute austerity.[1]

Narratively, these images represent a fantasy that the film's protagonist, the director Niccolò Farro (played with terrific aloofness and self-involvement by Tomas Milian), has of the film he will make in response to his failure to find 'the woman, the facts and the places' – and, hence, the inspiration – necessary to complete another project. The rest of the film depicts this failed quest, but in the end, having suffered through break-ups with two different lovers/actresses/potential characters in what seems to be a matter of weeks, Niccolò returns to his posh Roman flat, sets himself in the sun and mentally projects – as if on the glowing, internal screen of his closed eyelids – this highly fictionalised short about space travel, complete with a musical accompaniment reminiscent of Ligeti's choral atonality in *2001: A Space Odyssey* (1968) and the postmodern, New Age mysticism of Vangelis's *Blade Runner* (1982) score.[2]

In his 1984 review of the film, William Kelly aligns this ending with the motif of flight that we see used throughout Antonioni's work (ranging from the literal flight of model rockets in *La notte* (1961) and aeroplanes in *L'eclisse* (1962) and *Zabriskie Point* (1970), to the more figurative, spiritual and metaphysical 'flights' of characters into other worlds or into oblivion – Giuliana's island fantasy in *Il deserto rosso* (1964), the identity shift of Locke in *Professione: Reporter* (*The Passenger*, 1975), the disappearances of Anna in *L'avventura* (1960) and Piero and Vittoria in *L'eclisse* and so on).[3] The end of the film, then, represents some kind of flight or escape from external, objective reality into what Niccolò seems to hope will be a freer, internal, subjective realm of imagination – one precisely away from the creative 'crisis' in which he finds himself in reality. Niccolò's science-fiction-imbued imagination, then, is figured as both a solution to his impasse and an escape from it.

In Antonioni's work, Kelly argues, the motif of flight usually refers to a contemporary lack of ethics, responsibility and purpose. However, the act of flight itself is often depicted as a false or temporary liberation from the constraints of the phenomenologically and morally 'real' modern world – which, as we know from several interviews and statements (most famously one made at the Cannes Film Festival in 1960), Antonioni considers to exist in a highly dissonant and asynchronous relation with the human subject.[4] Flight, escape and imagination, in other words, all prove in Antonioni to be inadequate solutions to what is a more fundamental, historico-ontological problem. What results is what Seymour Chatman calls, 'collective banality', or, in Kelly's language, 'the sterility, or failure, of imagination, wherein our endeavors in the arts and sciences have fallen prey to myopia'.[5]

But the images at the end of *Identificazione di una donna* – and, indeed, as I will show, throughout the entirety of the film – posit a very different origin or driving force for this historical myopia than that which we see throughout the rest of Antonioni's oeuvre, one that, perhaps for this reason, has yet to be examined in relation to this film. The film's end is, without question, framed as a kind of mental flight on Niccolò's part. The images that we see are very deliberately and obviously coded as internal and subjective. What is crucial to note, however, is the extent to which this 'inner mind' has been invaded by external images. Niccolò's imagination is presented not as a site of autonomous and individualised image *production* (think of Guido's mental landscapes in Fellini's $8^{1}/_{2}$ [1963] by comparison, or even Daria's explosive fantasies at the end of Antonioni's own *Zabriskie Point*), but rather as just another site of image *consumption*.[6] The privileged access we are given to Niccolò's daydream reveals not an auteur's creative and unique mental world, but rather a series of regurgitated – perhaps we might say, using a more contemporary parlance, *reconditioned* – mass-media images, complete not only with specific generic markers, but also with signs of their own status precisely as constructed, as pop cultural and as derivative. The very projections of Niccolò's mind, in other words, present as a sort of B-film, complete with amateurish production values that foreground a blatantly obvious use of miniatures and chroma key technology, with ghostly, electronic smears of abstract, technological colour reminiscent of Antonioni's recent video experiment, *Il mistero di Oberwald* (*The Mystery of Oberwald*, 1980), and with a score that amounts to sci-fi pastiche. All of this suggests a subjective world that has been completely saturated or colonised by pop culture, media images and technologies of representation.[7] The space between subject and world, so vital an area of philosophical and formal investigation in Antonioni's earlier, more phenomenological-existentialist works, is here posited less as a boundary fraught with

217

Niccolò's imagination
of flight, heavily
mediatised by the
visual language of low-
budget space films
(*Identificazione di una
donna* [1982])

angst, desire, illusion, liberation and mystery, than as a permeable membrane
through which images produced for mass consumption ceaselessly flow. While
Antonioni's earlier films seem invested in a kind of deconstruction of the subject's
(and the camera's) apprehension of reality itself (and in the cinematic event that this
confrontation creates), here this entire process is mediated by the force of extra-
diegetic and extra-subjective images.[8]

The theme of collapsing boundaries – between subjective and objective, imagined and real, ideal and actual – abounds in the critical literature on the film.[9] Sam
Rohdie, for example, writes: 'real women and images of a woman multiply and disintegrate, to the point not only of their but of the narrative's extinction'. According
to Rohdie the film is 'doubly decentered: in the fiction that is sought within it, and
in the fiction that it is, as if simultaneously one is watching two narratives in search
of something which is never found and which is not even clear, but on which, nevertheless, their own narrative shape depends'.[10] What this tells us is simply that, as
elsewhere in Antonioni, meaning takes shape uncertainly and around an absent
centre. In this argument, *Identificazione di una donna* departs from the earlier work
only in the sense that it splits itself into a narrative and a meta-narrative.

What has yet to be examined in analyses of this film, however, is the crucial role
not just of questions of representation and reflexivity in general, but of mass media
and popular culture in particular. The decentring that we witness in *Identificazione
di una donna* must be seen not only as an extension of Antonioni's overall moral,
philosophical and aesthetic project (although it is this as well), but also as a response
to a new historical situation. This historical situation, as I will detail shortly, was
one defined by the sheer proliferation of media images and technologies of telecommunications that resulted from specific shifts in the Italian media landscape throughout the 1970s and 80s. It is its approach to image and media saturation that makes
this a properly *historical* film. *Identificazione di una donna* deals with the image not
only in abstract, universalising – almost Baudrillardian – terms, but also in highly
local and specific ones. What I will be arguing throughout this essay is that every bit
as much as it records Niccolò's personal and professional investigation of various

women, *Identificazione di una donna* also records Antonioni's cinematic investigation of an emergent media phenomenon in Italy in the 1970s and early 80s – namely, the presence, for the first time in the country's history, of a deregulated, national, commercial television system.

On 20 October 1984, under the direction of its nominally Socialist president, Bettino Craxi, the Italian Council of Ministers passed *decreto legge* number 694 concerning 'urgent measures for radio and television' in response to regional court-ordered blackouts of certain television stations. This decree, in tandem with *decreti legge* numbers 807 of 6 December and 223 of 1 June of the following year, would ensure the permanent legalisation of private ownership of national television stations for the first time in Italy's history. These three laws would come to be known as the *decreti Berlusconi* (the Berlusconi Decrees) after real-estate and media mogul Silvio Berlusconi.[11]

This would mark a crucial step in a long trajectory towards media saturation that began with the introduction of television by RAI (Radio Audizioni Italiana) in 1954. RAI began television broadcasting with a limited coverage area, a single network, complete governmental oversight and control, and a monopoly over all television transmissions until an arbitrarily set date of 15 December 1972. From its origins as a wing of the Christian Democrat executive branch, Italian TV was already connected to consumerism, privatisation and bourgeois power. Duplicating the radio-financing practices established under fascism, early television would be funded not through tax revenue (i.e., by the government), but via the private sector – by TV viewers on the one hand (in the form of licence fees) and advertisers on the other. Television's content would, in addition, articulate the ruling party's chief ideological values – linguistic uniformity, modernisation, the free market and, of course, the importance of Church and family.[12]

But it was not until the 1970s and 80s that television began to become a central aspect of the everyday life of the vast majority of Italians. This was due not to any specific governmental decision, but rather to the failure of regulation and the triumph of the free market. When 15 December 1972 arrived and the state's monopoly expired, a series of debates ensued about the future of television surrounding the question of regulation. After two and a half years of polemics (and stalling) by both the pro-corporate Right and the pro-regulation Left, a compromise was finally reached on 14 April 1975 that would allow RAI to retain its monopoly, but on the condition that control of the organisation be split amongst the various parties represented in parliament based on the number of seats held by each.

The government-controlled media utopia intended by this compromise was not to be, however. During the period with no regulatory framework (from December 1972 through April 1975), the Italian media landscape would be irreversibly altered. Seeing an opportunity for profit in the absence of regulation, a number of businessmen opened small, local, completely unregulated and *for-profit* TV stations

219

throughout the country. One by one, the government would attempt to shut these stations down through litigation, but this practice would prove to be ineffective, costly and, thanks to a 1976 Constitutional Court ruling, illegal as well. When the smoked cleared this time, RAI would be awarded a legal monopoly over all *national* broadcasting, but the government would retain no control whatsoever over *local* broadcasting. For-profit, local stations would be able to continue broadcasting – and expanding – throughout the peninsula.[13]

Among the entrepreneurs who benefited most from this ruling was, of course, Berlusconi. Since the court never stipulated *how many* local stations any single individual owner could control, Berlusconi shrewdly bought several of them and used trucking lines he already owned to distribute videocassettes with prepackaged content (mostly American shows intercut with Italian advertisements) to be aired simultaneously on all of his local stations. In this way, throughout the mid- to late 1970s and into the early 80s, Berlusconi, a private businessman, was able to defy the government and unify and consolidate his own 'public' – one that represented, according to Giuseppe Richieri, 30 to 40 per cent of all television viewers.[14] Fininvest, Berlusconi's holdings company (and Mediaset, its media holdings subsidy), established and purchased stations like Canale 5 (the heir of Berlusconi's Milan regional Telemilano), Rete 4 and Italia 1 that are still thriving in the twenty-first century.

Henceforth, Italy would have a 'mixed system' of ownership: the state would retain ownership of the RAI networks, but in theory anyone with enough capital (and the right connections) could reach a national audience. In practice, however, Berlusconi would monopolise the private market (and use it to propel himself into political office and legal immunity), and Italian state television would now be forced to compete with him for massive and ever-increasing sums of national advertising revenue. Television on the whole – regardless of its public or private ownership status – thereby became, in the words of Elena Dagrada, 'no longer … an educative instrument but … an integral part of the culture industry'.[15]

The effects of these institutional/industrial shifts were felt immediately. Berlusconi perceived – and indeed helped to produce – an emergent set of tastes, desires, ideologies and identities among Italians (the same ones that show up so visibly in *Identificazione di una donna*). His stations would be the first in Italy to rely on then cutting-edge marketing techniques (such as so-called 'narrowcasting') to organise their schedule grid. Using audience targeting and at every opportunity referring to and addressing its viewers not as colonised subjects (as the leftists of the time, among whom we can still count Antonioni despite his lack of orthodoxy, would have it), but rather as agents of free choice, Mediaset would strategically position itself as a beacon of individualism.[16] While Mediaset's broadcasts in Turin, Rome and Pescara were blacked out, the remainder of Berlusconi's networks decried the government's actions as restrictive not of corporate but of individual liberty.

Italian citizens, the broadcasts claimed, were at dire risk of losing their fundamental, 'freedom of the remote control' (*libertà di telecomando*).[17]

Disregarding its obvious hyperbole, this phrase reveals the close relationship in popular discourses of the time between new media forms and new subjectivities. Indeed, as Richieri notes, commercial television catered to a relatively 'new' audience within Italy's media history, viewers who associated the medium with certain ideals of liberty, who 'had been freed from financial hardship, were better educated and more independent in their views, and had more free time and wanted a wider range of information, culture and entertainment'.[18] Commercial television also produced a set of new viewing habits. Between 1977 and 1983, due to the growth of private networks, television dramatically increased its share as an outlet for advertising (from 18 to 53 per cent of all advertising costs nationwide). Of the 700 billion lire spent on television advertising in 1982, 415 billion (59.3 per cent) went to the private networks, 80 per cent of which went to Mediaset's stations (a number which exactly matches their viewership share – 80 per cent – among the privates), and much of which filtered through Publitalia, Fininvest's advertising firm and the largest in Italy.[19] Since advertising was the sole source of income for the private networks, stations like those owned by Mediaset vastly expanded their daily transmission periods in order to reach fringe audiences and attain a greater presence in the lives of already loyal viewers.[20]

Private networks were also able to make deeper inroads into their viewers' daily routines by adopting the American style of 'flow' first described by Raymond Williams.[21] As Mauro Wolf described the situation in 1986, with television deregulation,

> television and television time have been transformed into something co-extensive with the viewer's biographical time. This flow or sequence of programmes is not designed as something different from the subjective time and life of the viewer, but rather as something with which the spectator can become synchronized, and into which he or she can be inserted day or night. … A medium which used to be associated above all with leisure time is now assuming the role of a 'bystander' in everyday life, of an observer of common experiences, and of a companion in the viewer's daily life.[22]

Throughout the late 1970s and early 80s, in other words, television began to saturate the rhythms of everyday life. There were now double the number of broadcast hours (with some stations broadcasting twenty-four hours a day for the very first time), a vast increase in advertising slots, direct sales programmes and an emergent market for TV by-products like books, periodicals, LPs, posters, figurines, dolls and board and videogames. The consumerist images of mass culture, via the long arm of television, were moving beyond the screen to become a part of the very fabric of everyday life – of its practices and objects, its concepts and experiences.

The show that most clearly expressed private television's new role in Italian society was Canale 5's *Buongiorno Italia*. Airing for the first time in 1980 and directly inspired by ABC's *Good Morning, America*, *Buongiorno Italia* adapted the *programma contenitore* format (the 'hold-all' or 'variety show') usually reserved for leisure time in the evenings after work, to the morning hours. The morning variety show format was radical enough at the time that Mike Bongiorno, the host of *Buongiorno Italia*'s quiz show segment, *Bis*, and unarguably the largest television star in Italy's history to that point, opened the first episode of the segment with a speech explaining the move:

> Today is a very important day for us at Canale 5, and for me in particular since it is my very first morning show. As you know, this is the first day on which Canale 5 is running this band of programming in the morning called *Buongiorno Italia*, and as you've already heard many times, we are doing it ... for the elderly, for grandmas and grandpas, for young children, for those who are unfortunate enough to be in the hospital so that way they can have something to pass the time in the morning, and naturally, of course, also for every other person who happens to be out and about and, when they have five minutes at a bar or some place, want to look in on what we're doing on Canale 5.[23]

As this monologue reveals, like *Good Morning, America*, *Buongiorno Italia* attempted to infiltrate the daily habits of all Italians. And as with *Good Morning, America*, it would use an ideology of liveness – not just in the temporal sense of concurrence or simultaneity of broadcasting time and viewing time, but also in the more phenomenological/ontological sense of 'being there', everywhere – to accomplish this.[24] What is also important here is the enormous extent to which television maps spatio-temporal categories such as liveness onto the social body itself, all in the name of reaching deeper and deeper into the individual lives that comprise that social body. Simply put, Italian television was attempting at this time – and for the first time – to be everywhere at all times, to become one with everyday life and to be isomorphic with society itself.

If the late 1970s and early 80s can be seen as a privileged moment in an ongoing process of Italian televisualisation, one in which the fundamental social, subjective and phenomenological shifts which television entails are made visible in various areas of cultural production, then it is precisely this transition that *Identificazione di una donna* tracks. Not only are questions of media, technology, recording, surveillance and representation foregrounded within the film's diegesis, but in more subtle ways that I will discuss below, a representational and discursive tension haunts the film's very textuality as well. This tension, I will argue, can be traced to the sudden and vast expansion of mass media in Italian life. The film's arrangement of sound and image – its form and style – demonstrates certain contradictory effects precisely around acts of looking, perceiving and recording, ones that do not so much, as in the earlier Antonioni, open onto questions of being as such, as they reveal a filmic discourse that has been contaminated by the images and techniques of a vaster media universe.

In this sense, what is bad about the film – its seeming uncertainty, its unmotivated and uninspired lack of narrative cohesion, its stylistic sloppiness, its grotesque sexuality, its vulgar pop-influenced music – is also what is most interesting about it. Indeed, this formulation of *Identificazione di una donna* as a 'bad' or vulgar film intentionally flies in the face of the opinion shared by many of the film's initial critics – namely, that it was a film of great formal grace and delicacy; in short, an *Antonioni* film. Giving voice to a global critical community that lauded the film's supposed formal perfections and collectively celebrated the return of this master auteur after a long hiatus, Seymour Chatman has written that the film 'has all the familiar compositional brilliance of an Antonioni film. The framing is elegant as ever. Proportions are marked off crisply by the horizontals and verticals of door frames and windows and other architectural details.'[25]

With all due respect to Chatman and others, I simply and fundamentally disagree with this position. Despite certain, isolated moments of formal beauty, I find *Identificazione di una donna* to be a particularly ugly, even vulgar film by any standard, not just that of Antonioni. However, this does not make it any less interesting or critically useful (quite the contrary, as I argue throughout this essay), just less attractive. The film's science-fiction finale with which I began this essay, constructed as it is out of the debased, vulgar imagery of popular culture, only makes explicit what has been one of the film's central concerns all along, namely, the changing status of the 'image' – cinematic and photographic, but mental and imaginative as well – in a world entirely saturated by them. *Identificazione di una donna* launches its critique of television, in other words, not from any critical *distance*, but rather right from within the thick of popular imagery. In this sense, in its textual appropriation of the popular, the film discursively bears out Martin Heidegger's famous dictum that television represents 'the abolition of every possibility of remoteness'.[26]

Indeed, *Identificazione di una donna* is a film that seems to be unable to keep its distance from the popular, and to be always on the verge of buckling under the weight of extra-diegetic images and signifiers. One place that this can be clearly seen – or heard, rather – is on the film's soundtrack. The film's musical score, much of which was composed by former Ultravox front man John Foxx, is strikingly unusual for an Antonioni film. Although Antonioni had used contemporary rock songs in his films before (Pink Floyd, the Rolling Stones and the Grateful Dead in *Zabriskie Point*, the Yardbirds in *Blow-Up* [1966] etc.), never before had he approved an original musical score that was so steeped in the language of the growing genre of 'pop'. Foxx's tawdry, New Age-influenced, electro-synth score – heavy on electric guitar and keyboards – has a highly alienating effect in this film. This is underscored by its disorientating diegetic status: on multiple occasions, sound fidelity is deceptively used to suggest that it is non-diegetic only for it to be retrospectively revealed as diegetic by the appearance of a turntable or stereo. In addition, Foxx's non-diegetic music is explicitly paralleled by similar pop music that is more obviously marked as diegetic throughout the film (coming from Niccolò's neighbour's apartment at the very beginning of the film, from his car later, from a teeny-bop fashion boutique in a trendy shopping area in Rome, etc.).

Despite its alienating qualities, Foxx's music is at times quite catchy (and is, perhaps, all the more alienating because of this).[27] In its excessive major key optimism, its abstraction and its instrumentation, in fact, it closely resembles the 'marketability' quotient of the musical scores of a number of foreign and domestic-Italian television programmes and advertisements of the era – the very popular *Hart to Hart* and even to some degree *Dallas* and *Cagney and Lacey* (all of which aired on Mediaset's stations), for example, along with Canale 5's disco show *Popcorn* and RAI's quiz show *Flash*, and many of RAI's and Mediaset's 1970s and 80s *sigle* (station liner theme songs).[28] Besides simply having the quality of catchiness (which, indeed, as anyone who has been unable to get a song 'out of their head' knows, represents a kind of colonisation of consciousness by popular culture), this music also directly links *Identificazione di una donna* to a larger media sphere in a manner that is quite divergent from Antonioni's earlier, more modernist works. While the latter may have extensively examined issues of image-making and representation on a philosophical and proto-political level, even to the point of including references to pop culture and music, they held themselves much further apart from pop culture than does *Identificazione di una donna* at the level of their own textuality and mode of address.

Here, there is no denying the extent to which the popular is integrated into the film's discourse at the level of sound and music. But what is crucial to note is the rather critical *mode* of this integration. In many places in the film, Foxx's score ends up being used – intentionally or not – in such a way as not to sharpen but to blunt the dramatic, stylistic, or philosophical effect of a given scene or shot. This is especially noticeable in moments when abstraction is introduced via oblique framing and

Eros, vulgarity and postmodern simulation in *Identificazione di una donna* (1982)

camera autonomy in ways that recall Antonioni's modernist experiments in the 1960s, only to then be undercut by the score's postmodern, pop sleaziness. We see this most frequently around the depiction of sex (here, Eros truly is sick, as Antonioni always insisted it was), but one especially notable example involving a more classically Antonionian scenario occurs early in the film when Niccolò, returning to his apartment after meeting his blackmailer at a gelateria, sits down to write in front of his open window.[29] Niccolò here is framed in a classic Antonionian composition: squeezed into a corner of the frame by a large window opening onto posh Roman suburbs and an empty sky, he jots in his notebook before leaning back and seemingly beginning, as we've seen so many times throughout Antonioni's work, to ponder, along with the camera itself, the thereness of the view, the window's role in framing it and the very act of looking itself. But while the visual drama of a shot like this would be underscored by silence in the earlier Antonioni (or simultaneously underscored and dislocated by abstract, electronic noise as in *Il deserto rosso*), here we have only driving, minimalist electro-pop, the kind that reminds us of all of the pop music we hear diegetically throughout the film's Rome. Furthermore, the shot is left on the screen far too briefly for Niccolò or the spectator to register its visual dynamics. Whereas in an earlier Antonioni film this shot would have far outlasted its strictly narrative value in order to register with the viewer in purely visual or phenomenological terms, here, after just a few beats, and immediately after Niccolò leans back, a cut gives us a very brief reverse shot before a dissolve begins a flashback to Niccolò's first encounter with Mavi. This combination of Foxx's pop-influenced music, the unbalanced, comparatively rushed style of editing (it is worth noting here, in passing, that Antonioni's role in the editing process was so central that he gave himself the sole editing credit for the first time in his entire career) and the presence of a narrative device like the flashback completely undercuts the more phenomenological and durational exploration of the shot itself.

I would like to argue that moments like this – and the film is absolutely brimming with them – reveal a tension between two discursive modes: on the one hand, a signature, authorial discourse that foregrounds Antonioni's classic phenomenological concerns (vision and the gaze, space and the subject, etc.) and, on the other, a more jittery and distracted visual discourse, one that is associated with the film's musical soundtrack and thereby a vaster field of pop-cultural production – which would, of course, have been dominated by television at this time in the ways I outline above – and one in which images seem nothing more than vague and disposable glances. The critical *distance* that Antonioni's earlier films expressed towards the popular, in other words, has here been replaced by a critical *inclusion* (Heidegger's lack of 'remoteness'). As this scene at the window demonstrates, while this critical inclusion of the popular is epitomised by the film's soundtrack (in addition to Foxx's score there are also pop songs by Orchestral Manoeuvres in the Dark, Tangerine Dream and Italian pop star Gianna Nannini, a kind of gutless, Italo-rock version of

Niccolò explaining his
arrangement of images
of women to his
second lover, Ida

Cyndi Lauper, complete with the working-class encoding, ambiguous sexuality and celebration of girl culture), it is highly visible in the film's visual discourse – its arrangement of images – as well.[30]

Indeed, *Identificazione di una donna* is, if nothing else, about the collection, placement, arrangement and use of images and representations. From the images of women Niccolò obsessively collects, posts and arranges to the x-rays that dot the walls of his sister's office, from Mavi's oft-appearing glamour shot that she places prominently on her own wall, to photographic mannequins and glossy magazines, this film's *mise en scène* is a riot of images and technologies of representation. For Niccolò the film-maker, then, making a film is not about producing new images (his sketches, after all, get him nowhere) as much as it is about navigating the whole series of already-existing images with which he is constantly bombarded. Similarly, for Antonioni the film-maker, it is no longer a question of inventing a new visual language to grapple – like some tragic hero of Enlightenment itself – with the impossibility of ever framing something correctly (and here we cannot help but think of a defeated but hopeful Vittoria shifting abstract objects around on a table within an open picture frame near the beginning of *L'eclisse*), but rather of finding the right, already-existing thing or image in a world that – as a result of the shifts in the role of mass media in everyday, Italian life that I outline above – was being filled with things and saturated with images at a rapidly increasing rate.

Although we barely see television appear in the diegesis, in other words, its presence as a mode of image production, distribution and, indeed, saturation haunts the film's discourse. The activity of looking itself, so intensified in the earlier Antonioni, is highly attenuated here. Antonioni's thorough, precise, rigorous and empirical combination of camerawork, *mise en scène* and montage is replaced with a style that is at times awkward, distracted and even a bit clumsy. This aspect of the film's style – indeed, its failures at the level of style – can, I'd like to argue, be seen as an attempt to engage critically with what John Ellis has famously referred to as television's 'glance'-based visual regime (as opposed to cinema's 'gaze'-based operations). As Ellis defines it,

226

> TV's regime of vision is less intense than cinema's: it is a regime of the glance rather than the gaze. The gaze implies a concentration of the spectator's activity into that of looking, the glance implies that no extraordinary effort is being invested in the activity of looking. The very terms we habitually use to designate the person who watched TV or the cinema screen tend to indicate this difference. The cinema-looker is a spectator: caught by the projection yet separate from its illusion. The TV-looker is a viewer, casting a lazy eye over proceedings, keeping an eye on events, or, as the slightly archaic designation had it, 'looking in'.[31]

Antonioni's camera does, at times, cast 'a lazy eye over proceedings' in *Identificazione di una donna*. This can be seen above all in the combination, used frequently throughout the film, of various types of camera movement (pans, tilts, tracks, cranes, etc.) with zooms (both in and out, sometimes within the same shot). Although this technique had been explored by other important art-cinema directors beginning in the 1960s (Visconti, Kurosawa, Bergman, etc.) and indeed by Antonioni himself (most famously in the final sequence shot of *Professione: Reporter*), here not only is it used with much greater frequency but, unlike in these earlier examples, its occurrence will often – much like the pop music I discuss above – counter a precise composition with a seemingly random irruption of anti-formalism.

This can be seen as early as the second shot of the film. While the first shot offers a disorientating, extreme high angle of a front door and vestibule before Niccolò enters, climbs the stairs and a well-defined upward tilt reframes him against his building's graceful arched ceilings, the second, which awaits him from a reverse angle at the top of the stairs, zooms in and pans right as he approaches, seemingly without any motivation except the reframing itself. This choice – along with the shot/reverse-shot that ensues between Niccolò and his neighbour's closing door (behind which jazzy contemporary pop music plays) – obliterates the architectural elaboration set up by the first shot, thereby undercutting Antonioni's modernist mode of looking. This pan-and-zoom has none of the pictorialist qualities of the telephoto lens in a film such as *Il deserto rosso* which, as Antonioni himself has said, was intended to 'get two-dimensional effects, to diminish the distances between people and objects, make them seem flattened against each other'.[32] Here, by contrast, the zoom simply makes the camera's gaze seem unstable and distracted. Similar moments occur throughout the film (as when the camera rests for a moment on a painting of Castel San'Angelo and St Peter's Basilica hanging on Niccolò's wall only to be seemingly 'distracted' by Niccolò's tossed sport coat which it suddenly zooms out and pan-tilts to follow, or when Niccolò first notices the abandoned bird's nest in his tree – ostensibly the part-inspiration for his spaceship fantasy that closes the film – and the camera tracks with him out to his terrace before suddenly 'picking out' the strange object and shakily panning and zooming towards it). What they all have in common is a kind of aesthetic indifference. The particular 'gaze' that

227

the zoom might entail is never problematised, foregrounded, or in any way explored here, nor does the camera seem to be seeking abstraction for its own sake. These shots instead articulate precisely the kind of careless vision that Ellis associates with a televisual – as opposed to filmic – regime of visuality.

Television and popular culture, in other words, insinuate themselves into the film's very discursive modes via the use of pop music, a general anti-formalism and a kind of narrative lostness (that is also reflected in the film's rather episodic, segmented and disorientating organisation of narrative temporality). The recognition of a discursive presence of television might be used to explain a number of other things about the film as well – its blue-white, shadowless interior lighting, for example, which references a highly efficient, televisual mode of production (where simply getting images is far more important than composing or lighting them artistically), its moments of overdetermined melodrama (such as when Mavi tearfully watches Niccolò through her girlfriend's window, or when mirrors and windows underscore Ida's announcement to Niccolò that she is pregnant by another man), and its heavy-handed use of flashbacks and dissolves. This is, of course, countered by remnants of Antonioni's modernist impulses (an interest in fog, horizons and the unrepresentability of nature, an elliptical temporality, a general self-reflexivity around looking, windows and frames, etc.). Together, the tension between these two tendencies is what is responsible for the film's rather unusual, fractured discourse.

228

*　　*　　*

Returning, then, to the final moments of the film with which I opened this essay, we might ask, given the particular history that I've outlined and the terms of visual discourse set up by the film, what a fantasy or flight *into* the visual regime of pop culture means for Niccolò – and for Antonioni – in a film made at the beginning of the 1980s. As Ivo Franchi has noted, like earlier Antonioni protagonists such as Thomas in *Blow-Up* and Locke in *Professione: Reporter*, Niccolò 'has an almost maniacal need to "frame" situations and people. He tries to see, but because he relies upon outdated and inadequate means of understanding (*mezzi di conoscenza*), he can't.'[33] If here, however, unlike in the earlier films, the protagonist's inadequacy has something to do with the increased presence of mass-media images – and with those of television in particular – then, we might say that, like the film itself, Niccolò succeeds in the end precisely where he fails. Because he never finds his character, Niccolò is forced to adopt a new means of understanding, a new means of looking – one that, in the hyper-mediatised images of the tin-foil spaceship, effectively engages with, incorporates and assimilates in fantasy the image culture that Niccolò seems so unable to navigate in reality.

As for Antonioni himself, if the quest here has been – as it always has – to use cinema to articulate a changing object world, then he, like Niccolò, has succeeded through assimilation. What has changed about the object world in this case is the very role of images in it. Here, Antonioni produces a discourse that, in its very formal failures and uncertainties, seems to critically imbibe or assimilate pop culture and mass media. In *Identificazione di una donna*, in other words, Antonioni turns his cinematic phenomenology towards the identification of a medium – the medium of television, and in particular the forms, meanings and expanded presence it was beginning to take on as it moved into a commercial-corporate phase in Italy in the 1970s and 80s.

Notes

1. This is not the first time in his career that Antonioni has used the final moments of his films to institute a diegetic break. This occurs most famously in *L'eclisse* (1962), when neither Vittoria nor Piero show up for a rendez-vous and the camera is left to freely wander a centreless world of pure cinematic events; *Zabriskie Point* (1970), where various consumer objects are exploded in slow motion to a psychedelic, Pink Floyd score; and *Professione: Reporter* (*The Passenger*, 1975) when the camera cranes away from the film's dead protagonist in order to wander the surroundings of the hotel in which he has died. *Identificazione di una donna*'s ending, however, is the first in which we see an actual shift in recording medium (from cinema to video).

2. Seymour Chatman 'blames' the weakness of the ending purely on a lack of funding: 'The ship looks a bit forlorn, more like a meteorite than Voyager II. ... The sad truth may be that Antonioni's budget was too small for a more sensational effect. ... It is sad that Antonioni's budget did not permit him to end the film with the kind of finale that he wanted (and that it seems to need). For if the science fiction sequence had been realised with effects of the caliber of *2001*, *Star Wars*, or *Blade Runner*, one's feelings about Niccolò and his situation as an artist might be entirely different.' What Chatman seems to miss is both the obvious extent to which Antonioni foregrounds his poverty of means here and the intertextual references provided not only by the soundtrack but also by the cheap special effects themselves. In wanting to preserve Antonioni's image as a modernist auteur, in other words, it seems to be that Chatman misses the powerfully postmodernist gestures in this sequence. Seymour Chatman, *Antonioni, or the Surface of the World* (Berkeley and Los Angeles: University of California Press, 1985), pp. 222 and 237.

3. William Kelly, '*Identification of a Woman* by Michelangelo Antonioni', *Film Quarterly* vol. 37 no. 3 (1984), pp. 37–43.

4. Upon the release of *L'avventura* at Cannes in 1960, Antonioni outlined the film's – and his own – aesthetic project as one of articulating the contradiction between the progressive and scientific nature of human reality, and the regressive, rigid and retrograde experience of human morality. Antonioni famously wrote that man [sic] 'reacts, he loves, he hates, he suffers under the sway of moral forces and myths which

today, when we are at the threshold of reaching the moon, should not be the same as those that prevailed in Homeric times, but nevertheless are'. See Michelangelo Antonioni, 'A Talk with Michelangelo Antonioni on his Work' [1961], in *The Architecture of Vision: Writings and Interviews on Cinema*, ed. Carlo Di Carlo and Giorgio Tinazzi, trans. Marga Cottino-Jones (New York: Marsilio, 1996), pp. 21–47 (pp. 32–3).

5. Kelly, '*Identification of a Woman* by Michelangelo Antonioni', p. 42 and Chatman, *Antonioni*, p. 231.

6. Chatman, *Antonioni*, p. 219.

7. The somewhat degraded, pop saturation of this closing scene becomes clear when it is compared to the film's other 'fantasy' sequence (Mavi's flashbacks to her days learning sea rescue at college in Wales) and its other 'outer space' sequence (the close-up of the sun as seen through Niccolò's telescope). The former, equal parts documentary and Technicolor aesthetic indulgence (and similar in this way to the island sequence in *Il deserto rosso*), relies extensively on an art-film encoding, emphasising the awesome power of the sea through 'golden hour' shooting and the use of telephoto lenses and synch sound. The latter, on the other hand, refers to the highly esteemed scientific and technological visual language of the telescope with its promise of truth, knowledge and power.

8. For a fascinating take on the relationship between Antonioni's work – especially his early films – and phenomenology, see John Schliesser, 'Antonioni's Heideggerian Swerve', *Literature Film Quarterly* vol. 26 no. 4 (1998), pp. 278–87.

9. In addition to Kelly's piece, other worthwhile literature of particular interest to *Identificazione di una donna* includes Gideon Bachmann and Michelangelo Antonioni, 'A Love of Today: An Interview with Michelangelo Antonioni', *Film Quarterly* vol. 36 no. 4 (1983), pp. 1–4; Gualtiero De Santi, '*Identificazione di una donna* di Michelangelo Antonioni', *Cineforum* vol. 22 no. 12 (1982), pp. 31–8; Áine O'Healy, 'Oedipus Adrift: Unraveling Patriarchy in Antonioni's *Identificazione di una donna*', *Romance Languages Annual* (1989), pp. 56–61; Seymour Chatman and Michleangelo Antonioni, 'Antonioni in 1980: An Interview', *Film Quarterly* vol. 51 no. 1 (Autumn 1997), pp. 2–10; as well as various interviews and writings in Antonioni, *The Architecture of Vision*, the strong essays collected in Maria Orsini (ed.), *Michelangelo Antonioni. I film e la critica 1943–1995: un'antologia* (Roma: Bulzoni, 2002), pp. 281–92, and Bert Cardullo (ed.), *Michelangelo Antonioni: Interviews* (Jackson, MS: University Press of Mississippi, 2008).

10. Sam Rohdie, *Antonioni* (London: BFI, 1990), pp. 43 and 188.

11. Historical data and facts in this section are drawn from Giuseppe Richieri, 'Television from Service to Business: European Tendencies and the Italian Case', in Phillip Drummond and Richard Patterson (eds), *Television in Transition: Papers from the First International Television Studies Conference* (London: BFI, 1986), pp. 21–35; Giuseppe Richieri, 'Hard Times for Public Service Broadcasting: The RAI in the Age of

Commercial Competition', Philip Schlesinger, 'The Berlusconi Phenomenon', and Mauro Wolf, 'The Evolution of Television Language in Italy Since Deregulation', in Zygmunt G. Baranski and Robert Lumley (eds), *Culture and Conflict in Postwar Italy: Essays on Mass and Popular Culture* (New York: St Martin's Press, 1990), pp. 256–94; David Forgacs, 'Cultural Consumption, 1940s to 1990s', in David Forgacs and Robert Lumley (eds), *Italian Cultural Studies: An Introduction* (Oxford: Oxford University Press, 1996), pp. 273–90; Christopher Wagstaff, 'The Media', in Zygmunt G. Baranski and Rebecca J. West (eds), *The Cambridge Companion to Modern Italian Culture* (Cambridge: Cambridge University Press, 2001), pp. 293–310; Paul Ginsborg, *A History of Contemporary Italy: Society and Politics, 1943–1988* (New York: Palgrave Macmillan, 2003); and Paul Ginsborg, *Silvio Berlusconi: Television, Power, and Patrimony* (London: Verso, 2004).

12. The phrase 'educative model' is from Elena Dagrada, 'Television and its Critics: A Parallel History,' in Forgacs and Lumley, *Italian Cultural Studies*, pp. 233–47.

13. Wagstaff, 'The Media', p. 294.

14. Richieri, 'Hard Times for Public Service Broadcasting', p. 260

15. Dagrada, 'Television and its Critics', p. 244.

16. Wagstaff, 'The Media', p. 296.

17. Ginsborg, *Silvio Berlusconi*, p. 38.

18. Richieri, 'Hard Times for Public Service Broadcasting', p. 259.

19. Richieri, 'Television from Service to Business', p. 32.

20. Ibid., p. 29

21. This is first developed in Raymond Williams, *Television: Technology and Cultural Form* (Hanover, NH: Wesleyan University Press, 1992).

22. Wolf, 'The Evolution of Television Language in Italy Since Deregulation', p. 287.

23. Trans. by MS. The original text of Bongiorno's speech is, 'Oggi è un giorno molto importante per noi di Canale 5 anche per me in particolare perché per la prima volta faccio un programma di mattino. Ma come sapete questo è il primo giorno in cui Canale 5 inizia questa fascia di mattino che si chiama *Buongiorno Italia* e, come vi è già stato detto parecchie volte, dedicata … alle persone anziane, i nonni, le nonne, i bambini, a quelle che stanne negli ospedali sfortunatamente così avranno un passatempo al mattino e poi naturalmente anche a tutte le altre persone che sono in giro fuori casa, magari quando hanno cinque minuti si fermano lì al bar e seguiranno quello che facciamo noi a Canale 5.' Accessed 15 July 2010 at http://www.youtube.com (clip removed). Bongiorno was such an influential presence that Umberto Eco effectively equated him with all of Italian popular culture in an essay entitled, 'The Phenomenology of Mike Bongiorno'. See Umberto Eco, *Misreadings*, trans. William Weaver (New York: Harcourt, 1993), pp. 156–64.

24. Jane Feuer, 'The Concept of Live Television: Ontology as Ideology', in E. Ann Kaplan (ed.), *Regarding Television* (Los Angeles: American Film Institute, 1983), pp. 12–21.

25. Chatman, *Antonioni*, p. 34.

231

26. Martin Heidegger, *Poetry, Language, Thought*, trans. Albert Hofstadter (New York: Harper & Row, 1971), p. 163.

27. On 'catchiness' and its relation to the marketability of music in the 1980s, see Don Traut, ' "Simply Irresistible": Recurring Accent Patterns as Hooks in Mainstream 1980s Music', *Popular Music* vol. 24 no. 1 (2005), pp. 57–77.

28. Clips of the Italian material – *Popcorn*, <http://www.youtube.com/watch?v= QKTObUjkksA)>; *Flash*, <http://www.youtube.com/watch?v=1g6H7RAk8nc)>; and RAI *sigle*, <http://www.youtube.com/watch?v=11qEKwlN-Mg&feature=related>, <http://www.youtube.com/watch?v=vGyANXj3sAo&NR=1)> – are available on YouTube (all accessed 20 July 2010).

29. Antonioni's oft-quoted formulation 'Eros is sick', can be found in 'A Talk with Michelangelo Antonioni on His Work', p. 34.

30. Antonioni also worked with Nannini on the music video for her song 'Fotoromanzo'. See <http://www.youtube.com/watch?v=JT_CTOllIDA>. I thank Jacopo Benci for this reference.

31. John Ellis, *Visible Fictions: Cinema, Television, Video* (New York: Routledge, 1982), p. 137.

32. Quoted in Seymour Chatman, *Antonioni: The Complete Films*, ed. Paul Duncan (Köln: Taschen, 2004), p. 92.

33. Quoted in Orsini, *Michelangelo Antonioni*, p. 283.

Ecologies

Karl Schoonover

ANTONIONI'S WASTE MANAGEMENT

One of Antonioni's first films, the documentary short on garbage collection *N.U.* (*Nettezza Urbana*, 1948) stakes a claim: some subject matter is so ordinary that it requires a revision to the act of seeing for visual comprehension to begin. Where trash goes and who handles it is mundane, so taken for granted that it has become invisible to us, the viewers addressed by the film. The voice-over narrator begins, 'Over the course of a day, we encounter so many people and things and activities that seem familiar and routine but which we actually know little about – only the little that directly affects our lives. Everything else is foreign to us.' The film focuses on trash and its collectors as a means of retraining our vision along these lines: to see this foreignness in the everyday, to look beyond what we have assumed are the direct forces guiding our lives. What is at stake is the visibility of waste management. This doesn't just mean showing the garbage itself. It also means exposing our visual, ideological relationship to the world.

One of the film's most remarkable shots demonstrates how this film hopes to effect this change. It begins with the voice-over narration asking how the street cleaners see the life of the city. On the screen, the camera follows a man in a middle-class suit jacket walking by with a large bouquet of flowers. As his body traverses the screen, a small wooden structure obstructs our view of him and the camera comes to stop on a shack that looks something like a newsstand. The back door of this structure swings gently open, as if it has been caught by a wind. Inside the shack's dark interior we see a large dirty scrap of paper dancing, perhaps also stirred by the passing breeze. After a few seconds of watching this simple, poetic movement, a human figure emerges from the darkness and from under the paper. The voice-over tells us that this man is one of the street cleaners just waking for his day, and then the film moves on to another scene. In this crushingly eloquent shot, the camera moves our attention from one kind of human living to another. The shot attunes our vision to the grace of this ulterior mode of life. Just before this shot, the film alludes to a cultural bias of perception – one that threatens to dehumanise the street cleaner and remove him from our view: 'They seem like some inanimate part

236

A series of frame grabs from a shot in *N.U.* (1948)

of the city.' The brief poetic moment of this shot suggests that human agency has been replaced by what looks like an inanimate force – the random accident of the wind swirling with the abandoned piece of refuse. This moment seems to awaken another tempo, a different determinism, a new visuality. At first, this shot appears to toss us between narrativism and formalism. It betrays two modes of narration. On the one hand, it narrates our desire to know, to understand fully through seeing it all, through following the active vectors of agents. On the other hand, it works to dissolve those impulses, asking us to experience what it feels like to see without wanting *to know* so badly, to watch and not immediately reconcile what we see to what we already know of the world. Antonioni attempts to retrain the eye in this shot through a blurring of agency: what opens the structure's door is unclear, it seems like coincidence, but in this moment there is a suspension of cause and effect. We are asked to simply take in this microevent. And in doing so, the film invites us to occupy a temporality in which the utility of built structures and the purpose of made objects seem inconsequential, or at least less apparent – one in which things loosen themselves from the teleology of human intention and potential use. It is this microevent's elaboration of objects as waste that enables forms to fall away from their perceived function.

Here *N.U.* tells us something important about all of Antonioni's films. Waste is always at the threshold between the diegetic world and formal experimentation. It marks the place where narrative gives way to formalism, figurative signals non-figurative, realism dissolves into modernism. Refuse is a vestige of the narrative world that suddenly requires a different kind of seeing and understanding. And yet the gesture of this shot is quite telling, for, like all of Antonioni's films, it never fully gives way to abstraction. It can't seem to fully escape a world of objects. It remains both doomed to a world of things and committed to the people who must inhabit that world. In the following essay, I track an evolving dialectic between the modernist image and the politics of waste across three decades of the director's films. These films' thematic emphasis on the management of refuse must, I believe, be considered in the context of the formal excesses so often associated with Antonioni's style and art cinema in general. Waste is not just a theme of his films; it is a material process that serves as their methodological foundation. Their particular use of waste requires us to understand not only a specific late-capitalist mode of visuality (an eye trained to find coherence in a world cluttered with commodities) but also comments on that visuality. In other words, to understand these aesthetics is to understand Antonioni's anomalous environmentalism.

The Criterion Collection's Blu-Ray DVD edition of *Il deserto rosso* (1964) includes *N.U.* in its carefully selected supplements, positioning it as a key source text. And while it is convenient to have this remastered version of the short film on the DVD, it has long been a critical commonplace to suggest that *N.U.*'s formal impulses foreshadow a distinctive directorial style that would only fully emerge a

237

decade later in Antonioni's four masterpieces of the early 1960s.[1] Widely regarded by contemporary viewers as an unprecedented expansion of the cinematic image's expressive range, Antonioni's style seems exemplified by excessive images that refuse to guarantee narrative or semantic utility: the detached, somewhat opaque visual narration of a meandering and distractible gaze (*L'avventura*, 1960); the periodic filling up of the frame with the relative emptiness of an under-populated urban landscape left fallow (*La notte*, 1961); a temporal distension of narrative to explore the inexorable visual surreality of ordinary objects (*L'eclisse*, 1962); the dwarfing of human figures by the landscape and the composition of shots (*Il deserto rosso*, 1964). In tracing these formal tendencies back to *N.U.*, critics mention only briefly an overlapping of theme, loosely gesturing towards a connection between *N.U.*'s garbage and *Il deserto rosso*'s toxic landscape. What matters most to these commentators about *N.U.* is its move away from content, away from neo-realism's fetishistic relationship to profilmic material and towards a pure formalism. I would like to complicate this trajectory, deflect its teleology towards final and complete abstraction. If *N.U.*'s stylistic prescience tells us anything, it tells us that Antonioni's formal relationship to the image, to composition and to the non-figurative was always negotiated from the powerfully insistent presence of refuse, the material of waste and remnants. For example, in a key gesture shared by this early documentary and *L'avventura* – the tossing of paper – we find a complex dialectic of form and content, one that in both films declares an abandonment of narrative authority, an invocation of the randomness of life and a reflection on modernity's inherent relation to and production of excess. The toss of the paper begins a movement away from formal documentary narration. As *N.U.*'s voice-over recedes, re-enacted vignettes are replaced with a looser observational approach to the image, and the otherwise formal (waltz-like) piano music gives way to a jazz and blues of brass and wind instruments. Jazz signals experimentation as use and reuse, rifts and borrowings, improvisation as the expansion of a formal scale of certain elements to the detriment of linear progression, economic trajectories towards endpoints, and clear pacing.[2]

In what follows, I explore how this pictographic (almost documentary) interest in refuse stands at the base of Antonioni's most famous aesthetic excesses. In the essay's first section, I examine his *mise en scène* of refuse in several films in the context of a wider cultural politics of waste, from the obligations of quasi-neo-realist 'rubble' to a sublime of toxic dumping. In section two, I turn to examine one particular element of his *mise en scène* of waste: his compulsive interest in the dirtied or deteriorated surface. I connect his treatment of walls to theories of surface and looking. In the final section, I put pressure on the productive – or plastic – qualities of waste across Antonioni's work. Trash and refuse allow his films a formal means of expression, but I am also interested in the politics of this investment, a modernism that turns to waste as a means of producing a more plastic image. His films qualify as a truly 'plastic' cinema whose agile geometries, reflective opacities and even saturated colours are enabled by the consequences of a built world. Recognising his works as 'by-products' helps us to see Antonioni's attention to the social, environmental and even political conundrum of late capitalism's inescapable excess, and at the same time points to his keen self-reflection on cinema as modernism's rapprochement of waste and the aesthetic.

Detritus

A hyperbolic upsizing of large-scale industry's infrastructure in Europe ushered in the economic miracle, 'il boom', or what Victoria de Grazia has called the era of 'market empire'. Pumped up on the potential of nuclear energy, the greater accessibility to petroleum and the infinite multitasking of petroleum's flexible by-product, plastic, the new era of plentitude promised to whisk away postwar squalor with an array of dazzling commodities.[3] Yet plenitude also came with a new kind of trash. This miraculous moment of productivity and unprecedented abundance brought with it a stubborn kind of waste. Detritus no longer decomposed; it threatened to fill our lives, crowd us out and outlast us. This ubiquity of trash seems like a symptom of a world system that raised the standard of living without ever considering the potential dangers of overproduction and overdevelopment. The permanence of new forms of garbage took us by surprise: these new materials not only refurbished our standard of living, but also overspilled, contaminated and leached into our environment and bodies. Living with toxic waste seemed to haunt commodity culture's promise to eradicate need.

239

For artists, then, trash was suddenly more than what we threw away; its prominence was materially and conceptually inescapable. It was the by-product of a historically specific new world order: refuse made visible the system of value that late capitalism would prefer be left invisible. Late modernity's means of progress seemed always to produce waste. Its modes of development and innovation were ultimately more ways of making trash. As market value in global capitalism increasingly demanded overproduction, a rubbish-laden cinema became unavoidable. Speaking about *Il deserto rosso* in his canonical interview with Godard, Antonioni evokes this current condition:

> Our life, even if we don't take account of it, is dominated by 'industry'. And 'industry' shouldn't be understood to mean factories only, but also and above all, products. These products are everywhere and they enter our homes, made of plastics and other materials unknown barely a few years ago; they overtake us wherever we may be.[4]

In this context, Antonioni's cinema operated as an alternate system of waste management, one that refused to disappear commodity culture's dirty secrets and instead revelled in its non-reproductivity or what Bataille understands as non-utilitarian 'expenditures'.[5] Antonioni's films approach the cinema as a medium that not only works with waste but also needs waste to work. His films thus belong to a larger trajectory of waste cinema: from the prophetic shimmering surfaces of bayou waterways in *Louisiana Story* (Flaherty, 1948) and the ecstatic imbrications of fetishism with dumping in *Xala* (Sembene, 1975), to the queering of fallowed urban spaces in the early 1970s films of Brazilian conceptual artist Hélio Oiticica or Tsai Ming-liang's *I Don't Want to Sleep Alone* (2006). Antonioni's films are remarkable participants in this late modernist tradition in terms of how they suggest that their elaboration of formal excess remains inseparable from the economics of waste. In their use of refuse as a means of expanding the aesthetic registers of cinema, these films challenge our culturally determined systems of value and productivity. Not only do various forms of waste populate his cinema, including textual excess, aesthetic surplus, affective overages, cultural detritus and garbage, but his films also turn to trash as a means of questioning the broader politics of production. His images refashion categorical distinctions between utility or functionality and the defunct or withered. For this reason, a thematic reading of motifs of waste is inadequate. Such a reading would allegorically instrumentalise content, shearing it away from its dialectical tension with form. Like modern plastics that are created from petroleum refuse, Antonioni's cinematic images are by-products of waste. The flexibility, vibrancy and abstraction of form result from the indelible imbrication of image and content at a molecular level. For this reason, content is never fixed; waste seems unable to hold a single meaning or valuation. Barthes identifies this semantic complexity as Antonioni's 'leakage of meaning'.[6]

We should also note several of the more important films to be influenced by Antonioni's visual style. Todd Haynes's *Safe* (1995), Samira Makhmalbaf's *The Apple* (*Sib*, 1998) and Jia Zhangke's *Still Life* (*Sanxia haoren*, 2006) also suggest that the political and philosophical realities of living in a late-capitalist world stem from social, civic and economic systems increasingly burdened with the job of hiding 'waste'. Classical Hollywood film participates in a similar obfuscation, creating a formal system that attempts to do away with any unnecessary details. Kristin Thompson understands Hollywood narrative as often defining its form around 'the rejection of excess, the reluctance to consider the uneconomical or unjustified'.[7] Conventional definitions of the neo-realist aesthetic, such as those proposed by Bordwell and Thompson, tell us that postwar Italian films give screen time and narrational emphasis to activities that Hollywood film banished for their lack of narrative importance (the camera inexplicably follows a secondary character making coffee in real time; a climactic chase scene is derailed when a boy begins to urinate). Neo-realism was a cinema of missed opportunities, of the over-ripeness of idle time and the unfairness of accidental or inadvertent victimisation. And it was simultaneously a cinema that revealed (unveiled) human potentiality in these moments that

240

seemed sparkling with contingencies and possibilities. It is between these two poles that Antonioni's waste cinema emerges.

At times, Antonioni's films engage with issues of excess and waste as the unavoidable consequence of modern production and supposed postwar plentitude: *Tentato suicidio* (1953), the short docudrama that Antonioni made for the omnibus feature, *L'amore in città*, suggests that the 'dopoguerra' has populated Italy with young women who do not want to (re)produce. As these women tell their stories of destitution and nihilism, we discover that many of them live in the housing projects and lower-income zones of Rome. An environment of waste has begun to wear on the film's subjects and, by implication, the film questions the fortitude of the post-war subjectivity so often associated with neo-realism's heroes. *Il grido* (1957) also engages with neo-realism's aesthetic legacy, purposely blurring the distinction between a life unjustly wasted and suicide. As such, these two films, along with another film from the 1950s, *I vinti* (1953), which I discuss below, disallow us from attributing any easy optimism to *N.U.* To see this film as a happy allegory of reuse and recycling would be as misguided as insisting on a completely dystopic reading of *Il deserto rosso*.

Antonioni's career spans a period of significant decline for both Classical Hollywood's and neo-realism's narrative forms. His most famous and influential work came to exemplify a new moment for the cinema, a time when critics and some audiences embraced the art film. A coherent aesthetic and excess developed with the art film, as imagistic abundance, hyperbolic *mise en scène*, or distended temporality or slowness. Landscape is the aspect of Antonioni's excessiveness where critics most frequently identify a thematic interest in waste and the costs of industrialisation. Recently, however, the more interesting analyses argue that the landscape allows an aesthetic transaction in which the cinematic image becomes not only a venue displaying documents of a polluted world. That image also undergoes a wasting away, as if it is unable to sustain itself. Closely reading *Gente del Po* (1943/1947), Noa Steimatsky describes this film inaugurating Antonioni's characteristic aesthetic: 'an emerging principle of dissolution, recession, abstraction that inflects the short documentary at every level'.[8] The film's distinctive visual devices – including the blotting out of depth, this use of smoke to efface a shot, the emphasis on the blank greyness of the river – 'turn attention to the grasp of the landscape *as* cinematic image *in process of being drained*'.[9]

In *L'eclisse* (1962), depictions of a stock market crash encourage the viewer to transpose the problem of surplus value to the film's emphasis onto landscape. Angelo Restivo finds a 'sublime of … the unthinkable catastrophe of technology' in the film's locations, reading the mushroom shape of the water tower to signal the mushroom cloud of the atomic bomb.[10] In more overt and fascinatingly cumbersome terms, *Zabriskie Point* (1970) attacks real-estate developers by visualising a cataclysmic end to their construction schemes. Torture and human death are framed as a disturbingly modern form of refuse in *The Passenger* (1975): a scene of torture is introduced scenically by rubble, and blurry extra footage from a film found in piles of film reels reveals an execution. The scale of the archive seems on the brink of an immensity that would obliterate our ability to find any meaningful registration of human life. Late modernity (and the specificity of globalisation's geopolitics) threatens to dissolve the distinction between human life and refuse.

Antonioni's films and their indulgence of waste are crucial for how they question neo-realism's instrumentalisation of contingency as much as they frustrate Hollywood linearity and causation. A kind of wasting of time preoccupies their narrative structure (e.g., wandering in *L'eclisse* and *La notte*). Unwilling to move past the temporalities of idleness and ennui, these films overdraw the economy of Hollywood narrative while cashing out the investments of neo-realism. We might think of these excesses as a kind of visual noise, since they serve neither narrative nor realism.[11] For example, odd details take up an inexplicable centrality in *Identificazione di una donna* (1982): routine urination, the void under an old house or a nest forgotten by its builders. These details abuse any sense of economy, both too inconsequential to serve the plot and too bloated (in the diegesis) to serve as discrete symbols. However, they underscore the film's aesthetic (and ideologically consequential) untethering of reproduction, productivity and virility by making uncomfortably obvious the excesses of the male gaze in this film. Perhaps these are the features that caused Vincent Canby to deem it 'an excruciatingly empty work'.[12]

242

In *The Passenger*, Jack Nicholson's character David Locke is a television reporter who has tried to trade in his identity and swap it for a new one. Towards the end of the film, as he begins to realise the true impossibility of exchanging his identity, he invokes our relationship to time, history and identity through an analogy of carefree waste production and removal, 'Wouldn't it be better if we could just forget old places? Forget everything that happens and just throw it all away, day-by-day? Unfortunately the world doesn't work that way.' Here Antonioni identifies the modern impulse to toss everything away, a desire to make our world disposable without consequence. This world, never haunted by vestiges of the past, is already an impossibility. Is the throwaway temporality that David wishes for a desire for renewal through a kind of presentist assertion of the now? Is this a call for a Bergsonian durée? Or does it simply ask for a blind obliteration of history? As he continues to contemplate this issue, David suggests that the world can be neither a clean slate nor can it ever truly build on past mistakes. 'Well, it doesn't work the other way either. People believe what I write because it conforms to their expectations.' We are able to digest only that which we already know. Our sense of the future is limited by the build-up of our past experiences. We could say that, through David, Antonioni gives voice to his own philosophy. But it would be more correct to say that David's words articulate the paradox from which Antonioni's style works to break free. To understand a truly modern world is to neither embrace history nor to negate it. There's no blank past and no blank future. We always live with the messiness of meaning in a way that resists historicism and teleology.

Barthes addresses Antonioni in precisely these terms: 'Throughout your work, basically, there is a constant critique, at once painful and demanding, of that strong imprint of meaning known as destiny.'[13] Waste constantly checks what is possible against what is known, and thereby always conspires against teleological prognostications. Like the return of the repressed, waste always tugs on the purity of a given moment, exposing the relativism of its meaning. It preserves the uncertainty of our destiny, and in Antonioni's films wasted time, wasted images, wasted shots, function precisely to guarantee that unknowability. Antonioni's treatise on waste – if we can call it that – presents a much more profound and honest environmentalism than the current rhetoric that seems to require apocalypse and other doomsdays to make the value of nature and humans meaningful and visible.

Barthes saw Antonioni as combating reification, or what Barthes calls the 'hypostasis of meaning' that is at the root of nothing less than the worst of human atrocities. 'All of those wars, repressions, terrors, genocides, for the sake of the triumph of a meaning.'[14] Insistence on the truth, on *a* truth, can result only in violence. Antonioni offers his viewers a particular kind of vision that was able to 'undo the fanaticism of meaning', a particular aesthetic that was able to combat 'this terrorist operation [that] generally goes under the name of realism'.[15] Nowhere does this happen more boldly than in Antonioni's recasting of the film image as surface itself.

243

Marred Surfaces

Antonioni's image is not an excavation. Unlike that of Hitchcock, his image does not ask to be penetrated; it has no deeper narrative significance that emerges from yielding to a piercing gaze. His films trigger an anti-hermeneutic gaze that stops at the surface. Barthes describes Antonioni's gaze as a kind of scanning: Antonioni 'scans, like a very sensitive instrument'. The cinema that results from this gaze 'is not a fixed reflection, but an iridescent surface'. Through this kind of surface Antonioni's image achieves the undoing of meaning, a refusal of the 'hypostasis of meaning'.[16]

On a metaphorical level, surfaces put up a similar resistance to deeper meanings. Towards the end of *The Passenger*, various pursuers are closing in on David. In front of the white walls of a small Spanish town, he sits on a street curb inspecting what looks to be a blossom from a geranium plant. In a closer framing, we see him take the small red flower and carefully insert it into a small crack in the plaster wall behind him. He looks at this bright red speck in the field of blankness for a moment, and then, in a violent shift in mood and body language, he smashes the flower in the wall. The wall crumbles, and the flower's red pigment has left a small smudge in the wake of David's hand. Despite the unexpected force of his hand, the wall's surface doesn't surrender to depth. The original crack only gives way to more cracks. Below its plaster is just plaster of a slightly different shade and texture. The wall stubbornly refuses to develop into anything more and yet the grammar of the film forces us to take this wall as important or at least obstinately present. After David leaves the shot, the camera holds on this marred surface for a few seconds, asking us to contemplate its emptiness and lack of narrative information.

It is crucial to see this relatively late assertion of formalism in the attention to a marred surface in the context of both this film's larger spatial politics and the appearance of similar surfaces in earlier films. Surfaces spread out in Antonioni's films, expanding to take over the frame rather than opening to depth. Surfaces threaten to blot out character and plot. Their spreading out leads nowhere that would provide geographical traverse or narrative traction. The image reclaims cinema's two-dimensionality, returning the screen to being a flat surface.

The stubbornness of the surface also appears in a much earlier film, *I vinti*. This film investigates a contemporary phenomenon of senseless murders by young middle-class youth, who seem to value celebrity more than human life. The film has three sections, each set in a different European country. In the 'France' segment, the ruins of a château offer the setting for the first senseless murder. The crumbling walls of the *ancien régime* function to anchor a contrasting element in the film's transformation. Old Europe that is left in rubble is complemented by the death of the film's supposedly moneyed character. The young man dies in a melodramatic fashion, splayed on the 'stage' of the old grand stairs of the château. But in the next scene this suffering body loses its centrality in the frame. The body continues to teeter on the brink between life and death but has been denied a compositional centrality – left in the corner of the frame and discarded by the side of the road. A man who finds this imperilled but still breathing body handles it with an erratic roughness, dropping it face down on the ground before getting help. This still-moving body is a kind of half-dead animal: tossed aside as refuse even before its demise is certain, as road kill that cannot be redeemed as a martyr. With nightfall and the descent of the image into darkness, something far more ruinous than rubble comes to occupy this film. The murderous impulses of a sick generation have manifested a kind of foreboding refuse that now changes the terms of the image itself, pulling it towards abstraction and dissonance rather than life.

Waste functions in another crucial way in this film. The damaged or stained walls of this film gain prominence at certain key moments in each of the narratives. In their definitions of Antonioni's aesthetic, Angelo Restivo and Noa Steimatsky each draw attention to the scarred surface of the image and to the predominance of the stain.[17] The walls of *I vinti* carry such markings. The French teens responsible for the murder at the château return to their middle-class apartment in Paris. In the chiaroscuro of the building's dingy hallway, light suddenly illuminates not just our anti-heroes but the wall on which its marbleising effect (or veins of actual marble)

A marred surface from the 'Francia' section of *I vinti* (1952–53)

looks suddenly like dirty marks, desperate gashes made by fingernails, bloody fingers, the veins of a distended organ. This ornamental interior now looks like a soiled, sordid surface that dominates the centre of the frame as the main character proclaims their dismal defeat, 'It's over.' The imperfect surface finds illumination in this crucial moment of truth. It is a wasted space, and not fully reconcilable to the narrative. As with the grey fruit in *Il deserto rosso*, *mise en scène* seems too easily contaminated, the site of a leakage. The wall is not exactly a reflection of men's moods, nor is it a neo-realist surface testifying to the distressed humanity of Europe. In its combination of emptiness *and* abstraction, we find the atonality of the senselessness of wasted lives: all mix together on the violenced surface of wall. Like the echo of footsteps in the hall, which seems more appropriate for a bad horror film, this wall aesthetically dominates the diegesis, upstaging the characters' remorse and rejection; it is a formal element of the scene that seems to speak out of turn, asserting more than the characters themselves can.

245

The 'England' segment of the film also centres on a maladjusted middle-class youth named Aubrey who murders to gain attention and celebrity. In a moment of utter defeat, Aubrey grapples with the possibility that the infamy gained from murdering offers no redemption or transcendence. As with the marred wall in the 'Paris' section, the frame here reveals and revels in a large gash in the plaster above Aubrey's head. This wall carries an odd insistent presence in the shot. This surface isn't really a background; it is an integral part of the shot.

Perhaps the most remarkable of these marred surfaces occurs in the 'Italy' section.[18] The narrative focuses on Claudio, a wealthy college student drawn into a life of terrorism. Throughout the film, he is on the run after blowing up an ammunitions factory. In the explosion, he received a head trauma whose after-effects seem to wear on him in many scenes and will eventually lead to his death at the end of the film. Seeking cover at the apartment of his girlfriend, Marina, he discovers that she is having a party. Together they escape the party and, on the way out, he explains his absence as they walk through the various hallways, foyers, courtyards and parking structures of her posh apartment complex. The background of shots devolves formally across one sequence, descending through a series of more and more minimalist designs that result finally in a total lack of order on the interior walls of the apartment complex's parking garage. As Claudio explains his political entrapment and the futility of his life, we realise the modernist decoration of the apartment complex has given way to a damaged and marred wall. 'But now I am alive at my own funeral. Everything I've done is for nothing. No use.' Like those in the film's other stories, the wall here is littered with marks, cracks and scratches. It also contains black circular stains from car exhaust fumes. In the transition from patterned and geometrical background to marred surface, we find an allegory of modernist aesthetics, the move from geometrical modernism built from pure forms and simple lines to a putrid modernism built from the residues of a toxic world.

Antonioni gives us a way of reading waste, a protocol for our encounter with modernity, a means of finding lyricism in an era when surfaces no longer yield to depth. Ezio Manzini has written extensively on the late twentieth century as a period

A progression of background surfaces from the 'Italia' section of *I vinti* (1952–53)

when the very notion of materiality has changed. According to this media theorist and industrial design historian, late twentieth-century humans do not perceive materiality in the same terms as earlier humans, and this is primarily because of the invention of radically new materials. While Manzini is most concerned to track how industrial design reworks and responds to our sensory understanding of the object, it is interesting to consider how Antonioni's attention to surfaces may qualify as examples of 'the emblematical images of the present-day world [that] reveal an environment tendentially dematerialised'. 'Once upon a time,' Manzini writes, we encountered the world as 'a universe peopled by shapes that filled space with their three-dimensional solidity, shapes that were obstructively physical, whose "truth" lay in their structure, their working, in the intrinsic quality of the material of which they were built'. Our relation to the ontology of objects has been radically revised in an era defined by the 'prominence of the surface'. In an age when manufactured objects appear to outnumber or at least upstage natural things, the role of surface is 'no longer linked to the properties of the underlying ones but has a degree of autonomy'. The second dimension has begun to trump the third dimension. The outer skin of things has no necessary parallel or connection to what's inside. 'The impossibility of knowing just which of all the infinite combinations of different materials, made possible and available by modern technology, lies beneath the surface of the article we are looking at leads to a kind of blunting of the image. The surface gives no hint at anything beyond itself.' Surface becomes, for Manzini, 'a kind of screen'.[19]

In his compelling indictment of Pierre Jeunet's immaculate simulation of the French New Wave aesthetic as a series of digitally rendered surfaces, Dudley Andrew evokes Truffaut's contempt for Antonioni, with Truffaut accusing the latter of 'trying to turn every shot into a painting, draining his films of spontaneity'.[20] While it is true, as Andrew reminds us, that Antonioni painted the grass in making *Il deserto rosso*, there remains a certain contingency to even his most composed images. Antonioni understood any shooting scenario as a dialectic between the preplanned and the accidental. In the midst of one particular shoot, the refuse from four days of an actual garbage strike began to pile up, threatening to invade the story's diegesis. Rather than see the garbage as an inconvenient intrusion, Antonioni saw it as opening up the film in pictorial and non-narrative ways:

> Rome flooded with rubbish, piles of colored filth on the street corners, an orgy of abstract images, extraordinary pictorial fury. ... An unusual situation in which to insert a plot. But this was the time Italian censorship was campaigning against even slightly raw films, so you can imagine using this.[21]

For Seymour Chatman, Antonioni always aimed to register the outer layer of the world. His camera worked to 'render the effect of surface' and, in doing so, resulted in 'a *vision* of the world in its plastic particularity'.[22]

Plastics

A focus on waste in Antonioni's aesthetic also allows a powerful distinction to be drawn between his modernism and other modernisms. He does not bring refuse into the pictorial plane as an *objet trouvé*. Refuse is not a vestige of a past now inaccessible, nor is it the regurgitation of modernity's capitalist consumerist clutter in figures of decadence and superfluity (the typical 1960s rejection of commodity culture and crass materialism). It would also be wrong to see his aesthetic as a simple reversal of good for bad terms in which the toxic and the natural are inverted. *Il deserto rosso* remains somewhat ambivalent about whether waste brings ruin or not. Its world appears as much embellished by toxicity as it is burdened by it. The image refuses any simplistic eco-politicking on pollution. As Antonioni says in his interview with Godard:

> It simplifies things too much (as many have done) to say that I accuse this inhuman, industrialized world in which the individual is crushed and led to neurosis. My intention, on the contrary (moreover, we may know very well where we start but not at all where we'll end up), was to translate the beauty of this world, in which even the factories can be very beautiful. ... The line, the curves of factories and their smoke-stacks, are perhaps more beautiful than a row of trees – which every eye has already seen to the point of monotony. It's a rich world – living, useful. As for me, I hold that the sort of neurosis seen in *Red Desert* is above all a question of adaptation.[23]

Not purely apocalyptic, the sublime of a waste-laden world seems certain to Antonioni. More profound and more startling than man's harnessing of nature (seen in a planted rows of trees), an overly industrialised landscape is unavoidable. Waste always exists in Antonioni as a kind of non-negotiable presence, as something that cannot go away. Here one need think only of the birds at the end of the film, which have learned to fly around the poisonous yellow smoke, to understand the inescapable necessity of making a life alongside this persistent toxicity. The challenge is never constructed as waste removal but rather as what he calls adaptation: a reworking of the human subject in light of the environment. *Il deserto rosso* mourns not the loss of nature but humanity's current inability to adapt to the world.

The film itself attempts to model such an adaptability. As Angela Dalle Vacche has written of the film: 'Antonioni regards the industrial pollution of Ravenna as a positive experiment rather than just as a negative catastrophe, for the odd alterations of water and grass at the level of color produce a whole new set of emotional and artistic possibilities.'[24] We could say then that film's visual strength stems from its adaptation of waste. From this perspective, the film is itself a glorious by-product of the petrochemical industry, a form of aesthetic adaptation not unlike plastic.

Since the 1910s, film theorists have referred to any aesthetic approach to the image that results in a pictorial, more visual, more abstract film image in terms of an increased *plasticity*. Meanwhile, the idea of plastic as a material increasingly served as a metyonym for the simulacra over the twentieth century. For this reason, Barthes describes plastic as having a paradoxical ontology because it 'hardly exists as substance' and is defined only by 'its infinite transformation'. With this material's proliferation, 'the hierarchy of substances is abolished'.[25] In Antonioni's cinema, the idea of visual plasticity is overdetermined, precisely because it so frequently derives from waste. The ability of the image to become more colourful, more vibrant, more pictorial results not from postproduction process work but rather from the repurposing of a landscape of waste. So while *Il deserto rosso* is neither Roger Vadim's *Barbarella* (1968) nor Oskar Fischinger's *Motion Painting, No. 1* (1947), this is a plastic film. The image's system of waste management is basically a plasticising of the world.

An early documentary of Antonioni's not included on the 2010 Criterion Collection discs but equally important in how it anticipates the visual style of *Il deserto rosso* is *Sette canne, un vestito* (*Seven Reeds, One Suit*, 1949). This short film explains how rayon is made, following the industrial engineering of organic materials into plastic fibres. The story of synthetic fabrics is told in a fairly straightforward and orderly fashion. However, it contains several sequences when this traditional mode of explication veers towards an exuberant formalism. In certain passages, a new synthetic product empties out the image, delivering a kind of radical blankness as large sheets of materials emerge from chemical baths or are carried by highways of conveyor belts. The willingness of these shots to envelop the image in total emptiness demonstrates the aesthetic logic whereby industrial forms bring the abstract, non-figurative and excessive to the image. The factory's steam consumes the figures of workers as in *Il deserto rosso*. This industrial fog not only erases the human form, smothering out our ability to see the workings of a human agency, it also banishes any informational aspects of the image. At the same time, this film makes the process appear truly magical. Introduced by the voice-over narration as 'a fairytale of modernity, a fable taken from the book of the magic of the chemical industry's processes', this film shows us sights that are still astounding in the way they capture an alchemic transfiguration of materials taking place before our eyes. The moment when liquid turns into threads is astonishing. What we witness is more than a simple chemical reaction. This is not simply the merger of two substances to create an easily anticipated spectacle of explosion – like childhood volcanoes of baking soda and vinegar or yeast and sugar water. This is the transformation of a liquid into a solid. One kingdom of materiality becomes another. Like cinema's central illusion of moving bodies generally, there is something uncanny happening to materiality as we know it. This sequence speaks to the most primal moments of the cinematic, such as the Lumières playing their film *Démolition d'un mur* (1896) backwards.

We should remember that for the historian Manzini, new synthetic materials trigger a shift in how humans recognise and understand surfaces. These new materials allow a divorcing of inner and outer. Plastic is the emblematic material of this transformation. Plastic is both the most reviled and the most revered material of the mid-twentieth century, the most productive and the most wasteful (and waste generative), the most spectacular and the most ordinary, the most inherently human (made from human intervention at a molecular level) and the most inorganic. More than perhaps any other material, plastic enabled a sense that the plenitude of the world had returned after the war: lots of lost goods were replaced quickly, and colour came back into the face of Europe.

In the interview with Godard mentioned above, Antonioni describes this transformation of European society differently. Here we find the commodity consumerism of the economic miracle treated as a catastrophic flood: Europe's total immersion in a world of synthetic products creates a crisis that 'like a torrential river, swelled a thousand tributaries, divides in a thousand arms in order, finally, to submerge everything and spread everywhere'.[26] Industrial materials and commodities flood the market but also our perceptual field. And while Antonioni is most often celebrated for paired down and sparse compositions, *Il deserto rosso*'s compositions often follow this flooding effect, albeit in one colour as the title would suggest.

As we look at *Il deserto rosso*, we find that the plasticity of the image enabled by waste, pollution and detritus carries no clear positive or negative value. There are particular images that suggest apocalypse, destruction and dystopia. But the image refuses to reify the meaning of humanity's impact on the earth. I am not suggesting the film is optimistic about technology, the environment or the human condition. Rather, in refusing origins and end points, the imagistic (and aural) plasticity of the film is quite like the substance of plastic itself: the substance, which appears promiscuously, belongs to no particular genus of materials and to every one of them at the same time. It is a material whose ontology suggests no natural status: it exists as a gas, a liquid, a solid; a fabric, a supporting beam, a sub-particle.

Without naming plastic, Dalle Vacche seems to describe a key feature of the plastic age in her description of *Il deserto rosso*'s aesthetic:

> this metamorphosis from industrial ugliness to beautiful design hides a fear [that] … one might slip into pleasurable numbness … leveling all differences into quick gratification, much in the same manner that the massive production of consumer items in the fifties fostered the illusion of a happy, classless Italian society.

After describing the film's visual language of rusty cables, clutter, dead things, she says,

> While all these elements could function as practical objects, with their outlines and bulky shapes repeating the themes of measurement and sturdiness already encountered in the

opening architectural outdoor shots, the components of the ship, to our surprise, transfigure themselves into elegant design. It is as if heavy, mundane technology had become subordinate to a light aesthetic exercise.[27]

Here we find a perfect account of transfiguration as a form of repurposing. The image emerges as a kind of industrial by-product – a unique medium for how it allows for a greater manipulation and elegant transfiguration. Without naming it, this description echoes the manufacture of plastic: an ability to turn a heavy, sticky, unctuous substance (petroleum) into a 'light aesthetic exercise'.

Dalle Vacche encourages us to read this film alongside particular art-making practices from the period that suggest 'art can be born out of waste' – such as *Art Informel*, tachism, action painting – and which use decay and regeneration as a means of reinventing the image. This is not simply aesthetic innovation for Dalle Vacche, for she sees these new techniques as allowing for 'microscopic analysis of historical change'. In particular, she identifies colour as the site of *Il deserto rosso*'s microscopic historiography, and suggests that the film puts forward colour as 'the abstract language of the future'.[28] The idea that colour can be imagined as an abstract language of the future is thanks to plastics. The versatility and variability and variety of colours (and their ability to perform like language – which requires an intense flexibility) is something only the plastic age could image. The history that plastic itself lives is one that we might say is molecular change. Understanding historical change occurring molecularly is something that the age of plastics made imaginable, necessary and possible. It is also a central part of the cultural imaginary of the new physics of the late twentieth century.

In his 'letter' to Antonioni, Barthes assesses the role of the artist in society in a description that seems particularly prescient today and that makes the discourse of waste in the films that I have been describing relevant.

251

> The artist is threatened ... by a collective feeling, ever latent, that society can do without art. Artistic activity is suspect because it disturbs the comfort and security of established meanings, because it is expensive and yet free, and because the new society in search of itself, whatever the regime it lives under, has not yet decided what it should think about *luxury*.[29]

Here, in Barthes's musings, we find something radical – a sense that the idea of art is tied not only to politics but also to the political parameters imagined for waste and excess. If art is to be the icing on the cake, if it is to exist as an epiphenomenal piling on, then it remains shackled to its uselessness. It remains always already defunct. But Antonioni seemed aware, as Barthes suggests here, of the dangers of deciding absolutely what falls into the category of excess and what falls into the category of necessity. The uncertainty that his work fosters asks us to experience the place that abandons or ignores questions of necessity. What does it mean to live in a world so unmagical that every single thing (animate or inanimate) must parade its utility? Would a world rich with only necessary objects be anything other than tyranny? In his explorations of excess and waste, Antonioni makes the costs of such a tyrannical world clear. At the same time, his waste aesthetics makes what seems like that world's inescapable ecological apocalypse less inevitable, if only in an instant. In reminding us that what counts as productive is almost always politically and ideologically defined, his films also suggest that the aesthetic is the register by which we can exuberantly and emphatically question productivity's definition. If we can see the world as something more than just needs, we will once again see the world as humans see it.

Notes

1. Seymour Chatman, *Antonioni, or the Surface of the World* (Berkeley: University of California Press, 1985), pp. 8–9; Sam Rohdie, *Antonioni* (London: BFI, 1990), pp. 111–12.

2. This film's use of jazz echoes a wider pattern of referencing jazz in postwar Italian culture. An often appropriated cultural form in this period, jazz appears frequently in neo-realist films and is often accompanied by a problematic racialisation. These overdetermined citations all too easily signal the exuberant liberties of American culture, the mythic struggles of African Americans and the controlled sexual exoticism of upper-class nightclub culture. In *N.U.*, jazz functions in a slightly simpler fashion. My point here is that this film's obvious move away from clear explication and towards a looser and more experimental approach is associated with jazz and not with other genres of modernism.

3. The nuclear industry regards Italy as a pioneer of civil nuclear power programmes. The first power plants were built in the late 1950s after over a decade of vigorous industrial development and promotion.

4. Jean-Luc Godard and Michelangelo Antonioni, 'Michelangelo Antonioni' [Interview], in Andrew Sarris (ed.), *Interviews with Film Directors* (New York: Avon, 1969), pp. 21–32 (p. 24).

5. Georges Bataille, 'The Notion of Expenditure', in *Visions of Excess: Selected Writings, 1927–1939* (Minneapolis: University of Minnesota Press, 1985), pp. 116–29.

6. Roland Barthes, 'Dear Antonioni …', in Geoffrey Nowell-Smith (ed.), *L'avventura* (London: BFI, 1997), pp. 63–8 (p. 65).

7. Kristin Thompson, 'The Concept of Cinematic Excess', in Philip Rosen (ed.), *Narrative, Apparatus, Ideology: A Film Theory Reader* (New York: Columbia University Press, 1986), pp. 130–42 (p. 136).

8. Noa Steimatsky, *Italian Locations: Reinhabiting the Past in Postwar Cinema* (Minneapolis: University of Minnesota Press, 2008), p. 33.

9. Ibid., p. 35. Emphasis in the original.

10. Angelo Restivo, *The Cinema of Economic Miracles: Visuality and Modernization in the Italian Art Film* (Durham, NC: Duke University Press, 2002), p. 120.

11. Actual aural noise is another key component of Antonioni's waste aesthetics. Valentina's audio essay in *La notte* describes how noise pollution threatens the integrity of human subjectivity and thus reflects on the film's title sequence (aerial shots of urban landscape keyed to a jarring electronic music score) and the loudness of the traffic jam in an early scene. The film also anticipates the use of sound in *Il deserto rosso*.

12. Quoted in Peter Brunette, *The Films of Michelangelo Antonioni* (Cambridge: Cambridge University Press, 1998), p. 25.

13. Barthes, 'Dear Antonioni …', p. 65.

14. Ibid., p. 64.

15. Ibid., pp. 67, 65.

16. Ibid., pp. 64, 65.

17. Steimatsky, *Italian Locations*, Chapter 1; Restivo, *The Cinema of Economic Miracles*, Chapters 6 and 7.

18. Here I am working with the original version of the film, which can be found on the Minerva DVD. For more on how the harsh indictment of critics at the film's premiere at the Venice Film Festival led to this dramatic excision and revision of the plot to concern cigarette smuggling rather than terrorism, see Benci's essay in this volume.

19. Ezio Manzini, 'Objects and Their Skin', in Penny Sparke (ed.), *The Plastics Age: From Modernity to Post-Modernity* (London: Victoria and Albert Museum, 1990), pp. 115, 115, 116, 119, 120, 119.

20. Dudley Andrew, 'Amélie, or Le Fabuleux Destin Du Cinéma Français', *Film Quarterly* vol. 57 no. 3 (2004), pp. 34–46 (p. 38).

21. Michelangelo Antonioni, 'Introduction', *Screenplays of Michelangelo Antonioni: Il grido, L'avventura, La notte, L'eclisse*, trans. Roger J. Moore and Louis Brigante (New York: Orion Press, 1963), pp. viii–xviii (p. x).

22. Chatman, *Antonioni*, pp. 3, 7. Emphasis in the original.

23. Godard and Antonioni, 'Michelangelo Antonioni', p. 23.

24. Angela Dalle Vacche, 'Michelangelo Antonioni's *Red Desert*: Painting as Ventriloquism and Color as Movement (Architecture and Painting)', in Angela Dalle Vacche and Brian Price (eds), *Color: The Film Reader* (London: Routledge, 2006), pp. 183–91 (p. 187).

25. Roland Barthes, *Mythologies* (New York: Hill and Wang, 1972), pp. 98, 97, 99.

26. Godard and Antonioni, 'Michelangelo Antonioni', p. 24.

27. Dalle Vacche, 'Michelangelo Antonioni's *Red Desert*', pp. 185–6, 185.

28. Ibid., pp. 187, 188, 187.

29. Barthes, 'Dear Antonioni …', p. 68. Emphasis in the original.

Karen Pinkus

ANTONIONI'S CINEMATIC POETICS OF CLIMATE CHANGE

I

The question of cinematic representation has surfaced urgently with regard to global climate change. Climate change sceptics, although probably few in number, are often granted equal time in the media's claims to a *par condicio*.[1] Sceptics may call for empirical evidence to support a 'theory' of warming. For the general public, at least, such evidence could or should come in cinematic forms; ideally forms that could narrativise, arouse empathy and, by necessity, encapsulate geological change – which occurs normally over unfathomable scales of time – into a format that can be absorbed by the human eye and brain. As opposed to pollution in a generic sense, climate change is essentially a temporal problem: greenhouse gases (primarily carbon dioxide) are released into the atmosphere naturally, but in the past several hundred years the rate of release has reached unprecedented velocity. Greenhouse gases are both invisible (posing a peculiar challenge to cinematic representation) and global, in the sense that their effects are felt everywhere and not just in the areas of intense production. How is cinema to respond authentically to the imperceptible, dispersive, global nature of climate change?[2]

Climate science needs cinema as uncinematic, in the sense that Kracauer means when he writes that a genuine cinema is made of images that do not corroborate but instead 'question our notions of the physical world'.[3] Given the urgency of swaying public opinion, could we say that cinema must suspend its essence – for now – and take on a more instrumental role to serve a greater good, perhaps to resume its authenticity in less chaotic times? Or can cinema retain its essential qualities and help us think about climate change in its profound complexity?[4] These are questions that Antonioni addresses better than any other cineaste even if the particular term, with all of its present nuances, was not available to him.

Let us begin then with the potential of cinema to represent climate change taken in its specificity, and as opposed to a more generic sense of environmental degradation that is so prominent in the broad panorama of the history of cinema from experimental science-fiction dystopias to mainstream Hollywood comedies. Inasmuch as cinema itself stands for 'technology' or 'progress' it is always already opposed to Nature, understood as what is outside of or untouched by the human. Even early cinema reflects the anxiety of a medium that necessarily involves a difference from the natural, whether this is understood in positive or negative terms. And again, this essay wishes to think in particular about climate change, a phenomenon that is, per se, entirely natural.

In recent years a number of films have addressed climate change with various degrees of specificity. *The Day After Tomorrow* (Roland Emmerich, 2004) was criticised and even censored by the right for its 'liberal views'; and by scientists for its lack of accuracy, for its failure as 'corroboration' especially with regard to the temporality of 'climate shift'.[5] So while the potential effects of increased greenhouse gas emissions on ice sheets, ocean currents, hurricanes and extreme weather patterns in the film may have been informed by accepted science, Emmerich had to contain and constrict change within an absurdly brief period to satisfy narrative demands. In the film the passage of time is indicated with editing of the most conventional sort. Spielberg's *A.I.* (2001) also uses traditional editing techniques, voice-over and music to indicate that an immense period has elapsed between the last presence on camera of a human being and the discovery/reanimation of David and Teddy by aliens. Moreover, the aliens confirm the time lapse through (subtitled) dialogue. Interestingly, though, the aliens grant David's wish to return to the space-time of his Oedipal bonding with 'his mother'. In other words, the film moves back in time through what is clearly posited as simulation, putting into question the scientific legitimacy of the 'present' as prophetic fulfilment of anthropogenic climate change.

Outside of narrative film, time-lapse documentary (melting glaciers, rising sea level and so on) provides an interesting response to the call for representation. Time-lapse is essentially a formalist project that refers back to the very earliest moments of (pre)cinema. A series of what are essentially photogrammes are linked together to form a sophisticated flipbook. That this effect can be achieved by the most advanced digital technologies does not negate the fact that the viewer is confronted with two still images taken by a static camera as a means of juxtaposing two different temporal states of the same spatial coordinates.

Along these lines, a number of recent overviews of climate change refer to paintings as visual representations or documents of change. Pieter Brueghel's painting *Hunters in the Snow* (1565) is cited as an example of the 'little ice age' (c. 1450–1850) in Europe since the landscape appears quite snowy compared with the average winter in the present.[6] Canaletto's paintings show water levels in the Venice lagoon that can be viewed next to photographs taken beginning in the nineteenth century. In both cases, the paintings were made before modern scientific measuring equipment. As images they are static, and compared with other more recent images or measurements they function qualitatively as evidence in the same way as the photogrammes of time-lapse documentary, except that the intervals between images are rather long.

This essay puts forward Michelangelo Antonioni as the cinematic poet of 'climate change'. A good deal of scholarly work has been devoted to exploring Antonioni's relation to architecture, space, landscape, ecology and 'the environment'. This latter term deserves some analysis before we proceed.[7] The Italian word *ambiente* refers simultaneously to both interior/set design and the *Umwelt* – what is 'out there' beyond the human, perhaps Nature itself in the most reified and clichéd sense. This web of meanings is especially intense in Antonioni where a film's *ambiente* may refer to the locations scouted so carefully, the sets designed/altered by an architect or art director (Antonioni worked often with Piero Poletto) and the 'natural landscape' inhabited by his characters.[8]

It bears mention here that 'landscape' (*paesaggio*) was indeed the subject of debate in the context of policies and politics of cinema during the fascist period. On the one hand, landscape understood in the most basic sense as location shooting might seem to imply an apolitical realism. On the other hand, the Regime undertook the creation of an agrarian or rural cinema – in part or at times as propaganda to support undertakings such as land reclamation; in part as a means of exalting peasant life. The various positions towards landscape are too complex to summarise in a single position and indeed 'landscape' is a mobile signifier during fascism that can be deployed in multiple directions. For instance, Bolognese journalist Leo Longanesi, a strong supporter of fascist ideology particularly in its early, revolutionary phase, as well as of the aesthetic movement known as *strapaese* (supercountry), called for a 'natural and logical Italian film', developed from attentive observation of peasants and their dwelling on the land.[9] In this context '*strapaese* cinema' sounds strangely like something that would emerge in the distinctly antifascist project of neo-realism. On the pages of his magazine, *L'Italiano*, Longanesi imagined an Italian filmic landscape distinctly different from American landscapes, too dominated by spectacle and serving as mere backdrop to the foregrounding of stars framed in close-ups. *Strapaese*, in painting (and in an ideal cinema), would employ natural, atmospheric details to promote rural life over industrialisation and international modernism. To be clear, then, *strapaese* was not so much an official policy (especially since it opposed much of the imperialist and rationalist imagery of public monuments and architecture supported by the Regime) as it was a reactionary aesthetic movement that coincided, at times, with Regime goals.

Emily Braun's work on Giorgio Morandi is crucial in underscoring the complex and contradictory position of *strapaese* or landscape more generally as potentially politicised. Morandi (not unlike Antonioni in certain critical traditions) is usually considered a formalist whose still lives and landscapes exist in idealised spaces. Yet the Bolognese artist was supported by and supportive of key proponents of *strapaese*, including Longanesi. As Braun notes, it is difficult to read any

The Po as 'landscape' in Visconti's *Ossessione* (1943). It is only at the end of the film that the environment and actors merge

overt rhetorical statements into his muted scenes of hillsides or bottles. Yet his work is characterised by a 'conservative position of intransigent sameness' and the same terms could be applied to the ideal of an unchanging, pure Italian landscape.[10]

'Landscape' was also in circulation in the *Cinema* group with whom Antonioni was associated for a brief period in the early 1940s, and it is often mentioned in the coincidence of Visconti's *Ossessione* (*Obsession*) and Antonioni's *Gente del Po* (*People of the Po*), both shot around Ferrara in the Po River Valley in 1943. Giuseppe De Santis, who collaborated with Visconti, wrote a well-known essay in *Cinema*, 'For an Italian Landscape' ('Per un paesaggio italiano').[11] Here he posited a psychophysical correspondence between landscape and cinematic characters that seems to hold the seeds of a neo-realist (and hence anti-fascist) approach to film-making.

From a broader perspective, the very idea of landscape implies a flattened backdrop that pre-exists the arrival of the cinematic *équipe* – it is thus static, codified, contained and mastered space.[12] For De Santis landscape and human presence are two fixed elements that must come together for genuine cinema. He laments the fact that while such interaction has been successful in other national cinemas, the problem 'is never resolved in Italy'.[13] It would seem that an authentic cinema would situate characters in the landscape, and thus bring out the genuine national characteristics of both. In his photo-essay, 'For a Film on the River Po', also published in *Cinema*, Antonioni is much more interested in the possibilities of cinema (and photography) to actually shape not landscape in De Santis's sense so much as the *ambiente*. And, as his film career develops, Antonioni increasingly embraces the aleatory in location shooting. He explains:

I arrive on location in a fixed state of 'virginity.' I do this because I believe the best results are obtained by the 'collision' that takes place between the environment [*ambiente*] in which the scene is to be shot and my own particular state of mind at that specific moment. I don't like to study or even think about a scene the night before, or even a few

257

days before I actually start shooting. And when I arrive there, I like to be completely alone, by myself, so that I can get to feel the environment without having anybody around me. The most direct way to recreate a scene is to enter into a rapport with the environment itself; it's the simplest way to let the environment suggest something to us.[14]

In the broadest sense, then, one cannot distinguish in the statement above between landscape, location, meteorological conditions and even the film's themes or content inasmuch as for Antonioni these develop in relation with *ambiente*. Ambience (*ambiente*) comes from the Latin root *ambo*, meaning both (of something), as in ambidextrous or ambivalent.[15] Yet the idea of 'both' is elided in common usage of 'ambience'. 'Both' loses any specificity and comes to signify 'around' (which is, in fact, the root of 'environment') as when we speak of 'ambient poetics'. For Timothy Morton,

> ambient poetics could apply as easily to music, sculpture, or performance art as it could to writing. Ambience, that which surrounds on both sides, can refer to the margins of a page, the silence before and after music, the frame and walls around a picture, the decorative spaces of a building [*parergon*], including niches for sculpture.[16]

In particular, Morton notes, rendering, the making consistent of an atmosphere, is important in cinema. Ambience is 'more or less palpable, yet ethereal and subtle',[17] invisible and yet material. Ideally, rendering leads to an audience's direct immersion in a film's environment. This is certainly the case with Antonioni's *Il deserto rosso* (*Red Desert*, 1964): as soon as we are pulled in we become almost simultaneously disorientated.

Films – and here Antonioni appears again exemplary – may express or be expressed by a certain atmosphere (*atmosfera*) but this term is rarely used to describe the physical location of shooting in either Italian or English. Film sets may be characterised by a particular 'climate' but this term is clearly not used in the geological or meteorological sense.[18] So while this is not the place to develop a detailed philological analysis of the very terms above, not to mention, for instance, *milieu*, it is essential to realise that Italian uses the same word in common speech to refer to both a film set and 'Nature' as an object.[19]

II

Early in his career, in 1940, Antonioni wrote a response to an essay by writer and journalist Guido Piovene published in the authoritative daily newspaper, *Corriere della Sera*. Piovene's essay consisted of notes for a possible novel (or a film) about a change in the climate of Greenland due to a shift in the Gulf Stream. He had read of a persistent, long-term freezing that forced most residents of a particular village to relocate, but the details of this event are vague in his mind.[20] Antonioni's response reproduces Piovene's notes (whose realisation 'should be imagined … in Technicolor') followed by his own embryonic treatment for an imaginary film – 'Green Land'.[21] The piece is extraordinary for several reasons: the 'translation' from prose notes for a piece that carried the potential to be either literary or cinematic to prose notes for a film (unrealised); the insistence on colour more than twenty years before his first colour film, *Il deserto rosso*; and the crystalline sensitivity to the limits and potential for cinematic narration of climate change. As Antonioni puts it: 'The subject matter itself had led me to think that film might be the idiom in which the piece could find its most faithful and effective representation … to express the subtle transition of countries and peoples.'[22]

Piovene begins his notes with the conditional tense characteristic of an outline ('My farmers *would* live above the sand dunes …' and so on [my emphasis]). About a third of the way through he switches to a narrative present: 'Now one day, some-one from this homestead [the seaside settlement of the displaced], grazing his horses, stops with a jerk.' The author frequently inserts his own presence ('I imagine …'; and at one point 'I cannot forget …') as if he were an eyewitness to the events. The change takes place over a long time but is documented in one generation of inhab-itants. At the end the townspeople leave Greenland by sea. Piovene uses the prose of a *récit* or tale, and even Antonioni ends his piece with the fragment: 'Once upon a time, there was a green land …'.[23]

Following Piovene, Antonioni proposes observing episodes in the lives in the people from a village who are forced towards the sea (and eventually, off the land) by ever-increasing glaciers. The villagers experience moments of revelation followed by periods in which they appear unaware of any shifts in the environment. Indeed, Antonioni affirms:

> The writer [Piovene] doesn't say how much time elapses between the first symptoms of
> the freeze and the departure of the population. A lot, one presumes, if 'the days of past
> wealth' are able to emerge 'from the memories of the living' and become a 'heroic
> mythology': reality doesn't become myth that quickly … But I think that in a film you
> would have to speed things up, in order to make it more dramatic.[24]

Another possibility, he admits, would be to film several generations by using differ-ent actors for the same role. In any case, we are still here within the realm of human memory and action, of 'humanism'.

In his treatment Antonioni is acutely aware of colour: 'not to be flamboyant or as mere decoration but as an integral part of the story'.[25] In fact, colours are pre-cisely what indicate change rather than, say, special effects, editing or voice-over. Are they psychophysical correspondences?[26] This is what Antonioni implies when

259

he writes that colour will 'represent psychological developments, the drama itself – visually'.[27] He uses the terms the 'current state of colour technology',[28] implying that it will inevitably advance, progress.

Piovene's notes are not based on research. On the contrary, he explicitly refuses to look up 'Greenland' in any reference source or to learn facts about the climatic cooling since he is only interested in images. And in a footnote to his piece, Antonioni notes:

> As for historical background – to which it would be as well not to attribute too much importance – the following quote should provide enough information ... 'In the history of inhabited countries, they say that the east coast of Greenland was once dotted with towns, villages, and vegetation. They also say that a 'sudden change' in the Gulf Stream which gives life to these northern lands was responsible for its death.[29]

Antonioni readily admits: 'I do not know the North, even less how it was in those days.'[30] It is almost as if any data concerning the dates, timeframe, or specific geological phenomena associated with change would actually impede the director's eventual ability to represent it on film. Facticity and filmic representation seem paradoxically incompatible.

In imagining how he would convince a producer to make this film Antonioni engages in some rather clichéd prose about the fearsome forces of Nature and 'the eternal myth of man engaged in a struggle with the elements'.[31] Such writing is not only uncharacteristically banal, it suggests a banal film; one in which Nature (or climate change) is only thinkable through its impact on characters ('like all Nordic people she [a character he imagines] is deeply attached to Nature'[32]). Perhaps the reification of Nature is a tactic to pitch the film and as such it is precisely driven by the very conditions of compromise that the director would not, ultimately, wish to make. In other words, Antonioni's 'Green Land' can be read as a piece of writing about what Kracauer might call 'genuine cinematic content' confronting the economic reality of the market. It is a wish (here, reader, are my notes for a film, jotted down in the most preliminary way, like a dream) fulfilled (I have produced my film, here, on paper).

III

Antonioni again addressed cinema's privileged relation to (climatic) time first in a preparatory photo-essay published in *Cinema*, 'For a Film on the River Po', and then in his short documentary *Gente del Po*. As is well known, the director filmed in 1943, but he was forced to abandon the project until after the war. By this time much of the footage had been ruined, lost or sabotaged and the nine-minute film released in 1947 is severely truncated with respect to the original plan. It is clear that the Po, with all of its particular nuances for Antonioni, provided an ideal locale for the director to explore the special relation of cinema to (environmental) change and human adaptability.[33] According to Noa Steimatsky, even before he began shooting, Antonioni's essay on the proposed film 'raises questions on the ways in which location shooting complicates the relation of fiction to documentary'.[34] Focusing on the photographs (presumably taken by Antonioni himself), she notes that film emerges as particularly suitable for measuring change. At the same time, any documentary risks indulging in clichés about nature and the (changing) landscape. A documentary on the Po risks positing the Po as the essence of a people and solidifying place in some mystified form of a pathetic fallacy. Of course stills such as those included with the *Cinema* essay can show change if positioned in sequence, in a way that film cannot except through techniques like superimposition, captioning, fades, sepia-toned stock and so forth. How can Antonioni document change in the context of a tension between the fascist domination of space implied by the aerial photograph and the emerging neo-realist vernacular?

Steimatsky rightly points out that while Antonioni's (photo-)essay suggests that the world around the Po has become modern and industrialised, he does not call for a return a pre-industrial past. Rather, he advocates adaptation, just as he will do in *Il deserto rosso* many years later. More specifically, in Antonioni 'cinema is instrumental in this process of adjustment' by its unique ability to mediate between 'modern environment and human perception'.[35] Perhaps this resonates with a Heideggerian habituation, or dwelling in the environment, vulnerable to a critique of radical passivity in the face of devastation. In some sense, the author anthropomorphises the river (as the despot of the valley). Yet there is something in Antonioni's films that pushes beyond simple human(ist) resignation. What?

Perhaps the auditory can provide a way into thinking about this question. Obviously, in the case of *Gente del Po* Antonioni was limited by the footage he had (unless he wanted to reshoot scenes after the war), but the soundtrack could be altered and imposed later and its relation with the images serves as an index of difference, temporal and otherwise. Moreover, the soundtrack itself is not unified. We could classify the sound in *Gente del Po* into several types. First, for the most part the music for the film is rather traditional and orchestral (except for a brief interlude in which an accordion is heard playing a 'folk' tune – a tune of the people). Second, the voice-over is the only 'human' sound heard during the film. We see the people's lips moving as in a silent film, but we never hear them. Only once does the voice directly address us: 'Look at that young man!' But there is a delay – we don't see any young man. Soon he enters the frame and there was no need to tell us to watch him. We have no choice, and we fully understand what he is doing without help. If we know something of the history of the war's interruption we could speculate that the voice-over is disjointed from the images and that the silently moving lips speak to a

261

pathos of loss and separation and even without 'historical knowledge' we might perceive something strange about the documentary's auditory component.

Third, the soundtrack includes diegetic sounds. Of this type, some are unmediated – we see a barge blowing smoke and hear, at the same time, a barge whistle. However, as with the voice that announces a young man who enters the frame after a slight delay, other sounds pre-announce a visual event. That is, we hear a train whistle and then see a train (Antonioni will use the same technique in his next documentary, *N.U.* [1948], and the ambiguity of the temporal discordance between sound and visuals will surface in a particularly dramatic scene in *Il deserto rosso*, as we will see). Or we may be asked to make a leap of faith: we hear church bells and see a church, but we have no reason to assume that this church, at this precise moment, produces the sound of bells ringing.

Similarly, Antonioni imposes onto his footage 'natural' sounds such as thunder or wind. The visuals on screen suggest that a storm is at hand but the sounds we here cannot be verified as originating from a particular source or locale. And it is precisely this unverifiability – even the director himself is not in control of all sensory elements – that I suggest opens to a kind of humility that transcends cynical acceptance. While we hear ambient wind, we see footage in which water blotches break down the borders that we would expect to separate the inside and outside of a film, the film from its 'environment' in the most unthought or generic sense.

Ultimately, however, *Gente del Po*, as its title suggests and like 'Green Land', was meant to be a film about people.[36] In fact, the director admitted that while he may have set out to make a film about the river, 'I was completely taken with those people.'[37] To depict on film the conditions of the climate was itself risky in the context of fascism since then, as now, adaptation to what is 'external' was considered a question of national strength. The director noted: 'Our cinema had carefully avoided representing those situations [flooding, mudslides], as the fascist government had prohibited them.'[38] Ironically, because of the loss of footage (due to

Water blotches.
The interpenetration of inside and outside of the film stock in *Gente del Po* (1943/47)

flooding and excessive humidity in Venice where the film was stored), or because the scenes of meteorological violence were sabotaged by fascist censors, the narrative thread is lost and the film emerges as rather abstract.[39] *Gente del Po*, beyond any considerations of its form and content or (self-)censorship, is also a film about the materiality of film and its subjection to the *ambiente*.

IV

Il deserto rosso, Antonioni's first colour film, is about ecological devastation. This is the film's subject, in other words, its manifest content. Yet the director proleptically anticipates climate change in all of its radical specificity, linking it with colour and sound, and positing cinema as the medium best equipped to capture its peculiar temporality. In other words, although he did not have access to the 'science' that has now verified the devastating effects of sped-up release of carbon dioxide and other anthropogenically produced greenhouse gases, Antonioni thinks about the strange time and space of climate change – profoundly.

Let us begin with a few words about the director's views on technology and progress so that we can move beyond to the film itself. Antonioni was no Luddite, as he consistently makes clear in various writings and interviews. 'Factories are extremely beautiful,' he says in what sounds like a quasi-Marinettian outpouring:

263

> So much so that in many architecture competitions the first prize often goes to factories, probably because they are places that offer the imagination a chance to show itself off. For example, they can profit from colours more than normal houses can. They profit from them in a functional way. If a pipe is painted green or yellow it is because it is necessary to know what it contains and to identify it in any part of the factory.[40]

And as Gilles Deleuze concurs:

> Antonioni does not criticise the modern world, in whose possibilities he profoundly 'believes': he criticises the coexistence in the world of a modern brain and a tired worn-out neurotic body. So that his work, in a fundamental sense passes through a dualism which corresponds to the two aspects of the time-image: a cinema of the body, which puts all of the weight of the past into the body, all the tiredness of the world and modern neurosis; but also a cinema of the brain, which reveals the creativity of the world, its colours aroused by a new space-time, its powers multiplied by artificial brains.[41]

Giuliana's exhaustion in *Il deserto rosso* is clearly contrasted with her son's fascination for robots and erector sets; and with the technophilic pans through the factory interiors. For Deleuze it is precisely through colour that Antonioni celebrates

the positive potential of modernity. The director himself noted that the objects produced by an industrial society are in colour and therefore colour film stock is appropriate for a film about such a society. Moreover, because, as I have noted, film itself
represents technological progress regardless of subject matter, to make a film (about
ecological devastation) is already to adapt to and avow human participation in
change.

It is unclear – and perhaps impossible to gauge – if the 'background' of the
industrial zone around Ravenna suggested the film, or if Antonioni had an idea for
a film and happened across an ideal 'background'.[42] Rather, it might be more accurate to speak of an organic, developing interaction. In interviews, he spoke of two
worlds coming into conflict. There are some characters that adapt well to a 'new
"way" of life'[43] and others, like Giuliana, who do not. 'And thus we witness a sort
of process of natural selection: the ones who survive are those who manage to keep
up with progress, while the others disappear.'[44] Moreover, he notes that the only
scene in which he did not manipulate colour is the fairytale Giuliana tells her son
(filmed in Sardinia) because this is a world that has not (yet) been transformed by
industry. In essence, then, we are still talking about a rather fixed view of nature as
something static, a background to cinematic action.

In fact, the landscape around Ravenna which Antonioni chose as the background for his film and/or which suggested the film to him serves a rather instrumental purpose given its peculiar multiple cultural signifiers of energy and
nationalism. As background, it is important to note that Mussolini had attempted
– without success – to search for oil in Italy and its colonies. Petrol marketed during
the Regime – under the AGIP (Agenzia Generale Italiana Petroli – the state oil company) banner, for instance – as 'autarchic' or 'national' was, in fact, imported.[45]
Enrico Mattei was named President of the newly formed ENI (Ente Nazionale degli
Idrocarburi – the state holding company for research, production and transportation of hydrocarbons in the Po valley) a decade prior to the film. Mattei, supported
by the leftwing of the Christian Democrats, encouraged prospecting in Northern
Italy (where natural gas and methane were discovered, beginning the in 1940s) as
part of a strategy of 'defense of the interests of the collective against the interests of
capital'.[46] When a large field of methane was discovered near Ravenna, Mattei set
up a series of petrochemical plants – those seen in the film – primarily for plastics,
synthetic rubber, carbon black (used in tyres) and fertilisers. These products were
exported to the Soviet Union, China and other countries. In a speech given in
Urbino in 1962 (several months before his still-mysterious death in a plane crash),
Mattei spoke of hydrocarbons as a means of promoting industry in underdeveloped
areas:

> It is sufficient to recall the immense constructive force that Eni has and continues to
> realise with the petrochemical plants in Ravenna ... In the depressed area around

Ravenna, the Anic plant has had a propulsive effect on the economic recovery. Remember that industrial and economic activity in the province of Ravenna has more than doubled between 1951 and 1961, significantly more than any other Italian province.[47]

This is the political background against which Antonioni films. Early viewers of *Il deserto rosso* might not have been aware of the precise use of the factories in the film, but they would certainly read them as symbols of the economic boom, the Christian Democrat compromise between state and private capital; and as symptoms of the deleterious after-effects of (rapid) industrialisation. For our purposes, moreover, the petrochemical factory, electric plant and even the AGIP hotel where Corrado stays are tied to fossil fuels and greenhouse gases.[48] Even if Antonioni was not aware of the ways in which these were contributing to a change in the climate, the film reflects proleptically on (invisible) gases and energy in significant ways.

Still, the mere indication of this broad context would fall into the realm of landscape-as-theme, were it not for the film's developments of an ambient poetics. To begin, then, the plants in the film were not only noisy, they also produced an unbearable stench that the film crew must have been subjected to during shooting. Synaesthesia penetrates and even saturates the film stock itself.

Il deserto rosso, like all of Antonioni's earlier works, including, of course, *Gente del Po*, was shot on (analogue) film stock. Yet the director both predicted and celebrated the fact that video would soon supplant film as the future of cinema, mostly because it offered the potential to manipulate colour 'electronically' and not just in developing. He also felt that videotape, while vulnerable in certain respects, would have a longer shelf life than film.[49] In 1980 he noted:

> Magnetic tape has every advantage over traditional film. Less than a decade from now it will be the only medium available, and this for the economic and artistic benefit of all. In no other field more than the electronic do poetry and technology walk hand in hand.[50]

Of course, by 'electronic' in this context Antonioni does not mean 'digital' although he did look forward to new distribution channels such as cable television. Rather, he is speaking of a medium that was developing simultaneously to supplant the more expensive and physically limiting film stock as a means of capturing reality (capable of being manipulated, however, in the editing process) and as a means of manipulation (experimental, avant-garde) for its own sake. Leaving aside a series of debates about the sustainability of digital dematerialisation, magnetic tape (the backing is usually acetate, polyester, Mylar or polyvinyl chloride – petrochemical products!) is no more or less environmentally friendly than film stock. Tape, like film stock, is wound on a reel in quantity limited by the apparatus. It is coated on one side only with tiny magnetic particles that arrange themselves into what are called 'domains' based on the light (or sound) waves by which they are bombarded. Tape is certainly not invulnerable – over time the particles can drift apart from the backing (although Antonioni was of a generation that did not have to face this issue) and depending on the reels and storage, particles can drift from one track to another (cross-talk) or seep through to contaminate what is stored behind a given piece of tape (print-through). Like film, tape is also subject to alteration by humidity. But Antonioni did not think of tape as a perfect replacement for film stock – he was indeed intrigued by the aleatory and creative possibilities it offered at various stages of film-making. In essence, however, the term 'electronic' does not adequately describe any sort of qualitative difference between film and tape: in both cases light waves hit the surface of the medium through a lens. Although film must be treated for the image to emerge in positive, in both cases the source (or signal) is an analogue one.

Magnetic tape is also the medium used to both generate and record 'electronic music' such as is heard (sparsely) throughout *Il deserto rosso*, composed by Vittorio Gelmetti. The term 'electronic music' in this context does not mean digital or even synthesis.[51] Rather it refers to sounds that are generated electronically (for instance, by an oscillator) and then 'translated' into sound waves by an amplifier. Even if 'real' or 'acoustic' sounds are captured and put to tape and then manipulated (through time variation, splicing, etc.) the source remains an electronic signal. In short, electronic music may have (had) recourse to acoustic sounds earlier in the conceptual process, but it derives from a signal that is electronic, and composers embrace this distinction rather than lamenting a diminished or lost original. Even the female voice that is imposed over Gelmetti's music sounds rather electronic, like a Theremin.

In a primer on composing electronic music Allen Strange notes: 'It is often said that electronically generated sound lacks "life," or is less "humanistic" than acoustically-produced sound.'[52] The latter can be said to differ from the former in its truly transient (or ambient) state, with many different variations that tend to make us hear sound as 'live'. The use of an oscillator as the source of signal results in a greater degree of stability, less transience. To compensate for this, Strange explains, composers may use reverb, but '[t]rue reverberation is the result of variations in arrival time of a particular sound caused by multiple reflections from several surfaces'.[53] In the opening credit sequence, and indeed throughout *Il deserto rosso*, Gelmetti's electronic sounds, which may or may not correspond to movement on-screen, are alternated with 'live' voices and sounds that move freely throughout the environment. The sound editing confuses any sense of space and time that we might associate with the factories and labour.

Electronic music is used for both ambient and diegetic sounds in *Il deserto rosso*. Over the credits we hear sounds – perhaps best described as pings, hums and blips – and view images of the factory. We do not, however, see any mechanical movements, only the smoke that emerges from the factory and blends with fog in the

The first moment of diegetic sound in *Il deserto rosso* (1964), corresponding to a belching smokestack

atmosphere. The ear may take in the sounds as electronic and link them, through an intellectual connection, with the factory but there is still a sense of disjuncture that is easily tolerated, perhaps, only because we are concentrating on the information in the credits. Yet the only movement on screen is supplied by the drifting smoke and the atmospheric fog (as well as very slight camera jerks). In a sense, then, the viewer, with varying degrees of consciousness, is left to link ambient sounds with smoke; or to exist in a state of disaggregation and confusion.[54] Immediately after the credits Antonioni brings us to diegesis through abstraction. We see a belching smokestack and hear a corresponding rhythmic pulse. Indeed, throughout the film the soundtrack will alternate between sounds that correspond to machinery, car or boat horns, human actions, or, on occasion birds or the sea; and ambient electronic sounds that emerge at moments of emotional intensity with no apparent motivation or source.

267

In one scene, as Giuliana and Corrado leave her store, she collapses with exhaustion in a chair next to a produce cart. At this point, we share with her (and possibly with her alone) the experience of hearing electronic sounds. A series of over-the-shoulder shots/counter-shots helps to provide a context: they are on the deserted, grey street where Giuliana has her store and at least this is familiar, even if we may wonder why the *fruttivendolo* would choose this quintessentially metaphysical spot to sell his produce. Indeed, the produce is painted here so it appears as if covered with post-nuclear ash. The combination of ambient sounds, painted

Produce on cart appears as if covered by post-nuclear ash, *Il deserto rosso* (1964)

props and colourised stock take us to a realm of hypothesised disaster as in the suggestive ending of *L'eclisse* (1962). But just as we may feel some sense of locatedness – however unpleasant the scene – an abrupt cut takes us to a different location, one the where colours are brighter and more 'true'. The only continuity is that again the couple moves near a produce truck. As they pass by, we hear a ping as the seller places something on a scale. And although this lonely ping does not, logically, correspond to the sound we would expect from a scale, it is linked to a movement and, thus, potentially diegetic in a way that the blips of the previous scene are not. The ping is a sonic *hapax* – we will never again hear the same sound, in any context. It registers not only estrangement, but also a sense of loss, of the impossibility of turning back (the film).

The problem of sound, verification and temporal disjunction emerges at another moment in *Il deserto rosso* when Linda tries to match a quarantine flag with the cry (*il grido*, also the name of Antonioni's own 1957 film shot in the Po valley) that she (and we) heard 'a little while ago'. But her husband speaks condescendingly to her, saying that the boat has just arrived so it is impossible that she heard a cry emanating from it ('*Chi vuoi che abbia gridato?*'). The ambiguity of the situation triggers a crisis in Giuliana as it also forces us to think back in the film – to a place we are, however, unable to access, assuming we are watching it on a movie screen and not on a home device. In *Il deserto rosso* ambient sounds and spaces are conceptually linked. Giuliana hears and reacts to sounds that other characters seem unaware of. Similarly, the short takes and lack of continuity in some of the editing make it difficult to locate oneself in space.

The Northern Cross radio telescope that Giuliana and Corrado visit – under construction at the time of filming – is still active in Medicina. It is a parabolic radio receiver that is primarily meant to listen to very weak radio waves from the cosmos, another force, like greenhouse gases, that is both invisible and inaudible to humans. As Giuliana and Corrado walk towards the array we hear a persistent ambient hum. This noise could either stand for the sound of film scrolling through a projector (the kind of hum that we experience if we are watching the film in an intimate setting or *cinema d'essai*, but not in a modern theatre). However, this 'theory' is disproved quickly. The humming sound intensifies as the camera moves closer to the array itself. Perhaps, then, it emanates from some machine involved in the construction, which we never see (or, what is far less logical but certainly more poetical, from the sound of distant radio waves amplified). After Corrado finishes speaking with the worker and returns to Giuliana, the sound abruptly stops. We are supposed to pay attention to the dialogue of the actors, now in a medium shot, as in a traditional film. Our theories about the sound no longer matter as we are drawn into human drama. In fact, however, this most 'electronic' of constructions is meant to listen to acoustic sounds. The array is a found object in the landscape that Antonioni is able to exploit, and the sound without a given source first

Bodies emerge on film
from behind a thick
curtain of fog as if
conjured up from
nothing, *Il deserto rosso*
(1964)

appears purely environmental, but then the film-maker can turn it off as quickly as he can cut to a new locale.

As with ambient sound, in *Il deserto rosso* the materiality of film is not incidental but rather crucial to meaning. At several points in the film ships pass through the canals, their prows appearing from off-screen and moving from left to right. These images are disconcerting because of the proximity of the ships to structures on land, but also because we do not see them coming – they emerge from the fog like the human figures so that we can no longer be certain we are watching a realist film. The human actors emerge from the fog as if from behind a thick curtain. Giuliana walks into the frame, her body contrasting with an abstract swathe of colour. The unfocused areas that highlight certain other parts of the photogrammes result from very short takes. Antonioni uses lenses and filters and he paints the 'signals' that he is going to 'record' but in the end they are still the equivalent of 'acoustic' signals hitting analogue film. Colours are bound to fade as analogue film degrades and it seems as if *Il deserto rosso* already anticipates loss of information – it is already nostalgic about such loss.[55] That is, Antonioni celebrates the immediate vibrancy of the colour process and at the same time, signals to the viewer that film is ephemeral and subject to wear – an idea that is clearly disavowed by Technicolor gems such as Hollywood musicals.

Giuliana and Ugo's house is located in what was planned to be a worker's village for the Enel-Sade electric power station. The crew wanted to reproduce the sense of the houses on the small industrial canal as being open, yet they faced the obstacle that the equipment would not fit inside. By a happy coincidence, the village was going to be demolished, so Antonioni was able to tear down walls to gain the desired effect. As Flavio Nicolini writes, the director's aim was to create an 'environment that was cinematically equivalent to the existing one'.[56] We could read this statement to mean, simply, that Antonioni wanted to make a realist film, and that the reality he confronted around the port of Ravenna was itself so polluted as to be ambientally ambivalent. But it seems to me that this short-changes the impact of the film. Instead, Antonioni wanted to make an ambient film, one with the environment as its content but also as its form. By highlighting the temporal disjunctions through his use of sound and spatial disjunctions, by the embrace of fog in/on the film, he

269

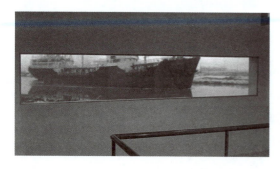

Ship passing through
the Enel-Sade canal
filmed from inside Ugo
and Giuliana's house,
Il deserto rosso (1964)

undoes any sort of certainty about borders between the visible and invisible or out-side and inside that would make us comfortable determining the film's *ambiente*. In *Il deserto rosso* we move far beyond debates about the politics of (national, region) landscape in the film journals. It is no longer possible to speak of a dialectical dif-ference between the (false, spectacular) close-up and the (genuine, pure, quintes-sential) landscape. The face – Giuliana's face – is no longer an object that stands out from a ground. Likewise, to say that Antonioni takes us into a realm of the ineffa-ble is not to say that he renounces action in the face of environmental problems. Rather, we realise, thinking with Antonioni, that there is no question of facing the environment since we are in it, of it.

So if climate science, as calculating, measuring and 'enframing', might beg cinema to suspend its essence in order to make us face – definitively – the effects of human (as opposed to 'natural') actions in the atmosphere (or on the *ambiente* more generally), Antonioni refuses to do so precisely in order to make us truly see that there is no definitive boundary between the human and what surrounds the human. He refuses to choose between the landscape as unchanging, genuine or even nation-alist backdrop for human interaction or even as the analogic embodiment of human emotions. Rather, his cinema is so thoroughly immersed in the environment or in the climate that it undoes any thought of the climate as an object that might be stud-ied in order to arrive at particular solutions. It is in this regard that Antonioni can be retrospectively crowned the cinematic poet laureate of climate change.

270

Notes

1. Robert Henson suggests that sceptics in the US currently number no more than a few dozen. Robert Henson, *The Rough Guide to Climate Change* (London: Penguin, 2009), p. 254.

2. Hollywood cinema certainly has means for separating different locales (think of the cuts and colouration in Soderbergh's *Traffic* [2000]) but the (geographical) temporal problem remains much more vexed.

3. Siegfried Kracauer, *Theory of Film: The Redemption of Physical Reality* (Princeton, NJ: Princeton University Press, 1997), p. 306.

4. The reader could note in these rhetorical questions echoes of Heidegger's 'question after technology'. Like technology (or technics) cinema has moved away from its essence towards a more instrumental mode, one that is widely accepted and hence 'technically correct' but not for that more essential and certainly less poetic. Heidegger seems a crucial thinker for Antonioni's films, even if the director apparently had only a superficial interest in the philosopher.

5. This is the term used by manly but humble scientist Jack (Dennis Quaid). Jack has no political agenda – he simply happens to observe a rapid 'shift' in the climate caused by trapped greenhouse gases from the past (a sign of what is to come if we continue our sins of emissions). This subtle terminological distinction allows the film to proceed as if climate 'change' has been a mere theory and as if there is still time for us to repent. That is, the film both posits climate change as a definite event to come, and yet disavows any particular 'political' position towards capitalist industry and consumerism that is the root cause.

6. See George Ochoa et al., *Climate: The Force That Shapes Our World and the Future of Life on Earth* (London: Rodale, 2005), p. 77; and Henson, *The Rough Guide to Climate Change*, p. 223.

7. I have discussed implications of the English word 'environment' in my essays: 'The Risks of Sustainability', in Paul Crosthwaite (ed.), *Criticism, Crisis, and Contemporary Narrative: Textual Horizons in an Age of Global Risk* (London: Routledge, 2010), pp. 62–78; and in 'Carbon Management: A Gift of Time?', *Oxford Literary Review*, no. 32 ed. Timothy Clark (July 2010), pp. 51–70. Also see Timothy Morton, *Ecology Without Nature* (Cambridge: Harvard University Press, 2007).

8. Antonioni's films may emerge not from character or story, but precisely from an *ambiente*, meant in the sense of a location, but also a certain ambiance, that is, a certain sense of being surrounded on both/all sides. For instance: 'A story can also be born by observing the environment [*ambiente*], which will then become the outline.' Cited in Giorgio Tinazzi, 'The Gaze and the Story', in Michelangelo Antonioni, *The Architecture of Vision: Writings and Interviews on Cinema*, ed. Carlo Di Carlo and Giorgio Tinazzi, trans. Marga Cottino-Jones (New York: Marsilio, 1996), pp. xxiii–xxvii (p. xxi).

9. Cited in Deborah Toschi, *Il paesaggio rurale. Cinema e cultura contadina nell'Italia fascista* (Milan: Vita e Pensiero, 2009), p. 3.

10. Emily Braun, 'Speaking Volumes: Giorgio Morandi's Still Lifes and the Cultural Politics of *Strapaese*,' *Modernism/Modernity* vol. 2 no. 3 (1995), pp. 89–116 (p. 106).

11. Reprinted as 'Towards an Italian Landscape', in David Overbey (ed.), *Springtime in Italy: A Reader on Neo-Realism* (London: Talisman, 1978), pp. 125–9.

12. A brilliant essay that discusses such questions is: Nigel Clark, 'Ex-orbitant Globality', *Theory Culture Society* no. 22 (2005), pp. 165–85. In terms of *Ossessione* I would argue that the Po tends to serve as a flat backdrop to characters' interaction until the

penultimate scene when it immerses Gino and Giovanna. It is this moment when Gino declares that he is finally liberated and the viewer also has the sense that cinema itself has moved beyond the more traditional melodrama of the earlier scenes in the film; almost as if Gino's proclamation is an announcement of the birth of neo-realism, or of a new cinematic moment.

13. De Santis, 'Towards an Italian Landscape', p. 125.

14. Michelangelo Antonioni, 'A Talk with Michelangelo Antonioni on his Work', in *The Architecture of Vision*, pp. 21–47 (p. 27).

15. See my *Alchemical Mercury: A Theory of Ambivalence* (Stanford: Stanford University Press, 2009) for a discussion of the disappearance of the specificity of the 'ambo'-prefix in common uses of 'ambivalence'.

16. Morton, *Ecology Without Nature*, p. 34.

17. Ibid.

18. The term '*clima cinematografico*' was used by Leo Longanesi to express a 'poetry expressed in backgrounds and scenery – a series of images capable on their own of arousing emotion'. Cited in Toschi, *Il paesaggio rurale*, p. 9.

19. For the significance of *milieu* as both 'middle' and 'environment' see Gilles Deleuze, *Cinema 2: The Time-Image*, trans. Hugh Tomlinson and Robert Galeta (Minneapolis: University of Minnesota Press, 1989), p. 71.

20. In this context it is worth recalling that scientists predict not all areas of the globe will warm with climate change (hence, this term is preferred to 'global warming').

21. We should note that at one point he had considered *Light Blue and Green* as the title for *Il deserto rosso*. He apparently rejected the earlier title precisely as it placed too much emphasis on colour.

22. Michelangelo Antonioni, 'Green Land', *Bianco e Nero* no. 10 (October 1940), pp. 959–72. Reprinted in Michelangelo Antonioni, *Unfinished Business: Screenplays, Scenarios, and Ideas*, ed. Carlo Di Carlo and Giorgio Tinazzi, trans. Andrew Taylor (New York and Venice: Marsilio, 1998), pp. 1–18 (p. 1).

23. Ibid., p. 17.

24. Ibid., p. 12.

25. Ibid.

26. Kracauer writes: 'Natural objects, then, are surrounded with a fringe of meanings liable to touch off various moods, emotions, runs of inarticulate thoughts; in other words, they have a theoretically unlimited number of psychological and mental correspondences.' Kracauer, *Theory of Film*, p. 68. Some of these meanings are phylogenetically inherited and can thus be explained by science. Others are culturally determined. And while I would argue that at some points Antonioni may force colours (or objects) to correspond to psychological states either through manipulation of the set, use of coloured filters or physically tinting film stock, at other points – in *Il deserto rosso* in particular – colour-effects break out of any such containment and begin to act on their own in uncontrollable and unexpected ways.

27. Antonioni, 'Green Land', p. 16.

28. Ibid., p. 17.

29. Ibid., p. 7.

30. Ibid., p. 11.

31. Ibid., p. 7.

32. Ibid., p. 13.

33. For instance, Rohdie writes: 'The river not only had a social-populist interest for him, which he expressed in the article ['Per un film sul fiume Po'], but a visual and philosophical one ... Antonioni used the river and its mists and fogs to distort shapes and surfaces, to blur and alter perspectives, and to create an atmosphere of uncertainty and fragility.' And he continues, 'In part, the appeal of the Po for Antonioni in his article-treatment is the mutability of the river: full to the point of flood in winter, dry, emptied out, in late summer. His interest is in the visual possibilities offered by change rather than in their philosophical or social implications.' Sam Rohdie, *Antonioni* (London: BFI, 1990), p. 26.

34. Noa Steimatsky, *Italian Locations: Reinhabiting the Past in Postwar Cinema* (Minneapolis: University of Minnesota Press, 2008), p. 2.

35. Ibid.

36. 'Po di Volano belongs to the landscape of my early childhood. To the Po of my youth. The men who would pass on the levees, dragging along the barges with a rope at a slow, rhythmic pace; and later the same barges dragged along in a convoy by a tugboat, with the women intent on cooking, the men at the helm, the hens, the clothes hanging out – true wandering houses, touching. They were images of a world of which, little by little, I was becoming conscious. That landscape, which until then had been a landscape of things, motionless and solitary – the muddy water, full of whirlpools, the rows of poplars that would get lost in the fog, the Isola Bianca which, in the middle of the river at Pontelagoscuro, divided the current in two – that landscape was moving, it was filling up with people and regaining strength. The things themselves were claiming a different attention, acquiring a different significance. I looked at them in a new way, I was taking control of them. Beginning to understand the world through the image, I was understanding the image, its force, its mystery.' Michelangelo Antonioni, 'Preface to Six Films' [1964], in *The Architecture of Vision*, pp. 57–68 (p. 65). Tinazzi confirms that Antonioni's desire was the make a film about fishing and fishermen rather than a place or *ambiente*. Giorgio Tinazzi, *Michelangelo Antonioni* (Florence: La Nuova Italia, 1974), p. 11.

37. Aldo Tassone, 'The History of Cinema is Made on Film' [1979], in *The Architecture of Vision*, pp. 193–216 (p. 193).

38. Ibid., p. 194.

39. The director put forward the theory of sabotage in a 1985 interview. See Michelangelo Antonioni, 'Identification of a Filmmaker' [1985], in *The Architecture of Vision*, pp. 245–56 (p. 253).

273

40. Tassone, 'The History of Cinema is Made on Film', p. 203.

41. Deleuze, *Cinema 2*, pp. 204–5.

42. A piece published in 1964 fails to help us determine if the setting, the desire to make a film in colour, or the desire to make this particular story came first: 'I always thought of *Il deserto rosso* in color. The idea for it came to me as I was going through the countryside around Ravenna ... The violent transformation of the countryside around the city has had a strong effect on me. Before, there were immense groves of pine trees, very beautiful, which today are completely dead. Soon even the few that have survived will die and give way to factories, artificial waterways, and docks. This is a reflection of what is happening in the rest of the world. It seemed to be the ideal background for the story I had in mind – naturally, a story in color.' Michelangelo Antonioni, '*Il deserto rosso*' [1964], in *The Architecture of Vision*, pp. 283–6 (p. 284). In an interview (in French) included on the Criterion DVD, Antonioni notes that the *milieu* rather than the character(s) were at the origin of the film.

43. Ibid.

44. Ibid., p. 285.

45. While France and England had established national oil companies earlier (CFP, with its own source of supply from the beginning, and BP, respectively), Mussolini did so only in 1926, the same year as the radical revaluation of the lira. AGIP (Agenzia Generale Italiana Petroli) had as its goals to conduct exploration for possible energy sources and develop refineries in Italy; and to market oil found elsewhere as 'national'. In its early years AGIP did manage to acquire a number of oil companies in Romania and Albania as well as Iraq. Some key discoveries of the postwar period include: a methane field in Caviaga (Milan), 1944; a natural gas field near Cremona, 1947; and one at Cortemaggiore, 1948. This latter field was so important that petrol sold in AGIP stations was called 'supercortemaggiore', even though most of it was imported.

46. Nico Perrone, *Enrico Mattei* (Bologna: Il Mulino, 2001), p. 46.

47. Cited in ibid., p. 67.

48. Simultaneous with the developments of Eni, AGIP expands service stations and modernises services for consumers. Enrico Mattei assigned a great deal of importance to the standardisation of the AGIP brand. In a scene from Francesco Rosi's 1972 film, *Il caso Mattei* (*The Mattei Affair*), Gian Maria Volonté as Mattei goes ballistic after inspecting a dirty bathroom in an AGIP station in Sicily. According to Enrico Menduni, however, Mattei's modernist 'good design', while it may have helped establish the AGIP brand as perfectly uniform, also missed an opportunity to stimulate hyper-consumerism. Interestingly, the AGIP style is also Antonioni's style in various films – a cold modernism that frames characters in rectangles. Writing of the AGIP stations and roadside restaurants, Menduni notes: 'They exhibit a rationalist quality of enlightened architectures, modernist and a bit cold, good design ... the clean lines of Swedish furniture, but they are almost all the same. Perhaps the modernism of Eni was too catholic to understand the sinful excesses of food and consumables that could take

place in a roadside restaurant.' Enrico Menduni, *L'autostrada del sole* (Bologna: Il Mulino, 1999), pp. 78–9. Thus we could say that Antonioni does not merely film against this 'found landscape'. Rather, he actively engages it in the formation of cinematic subjectivity.

49. Michelangelo Antonioni, 'The Director and Technology: "Take it From Me, This is the Future"' [1983], in *The Architecture of Vision*, pp. 352–5 (p. 355).

50. Michelangelo Antonioni, *Il silenzio a colori*, ed. Enrica Antonioni (Rome: Campisano Editore, 2006), p. 104. Trans. KP.

51. Robert Moog built his first synthesiser in Trumansburg, New York, the same year *Il deserto rosso* was made.

52. Allen Strange, *Electronic Music: Systems, Techniques and Controls* (Dubuque, Iowa: William Brown and Co., 1972), p. 86.

53. Ibid.

54. Thus, it is especially ironic that the trailer (featured on the 2010 Criterion DVD) for *Il deserto rosso* featured up-tempo jazz (as one might expect in a Dino Risi comedy) that plays for only a few minutes of screen time during the 'orgy' scene.

55. Carlo di Palma, Antonioni's director of photography who had worked on the colours of the original, helped restore the film in 1998. The BFI and Criterion DVDs are made from the restored print.

56. In the original: 'un ambiente cinematograficamente equivalente a quello esistente'. Flavio Nicolini, 'Deserto Rossso,' *Cinema nuovo* no. 168 (March–April 1964), pp. 147–50 (p. 150).

John David Rhodes

ANTONIONI AND THE DEVELOPMENT OF STYLE

To speak about Antonioni is to invoke the category and the problem of style, for, above anything else, it seems fair – if not, obligatory – to acknowledge, at the outset of any discussion of his work, that Antonioni is a stylist. He is a storyteller, yes: his movies all narrate, are committed in various ways to the labour of diegesis. In fact, as Seymour Chatman notes in the opening paragraphs of his book on Antonioni's work, the narrative contents of Antonioni's films 'do not differ markedly from those of network television's daily fare': they are mostly melodramas.[1] But, according to Chatman, Antonioni's 'subtleties of form make the content seem more abstruse than it really is'.[2] Chatman introduces, thus, a gap, or interval between Antonioni's style and his content. But if, as Susan Sontag argued, '[T]o speak of style' is to speak 'about the totality of a work of art', then such a division of the film's labour (form or style on one side, narrative content on the other) is a false division.[3] Antonioni's films are constituted by their style. Perhaps, even, the abstruseness of a simple story's formal elaboration is, if not the content of an Antonioni film, then surely the 'point' or the interest of the film. We know, for instance within seconds of the beginning of *L'eclisse* (1962) – as Vittoria (Monica Vitti) rearranges objects inside empty frames, postponing the conversation that will terminate her love affair that is ending as the movie begins – that we are being asked not just to look at what is made visible but to see *how* what is made visible is being made thus.

If we agree that style is not merely ornament, the 'dress' of thought (in Alexander Pope's phrase), and if we agree, in reference to Antonioni's cinema, that an interest in style – a consistent and consistently developing formal experimentation – ranks above an interest in story content, we will still not have said a great deal that is very specific about style or about Antonioni. I want to press on the matter of Antonioni's style with some insistence. By the matter of his style, I mean both the question or the problem of his stylistic individuality, but also the materiality of his style – how it comes into being through an attention to and contact with objects and landscapes. What I hope to demonstrate in this essay is that Antonioni's style 'develops' in relation to and as a way of analysing a landscape of economic

276

L'eclisse (1962)

development. The success of his mature cinema is its treatment of landscape and the humans and objects that populate it. This landscape (whether we are looking at the Po river delta, the suburbs of Rome, LA, or Beijing) is, moreover, distinctly a developing and developmental landscape. It is a landscape that is littered with and perforated by the evidence of globalised post-World War II economic growth and development. Antonioni's cinema develops alongside and in response and relation to development itself, especially in relation to Italy's unprecedented, vertiginous – and in many senses traumatic – economic and industrial expansion during what has been called the 'economic miracle' (or, more demotically, *il boom)* of the 1950s and early 60s. His style becomes a method not just of representing this landscape – and the unmappable totality (pace Fredric Jameson) that it metonymises – but of mediating and meditating on it, and also of mimicking some of its features.[4] The traces that economic development leave on a particular geographical landscape are always signs of how that landscape is sewn into a system of larger economic flows; that which is near and immediately at hand connects us – quite materially – to what is very far away, unreachable, unseeable. Style, in its sensuous proximity and immediacy (it is 'right there' in the image) and in its distantiating alienation (it forces us, iteratively, to register the image *as* image), behaves something like – and becomes a powerful language for representing – the nearness and the farness of capitalism's localised globalism and globalised localities. Style then, might not only be invoked as a useful language for talking about the totality of works of art, as Sontag claims, but also for talking about the much larger totality of social and economic materiality.[5]

Antonioni's style is the practice of a relative autonomy afforded by global capital to what has come to be known as 'art cinema'. The apogee of European art cinema's first major phase coincided with and was partially defined by Antonioni's major works of the late 1950s and early 60s. Along with that of Godard, Ingmar Bergman and Alain Resnais (to name only some of the major figures), Antonioni's work from this period came to embody art cinema's difficulty, its concentration on an anguished middle-class consciousness as it struggled to come to terms with a precipitous and dangerous modernity, particularly the modernity of the economic 'booms' of postwar European economies, stimulated as they were by American capital and the discovery and exploitation of cheap energy sources closer to home.

To circulate globally as art cinema, a film needs first to be marked as different from the 'normative' or 'classical' forms of narrative cinema. As Pasolini argued, art cinema – or, as he called it, the 'cinema of poetry' – was a mode of formal experimentalism in which the director's personal (but class-bound, and thus 'general') vision became visible, exaggerated. This experimentalism Pasolini saw as, among other things, a symptom of 'neo-capitalism'.[6] Style is the mutable substance, the vital resource – or better yet and more concisely, the commodity that is traded in the global circulation of art cinema. (Of course, as works of art, art films are never 'merely' commodities.) Style is what is desired, bought and sold in the art cinema. It is a particularism that enables the work to circulate in a global market, or – put in less pecuniary terms – in the global network of reception.

As Rosalind Galt and Karl Schoonover have recently argued,

> [A]rt cinema has from its beginnings forged a relationship between the aesthetic and the geopolitical, or in other words, between cinema and world. Thus, it is the critical category best placed to engage pressing contemporary questions of globalization, world culture, and how the economics of cinema's transnational flows might intersect with trajectories of film form.[7]

According to their understanding, art cinema's ability to mediate, think and criticise the geopolitical hinges on 'its sustaining concept of universal legibility'.[8] For it to be viable as an aesthetic (and economic) mode art cinema's 'forms and stories' must be 'comprehensible across languages and cultures'.[9] Galt and Schoonover are, of course, sensitive to the 'western/patriarchal/neo-colonial' implications that may subtend or be folded into such aspirations towards universal legibility. Refreshingly, however, they 'refuse to underestimate the potential of the international'.[10] Implicit, I think, in their argument, is the idea that art cinema's privileging of style – that style itself – might be a powerful medium for a productive thinking of the geopolitical.

Had Antonioni's films not struck the studio heads at Universal as both particular and (therefore) remunerative, he would never have been granted a three-picture deal to make *Blow Up* (1966), *Zabriskie Point* (1970) and *The Passenger* (1975) –

films that would be distributed to global audiences. (That these same studio heads probably regretted this decision is another story.) A particularised (cinematic) style is the prerequisite for the film's ability to insert itself into the global political economy. But style is also the means by which – the formal 'language', for lack of a better term – art cinema talks about this same political economy. As I want to try to argue in this essay, Antonioni's style develops in relation to the indices (scars, traces, refuse, monuments) of economic development (always both national and global) itself. The landscape of development is the object of his cinema's attention, and his cinema develops into a method of meditating on this same development.

Style and the Developmental Landscape

To begin to explain what I mean in claiming that Antonioni's style 'develops' in explicit relation to a landscape that is itself in or under development I want to take a fleeting moment in one of Antonioni's early documentaries, *Sette canne, un vestito* (*Seven Reeds, One Suit*, 1949), Antonioni's documentary about the rayon industry. Near the beginning of this short film, a slatted wooden cart full of reeds (*canne*) are hauled across the frame in a medium shot, and as the last cart disappears off frame left, we discover a modern factory gleaming in the background. While it was already clear that the reeds were being harvested by modern methods (the film opens with sweeping aerial vistas of factories, and we see a machine-powered thresher in use on the back of a cart), the humbleness of the carts laden with reeds is clearly juxtaposed with the striking modernity of the factory. (The voice-over describes the factory as '*un edificio maestoso*': a magnificent building.) The intrigue of this image is its mediation of foreground and background as two distinct but interconnected planes of a developmental, working landscape. The shot's style – the material disposition of its form – binds foreground and background together. Its modernity is materially connected to and materially connects that of the landscape. During the fascist period the rayon industry had been celebrated as one of the industrial-agricultural nexuses most ripe for exploitation in the effort to achieve economic autarchy.[11] The rayon industry functioned something like this shot in its synthesis of the natural and the technological.

Noa Steimatsky has written forcefully of how Antonioni, in *Gente del Po* (*People of the Po*, 1943/47), another early short documentary, but one that only survives in fragments, 'grasp[ed]' 'the landscape as a distanced, alienated terrain'.[12] This is a landscape at once natural and cultivated, agricultural and industrial. The economic activity (industrial and agricultural) along the Po river and throughout its delta were central to the story of Italy's rapid economic growth in the postwar period. In Antonioni's early films we are frequently invited to notice the contradictions of Italy's uneven modernity. For instance, another short documentary like *Superstizione* (*Superstition*, 1949) asks us to recognise the survival of an ancient

279

(almost pre-Christian) peasant culture inside that of modern postwar Italy. In Antonioni's early features the scenes that suggest Antonioni's mature aesthetic – his propensity for long takes, his manner of emphasising the landscape and architecture by holding shots after characters have left the frame, his careful manipulation of bodies and objects in the frame so that spatial relations are often difficult to read and backs are often turned towards the camera – are frequently set in a landscape that bears the traces of recent economic development, particularly of the implantation on the landscape of what David Harvey, following Marx, has called 'immobile capital': the infrastructural features of highways, airports, office buildings and the like.[13] In *Cronaca di un amore* (*Story of a Love Affair*, 1950), Antonioni's first feature, the style generally adheres to a 'classical' model of narration and formal design, despite its tendency to use much longer (and therefore fewer) takes than was the norm.[14] But according to Lorenzo Cuccu, the film's most stylistically 'exemplary' scene – that is to say, the one that most anticipates Antonioni's later style – is the one shot at Milan's *idroscalo*, the city's aquatic airport. In the interwar period, because of the scarcity of runways in Italy, seaplanes were the most common mode of aviation. By the time Antonioni came to shoot *Cronaca di un amore*, seaplanes had been superseded and Milan's *idroscalo* converted into a pleasure and sporting grounds. Paola and Guido, the films' central characters, drive to the *idroscalo*, where Guido shares with Paola the news that their past is being investigated. It is entirely empty of other human beings. Guido and Paolo sit near the water's edge on the low, raked concrete rows of seating that line the basin of the *idroscalo*. The rows dominate a shot of the two of them seated; the image borders on a mode of visual abstraction. Despite the purely formal visual interest of the location, the location

Cronaca di un amore
(1950)

also emits a sense of dense particularity. Even if we do not recognise this specific location, its specificity is felt. We can surmise that this is a place for watching some sort of aquatic spectacle. (Its use here looks forward to the use of the Olympic velodrome as a meeting point for Vittoria and Piero in *L'eclisse*.) This is the landscape of the changing face of economic development: a place that had functioned – until a past very proximate to the film's moment of production – as an infrastructural feature of the landscape (as immobile capital) and whose use now – in the film's present – has been superseded. In its new function as a site of pleasure and recreation, it seems to be subject to the extraction of a kind of surplus value. What is more significant, perhaps, is the fact that this locale either lends itself to or is appropriated by Antonioni as a means of stylistic display. If this scene looks forward to Antonioni's development as a film-maker whose style will make bolder use of landscapes and locations like this one, it is because of the way in which the scene achieves some degree of formal exaggeration through the visual cathexis of a landscape of development.

Il grido (*The Cry*, 1957) is widely considered to be a pivotal film in the development of Antonioni's style – 'the first film to show his mature style and preoccupations'.[15] Its emphasis on location shooting and working-class milieus connect it to the major currents of Italian neo-realism of the late 1940s and early 50s, but the film radicalises the *longueurs* of neo-realism while it pursues an increasingly abstract visual style and a nearly aleatory plot that follows the main character's peripatetic traversal of the landscape. This landscape is a return to the landscape of *Gente del Po*, the landscape of Antonioni's own childhood and young adulthood and, as mentioned already, a landscape of intense agricultural cultivation and intense industrial development. Although it has rarely been discussed in these terms, the film nearly thematises the problem of economic development and the impact such development leaves on the geographic environment.

Aldo, the film's protagonist, works in a sugar refinery. By establishing his work in these terms, the film locates Aldo – in quite a 'realist' and 'realistic' (verisimilar) manner – inside one of the mainstays of agricultural production in the Po river delta. The Italian sugar-beet industry dates back only to the late nineteenth century when the cultivation of sugar beets as a source for refined sugar was first subsidised by the Italian government. The industry enjoyed a boom in the early 1920s, but by the 30s its fortunes were already declining, in part as a result of competition from other growing regions outside Italy that enjoyed climates and geographies better suited for the crop than those of the Po river delta.[16] Aldo gives up his work at the refinery after his girlfriend Irma leaves him, following the news of the death of her husband who had long ago emigrated to Australia.

Il grido insists on the specificity of this place, of the Po river's flat expanse, the muddy levees that attempt to protect the agricultural plains from its annual floods, the nature of the work undertaken in this landscape, of the houses in which its

281

inhabitants find shelter. Despite Aldo's wanderings, he never leaves this place, and while the expanse of the landscape bleeds past the frame of the image, the film's space still feels bound by a law of centripetal movement. Aldo's wandering from Goriano only returns him to the same place by the film's end.[17] The facts of the film's setting and its characters' occupations, however, also allude and directly link the film to a larger flow of goods and people to places far away from Goriano and the Po river delta. The sugar-beet industry's own history and its subsidisation by the Italian state is a story of how competition in international markets can reshape the texture of a particular place. Irma's husband, the announcement of whose death begins the film, has made it out of this place – has obviously emigrated from Italy's depressed labour market to find better-paying work in Australia. (Emigration was such a typical fact of Italian existence, even during Italy's period of economic growth in the 1950s, that the film need not expend any real energy filling in the details of why he is in Australia.) Two more events in the film also mark explicitly the imbrication of this locality with global flows. First: in a brief scene shot on the levees of a canal, Aldo and another man discuss the possibility of emigrating to South America. They both carry brochures in which the process of emigration and finding work is spelled out; the brochures include a map of South America. 'Venezuela sure is big,' the man exclaims to Aldo. This exchange (like a number of other things in the film, including its location) looks forward to the recruitment of workers for emigration to South America in *Il deserto rosso* (1964). Second: in the film's concluding movements, after Aldo has returned to Goriano, we learn that the sugar-beet fields are being burned and bulldozed so as to make way for a new military airport. Angelo Restivo has remarked that the threat of the bulldozers and the voices raised against them mark 'the point at which historicity emerges in the text'.[18] (The beet fields themselves, of course, are a resolutely modern intervention in the landscape and are as much markers of historicity as their destruction.) William Arrowsmith wonders:

> What, after all, can happen to Goriano after the bulldozers have flattened the fields and slabbed them with cement? What happens to a sugar-beet factory like the one in which Aldo works once the fields are destroyed? What, in fact, happens to Irma and the others – the milkman, the egg lady, the old woman in the vegetable stall – who live in Goriano surely for reasons of *their own*? All these are images that transcend the separation of Aldo and Irma; much more is at stake than one couple.[19]

Arrowsmith is asking questions about what Harvey has called the 'spatial fix' of capitalism's perpetual development, destruction and redevelopment. The 'spatial fix' is the process by which:

> capitalism has to fix space (in immoveable structures of transport and communication nets, as well as in built environments of factories, roads, houses, water supplies, and

other physical infrastructures) in order to overcome space (achieve a liberty of movement through low transport and communication costs). This leads to one of the central contradictions of capital: that it has to build a fixed space (or 'landscape') necessary for its own functioning at a certain point in its history only to have to destroy that space (and devalue much of the capital invested therein) at a later point in order to make way for a new 'spatial fix' (openings for fresh accumulation in new spaces and territories) at a later point in its history.[20]

It is capitalism's restless development and Aldo's death that occupy the closing movements of *Il grido*. The tower of the refinery from which Aldo falls (or jumps?) to his death will face, presumably, its own death, or obsolescence in the unnarrated future of the film's diegetic world. It is instructive to recall that that the sugar-beet industry itself – here giving way to other, more rapid means of producing value – had wrought considerable changes on this landscape in a brief space of time. It was not an example of an ancient, 'timeless' practice of locally specific land cultivation, but was a heavily capitalised and state-subsidised industry.

In another visually striking sequence from the film, Aldo and Virginia, his lover for the duration of the middle part of the film, attempt to make love on bare ground, amid enormous wooden spools used to transport utility cables for electricity or telecommunications. The spools seem to have been stranded on what appears to be a newly built dirt road running alongside some agricultural fields. The spools read 'Pirelli elettrici'. Pirelli was a major manufacturer of rubber tyres and electric and telecommunications cables.[21] The rubber used in the manufacture of tyres and cables is, of course, a by-product of the petroleum industry, thus the spools link back to the petrol station that Virginia runs, where Aldo has been working, and where he and Rosina, his daughter, have been living as a provisional family with Virginia and her father. In the distant background of the image we see some bright new high-rise housing projects. These are the outskirts of Ravenna: the

283

Il grido (1957)

city is clearly expanding into the countryside, claiming it for conurbation. Rosina, Aldo's daughter, has been playing on her own, but she happens upon her father and Virginia in their embrace. The spools, as Chatman notes 'are not symbolic of anything in particular, but their shape and size seem just right to mirror the child's shock and consternation'.[22] I rather think that the spools have nothing to do with Rosina's interiority and more to do with the abstract rhythm of the visual surface of the film. What strikes me here, however, is not merely that Antonioni introduces visual abstraction into the most generic of psychoanalytic scenes (that of the 'primal scene'); I am interested, rather, in the fact that one of the film's most visually charged scenes takes place in and through – or rather assembles itself around and in relation to – the developing landscape. Insofar as the scene introduces a degree of abstraction (the visual design of the film existing autonomously, or 'for itself'), it does so in a rather complex way. On the one hand, the spools function as the main vehicles of pictorial abstraction. We register them as shapes, lumps of visual plasticity – too large, too close; they lend a kind of formal-stylistic immediacy to the scene (and, thus, also the distance or 'alienation' that abstraction produces). On the other hand, though, they are merely the un-noteworthy metonymic indices of the everyday reality of Italy's changing landscape. And yet, even as such, they register abstraction in a different sense from the pictorial: the spools are the literal materials of the abstracting nature of long-distance telecommunication and they are the objects produced by the petroleum industry's production and cancellation of distance – through long-distance travel, and through the oil economy, which both produces geographic differentiation (the cathexis – both real and imaginary – of the 'oil producing region', for instance) and globalised uniformity. In other words, the abstract and abstracting dimensions of Antonioni's style are bred out of and cannot be thought in isolation from a landscape of development, one that looks and feels both entirely local but is, we know simultaneously, forever punctured, punctuated and perforated by, sutured and inserted into the development of the global economic system.

284

The relation between a stylistic tendency towards visual abstraction that occurs in and through the materials – the actual building materials – of the developing landscape is evident quite powerfully in the films of Antonioni's 'trilogy': *L'avventura* (1960), *La notte* (1961) and *L'eclisse*. The opening dialogue and shots of *L'avventura* explicitly reference the encroachment of new building onto the property of Anna's (the disappearing 'central' character's) father's villa. The dome of St Peter's looms in the furthest background, but nearer to hand is a file of new middle-class apartment buildings. (Anna's father's real-life counterparts, the black aristocracy of Rome, were, in fact, themselves responsible for much of the aggressive overdevelopment of Rome's periphery. Many were all too eager to sell off to speculators the farm and woodland that surrounded their villas, or else to turn speculators themselves. Anna's father, who identifies himself as a diplomat, expresses a

L'avventura (1960)

jaded world-weariness. Whether this attitude derives from a disgust with or a responsibility for the speculation that so transformed the Roman landscape, the film does not tell us.) *L'avventura* moves into a much more accomplished and decisive mode of visual and narrative abstraction than that of *Il grido*, but it almost feels as if the later film, in granting us this brief but intentionally orchestrated glimpse of urban development, is taking care to imbricate its interest in the developing land-scape with that of the earlier film, as if to demonstrate the continuity of their inter-ests and investments (stylistic and thematic) across the geographical distance that separates the Po river delta from Rome and Sicily, where most of the rest of *L'avventura* takes place. Style, as a connective substance, running from *Il grido* to *L'avventura* and beyond, running from Ravenna to Rome, is something like the rubber electrical cables whose empty spools stud the periphery of growing Italian cities, north and south.

Or we might consider the notorious closing sequence of *L'eclisse* in which we are given a series of nearly abstract shots of the building site (and its requisite building materials) at the corner of the Viale del Ciclismo and the Viale della Tecnica in Rome's EUR district (a fascist World's Fair site that was redeveloped as a swanky bedroom community and white-collar workplace in the 1950s and 60s). Instead of the meeting between Vittoria and Piero that we had expected, the film gives us, for example, piles of bricks shot in such extreme close-up that they assume an almost entirely abstract visual interest. And yet we also register them – like the spools in *Il grido* – as nothing other than the stuff, the actual material of the developing suburbs. The tallest building in EUR, completed in 1962, is the ENI (Ente Nazionale degli Idrocarburi, or National Hydrocarbon Corporation) headquarters, which we glimpse earlier in the film. ENI was the chief engine of the Italy's petroleum industry. The building's steel and glass international mod-ernism is of a piece with Milan's more stylistically pronounced and memorable

285

L'eclisse (1962)

La notte (1961)

Pirelli Tower, designed by Gio Ponti and completed in 1958. *La notte*, the middle film of the trilogy, opens with a long, upward-tilting shot of the Pirelli Tower (juxtaposed with a Beaux Arts building in the shot's foreground), followed by two shots taken from its roof, both graphically abstract in their compostion, and then a stylistically virtuosic gesture: a long track *down* the surface of the Pirelli building. (The choice of the Pirelli building is not casual: it links back to the spools in *Il grido*, of course, but the building was – and remains – far and away the most daring modernist skyscraper in Italy.) The camera faces the building's surface, and in the reflection of its glass we see spread out before us the skyscrapers and highways that indicate Milan's rapid postwar urban and economic expansion. We could say the film's style constitutes itself by staring into and at – quite literally and insistently – the surfaces of objects whose existence is predicated on and proclaims Italy's accelerated entry into and competition in the global economy in the postwar period.

Abstraction as connection

Il deserto rosso, as Angelo Restivo remarks, is 'both a summation of past work and a movement forward toward something new'.[23] Restivo uses Lacanian gaze theory as a means of accounting for 'the very visibility of the economic miracle in *Il deserto rosso*'s *mise en scène* – as well as its utter incomprehensibility – that links Antonioni's *formal* experimentation (with the structures of the gaze within the tradition that is neorealism) with the text's encounter with history'.[24] Restivo argues that the historicity of the economic miracle's process of radical modernisation is explored by Antonioni as a site of unrepresentable, 'radical *loss*' registered via the director's 'understanding of the split between the eye and the gaze'.[25] For Restivo, who reads *Il deserto rosso* in the register of the sublime, Italy's unrepresentable modernity – 'a world totally and radically transformed by neocapitalism'[26] – appears in the film by way of 'stains', visual elements that metonymically linked to (or effects of) this modernity, but that are '*out of place*'.[27] These stains are the yellow gases that are emitted by the factory where Ugo works and the newspaper blown by the wind that wraps itself around Giuliana's legs momentarily near the shop she plans to open in Ravenna's Via Alighieri.

I am interested in approaching some of these same indices of Italy's radical transformation, but in slightly more prosaic terms. While I am entirely convinced of the usefulness and the appropriateness of the sublime as a heuristic for understanding the film's work, at the same time, I'm rather more interested in what is *there* in the image in its thereness. Rather than gesture only to the impossible-to-represent totality of global capitalism, the objects the film gives us to see and the manner in which it allows us to see them together constitute the terms of a visual rhetoric of connection and contact between places and spaces.[28] This totality will never, of course, be present in a film or to us as film spectators. However, the film's visual style becomes the agency through which the spatial dynamics of economic development are made visible. As Restivo's account of the film makes clear, the film registers the strain in the relation between what one could actually *see* of this reality (new commodities, new factories, the effects of pollution) and the larger totality that these visible indices point to. However, rather than emphasise their failure fully to represent this totality, I would prefer to consider how the film's style mediates this totality, and by mediate I do not mean that this totality is only estranged from us, but rather is, in effect, *put before us*.

While Giuliana is clearly the film's central character, much of her (and our) time in the film is spent following Corrado (Richard Harris) around in his attempts to recruit labourers to emigrate to South America. It was at exactly this moment in history that ENI was looking to expand its enterprise and to explore for oil in South America. Thus, despite the film's visually daring style – bordering as it does at times on almost complete visual and narrative abstraction – its narrative is in large part

287

*Il deserto
rosso*
(1964)

occupied by everyday facts of life under the economic miracle. These everyday facts involve excesses of nearness and farness. Factories and their noxious fumes and effluvia are too near, too present to the humans whose lives and landscapes they poison. And yet these real impositions on the natural and human landscape are only parts of larger forces that not only come from a distant elsewhere, but that also fling human beings away from where they have been used to live. I want to explore these visual and thematic dynamics in four passages from the film.

1) As what seems to be an erotic relation develops between them, Corrado takes Giuliana with him (somewhat inexplicably) on an errand to recruit a worker for emigration to Patagonia. In a sequence shot we see Giuliana and Corrado as they approach what seems to be a working-class housing estate. A small hangar-like building, in ochre-painted plaster is behind them as they walk across some lawn bisected by a planked sidewalk and a gravel path; to the left of the shot, along the path, a clump of three pink flowers on long green stalks adorns the scene. The film cuts to a reverse shot in which the camera has been positioned directly behind these pink flowers, now wildly out of focus and taking up more than a quarter of the entire screen. Behind them Giuliana appears quite small, but entirely in focus. In the next shot, taken from inside the apartment building, as Giuliana and Corrado open and walk through a large opaque glass door, we glimpse the flowers outside once more, now in deep space and in (relative) focus.

2) Later in the film, when Giuliana and Corrado visit an oil rig belonging to his company, we see Giuliana in a high-angle long shot, apparently taken from the large tanker anchored near the rig. She seems to be inspecting a large black pipe through which the oil from the rig is transported onto the tanker. Next, we see Giuliana in a high-angle medium close-up, the camera now positioned on the rig. She looks up at the large black pipe again, but then looks away, out towards the sea. As she does, the shot pans along the pipe and follows in close-up its sinuous course to the tanker, finally showing us

289

Il deserto rosso
(1964)

Corrado addressing the tanker's captain from a seat suspended out over the sea. (Presumably this seat is carrying him from the ship to the rig.) We can read the ship's name (*Lincoln*) and provenance (London). '*Arriverderci*', Corrado says. 'Bye-bye', the captain responds.

3) In the scene immediately following the one on the rig, Corrado makes a presentation aimed at recruiting potential emigrants to his new oil fields in Patagonia. The scene is shot in the warehouse of a factory where demijohns (giant glass bottles, usually encased in wicker and used in transporting olive oil and wine) are produced. As Corrado speaks to the workers in a large room, a giant map of South America is behind him. The scene is shot through alternating long and medium shots that show Corrado and the workers in shot/counter-shot fashion as he answers their questions. The camera, however, begins to abstract itself, visually, from Corrado's presentation. A tilting shot begins by showing us the crowns of some workers' heads (though out of focus) but continues to tilt upwards as its attention seems to be attracted by a bundle of electrical wires extruding from a sloppily patched, painted and time-weathered wall. Next we are given a close up of Corrado, the map behind him, as if the previous shot might have belonged to his point of view. Then follows a panning shot across the silent faces of the men and the mouths of the green bottles, as the idiotic off-screen chatter of the others in the room fills the soundtrack. Another shot of Corrado, then an out-of-focus shot of some of the men, then finally a close-up of a young worker who listens silently. This shot, however, tilts up, past his face, past stacks of wicker baskets for the demijohns, then up along the vertical extension of a bright blue strip painted on the wall behind.

In the shot that immediately succeeds this one, we see Corrado leaving the building through a door that opens onto a yard in which the empty demijohns are stored in imbricated stacked rows. They produce an element of intense pictorial abstraction in the same way that we have seen with *Il grido*'s spools and the building materials at the end of *L'eclisse*. The demijohns are particularly interesting here insofar as they metonymise the traditional commodities (oil and wine) associated with Italian agricultural labour and commerce. These workers are being plucked from an artisanal and ancient mode of work and trading in order to be inserted into the dynamised and more radically globalised world (oil) economy. Antonioni's style, however, links the use of these humble, more artisanal artefacts to the Pirelli electrical wires. Their deployment as material for stylistic expression, or articulation, asks that they be thought in terms of relation and difference. Style connects them (jars and spools), but they are also media of connection – through trade, communications and other modes of consumption.

4) The scene that immediately follows opens with a shot taken from inside Giuliana and Corrado's house, a modern construction (it is unclear if it is a flat or a detached dwelling) situated along Ravenna's docks. The camera looks out across the hallway of the upper storey and the stairwell, with its bright blue (the same colour as the stripe on the wall in the last scene) metal banister. A long horizontal window – an uninterrupted pane of glass – above the stairwell looks out onto the port and acts as a visual frame for

290

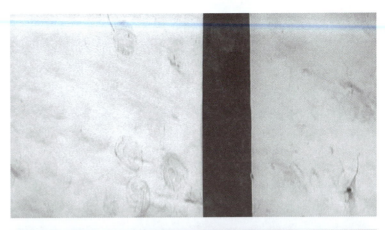

Il deserto rosso
(1964)

the traffic of large cargo ships outside. In this shot a large cargo ship takes up nearly the
entirety of the window; the window works to import the ship into the interior of the
house. The ship's enormous size and the window's perfect transparency work together to
confuse and collapse the spatial relations between them: both feel – and in a sense are –
compressed onto a single visual surface.

In each of these instances Antonioni's style operates in excess of what would
appear to be the basic demands of narration. The manner in which we see things
asserts a relative autonomy from the trajectory of the narrative. In each instance,
moreover, style (produced through a rigorously maintained system of shooting
and framing) is the means by which relations of distance and proximity are
insisted upon, inverted and hyperbolised. The process of hyperbolisation itself
could be traced as something that progresses across the films diachronically: as,
for instance, we move from the large Pirelli spools outside Ravenna in *Il grido* to
the gigantic Pirelli Tower in the centre of Milan in *La notte*. The stylistic processes
themselves also become increasingly hyperbolised – from a simple act of framing

Il deserto rosso
(1964)

in *Il grido*, to the technical virtuosity (itself produced by large-scale industrial means) in the downward tracking shot in *La notte*.

In the scene in which Giuliana and Corrado pay a visit to the worker's flat in the housing estate, the movement – across a single shot – of objects from large to small, background to foreground, focus to out of focus – absorbs our attention as much as any words that pass between the two characters at this moment. Antonioni's style here functions as a means of distancing and approximation. The nearly too-intimate encounter with the worker's wife (as this scene develops), who clearly does not want her husband to emigrate for fear of its impact on his mental health, operates as well through an economy of distance and proximity. She would keep her husband close; global capital would draw him far away, to Patagonia. Style operates similarly in the recruitment meeting at the bottle factory. The camera's abstracted attention to the abstract features of the factory's physicality (the blue stripe) would at first seem to drain the scene of its apparent 'social' contents. And yet, the style's flattening and distancing, its drawing near and pushing away might be said to literalise – at the level and on the surface of the image – the film's preoccupation with the distortions of near and far that occur under global capitalism.

The pattern of shooting in the scene on the oil rig actually connects us back to a moment in *Sette canne, un vestito*, another film about factory life and modern technology. In the earlier documentary – a film intended to educate its audience about the complexities of industrial production – the camera tilts upwards to follow the movement of rayon pulp through the pipes and tubes that carry the materials from one place in the factory to another. In this documentary the camera's curiosity about the 'plumbing' of the factory entirely makes sense in terms of the film's narrative-pedagogic intentions. In *Il deserto rosso*, however, while we note that the pipe is what carries the oil from the rig to the ship, the immediate sense evinced by the shot is one of abstraction, not didactic clarification. We would like to read the sinuous pan – a shot that theatricalises a kind of 'attention' to the rig's mechanics – as Giuliana's point of view, except that before the pan begins, we have already seen Giuliana turn away, out towards the sea. Thus, the panning shot describes neither the function of the machinery itself (as in *Sette canne, un vestito*) or, strictly speaking, Giuliana's point of view.[29] Instead, the shot demonstrates how Antonioni's style – as autonomous formal articulation – produces itself through an exaggerated attention to the material features of global development.

During the film's longest sequence, the half-hearted 'orgy' scene that transpires at a shack along a canal, a large ship moors itself nearby and runs up a flag that seems to suggest it is quarantined on account of some disease being carried by the ship's crew. Its unsettling appearance sends Giuliana into a nervous fit and forces this interminable scene to a conclusion. In the later shot of the picture window, the appearance of the ship outside the house (but pressed up against its window) initiates the discovery of Giuliana's son's paralysis (which she later learns – to her devastation – he is faking). The ship is thus a thematically charged object. As the actual means of transport of global commodities (whether crude oil or olive oil), the ship *connects* the problem of mental and physical illness (Giuliana's and her son's) to the problem of global capitalism. In making this connection, however, I run the risk of stating the obvious. The shot also – like all of these shots – makes a pronounced visual style – or visual style's pronunciation – the means of actually making these connections, of pressing things, goods, people, places, buildings, causes and effects up against one another. This particular shot is a compelling example of the film's use of the zoom lens as a flattening (and, I would say, an abstracting) agent. Antonioni remarked on this aspect of the film's style: 'I worked a lot in *Il deserto rosso* with the zoom lens to try to get two-dimensional effects, to diminish the distances between people and objects, make them seem flattened against each other.'[30] In each instance described above, as Antonioni's style asserts a kind of visual autonomy for itself, it actually acts to establish and assert the film's thematic investment in the problem of global economic development. Style presents an over-abundance of visual material that is entirely abstract, but that also asks us to read this visual abstraction as the legible sign of the abstraction of economic and social life.

In his controversial essay 'The "Cinema of Poetry"' Pier Paolo Pasolini made a handful of acute comments on some of the same scenes I have described above. These remarks he tosses out casually, mentioning that he did not 'want to linger' on these 'poetic' (the word is in quotation marks in the essay) aspects of the film. (He mentions the flowers [from example 1] and the 'insane pan [sic] from the bottom up along an electric blue stripe' [from example 2].[31]) Pasolini suggests that the film's '"obsessive framing" ... demonstrates the prevalence of formalism as a finally liberated and therefore poetic myth'.[32] Pasolini goes on to suggest that the film's formalism is made possible by Antonioni's identification of his own aesthetic vision of

293

the world with that of his 'neurotic' protagonist, Giuliana.[33] This last claim interests me less here than Pasolini's emphasis on the film's 'formalism' as 'poetic myth'. What I think Pasolini means is that formal exaggeration – which is to say *style* – becomes the foundational (mythic, organising) principle of the film's making (its *poeisis*).[34] This observation accumulates even more interest (for my purposes here) when considered in relation to Pasolini's subsequent comment, much later in the essay, that 'a renewal of formalism' (which he calls the 'language of poetry of film') has become 'the average, typical production of the cultural development of neo-capitalism'.[35] This latter comment identifies art cinema's (and Antonioni's) formalism (style) with the phase of 'neo-capitalism', or aggressive global development in relation to which it must be periodised. While Pasolini is nearly contemptuous of the 'late humanistic function'[36] of formalism (style), which he clearly sees as nothing more than a palliative effect of neo-capitalism, his strong linking of style and social materiality says more than he intends. For surely, as *Il deserto rosso* reveals across its duration, even if style is an index of global capitalism and even if it feeds itself on the indices of the same, it is also the material and substance through which the dizzying approximations, distantiations and abstractions of global capitalist development can begin to be apprehended.

'... that whiteness ... around a black point'

In 1963, a year before *Il deserto rosso* was released, Antonioni published a short essay, 'The Event and the Image', a suggestive piece of writing that has circulated frequently in critical discussions of the director's work. In the essay Antonioni hints at the means by which 'the cinema can acquire a new character', one that is 'no longer merely figurative'.[37] By this phrase Antonioni would seem to intend an approach to making cinema that is not only committed to narrative intelligibility, but that is open to tracking and tracing all those things left unaccounted for by narrative causality and the structures and forms of storytelling that have been relied on to picture such causality. Antonioni's vision of cinema is less causal, more relational: 'The people around us, the places we visit, the events we witness – it is the spatial and temporal relations these have with each other that have a meaning for us today, and the tension that is formed between them.'[38] Cinema would seem to name a disposition towards the world. Antonioni calls it 'a way of being in contact with reality'.[39]

Antonioni imagines this mode of 'contact' as a means of being 'committed morally in some way'. This moral commitment is construed in the following terms: 'our effort as directors must be ... that of bringing the data of our personal experience with that of a more general experience ... But even this effort will be sterile if we do not succeed in giving, by this means, a sincere justification of the choices which life has obliged us to make.'[40] These sentences conclude the first half (the first two paragraphs) of this essay. So far Antonioni seems to suggest that the film-maker's task is to be preoccupied with the relations *between and among* people, places and events; to bring one's own ('personal') methods of witnessing to bear on these things; but to put these personal methods and observations into conversation and connection with a broader audience. Basically he articulates a common under-standing of what we would call 'art cinema' – the cinema he was in the business of making – and its modes of ('personal') formal experimentation that were and are – however abstract – nonetheless committed to some level of communicativeness – or are, even, politically committed. The word for the director's 'personal' vision is, of course, style, and it is style that the art cinema, as an institutional mode, gives rela-tively free reign to. Style is – though it is not named here as such – the agency involved in picturing what Antonioni calls 'the tension' 'formed between' people, places and events.

In the second half of the essay – the two halves are denoted only by a gap between paragraphs – Antonioni shifts abruptly into a mode of writing suggestive of a film treatment or screenplay. All is present tense, a paratactic succession of details:

> The sky is white; the sea-front deserted; the sea cold and empty; the hotels white and half-shuttered. On one of the white seats of the Promenade des Anglais the bathing attendant is seated, a [black man] in a white singlet. It is early. The sun labors to emerge through a fine layer of mist, the same as every day. There is nobody on the beach except a single bather floating inert a few yards from the shore. There is nothing to be heard except the sound of the sea, nothing to observe except the rocking of that body. The attendant goes down to the beach and into the bathing station. A girl comes out and walks towards the sea. She is a wearing a flesh-coloured costume.
>
> The cry is short, sharp, and piercing. A glance is enough to tell that the bather is dead.[41]

Antonioni then narrates the exchanges that occur on the beach around the corpse as a small crowd gathers, in interest, and then disperses. Antonioni moves back into a more reflective mode. Here is the essay's final paragraph, which I quote in full:

> It was wartime. I was at Nice, waiting for a visa to go to Paris to join Marcel Carné, with whom I was going to work as an assistant. They were days full of impatience and boredom, and of news about a war which stood still on an absurd thing called the Maginot Line. Suppose one had to construct a bit of film, based on this event and on this state of mind. I would try first to remove the actual event from the scene, and leave only the image described in the first four lines [of the last quotation above]. In that white sea-front, that lonely figure, that silence, there seems to me to be an extraordinary strength of impact. The event here adds nothing: it is superfluous. I remember very well that I was

295

interested, when it happened. The dead man acted as a distraction to a state of tension. But the true emptiness, the malaise, the anxiety, the nausea, the atrophy of all normal feelings and desires, the fear, the anger – all these I felt when, coming out of the Negresco [Hotel], I found myself in that whiteness, in that nothingness, which took shape around a black point.[42]

This last paragraph is as close to an *ars poetica* as Antonioni would ever offer. On an initial reading, one is most struck by the rejection of the 'superfluous' event – the story – in order to penetrate the mystery of the 'shape around a black point'.[43] Antonioni announces an interest in the complex density of the image itself. This is an argument for the interest of style – for the priority of the *way of seeing* something over and above the something that one sees. But the context of this statement, the historical context of the memory from which it is borne seem to be crucial to understand what is being expressed here. This essay's argument for style emerges from the most radical geopolitical disturbance in modern world history – that of World War II. In this recollection, Antonioni is attempting to cross a border – a crossing made difficult by the contingent and stubborn nature of political borders themselves. He is travelling to make a film in another country. (He was travelling to act as an assistant director on *Les visteurs du soir* [1942].) He finds himself staying in a hotel – the Hotel Negresco, opened in 1913 – that had been built by and for an excessive experience of early twentieth-century capitalism but that had, by the time of Antonioni's stay, already succumbed to a period of decline.[44] The argument for style is borne out of the experience of the geopolitical. Style is also that force (or practice, attitude) that – in its mediation of near and far – makes the geopolitical appear while also abstracting itself from the immediate environment that occasions its appearance. Visual style permits the distance from which a dead corpse can be abstracted as a 'black point'. This formulation might well make us uncomfortable. One of the most important lessons of World War II, of the Holocaust is, of course, to refuse the conversion of dead bodies into the stuff of abstraction.[45]

It is, however, precisely this risk of abstraction, of style – of the distance, and nearness, the immediacy and estrangement – that Antonioni proposes. Style will have its dangers, its detractors, its shortcomings, its inappropriate assumption of more weight than it can bear. Style might be a way of being wrong, or being found wrong, charged as guilty. When Antonioni took his abstracting camera to China, at the invitation of the Chinese government in the 1970s, he shot the Chinese landscape (natural and manmade) in a way that was mostly consistent with his manner of shooting Los Angeles in *Zabriskie Point* (1970) just a few years earlier. But when the film, *Cina Chung Kuo* (1972), was released, Chinese bureaucratic officials repudiated the film and its director for slandering China by refusing to picture the greatest achievements of Maoist modernisation and focusing instead on the picturesque dimensions and traces of an extremely uneven development.[46] This was a charge against the self-sufficiency of artistic style as a means of accounting for (or as a means of recusing oneself from the obligation to account for) a larger social and economic totality. The film became the object of a international diplomatic brouhaha, with Chinese officials intervening in attempts to prevent the film from being shown at various European festivals. Rarely has style been the cause and the object of such consternation and governmental, bureaucratic attention.

We would be hard pressed to judge the legitimacy of the Chinese government's claims that Antonioni's film, among its many sins of omission and inclusion, 'skipped the stirring sights of collective labour and turned his camera solely on old people and a sick woman'.[47] But the controversy over *Cina Chung Kuo* reveals that, while it is true that 'socialism is not something you can see' (as one critic wrote accusingly of the film[48]), style puts the fact and the problem of socialism's appearance or non-appearance on display. In a sense, the Chinese officials – whether they knew it or not – were saying something true about Antonioni's cinema: it was often looking at what seemed to be the wrong things. But such looking constitutes his style. In abstracting vision from 'the event' and cathecting the 'shape around a black point', Antonioni's cinema, at its best, gives us an articulate visual language for the apprehension of our implication in the creative and destructive forces of global capitalist development. Unfortunately, Antonioni could not picture us outside the inexorable logic of development and its exploitation of peoples and landscapes. His style, however, does force on us an uncomfortable knowledge of the density of our entwinement with forces, objects and people – near and far. Through his style we do not see totality itself – as if we ever could – but we see the connective wiring that binds totality together. If the world will ever stand a chance of being better – that is to say, *other* – than it is, we will have to – as Antonioni did – *look* at it first, in better, more strange and demanding ways. Of course, *just* looking – looking alone – won't solve the crises of our catastrophic globalised late modernity. But looking with the abstracting force of Antonioni's style might help us to understand what we actually see when we look and to imagine what we would rather see in its place.

Notes

1. Seymour Chatman, *Antonioni, or the Surface of the World* (Berkeley and Los Angeles: University of California Press, 1985), p. 1.

2. Ibid.

3. Susan Sontag, 'On Style', *Against Interpretation* (New York: Dell, 1966), pp. 15–36 (p. 17).

4. See Fredric Jameson, *The Geopolitical Aesthetic* (London: BFI, 1992). Jameson's emphasis in this book is more on narrative content than on style, per se. Jameson's use of the notion of cognitive mapping (which he, of course, borrows from the urban

theorist Kevin Lynch) features prominently in the first chapter of his *Postmodernism, or the Cultural Logic of Late Capitalism* (Durham, NC: Duke University Press, 1991), pp. 1–54.

5. In work that is consonant with and, indeed, has informed my own thinking here, Rosalind Galt uses the concept of the 'pretty' to explore how certain types of images often dismissed as 'merely' decorative actually constitute a site of powerful political critique outside the forms of iconophobia that often inflect or undergird politicised film theory and film-making. See *Pretty: Film and the Decorative Image* (New York: Columbia University Press, 2011).

6. Pasolini makes these claims in his essay, 'The "Cinema of Poetry"', *Heretical Empiricism*, ed. Louise K. Barnett, trans. Ben Lawton and Louise K. Barnett (Bloomington and Indianapolis: Indiana University Press, 1988), pp. 167–86. Pasolini's essay was first delivered as a talk at the Pesaro Film Festival in 1965. I will discuss this essay later.

7. Rosalind Galt and Karl Schoonover, 'Introduction: The Impurity of Art Cinema', in Rosalind Galt and Karl Schoonover (eds), *Global Art Cinema: New Theories and Histories* (New York: Oxford University Press, 2010), pp. 3–27 (p. 3).

8. Ibid., p. 10.

9. Ibid.

10. Ibid.

11. On this subject see Jeffrey T. Schnapp, 'The Fabric of Modern Times', *Critical Inquiry* vol. 24 no. 1 (Autumn 1997), pp. 191–245. Given that the rayon industry's development was the object of such explicit nationalist support and attention under fascism, Antonioni's celebration of it in this film seems rather uncomfortably belated.

12. Noa Steimatsky, *Italian Locations: Reinhabiting the Past in Postwar Cinema* (Minneapolis: University of Minnesota Press, 2008), p. 38. Steimatsky's chapter on Antonioni, from which this quotation is taken, surveys the ambivalent nature of Antonioni's modernism, imbricated as it is with various and conflicting modes of regionalism and pictorial abstraction.

13. See David Harvey, *The Limits to Capital* (London: Verso, 2006), pp. 373–412 and Harvey, 'Globalization and the Spatial Fix', *Geographische Revue* no. 2 (2001), pp. 23–30.

14. Lorenzo Cuccu, *La visione come problema. Forme e svolgimento del cinema di Antonioni* (Rome: Bulzoni Editore, 1973), pp. 36–7. Chatman also singles out this scene and its location as exceptional: see *Antonioni*, pp. 17–18.

15. Chatman, *Antonioni*, p. 39.

16. For a thumbnail history of the industry up until the late 1930s, see C. J. Robertson, 'The Italian Beet-Sugar Industry', *Economic Geography* vol. 14 no. 1 (January 1938), pp. 1–15, esp. pp. 12–14.

17. Italian spectators and cinephiles are likely to notice that this landscape has made major appearances in the history of proto-neo-realist and neo-realist cinema: in Visconti's

Ossessione (*Obsession*, 1943), often considered the film that anticipated the major features of neo-realism, and Rossellini's *Paisà* (1946).

18. Angelo Restivo, *The Cinema of Economic Miracles: Visuality and Modernization in the Italian Art Film* (Durham, NC, and London: Duke University Press, 2002), p. 125.

19. William Arrowsmith, *Antonioni: The Poet of Images* (Oxford University Press, 1995), p. 29. Emphasis in the original.

20. Harvey, 'Globalization and the Spatial Fix', p. 25.

21. In 2005 Pirelli sold off its cable-manufacturing business to Goldman-Sachs, who renamed this division Prysmian. According to the company's own historical account, in 1950 the Italian state postal service gave Pirelli the contract to supply all telephone and television cables across the Italian penisula. See <http://www.prysmian.com/about-us/history.html> (last accessed 6 April 2011).

22. Chatman, *Antonioni*, p. 49.

23. Restivo, *The Cinema of Economic Miracles*, p. 126.

24. Ibid. Emphasis in the original.

25. Ibid., p. 140.

26. Ibid.

27. Ibid., p. 130. Italics in the original.

28. Insofar as postmodernism's love affair with the rhetoric of the sublime has provided the aesthetic mode in which we are made to feel most strongly the impossibility of imagining social totality, it has only hyperbolised what is the fact of any representation: the representation will always fail to provide an experience of totality. Postmodernism is not the phase of social reality in which representations were suddenly unable to account for the complexity of the world: they never could. Postmodernism, rather, is the moment at which that failure becomes the most absorbing thing about works of art, perhaps because even reason – and not just the imagination – begins to falter in its own account of advanced capitalism.

29. Pasolini believed the entire film ought to be understood as expressive of Giuliana's point of view. See Pasolini, 'The "Cinema of Poetry"', pp. 178–80.

30. Antonioni quoted in Seymour Chatman, *Antonioni: The Complete Films*, ed. Paul Duncan (Köln: Taschen, 2004), p. 92.

31. Pasolini, 'The "Cinema of Poetry"', p. 178.

32. Ibid., p. 179. The phrase 'obsessive framing' appears in quotation marks in the original because Pasolini has already used the term 'obsessive' to describe the film's framing in the previous paragraph. He is quoting himself.

33. Ibid.

34. Elsewhere I have attempted to come to terms with the larger argument of Pasolini's essay in regards to point of view, free indirect discourse and style. See 'Pasolini's Exquisite Flowers: The "Cinema of Poetry" as a Theory of Art Cinema', in Galt and Schoonover, *Global Art Cinema*, pp. 142–63.

35. Pasolini, 'The "Cinema of Poetry"', p. 185.

36. Ibid.

37. Michelangelo Antonioni, 'The Event and the Image', *The Architecture of Vision: Writings and Interviews on Cinema*, ed. Giorgio Tinazzi and Carlo Di Carlo, trans. Marga Cottino-Jones (New York: Marsilio, 1996), p. 51. This article was first published in Italian as 'Il fatto e l'immagine' in *Cinema nuovo* no. 164 (July 1964) and in English in *Sight & Sound* vol. 33 no. 1 (Winter 1963–4).

38. Ibid.

39. Ibid.

40. Ibid., pp. 51–2.

41. Ibid., p. 52.

42. Ibid., p. 53.

43. Geoffrey Nowell-Smith published an article about Antonioni that employed this phrase (as I do in this section of the essay): 'Shape Around the Black Point', *Sight & Sound* vol. 33 no. 1 (Winter 1963/64), pp. 15–20.

44. This information I gather from the Hotel Negresco's own website: <http://www.hotel-negresco-nice.com/un-peu-dhistoire> (last accessed 21 January 2011).

45. As Noa Steimatsky has shown, the abstracting dimensions of Antonioni's style are at least partly caught up in the abstracting nature of fascist *aeropittura*, a fascinating, if bombastic, nationalist and minor episode in the history of modern Italian painting. See Steimatsky, *Italian Locations*, pp. 1–39.

46. See <http://www.marxists.org/subject/china/peking-review/1974/PR1974-08d.htm> (last accessed 20 January 2011).

47. Ibid. Interestingly, most of the charges against the film have to do with a sense of injustice that Antonioni paid too little attention to the large, industrialised features of China's developing landscape and thus rendered a vision of China that was far less modern than was actually the case.

48. Antonioni quotes this critic in his preface to his book *Chung Kuo Cina*, ed. Lorenzo Cuccu in collaboration with Andrea Barbato (Turin: Einaudi, 1974), p. xv.

Bibliography

Achilli, Alberto, Alberto Boschi and Gianfranco Casadio (eds), *Le sonorità del visibile. Immagini, suoni e musica nel cinema di Michelangelo Antonioni* (Ravenna: Longo, 1999).

Alatri, Paolo, 'Ricordi e riflessioni sulla mia vita e la mia attività', *Dimensioni e Problemi della Ricerca Storica* vol. 9 no. 1 (1996), pp. 13–46, <http://w3.uniroma1.it/dprs/sites/default/files/214.html> (last accessed 27 August 2010).

Alicata, Mario and Giuseppe De Santis, 'Ancora di Verga e del cinema italiano', *Cinema* vol. 6/1 no. 130 (25 November 1941), p. 315.

Andrew, Dudley, 'Amélie, or Le Fabuleux Destin Du Cinéma Français', *Film Quarterly* vol. 57 no. 3 (2004), pp. 34–46.

Anelli, Maria Teresa, Paola Gabbrielli, Marta Morgavi and Roberto Piperno, *Fotoromanzo: fascino e pregiudizio. Storia, documenti e immagini di un grande fenomeno popolare (1948–1979)* (Milan: Savelli, 1979).

Anonymous, 'Questions à Antonioni' [interview, 1959], in Carlo Di Carlo and Giorgio Tinazzi (eds), *Michelangelo Antonioni: Entretiens et inédits, 1950–1985* (Rome: Cinecittà International, 1992), p. 33.

Antolin, Teresa, 'La contessa Maria Tarnowska e il conte Luchino Visconti', in Michelangelo Antonioni, Antonio Pietrangeli, Guido Piovene, Luchino Visconti, *Il processo di Maria Tarnowska. Una sceneggiatura inedita*, ed. Teresa Antolin and Alberto Barbera (Milan and Turin: Il Castoro/Museo Nazionale del Cinema, 2006), pp. 9–31.

Antonioni, Michelangelo, 'Concerning a Film about the River Po', in David Overbey (ed.), *Springtime in Italy: A Reader on Neo-Realism* (London: Talisman, 1978), pp. 79–80. Original Italian 'Per un film sul fiume Po', in *Cinema* vol. IV no. 68 (25 April 1939), pp. 254–7; reprinted in Orio Caldiron (ed.), *'Cinema' 1936–1943. Prima del Neorealismo* (Rome: Fondazione Scuola Nazionale di Cinema, 2002), pp. 117–20.

——, Foreword [1980], in Francesco Pasinetti, *Storia del cinema dalle origini a oggi* (Venice: Marsilio, 1980 [1939]), p. iii.

——, 'Dietro alla storia', *Volandum* vol. IX no. 7–8 (July–August 1940), pp. 83–6.

——, 'Green Land' [1940], in Michelangelo Antonioni, *Unfinished Business: Screenplays, Scenarios, and Ideas*, ed. Carlo Di Carlo and Giorgio Tinazzi, trans. Andrew Taylor (New York and Venice: Marsilio, 1998), pp. 1–18.

——, 'Incontri a Bengasi', *Volandum* vol. IX no. 9–10 (September–October 1940), pp. 107–11.

——, 'La settimana cinematografica a Venezia' [1940], in Anna Folli (ed.), *Vent'anni di cultura ferrarese: 1925–1945. Antologia del 'Corriere Padano'*, vol. II (Bologna: Pàtron, 1979), p. 175.

——, 'Taccuino volante. Introduzione alla Libia', *Volandum* vol. IX no. 5–6 (May–June 1940), pp. 55–7.

——, 'Vita impossibile del signor Clark Costa' [1940], in Michelangelo Antonioni, *Sul cinema*, ed. Carlo Di Carlo and Giorgio Tinazzi (Venice: Marsilio, 2004), pp. 155–60.

——, 'Distrazioni', in *Cinema* vol. 5/1 no. 115 (10 April 1941), p. 240.

——, 'L'ultima lezione', in Mimì Quilici Buzzacchi (ed.), *Nello Quilici. L'uomo, il giornalista, lo studioso, il maestro* (Ferrara: Nuovi Problemi, 1941), pp. 221–6.

——, 'Marcel Carné, parigino' [1948], in Michelangelo Antonioni, *Sul cinema*, ed. Carlo Di Carlo and Giorgio Tinazzi (Venice: Marsilio, 2004), pp. 111–47.

——, 'The White Forest' [1954], trans. Allison Cooper in Michelangelo Antonioni, *The Architecture of Vision: Writings and Interviews on Cinema*, ed. Carlo Di Carlo and Giorgio Tinazzi, trans. Marga Cottino-Jones (New York: Marsilio, 1996), pp. 84–8.

——, 'My Personal Experience' [1958], in Carlo Di Carlo (ed.), *Michelangelo Antonioni* (Rome: Cinecittà, n.d. [2005]), p. 14.

——, 'Making a Film is My Way of Life' [1959], in Michelangelo Antonioni, *The Architecture of Vision: Writings and Interviews on Cinema*, ed. Carlo Di Carlo and Giorgio Tinazzi, trans. Marga Cottino-Jones (New York: Marsilio, 1996), pp. 14–17.

——, 'Un entretien avec Antonioni', *Cinéma 60* no. 50 (October 1960), pp. 4–7.

——, 'A Talk with Michelangelo Antonioni on his Work' [1961], in Michelangelo Antonioni, *The Architecture of Vision: Writings and Interviews on Cinema*, ed. Carlo Di Carlo and Giorgio Tinazzi, trans. Marga Cottino-Jones (New York: Marsilio, 1996), pp. 21–47.

——, 'Introduction', in Michelangelo Antonioni, *Screenplays of Michelangelo Antonioni: Il grido, L'avventura, La notte, L'eclisse*, trans. Roger J. Moore and Louis Brigante (New York: Orion Press, 1963), pp. viii–xviii.

——, 'The Event and the Image' [1963], in Michelangelo Antonioni, *The Architecture of Vision: Writings and Interviews on Cinema*, ed. Giorgio Tinazzi and Carlo Di Carlo, trans. Marga Cottino-Jones (New York: Marsilio, 1996), pp. 51–3. Also published in *Sight & Sound* vol. 33 no. 1 (1963–4), p. 14.

——, 'Preface to Six Films' [1964], in Michelangelo Antonioni, *The Architecture of Vision: Writings and Interviews on the Cinema*, ed. Carlo Di Carlo and Giorgio Tinazzi, trans. Marga Cottino-Jones (New York: Marsilio, 1996), pp. 57–68.

——, 'The Red Desert' [1964], in Michelangelo Antonioni, *The Architecture of Vision: Writings and Interviews on Cinema*, ed. Carlo Di Carlo and Giorgio Tinazzi, trans. Marga Cottino-Jones (New York: Marsilio, 1996), pp. 283–6.

——, *Chung Kuo Cina*, ed. Lorenzo Cuccu in collaboration with Andrea Barbato (Turin: Einaudi, 1974).

——, 'The Director and Technology: "Take it From Me, This is the Future"' [1983], in Michelangelo Antonioni, *The Architecture of Vision: Writings and Interviews on Cinema*, ed. Carlo Di Carlo and Giorgio Tinazzi, trans. Marga Cottino-Jones (New York: Marsilio, 1996), pp. 352–5.

—— 'Almost a Confession' [1980], in Michelangelo Antonioni, *The Architecture of Vision: Writings and Interviews on Cinema*, ed. Carlo Di Carlo and Giorgio Tinazzi, trans. Marga Cottino-Jones (New York: Marsilio, 1996), pp. 127–9.

——, 'It was Born in London, But it is Not an English Film' [1982], in Michelangelo Antonioni, *The Architecture of Vision: Writings and Interviews on Cinema*, ed. Carlo Di Carlo and Giorgio Tinazzi, trans. Marga Cottino-Jones (New York: Marsilio, 1996), pp. 89–91.

——, 'Report about Myself' [1983], in Michelangelo Antonioni, *Quel bowling sul Tevere* (Turin: Einaudi, 1995), pp. 105–10.

——, 'Strada a Ferrara' [1978], in Anna Folli (ed.), *Vent'anni di cultura ferrarese: 1925–1945. Antologia del 'Corriere Padano'*, vol. II (Bologna: Pàtron, 1979), pp. 175–7.

——, 'Identification of a Filmmaker' [1985], in Michelangelo Antonioni, *The Architecture of Vision: Writings and Interviews on Cinema*, ed. Carlo Di Carlo and Giorgio Tinazzi, trans. Marga Cottino-Jones (New York: Marsilio, 1996), pp. 245–56.

——, 'Note su P. M. Pasinetti', in *Italian Quarterly* vol. 26 no. 102 (Autumn 1985), <http://digilander.libero.it/pmpasinetti/pdf/Antonioni_estratto.pdf> (last accessed 23 August 2010).

——, 'A Constant Renewal' [1987], in Michelangelo Antonioni, *The Architecture of Vision: Writings and Interviews on Cinema*, ed. Carlo Di Carlo and Giorgio Tinazzi, trans. Marga Cottino-Jones (New York: Marsilio, 1996), pp. 319–25.

——, 'About Myself and One of My Films', in Seymour Chatman and Guido Fink (eds), *L'avventura* (New Brunswick: Rutgers University Press, 1989), pp. 180–1.

——, *Fare un film è per me vivere. Scritti sul cinema*, ed. Carlo Di Carlo and Giorgio Tinazzi (Venice: Marsilio, 1994).

——, 'Le allegre ragazze del '24', in Michelangelo Antonioni, *I film nel cassetto* (Venice: Marsilio, 1995), pp. 55–62.

——, *The Architecture of Vision: Writings and Interviews on Cinema*, ed. Carlo Di Carlo and Giorgio Tinazzi, trans. Marga Cottino-Jones (New York: Marsilio, 1996).

——, 'Je commence à comprendre', *Positif* no. 483 (2001), pp. 47–8.

——, *Il silenzio a colori*, ed. Enrica Antonioni (Rome: Campisano, 2006).

——, Antonio Pietrangeli, Guido Piovene and Luchino Visconti, *Il processo di Maria Tarnowska. Una sceneggiatura inedita* (Milan: Il Castoro, 2006).

Arrowsmith, William, *Antonioni: The Poet of Images* (New York: Oxford University Press, 1995).

Bachmann, Gideon and Michelangelo Antonioni, 'A Love of Today: An Interview with Michelangelo Antonioni', *Film Quarterly* vol. 36 no. 4 (1983), pp. 1–4.

Barbera, Alberto (ed.), *Cavalcarono insieme. 50 anni di cinema e televisione in Italia* (Milan: Electa, 2004).

Barrell, John, *The Dark Side of the Landscape: Rural Poor in English Painting, 1730–1840* (New York: Cambridge University Press, 1980).

Barthes, Roland, *Mythologies* (New York: Hill and Wang, 1972).

——, 'Dear Antonioni ...' [1980], in Seymour Chatman and Guido Fink (eds), *L'avventura* (New Brunswick, NJ: Rutgers, 1989), pp. 209–13, also in Geoffrey Nowell-Smith (ed.), *L'avventura* (London: BFI, 1997), pp. 63–8.

Bataille, Georges, 'The Notion of Expenditure', in *Visions of Excess: Selected Writings, 1927–1939*, trans. Allan Stoekl (Minneapolis: University of Minnesota Press, 1985), pp. 117–29.

Baudrillard, Jean, *America*, trans. Chris Turner (New York: Verso, 1988).

Bayard, Pierre, *Le Plagiat par anticipation* (Paris: Minuit, 2009).

Bazin, André, 'The Ontology of the Photographic Image' [1945], in *What Is Cinema?*, trans. Hugh Gray, vol. 1 (Berkeley: University of California Press, 1967), pp. 1–12.

Ben-Ghiat, Ruth, 'Liberation: Italian Cinema and the Fascist Past, 1945–50', in Richard J. B. Bosworth and Patrizia Dogliani (eds), *Italian Fascism: History, Memory and Representation* (Basingstoke: Palgrave, 1999), pp. 83–101.

——, *Fascist Modernities: Italy, 1922–1945* (Berkeley and Los Angeles: University of California Press, 2001).

Benci, Jacopo, 'Michelangelo's Rome: Towards an Iconology of *L'Eclisse*', in Richard Wrigley (ed.), *Cinematic Rome* (Leicester: Troubadour, 2008), pp. 63–84.

Benjamin, Walter, 'Theses on the Philosophy of History', in Hannah Arendt (ed.), *Illuminations* (New York: Schocken, 1868).

——, 'Surrealism: Last Snapshot of the European Intelligentsia', in Peter Demetz (ed.), *Reflections* (New York: Schocken, 1978).

Bensky, Lawrence M., 'Antonioni Comes to the Point', *New York Times*, 15 December 1968, D23.

Berengo Gardin, Piero (ed.), *Alberto Lattuada fotografo. Dieci anni di Occhio quadrato, 1938/1948* (Florence: Alinari, 1982).

Berger, John, *A Fortunate Man* (London: Penguin, 1967).

Bernardini, Aldo, *Michelangelo Antonioni da 'Gente del Po' a 'Blow Up'* (Milan: Edizioni I Sette, 1967).

Bignami, Silvia (ed.), *'Aria d'Italia' di Daria Guarnati. L'arte della rivista intorno al 1940* (Milan: Skira, 2008).

Billard, Pierre, 'An Interview with Michelangelo Antonioni' [1966], in Bert Cardullo (ed.), *Michelangelo Antonioni: Interviews* (Jackson, MS: University Press of Mississippi, 2008), pp. 46–69.

304

Blair, Betsy, *The Memory of All That: Love and Politics in New York, Hollywood and Paris* (New York: Knopf, 2003).

Bois, Yve-Alain, 'A Picturesque Stroll Around Clara-Clara', *October* no. 29 (Summer 1984), pp. 33–62.

Boisson, Christine and Emmanuel Decaux, *Cinématographie* no. 84, special Antonioni issue (December 1982), pp. 30–3.

Bolter, Jay David and Richard Grusin, *Remediation: Understanding New Media* (Cambridge, MA: MIT Press, 1999).

Borrelli, Armando, *Neorealismo e marxismo* (Avellino: Edizioni di Cinemasud, 1966).

Bosworth, Richard J. B., *L'Italia di Mussolini, 1915–1945* (Milan: Mondadori, 2009).

Bourdieu, Pierre, *La Distinction, critique sociale du jugement* (Paris: Minuit, 1979).

Braun, Emily, 'Speaking Volumes: Giorgio Morandi's Still Lifes and the Cultural Politics of *Strapaese*', *Modernism/Modernity* vol. 2 no. 3 (1995), pp. 89–116.

Brenez, Nicole, 'Peter Whitehead: The Exigency of Joy', *Rouge* no. 10 (2007), trans. Adrian Martin, <http://www.rouge.com.au/10/whitehead.html>

Bresson, Robert, ' "Une mise en scène n'est pas un art": Robert Bresson rencontre les étudiants de l'Idhec (décembre 1955)', *Cahiers du cinéma* no. 543 (2000), pp. 4–9.

Brewer, Roy, *An Approach to Print: A Basic Guide to the Printing Processes* (London: Blandford Press, 1971).

Brunetta, Gian Piero, *Il cinema italiano di regime. Da 'La canzone dell'amore' a 'Ossessione', 1929–1945* (Bari: Laterza, 2009).

Brunette, Peter, *The Films of Michelangelo Antonioni* (Cambridge: Cambridge University Press, 1998).

Buchloh, Benjamin H. D., 'Conceptual Art 1962–1969: From the Aesthetic of Administration to the Critique of Institutions', *October* no. 55 (Winter 1990), pp. 105–43.

Burks, John, 'Fourteen Points to *Zabriskie Point*', *Rolling Stone* vol. 53 (7 March 1970), n. p.

Buskirk, Martha, *The Contingent Object of Contemporary Art* (Cambridge, MA: MIT Press, 2005).

Calabretto, Roberto, 'Giovanni Fusco: musicista per il cinema di Antonioni', in Alberto Achilli, Alberto Boschi and Gianfranco Casadio (eds), *Le sonorità del visibile. Immagini suoni e musica nel cinema di Michelangelo Antonioni* (Ravenna: Longo Editore, 1999), pp. 45–75.

Caldiron, Orio, 'Introduzione', in Orio Caldiron (ed.), *'Cinema' 1936–1943. Prima del Neorealismo* (Rome: Fondazione Scuola Nazionale di Cinema, 2002), pp. 9–14.

Calvino, Italo, 'Il mare dell'oggettività', in *Saggi 1945–1985*, vol. I, ed. Mario Barenghi (Milan: Mondadori, 1995), pp. 52–60.

——, 'Remarks on *L'avventura*', in Seymour Chatman and Guido Fink (eds), *L'avventura* (New Brunswick: Rutgers University Press, 1989), pp. 196–7.

Campany, David, 'From Ecstasy to Agony: The Fashion Shoot in Cinema', *Aperture* no. 190 (Spring 2008), pp. 40–7.

305

——, *Photography and Cinema* (London: Reaktion, 2008).

Canby, Vincent, 'No Life in Antonioni's Death Valley', *New York Times*, 15 February 1970, p. 81.

——, 'Screen: Antonioni's *Zabriskie Point*' [review], *New York Times*, 10 February 1970, p. 47.

Capanna, Alessandra, 'Palazzo dello Sport 1956–60', in Adachiara Zevi (ed.), *Una guida all'architettura moderna dell'EUR* (Rome: Fondazione Bruno Zevi, 2008), p. 34.

Cardullo, Bert (ed.), *Michelangelo Antonioni: Interviews* (Jackson, MS: University Press of Mississippi, 2008).

Carné, Marcel, 'When will the Cinema Go Down into the Street?' [1933], in Richard Abel (ed.), *French Film Theory and Criticism 1907–1939: A History/Anthology, Volume II, 1929–1939* (Princeton, NJ: Princeton University Press, 1988), pp. 127–9.

Casetti, Francesco, 'Elsewhere: The Relocation of Art', in Consuelo Ciscar Casabàn and Vincenzo Trione (eds), *Valencia09/Confines* (Valencia: INVAM, 2009), pp. 226–33.

——, 'Filmic Experience', *Screen* vol. 50 no. 1 (Spring 2009), pp. 56–66.

——, 'Back to the Motherland: The Film Theatre in the Postmedia Age', *Screen* vol. 52 no. 1 (Spring 2011), pp. 1–12.

Certeau, Michel de, *The Practice of Everyday Life*, trans. Steven Rendall (Berkeley: University of California Press, 1984).

Chatman, Seymour, *Antonioni, or the Surface of the World* (Berkeley and Los Angeles: University of California Press, 1985).

——, 'Antonioni in 1980: An Interview' [1997], in Bert Cardullo (ed.), *Michelangelo Antonioni: Interviews* (Jackson, MS: University Press of Mississippi, 2008), pp. 155–61; originally published in *Film Quarterly* vol. 51 no. 1 (Autumn 1997), pp. 2–10.

——, *Antonioni: The Complete Films*, ed. by Paul Duncan (Köln: Taschen, 2004).

Chatman, Seymour and Paul Duncan, *Michelangelo Antonioni: The Investigation* (Cologne: Taschen, 2004).

Chenet-Faugerat, Françoise, 'L'invention du paysage urbain', *Romantisme* vol. 24 no. 83 (1994), pp. 27–38.

Chiaretti, Tommaso, 'Antonioni ou le refus de la banalité', trans. Claire Clouzot, *Cinéma 60*, 50 (October 1960), pp. 12–21.

Chiarini, Roberto, 'Le origini dell'Italia repubblicana (1943–1948)', in Giovanni Sabbatucci and Vittorio Vidotto (eds), *Storia d'Italia. 4. La Repubblica, 1943–1963* (Rome and Bari: Laterza, 1997), pp. 3–126.

Cineteca Nazionale (eds), *La memoria del cinema. Restauri, preservazioni e ristampe della Cineteca Nazionale (1998–2001)* (Rome: Fondazione Scuola Nazionale di Cinema, 2001).

Ciucci, Giorgio, *Gli architetti e il fascismo. Architettura e città 1922–1944* (Turin: Einaudi, 2002).

Clark, Nigel, 'Ex-orbitant Globality', *Theory Culture Society* no. 22 (2005), pp. 165–85.

Coe, Brian, 'The Rollfilm Revolution', in Colin Ford (ed.), *The Kodak Museum* (London: Century Hutchinson, 1989), pp. 61–89.

Cook, Pam and Mieke Bernink (eds), *The Cinema Book*, 2nd edn (London: BFI, 1999).

Corber, Robert, *In the Name of National Security: Hitchcock, Homophobia, and the Political Construction of Gender in Postwar America* (Durham, NC: Duke University Press, 1993).

Corner, Paul, *Il fascismo a Ferrara, 1915–1925* (Rome and Bari: Laterza, 1974).

Cortázar, Julio, 'Blow-Up', in Julio Cortázar, *End of the Game and Other Stories*, trans. Paul Blackburn (London: Collins and Harvill Press, 1963), pp. 114–31.

Costa, Antonio (ed.), *Alberto Lattuada: Gli anni di 'Corrente'*, *Cinema & Cinema* no. 56 (September/December 1989).

Cosulich, Callisto, 'Rifiutato a Venezia, applaudito ovunque', in Tullio Kezich and Alessandra Levantesi (eds), *Cronaca di un amore. Un film di Michelangelo Antonioni* (Turin: Lindau, 2004), pp. 93–103.

Cotroneo, Roberto (ed.), *Giorgio Bassani. Opere* (Milan: Mondadori, 2001).

Cuccu, Lorenzo, *La visione come problema. Forme e svolgimento del cinema di Antonioni* (Rome: Bulzoni Editore, 1973).

Dagrada, Elena, 'Television and its Critics: A Parallel History', in David Forgacs and Robert Lumley, *Italian Cultural Studies: An Introduction* (Oxford: Oxford University Press, 1996), pp. 233–47.

Dalle Vacche, Angela, 'Michelangelo Antonioni's *Red Desert*: Painting as Ventriloquism and Color as Movement (Architecture and Painting)', in Angela Dalle Vacche and Brian Price (eds), *Color: The Film Reader* (London: Routledge, 2006), pp. 183–91.

De Berti, Raffaele, *Dallo schermo alla carta. Romanzi, fotoromanzi, rotocalchi cinematografici* (Milan: Vita e Pensiero, 2000).

De Salvo, Donna, *Open Systems: Rethinking Art c. 1970* (London: Tate, 2005).

De Santi, Gualtiero, '*Identificazione di una donna* di Michelangelo Antonioni', *Cineforum* vol. 22 no. 12 (1982), pp. 31–8.

De Santis, Giuseppe, 'Towards an Italian Landscape' [1941], in David Overbey (ed.), *Springtime in Italy: A Reader on Neo-Realism* (London: Talisman, 1978), pp. 125–9.

De Vincenti, Giorgio, *Il concetto di modernità del cinema* (Parma: Pratiche, 1993).

——, Giorgio, 'Conversazione sul cinema con Francesco Maselli', in Lino Micciché (ed.), '*Gli Sbandati' di Francesco Maselli. Un film generazionale* (Turin: Lindau, 1998), pp. 15–41.

Deleuze, Gilles, *Cinema 1: The Movement-Image*, trans. Hugh Tomlinson and Barbara Habberjam (Minneapolis: University of Minnesota Press, 1986).

——, *Cinema 2: The Time-Image*, trans. Hugh Tomlinson and Robert Galeta (Minneapolis: University of Minnesota Press, 1989).

——, *Lectures on Spinoza*. Available online at <http://deleuzelectures.blogspot.com/2007/02/on-spinoza.html>

Derry, Charles, *The Suspense Thriller: Films in the Shadow of Alfred Hitchcock* (Jefferson: McFarland Press, 1988).

Di Carlo, Carlo (ed.), *Michelangelo Antonioni* (Rome: Edizioni di Bianco e Nero, 1964).

——, *Il primo Antonioni* (Bologna: Cappelli, 1973).

——, 'Vedere in modo nuovo', in Carlo Di Carlo (ed.), *Il primo Antonioni* (Bologna: Cappelli, 1973), pp. 11–19.

——, *Michelangelo Antonioni 1942–1965* (Rome: Ente Autonomo Gestione Cinema, 1988).

——, 'Nota ai testi sul doppiaggio', in Michelangelo Antonioni, *Sul cinema*, ed. Carlo Di Carlo and Giorgio Tinazzi (Venice: Marsilio, 2004), pp. 166–7.

Di Carlo, Carlo and Flavio De Bernardinis, 'L'invenzione viscerale della modernità' [interview], *Segnocinema* no. 118 (2002), p. 17.

Di Majo, Luigi and Italo Insolera, *L'Eur e Roma dagli anni Trenta al Duemila* (Rome and Bari: Laterza, 1986).

Diffrient, David Scott, 'Autobiography, Corporeality, Seriality: Nanni Moretti's *Dear Diary* as a Narrative Archipelago', *Journal of Film and Video* vol. 61 no. 4 (2009), pp. 17–30.

Drucker, Johanna, *The Century of Artists' Books* (New York: Granary, 2004 [1994]).

Dubois, Philip, *L'Acte photographique et autres essais* (Brussels: Labor, 1990 [1983]).

Eco, Umberto, 'The Phenomenology of Mike Bongiorno', *Misreadings*, trans. William Weaver (New York: Harcourt, 1993), pp. 156–64.

Eisenstein, Sergei M., 'One Path to Color: An Autobiographical Fragment', *Sight & Sound* vol. 30 no. 2 (1961), pp. 84–6.

——, 'First Letter About Color', *Film Reader* no. 2 (1977), pp. 181–4.

Ellis, John, *Visible Fictions: Cinema, Television, Video* (New York: Routledge, 1982).

Epstein, Jean, 'Le Sens I bis', in *Bonjour Cinéma* (Paris: Éditions de la Sirène, 1921), pp. 27–44.

Farber, Manny, *Negative Space: Manny Farber on the Movies* (New York: Praeger, 1971).

Ferrero, Mario, 'Anticipazioni: Maria Tarnowska' [1946], in Michelangelo Antonioni, Antonio Pietrangeli, Guido Piovene and Luchino Visconti, *Il processo di Maria Tarnowska. Una sceneggiatura inedita*, ed. Teresa Antolin and Alberto Barbera (Milan and Turin: Il Castoro/Museo Nazionale del Cinema, 2006), pp. 424–5.

Feuer, Jane, 'The Concept of Live Television: Ontology as Ideology', in E. Ann Kaplan (ed.), *Regarding Television* (Los Angeles: American Film Institute, 1983), pp. 12–21.

Fink, Guido, 'Michelangelo Antonioni: A Biographical Sketch', in Seymour Chatman and Guido Fink (eds), *L'avventura* (New Brunswick and London: Rutgers University Press, 1989), pp. 17–28.

Flatley, Guy, ' "I Love This Country." Antonioni Defends *Zabriskie Point*', *New York Times*, 22 February 1970, D15.

Floyd, Kevin, *The Reification of Desire: Toward a Queer Marxism* (Minneapolis: University of Minnesota Press, 2009).

Folli, Anna, 'Introduzione', in Anna Folli (ed.), *Vent'anni di cultura ferrarese: 1925–1945. Antologia del 'Corriere Padano'*, vol. I (Bologna: Pàtron, 1978), pp. xv–xviii.

308

——, 'Michelangelo Antonioni' [interview, 1978], in Anna Folli (ed.), *Vent'anni di cultura ferrarese: 1925–1945. Antologia del 'Corriere Padano'*, vol. II (Bologna: Pàtron, 1978), pp. 333–6.

Ford, Colin, *The Kodak Museum: The Story of Popular Photography* (London: Century Hutchinson, 1989).

Forgacs, David, 'Cultural Consumption, 1940s to 1990s', in David Forgacs and Robert Lumley (eds), *Italian Cultural Studies: An Introduction* (Oxford: Oxford University Press, 1996), pp. 273–90.

——, 'Michelangelo Antonioni', in Paolo Bertetto (ed.), *Action! How Great Filmmakers Direct Actors* (Rome: minimum fax, 2007), pp. 201–13.

Forgacs, David and Stephen Gundle, *Mass Culture and Italian Society from Fascism to the Cold War* (Bloomington: Indiana University Press, 2007).

Foster, Hal, Rosalind Krauss, Yve-Alain Bois and Benjamin H. D. Buchloh, *Art Since 1900: Modernism, Antimodernism, Postmodernism* (London: Thames and Hudson, 2004).

Fotiade, Ramona, 'From Ready-Made to Moving Image: The Visual Poetics of Surrealist Cinema', in Graeme Harper and Rob Stone (eds), *The Unsilvered Screen: Surrealism on Film* (London: Wallflower Press, 2007), pp. 9–22.

Freccero, John, '*Blow-Up*: From the Word to the Image' [1970], in Roy Huss (ed.), *Focus on Blow-Up* (Englewood Cliffs, NJ: Prentice-Hall, 1971), pp. 116–28.

Freud, Sigmund, 'The Uncanny', in *The Standard Edition of the Complete Psychological Works of Sigmund Freud*, vol. XVII: *An Infantile Neurosis and Other Works*, ed. and trans. James Strachey (London: Hogarth, 1917–19), pp. 217–56.

Funnel, Peter, 'Visible Appearances', in Michael Clarke and Nicholas Penny (eds), *The Arrogant Connoisseur: Richard Payne Knight 1751–1824* (Manchester: Manchester University Press, 1982), pp. 82–92.

Galt, Rosalind, *Pretty: Film and the Decorative Image* (New York: Columbia University Press, 2011).

Galt, Rosalind and Karl Schoonover, 'Introduction: The Impurity of Art Cinema', in Rosalind Galt and Karl Schoonover (eds), *Global Art Cinema: New Theories and Histories* (New York: Oxford University Press, 2010), pp. 3–27.

Gambetti, Giacomo, *Cultura e politica nel cinema di Francesco Maselli* (Florence: Cecchi Gori Editoria Elettronica, 2009).

Gandy, Matthew, 'Landscapes of Deliquescence in Michelangelo Antonioni's *Red Desert*', *Transactions of the Institute of British Geographers* vol. 28 no. 2 (2003), pp. 218–38.

Garbin, Barbara, 'La 'saga' di Pier Maria Pasinetti: itinerario di uno scrittore veneziano e cosmopolita' (dissertation, Faculty of Arts, Ca' Foscari University of Venice, 1999–2000), <http://digilander.libero.it/pmpasinetti/indice_Garbin.htm> (last accessed 30 August 2010).

Garofalo, Francesco and Luca Veresani, 'Symbolic Arch for the E42', in Francesco Garofalo and Luca Veresani (eds), *Adalberto Libera* (New York: Princeton Architectural Press, 2002), pp. 107–9.

Gentile, Emilio, *Fascismo di pietra* (Rome and Bari: Laterza, 2007).

309

Giacci, Vittorio, 'Biografia', in Vittorio Giacci (ed.), *Michelangelo Antonioni. Lo sguardo estatico* (Rome: Fondazione Centro Sperimentale di Cinematografia/BA Film Factory, 2008), pp. 139–46.

——. 'Le regard évasif', in Carlo Di Carlo (ed.), *Michelangelo Antonioni, 1942/1965, L'Œuvre de Michelangelo Antonioni*, vol. 1, 2nd edn (Rome: Ente Autonomo di gestione per il Cinema, 1988), pp. 14–15.

Gili, Jean A., 'C'era una volta la cinefilia', in Gian Piero Brunetta (ed.), *Storia del cinema mondiale. V. Teorie, strumenti, memorie* (Turin: Einaudi, 2001), pp. 397–416.

Gilpin, William, *Essays on Picturesque Beauty* (London: Blamire, 1792).

Ginsborg, Paul, *A History of Contemporary Italy: Society and Politics, 1943–1988* (New York: Palgrave Macmillan, 2003).

——, *Silvio Berlusconi: Television, Power, and Patrimony* (London: Verso, 2004).

Giovannetti, Eugenio, *Il cinema e le arti meccaniche* (Palermo: Sandron, 1930).

Godard, Jean-Luc, 'Night, Eclipse, Dawn … An Interview with Michelangelo Antonioni', *Cahiers du Cinéma in English* no. 1 (January 1966), pp. 19–29.

Godard, Jean-Luc and Michelangelo Antonioni, 'Michelangelo Antonioni' [interview], in Andrew Sarris (ed.), *Interviews with Film Directors* (New York: Avon, 1969), pp. 21–32.

Goldwag, Arthur, *Isms and Ologies: All the Movements, Ideologies and Doctrines That Have Shaped Our World* (London: Quercas, 2007).

Gordon, Robert S. C., *Bicycle Thieves* (London: BFI, 2008).

Gray, Marianne, *La Moreau: A Biography of Jeanne Moreau* (London: Little, Brown and Co., 1994).

Grazzini, Giovanni, 'Antonioni: saper leggere dentro le cose', *Corriere della Sera* no. 5 March 1975.

Grierson, John, 'First Principles of Documentary' [1932–34], in John Grierson, *Grierson on Documentary*, ed. Forsyth Hardy (London: Faber and Faber, 1966), pp. 145–56.

Grossberg, Lawrence, *We Gotta Get Out of This Place: Popular Conservatism and Postmodern Culture* (London: Routledge, 1992).

Grossvogel, David I., '*Blow-Up*: The Forms of an Aesthetic Itinerary', *Diacritics* vol. 2 no. 3 (Autumn 1972), pp. 49–54.

Groys, Boris, *Art Power* (Cambridge, MA: MIT Press, 2008).

Guerri, Giordano Bruno, *Italo Balbo* (Milan: Mondadori, 1998).

Gundle, Stephen, *I comunisti italiani tra Hollywood e Mosca. La sfida della cultura di massa, 1943–1991* (Florence: Giunti, 1995).

Hagener, Malte, 'Where Is Cinema (Today)? The Cinema in the Age of Media Immanence', *Cinéma & Cie*, Special issue on 'Relocations', ed. Francesco Casetti, no. 11 (Autumn 2008), pp. 15–22.

Harvey, David, 'Globalization and the Spatial Fix', *Geographische Revue* no. 2 (2001), pp. 23–30.

——, *The Limits to Capital* (London: Verso, 2006).

Hedwig Kaiser, Tina, *Flaneure im Film. 'La Notte' und 'L'Eclisse' von Michelangelo Antonioni* (Marburg: Tectum Verlag, 2007).

Heidegger, Martin, *Poetry, Language, Thought*, trans. Albert Hofstadter (New York: Harper & Row, 1971).

Henson, Robert, *The Rough Guide to Climate Change* (London: Penguin, 2009).

Holland, Norman N., 'Not Having Antonioni', *The Hudson Review* vol. 16 no. 1 (Spring 1963), pp. 94–5.

Hutchings, Ernest A. D., *A Survey of Printing Processes* (London: Heinemann, 1970).

Insolera, Italo, *Roma moderna. Un secolo di storia urbanistica* (Turin: Einaudi, 1971).

Insolera, Italo and Alessandra Maria Sette, *Roma tra le due guerre. Cronache da una città che cambia* (Rome: Palombi Editori, 2003).

Iori, Tullia, 'Nervi e le Olimpiadi di Roma 1960', in Tullia Iori and Sergio Poretti (eds), *Pier Luigi Nervi, architettura come sfida. Ingegno e costruzione* (Milan: Electa, 2010), pp. 53–67.

Jacobs, Steven, 'Between EUR and LA: Townscapes in the Work of Michelangelo Antonioni', in Ghent Urban Studies Team (ed.), *The Urban Condition: Space, Community, and Self in the Contemporary Metropolis* (Rotterdam: 010, 1999), pp. 325–42.

Jameson, Fredric, *Postmodernism, or the Cultural Logic of Late Capitalism* (Durham, NC: Duke University Press, 1991).

——, *The Geopolitical Aesthetic* (London: BFI, 1992).

Johnstone, Stephen, 'Introduction: Recent Art and the Everyday', in *The Everyday* (London: Whitechapel, 2008), pp. 12–23.

Jones, Amelia, 'Seeing Differently: From Antonioni's *Blow-Up* (1966) to Shezad Dawood's *Make It Big* (2005)', *Journal of Visual Culture* vol. 7 no. 2 (August 2008), pp. 181–203.

Kauffmann, Stanley, '*Zabriskie Point*' [review], *The New Republic*, 14 March 1970, pp. 20–31.

Kelly, William, '*Identification of a Woman* by Michelangelo Antonioni', *Film Quarterly* vol. 37 no. 3 (1984), pp. 37–43.

Kezich, Tullio, *Federico. Fellini, la vita e i film* (Milan: Feltrinelli, 2007).

Kezich, Tullio and Alessandra Levantesi (eds), *Cronaca di un amore. Un film di Michelangelo Antonioni* (Turin: Lindau, 2004).

——, 'Personaggi e curiosità', in Tullio Kezich and Alessandra Levantesi (eds), *Cronaca di un amore. Un film di Michelangelo Antonioni* (Turin: Lindau, 2004), pp. 111–23.

Kinder, Marsha, '*Zabriskie Point*' [interview], *Sight & Sound* vol. 38 no. 1 (Winter 1968–69), pp. 26–30.

Kirk, Terry, *The Architecture of Modern Italy, Volume 2: Visions of Utopia, 1900–Present* (New York: Princeton Architectural Press, 2005).

Knight, Richard Payne, 'An Expedition into Sicily, 1777', unpublished diary (Weimar, Goethe-Schiller-Archiv MS 25).

——, *The Landscape: A Didactic Poem* (London: W. Bulmer, 1795).

——, *An Analytical Inquiry into the Principles of Taste*, 4th edn (London: Luke Hansard and Sons, 1808).

Kracauer, Siegfried, *Theory of Film. The Redemption of Physical Reality* (Princeton, NJ: Princeton University Press, 1997).

Kral, Petr, 'Traversée du désert: de quelques constantes antonioniennes', *Positif* no. 263, January 1983, pp. 30–5.

Krauss, Rosalind, *The Optical Unconscious* (Cambridge, MA: MIT Press, 1993).

Kristeva, Julia, *Powers of Horror: An Essay on Abjection*, trans. Leon S. Roudiez (Columbia: Columbia University Press, 1982).

Labarthe, André S., 'Entretien avec Michelangelo Antonioni', *Cahiers du cinéma* vol. 19 no. 112 (1960), p. 8.

Lacan, Jacques, Seminar XI: *The Four Fundamental Concepts of Psychoanalysis*, trans. Alan Sheridan (London: Hogarth, 1977).

Lambiase, Sergio and Tano D'Amico (eds), *Storia fotografica di Roma, 1950–62. Dall'Anno Santo alla 'dolce vita'* (Naples: Edizioni Intra Moenia, 2004).

Lange, Susanne, *Bernd and Hilla Becher: Life and Work*, trans. Jeremy Gaines (Cambridge, MA: MIT Press, 2007).

Lattuada, Alberto, *L'occhio quadrato* (Milan: Edizioni di Corrente, 1941).

——, 'Prefazione a *L'occhio quadrato*', in Piero Berengo Gardin (ed.), *Alberto Lattuada fotografo. Dieci anni di Occhio quadrato, 1938/1948* (Florence: Alinari, 1982), p. 15.

Lebeck, Robert and Bodo Von Dewitz (eds), *Kiosk: A History of Photojournalism* (Göttingen: Steidl, 2001).

Leonardi, Nicoletta (ed.), *Feedback. Scritti su e di Franco Vaccari* (Milan: Postmedia, 2007).

Leprohon, Pierre, *Michelangelo Antonioni* (Paris: Seghers, 1965).

Lev, Peter, '*Blow-Up*, Swinging London, and the Film Generation', *Literature/Film Quarterly* vol. 17 no. 2 (1989), pp. 134–7.

Levantesi, Alessandra and Francesco Maselli, 'Sui sentieri della memoria', in Tullio Kezich and Alessandra Levantesi (eds), *Cronaca di un amore. Un film di Michelangelo Antonioni* (Turin: Lindau, 2004), pp. 31–51.

Lietta Tornabuoni, 'Myself & Cinema – Myself & Women' [1978], in Carlo Di Carlo (ed.), *Michelangelo Antonioni* (Rome: Cinecittà, n.d. [2005]), pp. 22–32.

Lotman, Jurij, *Semiotics of Cinema*, trans. Mark E. Suino (Ann Arbor: University of Michigan, 1981 [1973]).

Macarthur, John, *The Picturesque: Architecture, Disgust and Other Irregularities* (London: Routledge, 2007).

Madesani, Angela, *Le icone fluttuanti. Storia del cinema d'artista e della videoarte in Italia* (Milan: Bruno Mondadori, 2002).

Magini, Manlio, *L'Italia e il petrolio tra storia e cronologia* (Milan: Mondadori, 1961).

Manceaux, Michèle, 'An Interview with Antonioni' [1960], in Bert Cardullo (ed.), *Michelangelo Antonioni: Interviews* (Jackson, MS: University Press of Mississippi, 2008), pp. 11–20.

——, 'Ravenne. Dans *Le désert rouge*: Pour la première fois Antonioni parle de son premier film en couleurs' [interview, 1964], in Carlo Di Carlo and Giorgio Tinazzi (eds), *Michelangelo Antonioni. Entretiens et inédits, 1950–1985* (Rome: Cinecittà International, 1992), pp. 183–6.

Mancini, Michele, Alessandro Cappabianca, Ciriaco Tiso and Jobst Grapow, 'The World is Outside the Window' [interview], in Carlo Di Carlo (ed.), *Michelangelo Antonioni* (Rome: Cinecittà, n.d. [2005]), pp. 48–63.

Manzini, Ezio, 'Objects and Their Skin', in Penny Sparke (ed.), *The Plastics Age: From Modernity to Post-Modernity* (London: Victoria and Albert Museum, 1990).

Maraini, Dacia, *E tu chi eri?* (Milan: Bompiani, 1973).

Margulies, Ivone, 'Exemplary Bodies: Reenactment in *Love in the City*, *Sons*, and *Close Up*', in Ivone Margulies (ed.), *Rites of Realism: Essays on Corporeal Cinema* (Durham, NC: Duke University Press, 2002), pp. 217–44.

Marien, Mary Warner, *Photography: A Cultural History* (London: Laurence King, 2002).

Marshall, Richard D., *Ed Ruscha* (London: Phaidon, 2003).

Martini, Andrea, 'I luoghi dell'intreccio (Antonioni viaggiatore)', in Giorgio Tinazzi (ed.), *Identificazione di un autore. Forma e racconto nel cinema di Antonioni* (Parma: Pratiche, 1985), p. 88.

Maselli, Francesco, 'I miei esordi con Michelangelo', in Alberto Achilli et al. (eds), *Le sonorità del visibile. Immagini, suoni e musica nel cinema di Michelangelo Antonioni* (Ravenna: Longo, 1999), pp. 147–52.

Maynard, Patrick, *The Engine of Visualization: Thinking Through Photography* (Ithaca: Cornell University Press, 1997).

Mazzotta, Giuseppe, 'The Language of Movies and Antonioni's Double Vision', *Diacritics* vol. 15 no. 2 (Summer 1985), pp. 2–10.

McCullin, Don, *Unreasonable Behaviour: An Autobiography* (London: Jonathan Cape, 1990).

Meccoli, Alessandro, 'Italiano di Ferrara, europeo di Venezia', *Ferrara. Voci di una Città*, 7 (December 1997), <http://rivista.fondazionecarife.it/articoli/1997/num.-7/italiano-di-ferrara-europeo-di-venezia.html> (last accessed 28 August 2010).

Mellor, David Alan, ' "Fragments of an Unknowable Whole": Michelangelo Antonioni's Incorporation of Contemporary Visualities in London, 1966', *Visual Culture in Britain* vol. 8 no. 2 (2007), pp. 45–61.

Menduni, Enrico, *L'autostrada del sole* (Bologna: Il Mulino, 1999).

Micciché, Lino, *Il cinema italiano degli anni '60* (Venice: Marsilio, 1975).

——, 'Antonioni visto da Antonioni' [1978], in Carlo Di Carlo and Giorgio Tinazzi (eds), *Michelangelo Antonioni. Entretiens et inédits, 1950–1985* (Rome: Cinecittà International, 1992), p. 87.

Minghelli, Giuliana, 'Haunted Frames: History and Landscape in Luchino Visconti's *Ossessione*', *Italica* vol. 85 no. 2–3 (Summer–Autumn 2008), pp. 173–85.

Moe, Nelson, *The View from Vesuvius: Italian Culture and the Southern Question* (Berkeley: University of California Press, 2006).

Moholy-Nagy, László, *Vision in Motion* (Chicago: Paul Theobald and Co., 1961 [1947]).

Montanaro, Carlo, 'Francesco Pasinetti', in Giovanni Di Stefano and Leopoldo Pietragnoli (eds), *Profili veneziani del Novecento*, vol. 2 (Venice: Supernova Edizioni, 1999), p. 54.

Montani, Pietro, *Bioestetica* (Rome: Carocci, 2007).

Moore, Rachel, *Hollis Frampton – (nostalgia)* (London: Afterall, 2006).

Morton, Timothy, *Ecology Without Nature: Rethinking Environmental Aesthetics* (Cambridge: Harvard University Press, 2007).

Mulvey, Laura, 'Visual Pleasure and Narrative Cinema', *Screen* vol. 16 no. 3 (Autumn 1975), pp. 6–18.

Muntoni, Alessandra, 'Piano E42, 1937', in Adachiara Zevi (ed.), *Una guida all'architettura moderna dell'EUR* (Rome: Fondazione Bruno Zevi, 2008), pp. 15–16.

Nancy, Jean-Luc, 'The Image – the Distinct', in Jean-Luc Nancy, *The Ground of the Image*, trans. Jeff Fort (New York: Fordham University Press, 2005), pp. 1–14.

Nelson, George, 'Marcello Piacentini' [1935], in George Nelson (ed.), *Building a New Europe: Portraits of Modern Architects – Essays by George Nelson, 1935–1936* (New Haven, CT: Yale University Press, 2007), pp. 29–37.

Nicolini, Flavio, 'Deserto Rosso', *Cinema nuovo* no. 168 (March–April 1964), pp. 147–50.

Nowell-Smith, Geoffrey, 'Shape Around the Black Point', *Sight & Sound* vol. 33 no. 1 (Winter 1963/64), pp. 15–20.

——, *L'avventura* (London: BFI, 1997).

O'Healy, Áine, 'Oedipus Adrift: Unraveling Patriarchy in Antonioni's *Identificazione di una donna*', *Romance Languages Annual* (1989), pp. 56–61.

Ochoa, George, Jennifer Hoffman and Tina Tin, *Climate: The Force That Shapes Our World and the Future of Life on Earth* (London: Rodale, 2005).

Olivieri, Mauro, '1925–1981: La città abusiva', in Alberto Clementi and Francesco Perego (eds), *La Metropoli 'spontanea'. Il caso di Roma* (Bari: Edizioni Dedalo, 1983), pp. 290–304.

Ongaro, Alberto, 'An In-Depth Search' [1975], in Michelangelo Antonioni, *The Architecture of Vision: Writings and Interviews on Cinema*, ed. Carlo Di Carlo and Giorgio Tinazzi, trans. Marga Cottino-Jones (New York: Marsilio, 1996), pp. 344–51.

Orr, John, *Cinema and Modernity* (Cambridge: Polity Press, 1993).

Orsini, Maria (ed.), *Michelangelo Antonioni. I film e la critica 1943–1995: un'antologia* (Rome: Bulzoni, 2002).

Orvieto, Angiolo, 'Spettacoli estivi: il cinematografo', *Corriere della Sera*, Milan, 21 August 1907.

Paci, Enzo et al., 'Dibattito su *L'eclisse*', in Carlo Di Carlo (ed.), *Michelangelo Antonioni* (Rome: Edizioni di Bianco e Nero, 1964), pp. 87–118.

314

Parigi, Stefania, 'L'avventura de *I vinti* – L'episodio italiano', in *I vinti* (Rome: Gianluca & Stefano Curti Editori, 2007), pp. 15–17.

Parr, Martin and Gerry Badger, *The Photobook: A History*, 2 vols (London: Phaidon, 2004 and 2006).

Pasolini, Pier Paolo, 'The "Cinema of Poetry"', in Pier Paolo Pasolini, *Heretical Empiricism*, ed. Louise K. Barnett, trans. Ben Lawton and Louise K. Barnett (Bloomington and Indianapolis: Indiana University Press, 1988), pp. 167–86.

Paton, William Agnew, *Picturesque Sicily* (New York: Harpers, 1902).

Paz, Octavio, 'The Ready Made', in *Marcel Duchamp in Perspective*, ed. Joseph Masheck (Cambridge, MA: Da Capo Press, 2002), pp. 84–9.

Penny, Nicholas, 'Richard Payne Knight: A Brief Life', in *The Arrogant Connoisseur: Richard Payne Knight 1751–1824*, ed. Michael Clarke and Nicholas Penny (Manchester: Manchester University Press, 1982), pp. 1–18.

Perrone, Nico, *Enrico Mattei* (Bologna: Il Mulino, 2001).

Phillips, Adam, 'The Value of Frustration: An Interview with Adam Phillips', with Jane Elliott and John David Rhodes, *World Picture* no. 3 (Summer 2009) <http://worldpicturejournal.com/WP_3/Phillips.html>

Piazza, Roberta, 'Voice-over and Self-narrative in Film: A Multimodal Analysis of Antonioni's *When Love Fails (Tentato Suicidio)*', *Language and Literature* vol. 19 no. 2 (2010), pp. 173–95.

Pietrangeli, Antonio, 'Verso un cinema italiano', *Bianco e Nero* vol. 6 no. 18 (25 August 1942), p. 315.

Pinkus, Karen, *Il Po del '900* (Bologna: Grafis Edizioni, 1995).

——, *Alchemical Mercury: A Theory of Ambivalence* (Stanford: Stanford University Press, 2009).

——, 'Carbon Management: A Gift of Time?', *Oxford Literary Review* no. 32, ed. Timothy Clark (July 2010), pp. 51–70.

——, 'The Risks of Sustainability', in Paul Crosthwaite (ed.), *Criticism, Crisis, and Contemporary Narrative: Textual Horizons in an Age of Global Risk* (London: Routledge, 2010), pp. 62–78.

Pirandello, Luigi, *Shoot!: Notebooks of Serafino Gubbio Cinematographer*, trans. Charles Kenneth Scott-Moncrieff (Chicago: Chicago University Press, 2005).

Piva, Manlio, 'P. M. Pasinetti: Alcune immagini di repertorio', in *Studi Novecenteschi. Rivista di storia della letteratura italiana contemporanea* vol. 61 no. 1 (2001) (Pisa and Rome: Fabrizio Serra Editore), pp. 221–41.

Ponti, Gio, 'Architettura 'nel' cinema – Idee', *Aria d'Italia* vol. 2 no. 7 (Summer 1941), pp. 25–6.

Price, Uvedale Sir, *Essays on the Picturesque as Compared to the Sublime and the Beautiful; and on the Use of Studying Pictures for the Purpose of Studying Real Landscape* (London: Mawman, 1810).

Quaresima, Leonardo, 'Da *Cronaca di un amore* a *Amore in città*: Antonioni e il neorealismo', in *Michelangelo Antonioni. Identificazione di un autore*, ed. Comune di Ferrara, Ufficio cinema (Parma: Pratiche, 1983), pp. 39–50.

——, 'Neorealismo senza', in Mariella Furno and Renzo Renzi (eds), *Il neorealismo nel fascismo* (Bologna: Compositori, 1984), pp. 47–73.

Quilici Buzzacchi, Mimì (ed.), *Nello Quilici. L'uomo, il giornalista, lo studioso, il maestro* (Ferrara: Nuovi Problemi, 1941).

Quilici, Folco, *Tobruk 1940. Dubbi e verità sulla fine di Italo Balbo* (Milan: Mondadori, 2006).

Rascaroli, Laura and John David Rhodes, 'Antonioni and the Place of Modernity: A Tribute', *Framework: The Journal of Cinema and Media* vol. 49 no. 1 (2008), pp. 42–7.

Reberschak, Maurizio, 'Cini, Vittorio', in Alberto M. Ghisalberti (ed.), *Dizionario biografico degli italiani*, vol. XXV (Rome: Istituto della Enciclopedia Italiana, 1981), pp. 630–1.

Renda, Francesco, 'Il movimento contadino in Sicilia', in Pasquale Amato et al. (eds), *Campagne e movimento contadino nel Mezzogiorno d'Italia* (Bari: De Donato, 1979), pp. 557–717.

Renzi, Renzo, *Album Antonioni. Una biografia impossibile* (Rome: Centro Sperimentale di Cinematografia, 1992).

Restivo, Angelo, *The Cinema of Economic Miracles: Visuality and Modernization in the Italian Art Film* (Durham, NC, and London: Duke University Press, 2002).

Rhodes, John David, 'Pasolini's Exquisite Flowers: "The 'Cinema of Poetry'" as a Theory of Art Cinema', in Rosalind Galt and Karl Schoonover (eds), *Global Art Cinema: New Theories and Histories* (New York: Oxford University Press, 2010), pp. 142–63.

——, 'The Eclipse of Place: Rome's EUR from Rossellini to Antonioni', in John David Rhodes and Elena Gorfinkel (eds), *Taking Place: Location and the Moving Image* (Minneapolis: University of Minnesota Press, 2011), pp. 31–54.

Richieri, Giuseppe, 'Television from Service to Business: European Tendencies and the Italian Case', in Phillip Drummond and Richard Patterson (eds), *Television in Transition: Papers from the First International Television Studies Conference* (London: BFI, 1986), pp. 21–35.

——, 'Hard Times for Public Service Broadcasting: The RAI in the Age of Commercial Competition', in Zygmunt G. Baranski and Robert Lumley (eds), *Culture and Conflict in Postwar Italy: Essays on Mass and Popular Culture* (New York: St Martin's Press, 1990), pp. 256–69.

Rickards, Jocelyn, *The Painted Banquet: My Life and Loves* (London: Weidenfeld & Nicolson).

Rifkin, Ned, *Antonioni's Visual Language* (Ann Arbor: UMI Research Press, 1982).

Roberts, John, *The Intangibilities of Form: Skill and Deskilling in Art after the Readymade* (London: Verso, 2007).

Robertson, C. J., 'The Italian Beet-Sugar Industry', *Economic Geography* vol. 14 no. 1 (January 1938), pp. 1–15.

Rohdie, Sam, *Antonioni* (London: BFI, 1990).

Rony, Fatimah Tobing, *The Third Eye: Race, Cinema, and the Ethnographic Spectacle* (Durham, NC: Duke University Press, 1996).

Sarris, Andrew, 'No Antoniennui' [1966], in Roy Huss (ed.), *Focus on Blow-Up* (Englewood Cliffs, NJ: Prentice-Hall, 1971), pp. 31–5.

Schatz, Thomas, *Old Hollywood/New Hollywood: Rituals, Art and Industry* (Ann Arbor: UMI Press, 1983).

Schlesinger, Philip, 'The Berlusconi Phenomenon', in Zygmunt G. Baranski and Robert Lumley (eds), *Culture and Conflict in Postwar Italy: Essays on Mass and Popular Culture* (New York: St Martin's Press, 1990), pp. 270–85.

Schliesser, John, 'Antonioni's Heideggerian Swerve', *Literature Film Quarterly* vol. 26 no. 4 (1998), pp. 278–87.

Schnapp, Jeffrey T., 'The Fabric of Modern Times', *Critical Inquiry* vol. 24 no. 1 (Autumn 1997), pp. 191–245.

Shiel, Mark, *Italian Neorealism: Rebuilding the Cinematic City* (London and New York: Wallflower, 2006).

——, 'Imagined and Built Spaces in the Rome of Neorealism', in Richard Wrigley (ed.), *Cinematic Rome* (Leicester: Troubadour, 2008), pp. 27–42.

Sontag, Susan, 'On Style', in Susan Sontag, *Against Interpretation* (New York: Dell, 1966), pp. 15–36.

——, *On Photography* (London: Penguin, 2002 [1977])

Steimatsky, Noa, *Italian Locations: Reinhabiting the Past in Postwar Cinema* (Minneapolis: University of Minnesota Press, 2008).

Stimson, Blake, *The Pivot of the World: Photography and Its Nation* (Cambridge: MIT Press, 2006).

Stock, Kathleen, 'Desires towards Fictional Characters', unpublished manuscript, University of Sussex, 2008.

Strange, Allen, *Electronic Music: Systems, Techniques and Controls* (Dubuque, Iowa: William Brown and Co., 1972).

Stumpf, Claudia 'The "Expedition into Sicily"', in Michael Clarke and Nicholas Penny (eds), *The Arrogant Connoisseur: Richard Payne Knight 1751–1824* (Manchester: Manchester University Press, 1982), pp. 19–31.

Summers, Rollin, 'The Moving Picture Drama and the Acted Drama: Some Points of Comparison as to Technique', in Stanley Kauffmann and Bruce Henstell (eds), *American Film Criticism: From the Beginnings to 'Citizen Kane'* (New York: Liveright, 1972), pp. 9–13.

Szarkowski, John, *The Photographer's Eye* (New York: MoMA, 1966).

Tassone, Aldo, 'The History of Cinema is made on Film' [1979], in Michelangelo Antonioni, *The Architecture of Vision: Writings and Interviews on Cinema*, ed. Carlo Di Carlo and Giorgio Tinazzi, trans. Marga Cottino-Jones (New York: Marsilio, 1996), pp. 193–216.

——, 'Conversation' [1985], in Michelangelo Antonioni, *The Architecture of Vision: Writings and Interviews on Cinema*, ed. Carlo Di Carlo and Giorgio Tinazzi, trans. Marga Cottino-Jones (New York: Marsilio, 1996), pp. 230–44.

——, *I film di Michelangelo Antonioni* (Rome: Gremese, 1990).

——, *I film di Michelangelo Antonioni. Un poeta della visione* (Rome: Gremese, 2002).

Thompson, Kristin, 'The Concept of Cinematic Excess', in Philip Rosen (ed.), *Narrative, Apparatus, Ideology: A Film Theory Reader* (New York: Columbia University Press, 1986), pp. 130–42.

Thurman-Jaies, Anne and Martin Hellmold (eds), *Art Photographica: Fotografie und Künstlerbücher* (Bremen: Neues Museum Weserburg, 2002).

Tinazzi, Giorgio, *Michelangelo Antonioni* (Florence: La Nuova Italia, 1974).

——, 'The Gaze and the Story', in Michelangelo Antonioni, *The Architecture of Vision: Writings and Interviews on Cinema*, ed. Carlo Di Carlo and Giorgio Tinazzi, trans. Marga Cottino-Jones (New York: Marsilio, 1996), pp. xxiii–xxvii.

Tornabuoni, Lietta, 'Intervista a Michelangelo Antonioni', in Caterina D'Amico de Carvalho (ed.), *Album Visconti* (Milan: Sonzogno, 1978), pp. 6–9.

Torriglia, Anna Maria, *Broken Time, Fragmented Space: A Cultural Map for Postwar Italy* (Toronto: University of Toronto Press, 2002).

Toschi, Deborah, *Il paesaggio rurale. Cinema e cultura contadina nell'Italia fascista* (Milan: Vita e Pensiero, 2009).

Tosi, Virgilio, 'L'organizzazione della cultura cinematografica', in Callisto Cosulich (ed.), *Storia del cinema italiano, VII. 1945–1948* (Venice and Rome: Marsilio/Fondazione Scuola Nazionale di Cinematografia, 2003), pp. 497–514.

Traut, Don, ' "Simply Irresistible": Recurring Accent Patterns as Hooks in Mainstream 1980s Music', *Popular Music* vol. 24 no. 1 (2005), pp. 57–77.

Trombadori, Antonello, 'Zavattini, Picasso e noi nel '49', in *La Repubblica*, 28 (October 1989), p. 10.

Tumiati, Gaetano, 'Quando Michelangelo si chiamava Nino', *Ferrara. Voci di una Città*, no. 17, December 2002, <http://rivista.fondazionecarife.it/articoli/2002/num.-17/quando-michelangelo-si-chiamava-nino.html> (last accessed 25 August 2010).

Turroni, Giuseppe, *Alberto Lattuada* (Milan: Moizzi, 1977).

Vidotto, Vittorio, *Roma contemporanea* (Rome and Bari: Laterza, 2006).

Virno, Paolo, *A Grammar of the Multitude*, trans. I. Bertoletti et al. (New York: Semiotext[e], 2004).

Vitella, Federico, 'Michelangelo Antonioni drammaturgo. *Scandali segreti*', *Bianco e Nero* vol. 70 no. 563 (2009), pp. 79–93.

——, *Michelangelo Antonioni. L'avventura* (Turin: Lindau, 2010).

Vittorini, Elio, *Conversazione in Sicilia* (Turin: Einaudi, 1975 [1941]).

Wade, John, *A Short History of the Camera* (Watford: Fountain Press, 1979).

Wagstaff, Christopher, 'The Media', in Zygmunt G. Baranski and Rebecca J. West (eds), *The Cambridge Companion to Modern Italian Culture* (Cambridge, UK: Cambridge University Press., 2001), pp. 293–310.

Walker, Beverly, 'Michelangelo and the Leviathan: The Making of *Zabriskie Point*', *Film Comment* vol. 28 no. 5 (September 1992), pp. 36–49.

Walpole, Horace, *Correspondence*, vol. XIX (New Haven and London, 1937–74).

——, *On Modern Gardening* (London: Brentham Press, 1975 [1780]).

Walton, Kendall L., *Mimesis as Make-Believe* (Cambridge, MA, and London: Harvard University Press, 1990).

Williams, Megan, 'Surface of Forgetting: The Object of History in Michelangelo Antonioni's *Blow-Up*', *Quarterly Review of Film & Video* vol. 17 no. 3 (2000), pp. 245–59.

Williams, Raymond, *The Country and the City* (Frogmore: Paladin, 1975).

——, *Television: Technology and Cultural Form* (Hanover, NH: Wesleyan University Press, 1992).

Wolf, Mauro, 'The Evolution of Television Language in Italy Since Deregulation', in Zygmunt G. Baranski and Robert Lumley (eds), *Culture and Conflict in Postwar Italy: Essays on Mass and Popular Culture* (New York: St Martin's Press, 1990), pp. 286–94.

Wollen, Peter, *Signs and Meaning in the Cinema* (London: Secker and Warburg/BFI, 1969).

Wölfflin, Heinrich, *Principles of Art History: The Problem of the Development of Style in Later Art* (Mineola, NY: Dover, 1932).

Zagarrio, Vito (ed.), *Cine ma tv. Cinema, televisione, video nel nuovo millennio* (Turin: Lindau, 2004).

——, *Cinema e fascismo. Film, modelli, immaginari* (Venice: Marsilio, 2004).

——, *'Primato'. Arte, cultura, cinema del fascismo attraverso una rivista esemplare* (Rome: Edizioni di Storia e Letteratura, 2007).

Index

320

323

List of Illustrations

Zabriskie Point, © MGM Inc.; *N.U.*, ICET; *L'amorosa menzogna*, Filmus/ Fortuna Film; *I vinti*, Film Costellazione Produzione/Societe Gen. de Cinema; *La signora senza camelie*, Ente Nazionale Industrie Cinematografiche; *Tentato suicidio*, Faro Film; *Il deserto rosso*, Film Duemila/Francoriz; *Blow-Up*, © MGM Inc.; *The Passenger*, © Comp Cin. Champion; *Sette canne, un vestito*, Artisti Associati/ICET; *Vertigine*, Michelangelo Antonioni; *Gente del Po*, Artisti Associati; *Superstizione*, ICET/Carpi; *Cronaca di un amore*, Vilani Film/Fincine; *Les Visiteurs du soir*, André Paulvé Productions; *L'avventura*, © Cino del Duca; *I tre volti*, Dino De Laurentiis Cinematografica S.p.A.; *Funny Face*, © Paramount Pictures Corporation; *Il Misterio di Oberwald*, RAI/Polytel International; *Identificazione di una donna*, Iter Film/Société Nouvelle des Établissements Gaumont/Raidue; *Ossessione*, Iniziative Cinematografiche Internazionale; *L'Eclisse*, © Robert and Raymond Hakim/Interopa Film/Cineriz di Angelo Rizzoli/Paris Film Production; *Il grido*, SPA Cinematografica/Robert Alexander Productions; *La notte*, Nepi Film/Sofitedip/Silver Films.